M000317319

THE POPE AND THE PROFESSOR

The Pope and the Professor tells the captivating story of the German Catholic theologian and historian Ignaz von Döllinger (1799–1890), who fiercely opposed the teaching of Papal Infallibility at the time of the First Vatican Council (1869–70), convened by Pope Pius IX (r. 1846–1878), among the most controversial popes in the history of the papacy. Döllinger's thought, his opposition to the Council, his high-profile excommunication in 1871, and the international sensation that this action caused offer a fascinating window into the intellectual and religious history of the nineteenth century. Thomas Albert Howard examines Döllinger's post-conciliar activities, including pioneering work in ecumenism and inspiring the "Old Catholic" movement in central Europe. Set against the backdrop of Italian and German national unification, and the rise of anticlericalism and ultramontanism after the French Revolution, *The Pope and the Professor* is at once an endeavor of historical and theological inquiry. It provides nuanced historical contextualization of the events, topics, and personalities, while also raising abiding questions about the often fraught relationship between individual conscience and scholarly credentials, on the one hand, and church authority and tradition, on the other.

Thomas Albert Howard is Professor of History and the Humanities and holder of the Phyllis and Richard Duesenberg Chair in Christian Ethics at Valparaiso University. His publications include *Remembering the Reformation: An Inquiry into the Meanings of Protestantism* (2016), *Protestantism after 500 Years* (co-edited with Mark A. Noll; 2016), *God and the Atlantic: America, Europe, and the Religious Divide* (2011), and *Protestant Theology and the Making of the Modern German University* (2009).

Praise for *The Pope and the Professor*

"Howard's book does not pretend to be the complete story of how Roman Catholicism evolved from Pius IX to Frances, but it does reveal—with impressive scholarship and lively prose—the fascinating drama of how that transformation began."

D. G. Hart, *The Wall Street Journal*

"Exemplary study."

Grant Kaplan, *First Things*

"Howard has produced distinguished histories of the Reformation, Protestantism, and the rise of the German universities. Looking for new worlds to conquer, he here stretches himself slightly to deliver an exhaustive study of the impact of the historical-critical method."

Patrick Madigan, *The Heythrop Journal*

"I strongly recommend this book for anybody interested in Catholicism's struggle with the modern world and in the process by which in the 19th century the church became more pope-centred than ever before."

John W. O'Malley, The Jesuit Review

"This exceptional and erudite book recounts the story of Ignaz von Döllinger (1799–1890), German priest, academic, theologian, and the man who challenged papal infallibility. . . . Howard's reading of the problems popes faced is fresh and surprisingly sympathetic."

Miles Pattenden, *Religion and Theology*

The Pope and the Professor

Pius IX, Ignaz von Döllinger, and the Quandary of the Modern Age

THOMAS ALBERT HOWARD

OXFORD
UNIVERSITY PRESS

OXFORD
UNIVERSITY PRESS

Great Clarendon Street, Oxford, OX2 6DP,
United Kingdom

Oxford University Press is a department of the University of Oxford.
It furthers the University's objective of excellence in research, scholarship,
and education by publishing worldwide. Oxford is a registered trade mark of
Oxford University Press in the UK and in certain other countries

First published 2017
First published in paperback 2019

Published in the United States of America by Oxford University Press
198 Madison Avenue, New York, NY 10016, United States of America

British Library Cataloguing in Publication Data
Data available

Library of Congress Cataloging in Publication Data
Data available

ISBN 978–0–19–872919–8 (Hbk.)
ISBN 978–0–19–880992–0 (Pbk.)

To Kenneth G. Elzinga and James Davison Hunter,
mentors and friends,
who helped me find my way when I was younger

Acknowledgments

Permit me to begin with what often comes last: any errors or general wrong-headedness in this book is entirely the fault of the author. With that unpleasant truth acknowledged, let me with great pleasure thank the many institutions and individuals that have contributed to making this book much better than I could by my own lights and efforts.

I have received generous funding from the German Academic Exchange (DAAD), the John Templeton Foundation through its Religion and Innovation in Human Affairs initiative, the Earhart Foundation, and the summer scholarship and faculty sabbatical programs at Gordon College. I am also grateful to Valparaiso University and its Provost Mark Biermann for granting me a leave in the spring semester of 2016, during which I was able to complete this project.

A number of professional organizations and universities have given me opportunities to present on aspects of this project and to receive constructive feedback, for which I am very grateful. These include the Radcliffe Institute for Advanced Study at Harvard University; the Centre for Research in the Arts, Social Sciences and Humanities at Cambridge University; the Interfaith Programme at Cambridge University; the Oxford Research Centre in the Humanities at Oxford University; the Ecclesiological Investigations International Research Network; Marymount University, Georgetown University; Pepperdine University; Louisiana State University; Loyola University Maryland; the University of Notre Dame, Baylor University; the Conference on Faith and History; the American Society of Church History; the American Catholic Historical Association; the Consortium on the Revolutionary Era, 1750–1850; and the Institut für Europäische Geschichte in Mainz, Germany.

An abiding pleasure of historical research is the opportunity to travel to and work in archives and libraries. This project has taken me to many wonderful sites, including the Archivio Segreto Vaticano (Rome); the Bistumsarchiv der altkatholischen Kirche Deutschlands (Bonn); the Handschriftenabteilung of the Bayerische Staatsbibliothek and the Bayerisches Hauptstaatsarchiv (Munich); the British Library (London); the Universitäts- und Landesbibliothek Bonn; the Universitäts-Bibliothek Frankfurt am Main; the Archives of Cambridge University Library; Harvard University's Widener Library; and the Andover-Harvard Theological Library (Cambridge, Massachusetts). For the patience, professionalism, and many courtesies of staff members at these fine institutions, I am deeply thankful.

With respect to individuals, I owe special gratitude to Franz Xaver Bischof of the University of Munich, where I spent several months in residence in the spring semester of 2013. Conversations with Professor Bischof and his past scholarship have been significant in shaping my own work. While in Munich, I had the good fortunate of lodging in the venerable Herzogliches Georgianum, for which I am especially grateful to its director, Winfried Haunerland. Furthermore, I would like to thank the encouragement, scholarship, and hospitality of the *Christkatholische* theologian Angela Berlis of the University of Bern, Switzerland. Anyone who treats Döllinger owes a debt to the rich corpus of Victor Conzemius, so I thank him, too, for his efforts over many decades. Finally, I owe a debt to Hubert Huppertz for his work in transcribing and hence rendering more legible many of the letters to Döllinger found in the Bayerische Staatsbibliothek in Munich.

I would like thank Ute Possekel, Richard Schaefer, and Ulrich Lehner, who read through the entire manuscript and helped save me from my ignorance and prejudices. Other individuals who deserve a word of gratitude include Gerald Ach, Claus Arnold, Gareth Atkins, Paul Bauman, Montgomery Brown, Mark D. Chapman, Janel Curry, Eamon Duffy, Günter Eßer, Massimo Faggioli, David F. Ford, Simon Goldhill, Marco Grilli, Mike Higton, Dominique Mamberti, Mel Piehl, Agnes Plabst, William Portier, Max Schreiber, Siegfried Thuringer, Laura Whitney, George Williamson, Johannes Wischmeyer, Imtrud Witsch, Jessica Wojtun, Donald Yerxa, and Johannes Zachhuber.

The interlibrary loan staff at Gordon College, and especially Lori Franz, deserve divine blessing for their many labors on my behalf. Likewise, my former, highly competent and long-suffering staff members at Gordon's Center for Faith and Inquiry deserve my heartfelt gratitude; these include Ryan Groff, Debbie Drost, Susanne McCarron, and Victoria Quay. Several of our student aides and "apprentices" at the Center also lent a hand along the way, so a robust thanks to Elizabeth (Libby) Baker, Katharine Stephens, Matthew Reese, Hilary (Sherratt) Yancey, and Mary Hierholzer. Not least, the blessedly meticulous Elspeth Currie did a remarkable job in helping me secure images and permissions and complete the bibliography.

Aspects of this book call attention to the history of the Papal States in central Italy. Some ideas for the book were hatched during stays at Gordon College's study-abroad program in Orvieto, Italy (once part of the Papal States), directed by John Skillen and Matthew Doll. I am grateful to them for creating an environment conducive to scholarly reflection.

Portions of the book have previously appeared as articles in journals. These include "Neither a Secular nor Confessional Age: Ignaz von Döllinger, Vatican I, and the Bonn Reunion Conferences of 1874 and 1875," *Journal of the Historical Society* 11 (March 2011): 59–84 and "A Question of Conscience: The Excommunication of Ignaz von Döllinger," *Commonweal* 141 (October 10, 2014): 14–20. I also contributed a chapter on Döllinger in Claus Arnold and Johannes Wischmeyer, eds., *Transnationale Dimensionen wissenschaftlicher Theologie* (Göttingen: Veröffentlichungen des Instituts für Europäische Geschichte Mainz, 2013). I am grateful to be able to reproduce material from these sources.

Tom Perridge and Karen Raith at Oxford University Press have been relentlessly encouraging of my work and are paragons of professionalism and good sense. I hope they, too, take satisfaction in the completion of this book.

Finally, I remain abidingly thankful to the support and assistance of my smart, helpful, and cherished wife, Agnes R. Howard, without whom...

This book is dedicated to Kenneth G. Elzinga and James Davison Hunter, mentors and friends, who helped me find my way during graduate school.

Thomas Albert Howard

Valparaiso, Indiana,
October 2016

Contents

List of Figures and Map

Figures

Map

List of Abbreviations

Archives

AAES	Archivio della Sacra Congregazione degli Affari Ecclesiastici Straordinari (Rome)
ASV	Archivio Segreto Vaticano (Rome):
	ASV NM—Archivio della Nunziatura di Monaco
	ASV SS—Archivio della Segreteria di Stato
	ASV CVI—Concilio Vaticano I
BAB	Bistumsarchiv der altkatholischen Kirche Deutschlands (Bonn)
BHSA	Bayerisches Hauptstaatsarchiv (Munich)
BL	British Library (London)
BSB	Bayerische Staatsbibliothek, Handschriftenabteilung (Munich)
CUL	Cambridge University Library (Cambridge)
UB	Universitätsbibliothek, Handschriftenabteilung (Munich)

Reference Works, Collected Editions, and Secondary Works

AAS	Pope Pius X, *Acta Apostolicae Sedis* (Vatican City: Typis Polyglottis Vaticanis, 1909ff.)
ADB	*Allgemeine Deutsche Biographie*, 56 vols. (Berlin: Duncker & Humblot, 1967–71)
ADSC	*Acta et decret sacrorum concililorum recentiorum: collectio lacensis*, 7 vols. (Freiburg im Breisgau, 1870–90)
AGP	Pope Gregory XVI, *Acta Gregorii Papae XVI: sicillcet constitutiones, bullae, litterae apostolicae, epistolae*, 4 vols. (Rome, 1901–4)
AK	J. F. von Schulte, *Der Altkatholicismus: Geschichte seiner Entwicklung, inneren Gestaltung und rechtlichen Stellung in Deutschland* (Giessen: E. Roth, 1887)
AP	Pope Pius IX, *Acta Pii IX Pontificis Maximi*, 9 vols. (Rome: Ex Typographia Bonarum Artium, 1854–78)
CCC	*Catechism of the Catholic Church* (Vatican City: Libreria Editrice Vaticana [Chicago: distributed by Loyola University Press], *c.*1994)
CE	*Catholic Encyclopedia: An International Work of Reference on the Constitution, Doctrine, Discipline, and History of the Catholic Church*, 15 vols. (New York: Robert Appleton Company, 1907–12)
DAB	*Dictionary of American Biography*, 22 vols. (New York: Scribner, 1928–58)

DBI	*Dizionario biografico degli Italiani* (Rome: Instituto dell-Enciclopedia Italiana, 1960ff.)
EC	*Enciclopedia Cattolica*, 12 vols. (Vatican City, 1948–54)
ESDD	*Enchiridion symbolorum definitionum et declarationum de rebus fidei et morum* (43rd ed., English bilingual edition edited by Robert Fastiggi and Anne Englund Nash [San Francisco: Ignatius Press, 2012])
EVP	Frank J. Coppa, ed., *Encyclopedia of the Vatican and Papacy* (Westport: Greenwood Press, 1999)
GG	Georg Denzler and E. L. Grasmück, eds., *Geschichtlichkeit und Glaube: Zum 100. Todestag Johann Joseph Ignaz von Döllinger, 1799–1890* (Munich: E. Wewel, 1990)
KGV	Klaus Schatz, *Konziliengeschichte: Vaticanum I, 1869–1870*, 3 vols. (Paderborn: F. Schöning, 1992–4)
KTD	Heinrich Fries and Georg Schwaiger, *Katholische Theologen Deutschlands im 19. Jahrhundert*, 3 vols. (Munich: Kösel-Verlag, 1975)
NDB	*Neue Deutsche Biographie*, 21 vols. (Berlin: Duncker & Humblot, 1953–2013)
ODCC	*Oxford Dictionary of the Christian Church* (3rd ed., Oxford: Oxford University Press, 1997)
ODNB	*Oxford Dictionary of National Biography*, 60 vols. (Oxford: Oxford University Press, 2004)
PE	Claudia Carlen, ed., *The Papal Encyclicals*, 5 vols. (Wilmington: McGrath, 1981)
RPP	Hans Dieter Betz, ed., *Religion Past & Present*, 14 vols. (4th ed., Eng. trans., Boston: Brill, 2007–13)
SCE	Eugenio Cecconi, ed., *Storia del Concilio Ecumenico Vaticano scritta su documenti originali. Antecendenti del Concilio.* 4 vols. (Rome, 1873–9)
TG	Franz Xaver Bischof, *Theologie und Geschichte: Ignaz von Döllinger (1799–1890) in der zweiten Hälfte seines Leben* (Stuttgart: Kohlhammer, 1997)
TRE	*Theologische Realenzyklopädie* (Berlin: De Gruyter, 1976–2004)

Periodicals

AHP	*Archivum Historiae Pontificia*
AHR	*American Historical Review*
AJT	*American Journal of Theology*
AMQR	*American Catholic Quarterly Review*
CH	*Church History*
CHJ	*Cambridge Historical Journal*
CHR	*Catholic Historical Review*
CnS	*Cristianesimo nella Storia*

CSSH	*Comparative Studies in Society and History*
DR	*Dublin Review*
EHR	*English Historical Review*
ER	*Ecumenical Review*
HBKD	*Historich-pölitische Blätter für das katholische Deutschland*
HJ	*Heythrop Journal*
HJB	*Historisches Jahrbuch*
HT	*History and Theory*
HZ	*Historische Zeitschrift*
IKZ	*Internationale kirchliche Zeitschrift*
JBM	*Jahrbuch der Bistums Mainz*
JCS	*Journal of Church and State*
JES	*Journal of Ecumenical Studies*
JHI	*Journal of the History of Ideas*
JHMT	*Journal for the History of Modern Theology/Zeitschrift für neuere Theologiegeschichte*
JHS	*Journal of the Historical Society*
JTS	*Journal of Theological Studies*
KD	*Kerygma und Dogma*
KJB	*Kurtrierisches Jahrbuch*
LS	*Louvain Studies*
MR	*Mercersburg Review*
NSJ	*Newman Studies Journal*
RHE	*Revue d'Histoire Ecclésiastique*
RP	*Review of Politics*
RQ	*Römische Quartalschrift*
SdZ	*Stimmen der Zeit*
TQ	*Theologische Quartalschrift*
TS	*Theological Studies*
ZBL	*Zeischrift für bayerische Landesgeschichte*
ZHF	*Zeitschrift für historische Forschung*
ZKG	*Zeitschrift für Kirchengeschichte*
ZKT	*Zeitschrift für katholische Theologie*

How heavy the papal mantle weighs.

　　—Dante, *Purgatorio*, canto xix

... that spark of conscience which was not even extinguished in the breast of Cain when he was turned out of Paradise.

　　—St. Jerome, *Commentary on Ezekiel*

Introduction

"As to Döllinger...the case is quite tragic."

—John Henry Newman

Few novels capture the nineteenth century's conflict between tradition and modernity better than Giuseppe di Lampedusa's *The Leopard*, set in Sicily during the tumultuous years of Italian unification. Toward the end of the book, one Chevalley, a representative of the newly-formed central government, travels to Sicily to ask the book's protagonist, the aging, affable aristocrat Don Fabrizio, to become a member of the Italian senate. Don Fabrizio declines, offering the following rationale:

> I am most grateful for the government for having thought of me, and I ask you to express my most sincere gratitude.... But I cannot accept. I am a member of the old ruling class, inevitably compromised with the Bourbon regime, and tied to it by chains of decency if not affection. I belong to an unfortunate generation, swung between the old world and the new, and I find myself ill at ease in both.[1]

The theme of a new, uncertain "modern world" or "modern age" emerging as a consequence of the French Revolution and its aftermath is, of course, not an uncommon one in the nineteenth century. The great Swiss historian Jacob Burckhardt (1818–97) once quipped that the nineteenth century began with a *tabula rasa* in relation to everything. For the positivist Auguste Comte (1798–1857), the Revolution represented a "salutary explosion" wiping away the decay of the Old Regime and preparing humanity for a higher development.[2] Since the Revolution, a writer in the Catholic *Dublin Review* bemoaned in 1869, "the framework of old royal Europe is breaking up, and men hardly know where to look to a new order.... [Perhaps] the glory of Christendom is passing away for ever."[3]

While the incipient "modern age" reshaped the political and social fabric of Europe, it also brought profound implications for the religious landscape. Unlike the American Revolution, which through the US Constitution's First Amendment (1791) sought a *modus vivendi* between the federal government and the diverse religious communities that had put down roots in North

America, the French Revolution launched a frontal assault on the age-old clerical powers of the *ancien régime*. While not without some support among the lower clergy, this assault had roots in the radical anticlerical thought of the Enlightenment, often signified in Voltaire's gibe, "Écrasez l'infâme" (destroy the infamy, i.e., the Catholic Church) and in Diderot's macabre proposition that liberty would not come to Europe until the last king was strangled by the entrails of the last priest.[4]

Indeed, when one considers the two defining revolutions of modernity, the American and the French, the religious aspect witnessed the sharpest contrast. American revolutionaries sought freedom *of* religion, as scholars today sometimes put it, whereas French revolutionaries—especially in the Revolution's radical phases in the 1790s—wanted freedom *from* religion—or at least deliverance from the age-old influence that the Catholic Church had wielded over state and society alike.[5] On the eve of the Revolution, as René Rémond reminds us, "all European societies were still confessional; everywhere religion was intimately interwoven with the life of society, allied with the ruling power and legitimizing it, a presence in all collective activities, governing social existence as well as private conduct."[6]

Today, in the geographical and mental "West" we live "on the other side" of modern democratic revolutions, which despite their differences entailed, whether slowly or suddenly, an unseating of the confessional world described by Rémond. The ideals of the late eighteenth-century revolutions constitute the very fabric of our world, what philosophers sometimes call our "social imaginary," the bedrock, often unexamined sensibilities that we have of what makes for right order, the way reality ought to be constituted and human nature understood.[7]

This book asks the reader to set aside the outlook of our own age, insofar as possible, and enter imaginatively into an older European world—but a world in distress and in the throes of fundamental transition. It asks the reader to consider an era when modern ideals were less established, when they did not possess a taken-for-granted status, but in fact were profoundly contested and threatened many time-honored ideals of the Old Regime—ideals such as hierarchy, legitimacy, loyalty, order, tradition, faith, and a long-established relationship between "throne and altar" that, if one had world enough and time, could be traced back to Emperor Constantine.

These ideals, of course, did not vanish after 1789. Far from it; they were powerfully and passionately reasserted across Europe after Napoleon's defeat in 1815 and today are generally associated with terms such as "Restoration," "Romanticism," and "Reaction" and with what historians recognize as the religious and specifically "Catholic Revival" of the nineteenth century.[8] Figures such as Count Metternich of Austria, René de Chateaubriand, Adam Müller, Friedrich Schlegel, Louis de Bonald, and many others sought to confute the optimistic, putatively naïve assumptions of the Enlightenment and Revolution and restore "throne and altar" to the position from where the Revolution had exiled it.[9] Others—and here the Savoyard Joseph de Maistre is the prime example—insisted that the Roman pontiff, the Pope (still standing in the person of Pius VII when Napoleon's day had passed), represented the authority of authorities, the indispensable cornerstone for securing lasting religious and political tranquillity. With like-minded thinkers, de Maistre helped revive "ultramontanism" (from *ultra* and *montes*, "over the mountains" to Rome), the assertion of extensive, centralized papal authority, one of the signature "isms" of the century, and one that would play a crucial role leading up to the First Vatican Council's pronouncement on Papal Infallibility, a focus of this book.[10]

But this is not the book's subject. From a high altitude, the subject might be described as the drawn-out twilight of "Christendom"—with particular reference to the institutional arrangements and structures of the Catholic Church, the papacy foremost, and its underlying theology and belief system. The book seeks to understand how this older body of religious ideas and practices found itself traumatized by and locked into fundamental conflict—a multiple-generation *Kulturkampf*—with "modernity," the European order taking shape as consequence of "the ideas of 1789."[11] Accordingly, in the first chapter we shall sketch the Catholic Church's confrontation with the French Revolution and Napoleon, before profiling several fervidly anti-modern popes, particularly Pius IX (r. 1846–78) or "Pio Nono," hands-down the most colorful and influential pope of the century, the longest reigning in the history of the papacy and one of the most controversial.[12]

But the first chapter is in part necessary stage-setting to contextualize a single, captivating individual and the complex set of issues and questions that his life raises—issues and questions no less relevant today in our own "post-secular" age.[13] This individual, "the Professor" in the title, is, of course, Ignaz von Döllinger (1799–1890). While not a household name today, Döllinger was among the most learned and influential scholars of his day: "Germany's most internationally celebrated theologian," according to the historian David Blackbourn.[14] Or in the words of Friedrich Wilhelm Graf, Döllinger was "the most significant German-speaking Roman Catholic theologian of his time."[15] When in the 1850s John Henry Newman founded a Catholic university in Dublin, the scholar he wanted above all others was Döllinger. "In gaining you," he wrote Döllinger in 1853, "we should gain the presence and countenance of a world wide [sic] reputation."[16] Supporters and critics alike referred to Döllinger as the first scholar in Germany, the "primus doctor Germaniae."[17] A writer in the *Edinburgh Review* opined shortly after Döllinger's death that "Döllinger has earned the esteem and veneration of the coming ages . . . as the greatest Catholic theologian and the most learned Church historian in Germany during the present century."[18] "He knew everything," the British Prime Minister William E. Gladstone, a personal friend of Döllinger, wrote before putting the pressure on future biographers: "If the tale of such a life is not rightly told, it will be a fraud upon mankind."[19]

While this book does not aspire to be a biography in the strictest sense, it does seek from the standpoint of intellectual history to examine aspects of the life and thought of Döllinger and their broader historical context, and from the bounty of his immense learning and varied life experiences to gain deeper insight into the aforementioned cataclysmic changes (and subtler continuities) of the nineteenth century.

L'AFFAIRE DÖLLINGER: A PREVIEW

But why Döllinger? How might his life and times enrich our understanding of the past and of the perennial human issues that the study of the past ought to evoke? Permit me to get ahead of myself with a brief preview.

Every educated person knows of Martin Luther's defiance of the Catholic Church in the sixteenth century and of the "Galileo affair" in the seventeenth. Both cases involved complex arguments about the Bible, ecclesiastical authority, conscience, and knowledge.[20] Few people today, however, recognize the significance of the "Döllinger affair" of the nineteenth century, in which comparable issues were at stake, but issues nonetheless distinctive to post-1789 Europe. Set against the backdrop of Italian and German unification, it involved an extraordinary cast of characters: in addition to Döllinger himself, Pope Pius IX; Pius's successor Leo XIII; the Archbishop of Munich, Gregor von Scherr; various papal nuncios in Munich and prelates in Rome; leaders in the Old Catholic movement; Ludwig II of Bavaria (the so-called "Fairy Tale King"); Prime Minister William Gladstone; John Henry Newman; and E. B. Pusey, leader of the Oxford Movement within the Church of England; and not least, John Emerich Edward Dalberg Acton or "Lord Acton," Döllinger's student and closest friend. (Acton made extensive notes for a biography of "the Professor," as he habitually referred to Döllinger, but this project, like so many others of Acton, remained an unfinished aspiration at the time of his death.[21])

By the middle decades of the nineteenth century, Döllinger had emerged as one of Europe's most eminent scholars, publishing numerous works and maintaining an extensive international correspondence in several languages. Ordained as priest in 1822, he spent the lion's share of his life in the Bavarian capital of Munich, where he received a professorship in 1826, later becoming Provost (*Stiftspropst*) of the Royal Church of St. Cajetan and a Privy Councilor to the crown, making him among the highest-ranking clergymen in Bavaria and among the closest to the Wittelsbach dynasty.[22] Decidedly ultramontane in his younger years, Döllinger became increasingly critical of the papacy of Pius IX by the eve of the First Vatican Council (1869–70), worrying in

1869-1870

particular about the intransigence and "Romanizing" tendencies of the Pope and his Jesuit backers.

Pius IX's well-known "Syllabus of Errors" (1864)—a list of eighty errors of the modern age that faithful Catholics should reject—directly condemned a number of ideas that Döllinger had advanced in an 1863 address, "On the Past and Present of Catholic Theology," delivered at a major congress of German Catholic scholars in Munich.[23] Hailed by Lord Acton as "the dawn of a new era" in Catholic thought, this address made clear Döllinger's preference for "historical theology," ascendant in the world-renowned German universities, over the "scholastic theology," favored by Rome and by leaders within the Jesuit order, a staunch supporter of the papacy at this time.[24] The thirteenth article of the "Syllabus," in particular, took direct aim at Döllinger, condemning those who assert that "the method and principles by which the Scholastic Doctors cultivated theology are by no means suited to the necessities of our times and to the progress of the sciences."[25]

While the "Syllabus" quickened Döllinger's opposition to Rome, the Vatican Council of 1869–70 with its well-known Constitution on Papal Infallibility, *Pastor aeternus*, practically unhinged him. Before and during the Council, writing under the pseudonyms "Janus" and "Quirinus" in one of Germany's leading newspapers, Augsburg's *Allgemeine Zeitung*, Döllinger had taken strong issue with papal centralization in general and Papal Infallibility in particular, convinced that historical scholarship taught that this teaching had no firm place in Catholic tradition and its formal definition represented, at a moment of great political uncertainty (Italian national unification and the demise of the Pope's temporal power), the irreversible elevation of some of the most questionable tendencies of the medieval papacy into official Catholic teaching.

After the dogma was defined on July 18, 1870, Döllinger, appealing to what Gladstone aptly called his friend's "historical conscience," refused to assent.[26] Soon thereafter, several rounds of emotion-laden letters were exchanged between Döllinger and Archbishop Gregor von Scherr of Munich, who had the unenviable assignment of obtaining Döllinger's submission. Significantly, the majority of German-speaking bishops, including Scherr, had voiced misgivings about Papal Infallibility prior to the Council, but all had submitted after the fact—some more willingly than others.[27] The final breach came on March 28, 1871 when Döllinger insisted to Scherr that "as a Christian, as a theologian, as a historian, as a citizen, I cannot accept this doctrine."[28] Scherr replied on April 2, 1871 that the matter "has now assumed the form of a direct revolt against the Catholic Church" and accused Döllinger of causing "much perplexity of mind and disquietude of conscience."[29]

After consulting with Rome and offering an ultimatum, Scherr, a former Benedictine abbot, presided over Döllinger's excommunication on April 17, 1871. (Some of Döllinger's writings had already been placed on the Index of Forbidden Books.) This period was the darkest in his life. "I have had only one sleepless night in my life," Döllinger later confided to a friend, "and that was when I was considering the impossibility of reconciling my conscience to the dogma of infallibility, thinking it over and over and coming to the conclusion that I could not."[30] It is noteworthy that Scherr, too, appealed to conscience. In an exchange with King Ludwig II of Bavaria prior to the excommunication, he regretted what he had to do, but asserted that the honor of his high office had placed upon him this "difficult duty of conscience."[31]

At this point, Döllinger, a septuagenarian, might have drifted from history's limelight were it not for the sympathy of King Ludwig II and much of Bavarian officialdom, the support of which assured him an enduring, indeed pedestalized, position in the intellectual life of Munich, which emerged as a major center of Catholic opposition to Papal Infallibility and to what some labeled "Vaticanism" or "Romanism."[32] In fact, the sizable number of Vatican-dissenting German Catholics—or emergent "Old Catholics," an enduring, articulate religious body too often unnoticed today—claimed Döllinger as one of their own, even as one of their founders and spiritual leaders, although he maintained an ambivalent relationship to this movement.[33] "Döllinger's name is now identical with the large movement called to life against Rome and Infallibility," as Berlin's *National-Zeitung* put it in a front-page story on April 12, 1871.[34] The "Döllinger movement," "Döllingerites," or even "Döllingerism" emerged as shorthand expressions to refer to central European Catholic opposition to the decrees of the Vatican Council.[35]

At the time of his excommunication, Döllinger's scholarly reputation and high-profile dissent from Rome turned him into an international *cause célèbre*, reviled in the ultramontane press as a heretic and apostate, but praised in other newspapers and journals the world over, not least in the United States and Great Britain, where liberals and Protestants tended to interpret him as a kind of Luther redivivus, leading a "new Reformation" within the Catholic Church, one with potentially "far-reaching and tremendous" implications.[36] As the *New York Herald* sized up the matter in May 1871:

> The Christian world is on the eve of a momentous crisis. The declaration of Döllinger [against Papal Infallibility] may mark a new era in the history of the Roman Catholic Church equal in importance to that of Luther in the sixteenth century.... It may give birth to a new religion under the name of a Reformed Catholic Church. We forbear giving any opinion as to the merits of the controversy on either side. We have only to consider the momentous prospects involved in the case.[37]

A harsh critic of Pius IX, the British Prime Minister William Gladstone became one of Döllinger's staunchest supporters at this time, corresponding with him frequently about religious and political matters.[38] Several universities, including Oxford, granted Döllinger an honorary degree for his defiance of Rome.[39]

Dismayed by the post-conciliar situation, Döllinger decided to put his energy into thinking about the unity of the Church or what today we would call "ecumenism"—a topic that already concerned him prior to the Council. In 1872, before dignitaries and scholars, he delivered in Munich's city museum a series of lectures on "the reunion of the Christian churches."[40] These formed the intellectual rationale behind two so-called "reunion conferences" in 1874 and 1875 held at the University of Bonn, another center of Old Catholic opposition to Rome.[41] Although heavily criticized by ultramontane Catholics, these conferences drew participants from Old Catholic, Eastern Orthodox, and Anglican churches together (alongside a handful of other Protestant attendees) to discuss causes of past divisions among Christians and ways for promoting unity in the future, in an effort to fulfill Jesus' mandate to his apostles in the Gospel of John 17:21 "that they all may be one."[42] /Bishops, archimandrites, abbots, priests, and scholars came from numerous European countries—and from Russia and North America—to deliberate under the direction of Döllinger, whom some trumpeted as "the most learned man in Europe." Not since the fifteenth-century Council of Florence had such a gathering of eminent Eastern and Western ecclesiastics and theologians taken place.[43] Although scantly remembered, the conferences in Bonn represent important harbingers of the Ecumenical Movement of the twentieth century and, to this day, the theological consensus that they produced serves as a benchmark for Old Catholic Christians the world over.[44] Their extensive coverage by the international press ought to make us question the misleading notion of the nineteenth century as a "secular age." As the *New York Times* summed up Döllinger's attitude at the 1875 conference: "[the meeting] is no child's play to him, but one into which he is throwing all the strength of his soul."[45] The events at Bonn, *The Guardian* reported in August 1875, was "commanding the attention of all Europe" and held "immense possibilities" for the future of Christianity.[46]

Despite the conferences' lofty, reunionist goals, some theological divisions remained insuperable. Widespread defection from the Eastern Orthodox occurred quickly. What is more, the Oxford Movement leader E. B. Pusey, who did not attend but closely followed the conferences, refused to endorse the doctrinal consensus achieved at Bonn, leading to further dissent among Anglican divines. Geopolitical factors intervened as well, as the coming of the Russo-Turkish War (1877–8) embroiled all of Europe in the so-called "Eastern Question," presaging tensions that would resurface in 1914. The tense build-up to this conflict also closed off a brief window of time under the liberal regime of Tsar Alexander II (r. 1855–81) that had facilitated Russian Orthodox participation at the Bonn conferences.[47]

Faced with such obstacles, Döllinger reluctantly abandoned the project, and turned to scholarly pursuits for the remainder of his life. Throughout the 1870s and 1880s, however, the Catholic Church recognized his redoubtable

scholarly authority and the large international following that he commanded—
not least among Old Catholics. Leo XIII (r. 1878–1903), successor to Pius
IX, quietly regretted the handling of Döllinger's excommunication, and
encouraged the effort to bring him back to Rome.[48] Many such efforts
took place; none succeeded. Neither decidedly *Old* Catholic nor *Roman*
Catholic, nor a convert to Protestantism or Eastern Orthodoxy, Döllinger
recognized his lonely status. "I am isolated," he wrote the papal nuncio in
Munich in old age.[49] Too respectful of Catholic tradition to become another
"Luther," as many continued to portray him, he led a devout and abstemious
life for the rest of his days. On the occasion of his ninetieth birthday
(February 28, 1889), letters of well-wishing poured in from around the
world.[50] He died on January 10, 1890 and was buried in Munich's "Old
South Cemetery."[51]

Presenting Döllinger as a modern-day Dante (an earlier critic of popes),
America's *Atlantic Monthly* in 1891 devoted thirteen pages to a retrospective
essay on his life.[52] A man of "world-wide fame," *The Times* of London hailed
him in an obituary, adding: "His learning was immense. It may probably be
said without exaggeration that he had as minute knowledge of the history of
the Church in every age as [Leopold von] Ranke had of the political conditions
of Europe in the 16th and 17th centuries."[53] "There he lies, as a corpse," the
priest-scholar Franz Xavier Kraus pensively reflected, "but how much more
seems to lie there, equally shattered and destroyed! Gone another bit of the
nineteenth-century world."[54]

NINETEENTH-CENTURY EUROPE AND
THE RETURN OF RELIGION

Shortly before his death, the eminent British historian Tony Judt (1948–2010)
published a collection of essays, lamenting how quickly we have forgotten the
events and lessons of the twentieth century.[55] If this can be said of the twentieth
century, it goes all the more for the nineteenth. This book aims, therefore, to
plunge the reader headlong into the *terra incognita* of this fascinating, "long"
century, which, as historians reckon, began with the storming of the Bastille in
1789 and ended in the trenches of the First World War. Döllinger's life spanned
practically the entire century. Having once seen Napoleon Bonaparte as a boy,
Döllinger died in the year that Kaiser Wilhelm II began to take a recently
unified Germany on an ominous, militaristic new course.

The present informs our vision of the past. This truism certainly applies to
understanding the nineteenth century. In our day, the recovery of "religion" as
a topic of inquiry has greatly assisted a more accurate appraisal of the century.

Too often in past scholarship, religious topics in post-1789 Europe have been ignored or treated dismissively by historians, sometimes disposed to impose an overdrawn narrative of "secularization" on the century.[56] But this tendency has happily ebbed. In fact, in his magisterial *The Transformation of the World: A Global History of the Nineteenth Century*, Jürgen Osterhammel has argued that religion "should occupy center stage" in a history of the century.[57] The historian Olaf Blaschke, moreover, has influentially proposed that, far from a "secular age," we might do better to think of the nineteenth century as a "second confessional era" in light of the persistence of Catholic and Protestant (and Jewish) "milieus" throughout Europe and lingering confessional animosities and prejudices.[58] Blaschke's words have received much deserved attention, and, while he might overstate the matter slightly, as I shall argue later, he is closer to the truth than those clinging to secularization narratives. Unfortunately, the latter persist in many general textbooks and in popular accounts of the century.[59]

Faithfully depicting the religious landscape of the nineteenth century, however, is not a simple task. This is especially true when examining figures such as Pius IX, a holder of one of the oldest religious offices in the world, and Döllinger, a church historian, regularly inclined to bring insights from, say, the third or thirteenth century to bear on analyses of his own day. For this reason, in what follows the reader should expect to encounter multiple levels of contextualization. By this, I mean that events and personalities will certainly be set within the context of historical forces and developments of their own times. But that alone would not suffice. Since the topics treated in this book are often implicated in deeper, complex issues in the European and Christian past, one must often plunge down far beneath the nineteenth century to make sense of a particular matter.

The topic of "Papal Infallibility" provides a clear example. Frequently, textbooks in modern history intimate that the dogmatic definition of this teaching in 1870 at the First Vatican Council amounted to little more than a ham-fisted, sour-grapes reaction to the modernizing and nationalistic forces of the nineteenth century, an act of fumbling resentment by Pope Pius IX and the Roman Curia to the Church's loss of the Papal States to Italian nationalists. This interpretation is not altogether beside the point, but it ignores a less obvious, more complicated theological history behind the idea of Papal Infallibility and the Council itself. To put the subject into a fuller historical context, one would have to know something about the "episcopal" organization of the Church's hierarchy in the Roman Empire, about complex issues in patristic and medieval theology, about the development of church canon law, about the Council of Trent (1545–63) and its response to Protestantism, and much more.[60] In opposing Papal Infallibility, Döllinger revisited many of these issues and developments to make his case; he engaged, as it were, in the discourse of a ongoing "tradition," which the philosopher Alasdair MacIntyre once nicely defined as an "argument extended through time."[61] To put the matter succinctly: one cannot understand the nineteenth century, especially in religious matters, by sticking to the nineteenth century alone. One must often dig deeper, following arguments and lines of inquiry into the intellectual and theological sediment of still earlier times.

An unfortunate side-effect of theories and narratives of "secularization" has been that religious actors themselves have too often been treated reductively. Scholars have not been disposed to "see things their way," but to "see through" their ideas and sensibilities and explain them only in reference to secular categories of analysis. This reflects a persistent attachment to some of the grand explanatory schemes of religion offered by figures such as Ludwig Feuerbach (religion as human alienation), Karl Marx (religion as ideological superstructure), Émile Durkheim (religion as social cohesion), Sigmund Freud (religion as coping-mechanism and/or neurosis), Clifford Geertz (religion as a network of symbols), Michel Foucault (religion as a mask for power), and others. Some of these schemes have yielded valuable insight, to be sure. Nonetheless, as Brad S. Gregory has compellingly argued, they often come with the presumption "that religion is not something that can be or ought to be understood in its own terms." As such, *explaining* subtly and sometimes readily yields to a more ideologically motivated *explaining away*, which in turn can evince what E. P. Thompson in an incisive locution once called "the enormous condescension of posterity."[62]

By contrast, this book attempts to take religious language and religious actors seriously, seeking to see their world from their standpoint and in light of their convictions and beliefs. It occupies itself, to quote Gregory again, "with understanding religious people on their own terms, or with reconstructing the ways in which they viewed themselves and their world or with depicting them in a manner in which they would have recognized themselves."[63]

Such empathetic retrospection does not imply approval or endorsement of a particular point of view. For many readers, some of the religious ideas encountered in this book—such as Papal Infallibility, the Trinity, the Holy Spirit, or the Immaculate Conception of the Virgin Mary—will appear strange, even ludicrous. This may be one's reaction. Fair enough. But one must be careful not to translate personal incredulity or bemusement into a hermeneutic of understanding. To understand, to achieve historical insight, one must seek to enter the mind-set, the mentality, of the historical actor, in all its vexing complexity and in its difference from the assumptions and convictions of subsequent generations. This fundamental task of historical inquiry, as diffi- cult as it is necessary, always proceeds through a tangled web of motivations, beliefs, ideas, impersonal forces, individuals, and institutions. Nonetheless, the historian's proper business is fidelity to the past in all its messiness and stubborn otherness, understanding the past qua past, not insofar as it measures up to or fails to meet present-day sensibilities.[64]

Empathetic historical inquiry of the sort I have just sketched does *not* mean abandoning normative concerns about the human condition for the "mere" task of understanding the past. To the contrary, I hope the topics covered in this book provoke thought on a number of normative matters that individuals face in their lives today.[65] In examining Döllinger's participation in a religious tradition, but then finding himself at odds with some of its developments, one recognizes a shared experience felt by countless individuals—even if most have certainly lacked the intellectual stature to undertake a full-scale operation of dissent the way Döllinger did during and after the First Vatican Council, as we shall see.

Whatever one finally makes of his excommunication, Döllinger's life, therefore, provides food for thought concerning a common human dilemma: when to submit to religious authority irrespective of one's personal convictions and when to follow one's conscience—what John Henry Newman famously called "the aboriginal Vicar of Christ"?[66] After the First Vatican Council, Döllinger found himself caught up in a fierce conflict between conscience and authority, between convictions resting on his scholarship, on one hand, and decisions taken at the Council, on the other. He worried that authority could run roughshod over conscience with deleterious effects, but he was also aware that conscience is not immune from wavering, distortion, and/or being poorly formed in the first place. "Conscience," as Thomas Aquinas wrote, "[is able] to witness, to bind or incite, but also accuse, torment, and rebuke."[67] The Christian New Testament contains numerous injunctions to serve God with a "clear conscience" or "good conscience," even as it also enjoins Christians to submit to proper religious authority.[68] Döllinger's candid, often painful wrestling with these theological and moral matters invites readers to deepen their own understanding of these all-too-human issues.[69]

DÖLLINGER, HISTORY, AND THE CATHOLIC CHURCH

It has been said of Döllinger that no scholar was more widely recognized during his lifetime and so quickly forgotten afterwards. The historical record corroborates this judgment. But Döllinger *should* be remembered as we reflect on this difficult century in Europe and the Catholic Church's history. Döllinger presents not only a case study in the conflict between conscience and authority, as indicated previously, but a study in the salience and transmission of some of the signature intellectual forces of his times. "No Catholic theologian in the nineteenth century," according to Johann Finsterhölzl, "more clearly felt, more sharply interpreted, and more passionately experienced both the progressive and reactionary forces in the Church than Ignaz von Döllinger."[70] Or, as the American theologian Walter Rauschenbusch put it a decade after Döllinger's death: "[Döllinger] played the foremost part in one of the crises in church history. In the forces that impelled him and the forces that flooded and broke against him, we see the great tendencies of [modern] history massed and condensed to dramatic vividness and swiftness."[71]

Although he was sometimes compared to Luther, especially among Protestant admirers, Döllinger had no intention of establishing a rival movement to the Catholic Church; he did not publicly burn the letter condemning him as Luther did, but accepted it, if with wormwood and resignation, deeming it an injustice, a sign not of his, but of the Church's shame.[72] To be sure, the Old Catholic movement in Germany drew a strong measure of inspiration from Döllinger's opposition to Rome, but, again, Döllinger maintained an ambivalent relationship to this movement—a point that shall be developed more fully in Chapter 4.[73]

Unlike the Galileo affair in the seventeenth century, where the issue at stake was the Church's relationship to the emerging natural sciences, Döllinger's case presents a conflict over the newfound authority and prestige of historical scholarship, especially as it had emerged in the German universities in the late eighteenth and nineteenth centuries. The ascendancy of historical forms of knowing—historicism (*Historismus*) as it is sometimes called—carried with it enormous implications for both exegetical and dogmatic theology and, by extension, for the authority of the magisterium and the practical workings of the Church.[74] "The new German science of history," as Lord Acton labeled it, emerged by mid-century as the "Copernicanism" of its day.[75] "Historical-mindedness," to use a term of Bernard Lonergan, has presented theology with one of its most difficult challenges in the modern age.[76]

By robustly embracing "history," Döllinger found himself on a divergent path from those neo-scholastic theologians oriented toward Rome who felt that a return to the scholastic doctors—Thomas Aquinas foremost—was the only way forward for the Church intellectually in the modern age.[77] History, Döllinger's critics maintained against him, presented a vertiginous relativism that, left unchecked by (scholastic) philosophy, would prove injurious to the faith. One of his outspoken critics, Archbishop Henry Manning of Westminster, even held that a principal purpose of the Vatican Council was to silence those who felt historical inquiry could challenge established articles of faith: "Are we to understand . . . that the rule of faith is to be tested by history, not history by the rule of faith?" Manning famously asked.[78] As "the intellectual head [*das geistige Haupt*] . . . against the Vatican Council," Munich's Archbishop Scherr remonstrated with Döllinger before his excommunication, "[you have] set *historical investigation above the Church*."[79]

Döllinger's career also presents a choice entry point for understanding the forces of nation-building and nationalism in the nineteenth century and how these forces came into conflict with the universalizing and centralizing tendencies of the Catholic Church (namely, ultramontanism). Prior to and after the Vatican Council, Döllinger believed in the Church Universal—the "one holy Catholic and apostolic church" of the Nicene Creed—but he also felt that the Church could and should have particular national (*völkisch*) expressions that merited a measure of autonomy from Rome. For this belief, he was sometimes accused by his ultramontane critics of "Febronianism," a movement in eighteenth-century, German-speaking lands, the proponents of which had questioned the temporal authority of the Pope and advocated greater independence for German bishops. (In essence, this was a German counterpart to French "Gallicanism," the exponents of which had long sought to pinion the papacy by asserting extensive French ecclesiastical independence from Rome.) Döllinger's inclination to extol the "German national genius" in contrast to the "backwardness of Rome" reinforced this view of him as a latter-day proponent of Febronianism.[80] But this, in turn, harkened back to a still older conflict between Rome and German-speaking lands within the Holy Roman Empire that one could trace back to the late Middle Ages, and is often regarded as a causal factor in the coming of the Reformation.[81] "As to Döllinger," as John Henry Newman wrote in 1871, "I think his case is only a portion of the long conflict between the Italians and the Tedeschi [Germans]. Each wishes to put down the other."[82] These deeper geographical and national(istic) factors will be duly considered when examining Döllinger's life and legacy, even if it would be misguided to reduce his conflict with Rome to these factors alone.

While often forgotten, Döllinger's legacy has nonetheless quietly lived on within the Catholic Church and within modern Christianity more generally. His historical inquiries led him to study the early Church and the early Church Fathers, whose authority he sought to elevate as a counterpoint to the authority of the scholastic theologians of the high Middle Ages and the influence of the decrees of the Council of Trent. In doing so, he foreshadowed the intellectual movement of *nouvelle théologie* on the European Continent in the twentieth century. Catholic thinkers affiliated with this movement—such as Henri de Lubac, Hans Urs von Balthasar, Marie-Dominique Chenu, not to mention the former Pope, Benedict XVI (r. 2005–13)—advocated a "return to the sources" (*ressourcement*) of the earlier tradition for the purpose of helping the Church think well and wisely about the challenges of the modern age—or what Pope John XXIII (r. 1958–63) famously called *aggiornamento*, "bringing up to date." This theological movement is of high significance for understanding the intellectual forces leading up to the watershed of the Second Vatican Council (1962–5).[83]

Döllinger's embrace of historical methods and criticism have also led some to see him as a precursor of the so-called "Modernist" theologians of the late nineteenth and early twentieth century. Thinkers associated with this "movement"—such as Alfred Loisy, Maurice Blondel, E. I. Mignot, George Tyrell, Friedrich von Hügel, and others—aimed to bring Catholicism into closer relation with modern philosophy and with the historical and social sciences generally as they had developed in the nineteenth century. Deemed to have irresponsibly accommodated to modernity, this movement was formally condemned by Pope Pius X (r. 1903–14) in the encyclical *Pascendi dominici gregis* (1907), leading to the so-called "Modernist Crisis" within the Catholic Church. Thinkers associated with Modernism languished in a cloud of disapprobation until a more salutary intellectual climate for assessing them came into being with the Second Vatican Council—although their legacy still divides Catholic theologians to this day.[84] Because of his excommunicated status, Döllinger was understandably not trumpeted by Modernist critics as a source of inspiration; but the lines of affinity between the former and the latter require little scrutiny to discern. In the entry on Döllinger in the *Catholic Encyclopedia*, published in 1909 amid the Modernist Crisis, it is revealing that the author felt the need to charge Döllinger, an "apostate," with "mental irregularity," "spiritual arrogance," and "profound mental confusion." "Seldom has it been so clearly proven," the entry concludes, "that whenever a man turns completely from a glorious and honorable past, however stormy, his fate is irrevocably sealed."[85]

In thinking about Catholicism (and Christianity more generally) in the twentieth century, one cannot help but see Döllinger as a forerunner of ecumenism, the search for Christian unity. As previously mentioned, mending the historic rifts within Christianity emerged after mid-century as one of his strongest commitments, and helps account for his anguished disapproval of what he felt were the unilateral, divisive actions taken by Rome at the First Vatican Council. His interest in questions of Church unity, particularly with healing the Western Church's rifts with Eastern Orthodox and Anglican Christians, contrasted sharply with the attitude of Rome in the late nineteenth and early twentieth century, even if it anticipated the pioneering efforts of Catholic thinkers such as the Jesuit Augustin Bea and the Dominican Yves Congar, who along with others helped lay the theological groundwork for Vatican II's epochal Decree on Ecumenism (*Unitatis redintegratio*) and for contemporary Catholic ecumenical engagement more generally.[86]

As much as Döllinger might have anticipated later developments in Catholic thought and theology, because of his excommunication, he is scantly recognized for his efforts. Notably, a number of figures in the twentieth century prior to Vatican II also found themselves marginalized (even officially silenced from speaking on certain topics) by the Church, only to find themselves rehabilitated in the post-conciliar period. Yves Congar himself presents a good case in point. He was mercilessly reviled by the Roman Curia in the 1940s and 1950s, but later made a Cardinal by John Paul II and today is widely recognized as a leading architect of Vatican II. Another well-known example is that of the American Jesuit theologian John Courtney Murray, banned from teaching on Church–state relations in the 1950s, only to have his ideas vindicated in the Second Vatican Council's Declaration on Religious Liberty (*Dignitatis humanae*).[87]

Döllinger has never been rehabilitated; he remains *excommunicato,* "handed over to Satan" in the older language of canon law.[88] He took his criticisms too far in the eyes of the Church's hierarchy, and had the misfortune of living in the age of Vatican I, instead of Vatican II. To return to Lampedusa's *The Leopard*, Döllinger might well have belonged to an "unfortunate generation, swung between the old world and the new" and often "ill at ease in both." Perhaps the most fitting thing that ought to be said of Döllinger (and in fact was said of him by John Henry Newman) is that he represents a "tragic" figure in the history of modern Christianity.[89] But this is also what makes him of interest from a historical perspective. And tragedy can serve important purposes. By peering into the tragic fate of another individual from another time, it helps us develop perspicacity with respect to our own times and the role that we are given to play therein. In this sense, "the Tragedy of Dr. Döllinger," if I may be permitted a moment of grandiloquence, holds the promise of a larger significance, serving as a well-placed window onto the irrevocable past, to help us live more thoughtful, examined lives in the present. If we study the past carefully with the tools of history—the very tools Döllinger championed—we might, indeed, learn something—but, again, not only about one individual and his fate, but about the passage of Christianity into the modern age, about the uses and limits of (historical) scholarship and its relationship to faith, and, not least, about the quandary of conscience and authority that, in some form or other, usually finds a way to visit us all.

1

"The World is Collapsing"

The Papacy, Memory, and Revolution

Who shall stay the devouring element? What nation shall escape, what throne, what altar?...It is not in the nature of things for revolutionary triumph...to forget its hate and dread of the Church.

—E. S. Purcell, *Dublin Review* (1860)

In 1797 and 1798, northbound caravans carrying precious works of art, ancient manuscripts, and historical artifacts made their way from the Italian peninsula across the Alps, bound for Paris. These were the spoils of the young Napoleon. Crossing the Alps, southbound, in 1796, he had in short order driven the Austrians from Lombardy, pushed into the Veneto, "liberated" Bologna and the Romagna. The rapidity and decisiveness of his victories allowed him to act with considerable independence from Paris. He oversaw the creation of two short-lived states in Northern Italy, the Cispadane and the Cisalpine republics, before turning upon Rome, the "center of fanaticism," home of the "the prince of darkness" (aka, the Pope) according to one member of the French Directory.[1]

Rome trembled. Forty-hour prayer vigils became the order of the day. Madonnas throughout the city were said to weep. But divisions existed within the clergy; many saw Napoleon as a sign of the Apocalypse; but some had warmed to the ideals of liberty and equality that he promoted with bayonet and canon. Pope Pius VI (r. 1775–99) stood among the former. The meager forces that he rallied to repel the upstart Corsican proved no match. Soon the Bishop of Rome was forced to sue for peace, the humiliating terms of which were finalized in the Treaty of Tolentino (February 19, 1797). The Pope was required to renounce all of the Holy See's historic claims to Avignon and Comtat Venaissin in France and its lucrative holdings in northern Italy; to pay 30 million livres, to close its ports to warships fighting against France, to release all political prisoners, and to hand over to France numerous works of art and pay for their transport to Paris.[2]

Soon "these doctrinaire [French] cannibals," one angry Roman reported, were "running around, catalogues at the ready, in museums and galleries and libraries." The *Apollo Belvedere*, the *Farnese Hercules*, the *Laocoön*, nine paintings by Raphael, two by Correggio, and many more were soon headed north as trophies of conquest, their transfer a powerful symbol of French might and of the dawning age of the modern state.[3]

But these were only part of a larger haul. Across northern and central Italy, French forces ransacked the Church's cultural patrimony. The four-horse *quadriga* was taken from St. Mark's in Venice.[4] Selections were taken from Ravenna, Rimini, Pesaro, and Perugia. At Loreto, in an outrage against popular piety, French forces seized treasures at one of the most-frequented shrines in the Catholic world: a house believed by the faithful to be that of the Holy Family at Nazareth flown there by angels to prevent desecration at the hands of Muslims; a picture of Christ Crucified said to be painted by St. Luke; and a hallowed wooden statute of the Virgin Mary. In a laconic communiqué to Paris, Napoleon reported: "We are masters of our Lady of Loreto." The Madonna was later sent to the Bibliothèque Nationale at Paris, with a cover letter from the Minister of the Interior, asking that it be placed "among the bizarre monuments of superstition and so help to complete the history of religious impostures."[5] A French general summed up the artistic conquests this way: "[art] which the French have taken from the degenerate Roman Catholic [is] to adorn the museum of Paris, and to distinguish by the most notable trophies, the triumph of liberty over tyranny, and of philosophy over superstition."[6]

The Pope and his court begged to differ. Even as the French incursions awakened reformist hopes in republican, Jansenist, and Jacobin circles in Italy, from the standpoint of Rome, the events of the late 1790s confirmed the rapacious and sacrilegious character of the *esprit de révolution* sweeping Europe and the need to rally around the Pope. The plundered artistic treasures and the confiscations at Loreto, in this light, concretely illustrate a much broader "cultural trauma" experienced by the papacy at this time. To understand the rise of ultramontanism in the nineteenth century—which Döllinger first embraced and then eschewed—and the outlook of Pius IX and his Curia, one must grasp what a bitter set of memories the trauma of revolution left on the papacy.

The history of revolutionary Europe and the Catholic Church, from 1789 until the founding of Italy and the First Vatican Council, is fairly well known. Too often, however, its telling suffers from a blind spot endemic to retrospection: it assumes certain outcomes—in this case, the triumph of nineteenth-century ideologies such as liberalism, nationalism, and secularism over clerical and royalist reaction. To properly understand the Döllinger affair, this cannot do. Instead, one must try to grasp Rome's perspective in these struggles, particularly its long-standing sense of itself as a divinely ordained spiritual *and* temporal pillar of the *ancien régime*. This perspective helps one see the papacy as it saw itself and not simply as an anachronism standing athwart history yelling stop, as so many textbooks suggest. It allows one to enter into the mind-set of the papacy as it wrestled with the revolutionary-Napoleonic era and its offspring: currents of anticlericalism, the movement of Italian unification or the *Risorgimento*, and the European-wide expansion of state power in the nineteenth century.

The concept of "cultural trauma" as it has been developed by contemporary social theorists offers helpful insight into these matters. A trauma of this sort, notes Jeffrey Alexander, occurs "when members of a collective feel they have been subjected to a horrendous event that leaves indelible marks upon their group consciousness, marking their memories forever, and changing their future identity in fundamental and irrevocable ways."[7] The revolutionary-Napoleonic onslaught constituted for the papacy such a "horrendous event," an unprecedented, violent disruption of established custom and order. This drawn-out, bitter experience shaped the "memory" of ultramontane Catholicism as it took shape in the nineteenth century. Elaborating on the connection between trauma and memory and linking them to identity-formation, Ron Eyerman observes that "collective identity formation, which is intimately linked with collective memory, may be grounded in loss and crisis, as well as in triumph. In fact, one way of dealing with loss is by attempting to turn tragedy into triumph."[8] The ultramontane triumphalism of the nineteenth century, both symbol and engine of the "Catholic Revival" of mid-century and of a more centralized papacy, did precisely this; it took the shock of the revolutionary assault and attempted, quite successfully, to fashion an ascendant, assertive Catholicism, which attracted both adherents and detractors.[9]

With an eye on the Döllinger affair after mid-century, this chapter aims to examine the tragedy and triumph, the trauma and memory-formation, of ultramontane Catholicism in the early nineteenth century. The chapter has a special focus on the institution of and discourse about the papacy from the French Revolution to the Italian *Risorgimento*, culminating in a profile of Pius IX or "Pio Nono." Given the immense historical territory, permit me to lay out several guiding questions. What bitter memories from the 1789–1815 era proved especially formative in shaping the identity of ultramontane Catholicism, and how did these memories resurface in later decades? After the Restoration of 1815, how did ultramontane theory about the papacy and the papacy itself develop? Significantly, ultramontane polemical defenses of the papacy—exemplified by Joseph de Maistre's well-known *Du Pape* (1819)— coincided with greater historical interest in the papacy, as evidenced by Leopold von Ranke's famous *History of the Popes* (1834–6). Since Döllinger frequently found himself grappling with forces of ultramontanism and historicism, these two works are particularly relevant. Finally, how does one account for the political and theological currents informing the papacy of Pius

IX from the time of the failed revolutions of 1848–9 until the eve of the First Vatican Council—decisive years for Döllinger's intellectual formation?

TRAUMA: THE FRENCH REVOLUTION
AND THE PAPACY

In Paris, at the Palais Royal on April 6, 1791, the Pope, "the ogre on the Tiber," was burned in effigy (Figure 1.1). His condemnation of the Revolution and breaking ties with France over the Civil Constitution of the Clergy (more on this later) had angered revolutionaries, who knew that his authority still carried weight with France's newly-minted *citoyens*. As had happened centuries earlier during the Reformation, unflattering caricatures of the Pope abounded. One popular image showed St. Peter turning Pius VI away from the pearly gates; another had the Pope blowing papal letters, in the manner of a child blowing bubbles, toward a figure of France who nonchalantly rebuffed them. Still cruder images showed French citizens wiping their behinds with papal letters.[10] The flaming effigy and these caricatures aptly symbolize the stand-off between "the Papacy" and "the Revolution" that developed in the 1790s; and they presaged the European-wide "culture wars" of the nineteenth

Figure 1.1. The Pope burned in effigy during the French Revolution.

Source: Artist unknown, Paris, 1791. Reproduced with permission from Bibliothèque Nationale de France.

century between ultramontane and anticlerical forces.[11] They also left bitter and enduring memories that shaped Rome's attitude toward what we today generally call "modernity."

Ironically, the revolutionary events of 1789 began with a religious procession. On May 4, at Versailles, the deputies of the Estates General marched behind a processional cross to the Church of St. Louis. Along with them journeyed the Blessed Sacrament under an ornate canopy carried by the Archbishop of Paris. Once at the church, a mass was sung and the Bishop of Nancy preached a sermon that lasted a full two hours. But later once the Third Estate (with many defecting lower-level curés) hived off from the Estates General, things went badly for the Church.[12] With France teetering on the brink of bankruptcy, the newly-formed National Assembly, meeting in the summer and fall of 1789, turned to the lands of the Church as a source of wealth. On November 2, the Assembly voted to sequestrate ecclesiastical property—a move that dwarfed the confiscations of Henry VIII during the sixteenth century. The sale of lands started the next month and continued years thereafter, saving the treasury of France and financing an increasingly anticlerical Revolution.[13]

The nationalization of ecclesiastical property produced a string of bad memories that would vex and haunt the papacy during the nineteenth century. Following the example of the "enlightened" Joseph II of Austria, revolutionaries turned next to the religious orders, which often enjoyed a closer connection to Rome than the secular clergy.[14] At a stroke in February 1790, monasteries and convents not engaged in "useful" work—such as caring for the poor or maintaining hospitals—were summarily abolished. If religious forsook their vows, they were eligible to receive a pension. Those who refused found themselves bunched together in a handful of surviving houses. The suppression of contemplative orders became a hallmark of the Revolution, both in France and abroad, spread by revolutionary armies and later under Napoleon.[15] Suppressions coincided with rising intellectual opposition to monks and nuns who were often regarded as parasites on society—a sentiment typified by Denis Diderot's *La Religieuse* (not published until 1795), which portrayed convent life in monotonous and lurid terms, a hatchery of psychological and sexual aberrations for young women, and a standing drain on the national commonweal.[16] "Philosophy has taught us long ago," a report of the Committee of Public Instruction (1792) read, "to suppress the monasteries.... All of these associations, intimately tied to the old episcopal regime,... were born under the auspices of superstition and steadily became more and more perverted by the nature and form of the teaching entrusted to them."[17]

Following on the heels of the suppression of the contemplative orders came the Civil Constitution of the Clergy (July 12, 1790)—an epochal, society-dividing reform that fundamentally altered the situation of the Catholic Church in France and, ironically, turned one of the most independent national church bodies into one of the most ultramontane in the coming century.

Acting only by its own authority, the National Assembly abolished more than fifty ecclesiastical sees and organized the rest according to the new eighty-three political units or *départements* of France. Roughly four thousand priests were dismissed. Clergy who had no pastoral function, such as cathedral canons, were eliminated. Bishops and priests became salaried civil servants. Citizens of the *départements*, including non-Catholics, would elect bishops, effectively depriving the Pope of canonical investiture. The Holy See was not consulted about these reforms, but presented with a fait accompli. The Assembly recognized the novelty of what they were doing, but also saw themselves as acting in continuity with the independent spirit of France's Gallican past, not to mention the Erastian spirit of eighteenth-century absolutist rulers such as Joseph II.[18]

Of fateful significance, the Assembly stipulated on November 27, 1790 that bishops and priests nationwide had to take a special oath of loyalty to the state and accept the new Constitution. This caused a commotion. Even by Gallican standards, the state seemed to be overstepping its bounds into the realm of conscience and matters of spirit. In the end, only seven bishops and about half the clergy agreed to the oath; the rest—the so-called "non-jurors" or "refractory priests"—declined. Further impetus to a developing schism within the Church came when Pius VI, who until this point had been quiet, came out vehemently against the Constitution, and the Revolution more generally, in his brief of March 10, 1791, *Quod aliquantum*: "The necessary effect of the constitution decreed by the Assembly is to annihilate the Catholic religion and, with her, the obedience owed to kings."[19] This was followed by the encyclical *Charitas* (April 13, 1791), in which the Pope deplored "the war against the Catholic religion which has been started by the revolutionary thinkers," adding that "these oaths should be regarded as perjury and sacrilege, unbefitting not merely the clergy but any Catholic; all actions which are based on these should be seen as schismatic, null, void, and liable to severe censure."[20]

When France found itself at war with the counterrevolutionary powers in the coming years, the schism of the clergy deepened. In the eyes of revolutionaries, refractory priests were seen in a harsh light, not only as obstreperous "conscientious objectors," but as a treasonous element within the fledgling body politic. With proponents of Revolution fearing a fifth column, many "refractory priests" were imprisoned. In late summer of 1792, the fear soon spread among Parisian populist militants—the infamous "sans-culottes"—that priests and loyalists to the crown were fomenting counterrevolution. Violent mobs descended on some of the jails, knifing the detainees to death. Between two and three thousand prisoners were slain in the so-called "prison massacres," among them three bishops and 220 priests.[21] Many priests went into exile. A law passed that required deportation for any priest publicly denounced by twenty "active citizens." Later it was reduced to six citizens.[22]

The climate of fear brought on by war and worries of a "danger within" helps explain the measures of *déchristianisation* after 1792, the radical attempt to displace Catholicism and replace it with a new *cultus* of reason, revolution, and republican virtue. What is more, the bloody, populist uprising in the Vendée region of western France, begun in March of 1793 and led by refractory priests, exacerbated the anticlerical and anti-religious hostility of this time.[23] In depositing subsequent traumatic memories for the Catholic Church, few periods are more significant than this one. Its main features include the replacement of the Gregorian calendar with the French republican calendar, which abolished the Sabbath, saints' days, and any reference to the Church; the renaming of street and place names, eradicating religious references and replacing them with ideals and figures of the Revolution; the holding of anticlerical parades in which the Church and the Pope were publicly mocked; the banning of clerical dress; the integration of the historic papal lands in Avignon and Comtat Venaissin into the Republic; the plundering of churches and monasteries to finance the revolutionary armies fighting abroad; and, not least, the deportation or execution of thousands of priests or religious suspected of disloyalty to the Revolution. What is more, many historic churches and monasteries, most infamously the great Abbey of Cluny, were almost completely destroyed during this time—their ruins often used for nearby building projects.[24] Finally, the well-known, if short-lived, transformation of the Cathedral of Notre Dame into the "Temple of Reason"—an occurrence that happened at other churches in France—became in the ultramontane imagination of the nineteenth century one of the most disturbing images from this period, a symbol of the danger, sacrilege, and hubris of "the ideas of 1789."[25]

The guillotining of Louis XVI and Marie Antoinette took place during these febrile years. The blade which severed the head of the king also severed any bonds of sympathy between the new regime and the Pope. In Rome, Pius VI proclaimed the decapitated king a "martyr" for the faith and arranged a requiem mass on his behalf at the Quirinal Palace. From this point onward, a firm link between the papacy and counterrevolutionary monarchs—the twin evils of "throne and altar" or "crown and church"—was made in the mind of revolutionaries. These events represent the death throes of the Gallican tradition. While the Revolution (especially once Napoleon took the reins) sometimes possessed a "Gallican" cast, as some have argued, the Church and monarchy that emerged after 1815 looked to Rome for direction in a way that had not been the case during the *ancien régime*.

The collapse of radicalism and the emergence of the Directory after 1794 moderated the course of revolution. Even so, anticlericalism continued apace. And although Napoleon's quest for power led him to temper the Revolution's assault on the Church, his invasion of Italy, welcomed by anticlerical Jacobins and Jansenists on the ground, brought the offensive against Catholicism to the very door of Rome. As we have seen, the temporal fortunes of the Pope were dealt a harsh blow by the Treaty of Tolentino (1797); this was accompanied by a wide-ranging attack on religious orders in northern and central Italy, their suppression, and the sale of their property to raise funds for the French satellite states. Rome and its immediate, contiguous ecclesiastical holdings were spared at first, but this proved to be short-lived. Pius VI was both aging and sick, and his temporal power had long been subject to criticism for he could neither adequately protect nor provide for his subjects in the Papal States. Throughout 1797, the French presence waxed in Rome with Frenchmen and their Italian supporters freely sporting the tricolor cockades and ridiculing the extant government.

The situation deteriorated when in December of 1797 a fracas occurred in Rome between republican revolutionaries and papal loyalists. A member of the latter fired a bullet that killed the French general Mathurin-Léonard Duphot.[26] The Directory demanded action against Rome and Napoleon gladly consented. Duphot was replaced by General Louis-Alexandre Berthier, who received orders to occupy Rome, remove the Pope, and set up a Roman republic. Paris buzzed with talk about terminating the papacy as an institution.[27] By early February 1798, Berthier's forces had entered Rome and occupied Castel Sant'Angelo. Pius VI had ordered relics to be carried around the city in processions. People thronged to St. Peter's and the other major basilicas to pray for deliverance. But on February 15, French forces took the city, largely unopposed. Republican sympathizers planted a tree of liberty on the Capitoline hill near the equestrian statute of Marcus Aurelius. Banners of "Religion and Liberty," "Sovereignty of the People," and "Equality and the Rule of Law" were unfurled. General Berthier tersely communicated to Paris: "Rome is Free." The Eternal City became essentially a French *département* on the Tiber. The octogenarian Pope was then informed that he would have to leave the city in three days. When Pius asked for permission to be left in peace to die in Rome, Berthier refused and allegedly responded: "One can die anywhere."[28]

The image of the frail Pope being escorted from Rome on an uncertain journey to his likely death proved jarring and enduring. In the short term, it helped inspire the counterrevolutionary Sanfedist (Holy Faith) uprising—an armed, peasant crusade, strongest in the southern peninsula led by Cardinal Fabrizio Ruffo (1744–1827), that greatly destabilized French suzerainty.[29] In the long term, the Pope's plight helped awaken European-wide sympathy for the papacy—as would the kidnapping of his successor, Pius VII in 1809— and thereby assisted in shaping the ultramontane imagination. On February 20, 1798 Pius was ordered into a carriage and sent to house arrest in a convent in Siena. At towns along the way, crowds comprising both the pious and the curious turned out to see the Vicar of Christ, "prisoner of Anti-Christ." In March of 1799, when the situation of the French seemed more precarious, he was moved from Siena across the Apennines to Bologna and then on to

Parma. When the Austro-Russian army descended on Lombardy in the hope of driving out the French, Pius was whisked across to Piedmont and then taken over the Alps to Briançon, to Grenoble, to Valence. The Directory had planned on taking him farther north. But at Valence, in the dilapidated Hôtel du Gouvernement, in a bed with a view of the Rhône river, he died on August 29, 1799, purportedly praying for his enemies.[30] "His death," wrote the revolutionary *Courrier Universel*, "has, as it were, placed a seal on the glory of the philosophy of modern times."[31]

*   *   *

The years 1799 and 1800 represent both a nadir and turning point in the history of the modern papacy. When Pius VI died, the College of Cardinals was in disarray. The Pope's temporal holdings had witnessed occupation and the disorienting spirit of revolution. In Paris and across Europe, anticlericals rejoiced that the head of reaction, "the ogre on the Tiber," seemed to be finished as an institution. Some members of the French Directory crowed about Pius being the "the last Pope."

But history is full of surprise twists. At arguably the lowest point of the papacy in modern times, a book, *The Triumph of the Holy See and the Church against the Attacks of the Innovators* (1799), appeared, offering an indication of ultramontane resistance and Catholic revival in the coming century and a sign of the will of papal loyalists to turn trauma into triumph. Unflappably asserting the case for Papal Infallibility (more on this later) and defending the temporal authority of the Pope, the work was penned by the conservative Camaldolese monk Bartolomeo Alberto Cappellari, who would become Pope Gregory XVI (r. 1831–46), a fortress of reaction and the predecessor of Pius IX.[32]

But in 1800 the conclave, meeting in Venice, selected a more conciliatory figure in Cardinal Luigi Barnaba Chiarmonte, Bishop of Imola, who took the name Pius VII (r. 1800–23) to show solidarity with his predecessor. With Rome occupied by the French, the Austrian Emperor Francis II and his Foreign Minister Thugut saw themselves as the savior of the papacy and had made provision for a quorum of cardinals to travel to the Benedictine cloister on the island of San Giorgio off the coast of Austrian-controlled Venice to hold their conclave. The outcome of this conclave is important for understanding Döllinger's conflicts with Rome later in the century because one of its central concerns was the future of the Papal States, especially the Papal Legations in northern Italy (Ferrara, Bologna, Romagna), without the economic production of which, many felt, the papacy could not sustain itself as a temporal power. Austria, it should be noted, possessed a countervailing interest to annex these lands to its empire. With the benefit of hindsight, some historians have argued that this might have been a propitious moment for the temporal power of the Pope to cease.[33]

But this did not happen. After deadlocking for three months over two candidates, Cardinal Ercole Consalvi (1757–1824) helped break the impasse by proposing Chiarmonte as a third option. Chiarmonte's relative youth at 58 and his belief, expressed in a much-circulated Christmas sermon of 1797, that the Revolution and the Church were not wholly incompatible, were held against him by some.[34] But he was a firm believer in the necessity of the Pope's temporal authority and in reclaiming papal influence in northern Italy, whether against France or Austria. Again, Austria desired a candidate with different views on this matter, so Francis II and Thugut regretted the outcome. They were so displeased, in fact, that they denied the cardinals use of Venice's glorious St. Mark's Cathedral to hold the papal coronation; it had to take place in the cramped monastery church and the piazza at San Giorgio. Curious Venetians gawked with telescopes from across the water.[35]

After the ceremony, Pius VII returned to Rome as the political winds shifted. Napoleon defeated Austria, again, at the battle of Marengo (June 14, 1800) and thus it was Napoleon, not Francis, with whom the new Pope would have to deal. Indeed, through military success and political intrigue, Napoleon's hour had come; the era of the French Directory had given way to the Consulate in France, and Napoleon's powerful personality was now at the center of French politics and would remain there until his defeat in 1814. For some time, Napoleon had recognized the limitations of past anticlerical policies for stable statecraft and wanted to improve relations with Rome. Much ink has been spilt attempting to pin down Napoleon's personal beliefs, but practically all agree that he regarded a pinioned Church as a pillar of his political legitimacy.[36] In a speech before the clergy in Milan, he made his new attitude clear: "A society without a religion is like a ship without a compass.... France has had her eyes opened through suffering, and has seen the Catholic religion to be the single anchor amid the storm."[37] Profoundly skeptical of one another, Napoleon and Pius VII nonetheless needed one another; Pius required Napoleon to restore Catholicism to France; Napoleon needed Pius to give his rule an aura of religious legitimacy, and to placate a society still deeply divided over the Civil Constitution of the Clergy (1791).

As is well known, Napoleon and the Pope, after much vitriol and fussing, agreed on the Church–state Concordat of 1801, and later Pius (reluctantly) attended Napoleon's imperial coronation in 1804, as immortalized in the famous painting by Jacques-Louis David. The Concordat resolved many of the outstanding problems between France and the Church, even if it fell short of what the Church desired. It recognized Catholicism as "la religion de la grande majorité" of the French people, but not as the official state religion. The revolutionary principle of freedom of worship was recognized, so long as public tranquillity was not disturbed. Bishops were to be nominated first by the Consul of France and then receive canonical installation by the Pope. Ecclesiastical properties not confiscated and sold off during the Revolution would be placed under the control of bishops, but the Church had to promise not to harass those who had purchased church lands during the Revolution. Additional articles made provisions for seminaries, recognized diocesan boundaries, and provided for clerical salaries, among other things.[38] The fact that the lost French papal lands of Avignon and Comtat Venaissin, not to mention the Legations in northern Italy, were not even on the negotiating table illustrates the weakened position of the Pope. In the end it was a bitter pill for the Church to swallow, but it found itself having to accept the bad to prevent the worst. "The two sides negotiated about different things," Owen Chadwick has nicely summed up; "the Pope was a religious man ignorant of politics. Bonaparte was an able politician for whom religion was an instrument of policy. The one could not get Catholic restoration without the complaisance of a revolutionary general, the other could not reunite France except by using the Pope whom he despised."[39]

After ratifying the Concordat and without consulting Rome, Napoleon attached to it several so-called "police regulations" or "Organic Articles." These restored the *placet*, the historical prerogative claimed by the French government to forbid the publication of bulls or briefs coming from Rome; banned nuncios (papal ambassadors) from exercising authority in the Church of France; made an appeal to France's Council of State the last resort in legal conflicts within the Church; prevented bishops from establishing seminaries or chapter houses without approval of the government; required teachers at seminaries to sign the Gallican articles of 1682, which stipulated that general Church councils were a higher authority than the Pope; ordered a single catechism and liturgy for all of France; and banned many feast days that did not take place on Sunday. All together, these regulations amounted to an extensive set of riders to the agreement, violating both the spirit and the letter of the Concordat. The Pope and Curia protested strongly, but did not make an effort to renege on the Concordat. The power of the modern state stood ascendant, implacable.[40]

During the reign of Pius VII, Napoleon pursued his interests in Italy. While a similar Concordat of 1802 improved Church–state relations in what had become the Italian Republic, the successor to the briefly-lived Cisalpine Republic, the situation below the Alps remained tense and fraught with difficulty. The Church had to cope with the often strident anticlericalism of Italian Jacobins and with Napoleon's importuning power politics. Following Napoleon's assumption of the title of emperor in France in 1804, the Italian Republic was transformed into the Kingdom of Italy with Napoleon himself as king (crowned in the Duomo of Milan) and his stepson Eugène de Beauharnais as viceroy. The Kingdom covered practically all of northern Italy, including parts of the Papal States. While the Pope enjoyed some autonomy around Rome, Napoleon regarded him and King Ferdinand, the Bourbon ruler of southern Italy and Sicily, essentially as his vassals. A medallion with the inscription of *Napoleon rex totius Italia* was issued; Napoleon baptized his son with the title "king of Rome."[41]

In 1805, with the ambitious Emperor reaching the height of his power, relations between Napoleon and Pius deteriorated. On June 8, 1805, Napoleon imposed on the Kingdom of Italy the French Civil Code (which, among other things, allowed for divorce) to the Pope's great displeasure. In 1806, Napoleon drove the Bourbons from Naples, placing first his brother Joseph and then his brother-in-law Joachim Murat on the throne. The Pope was now surrounded. Meanwhile, Napoleon found himself embroiled in the Wars of the Third and Fourth Coalitions, conflicts that would determine mastery of Europe. Although the Pope asked that he be allowed to remain neutral, Napoleon insisted that the entire Italian peninsula must support his so-called "Continental system," which imposed a European blockade against France's enemies. Pius refused to comply, writing Napoleon: "Your Majesty is immensely great, but you are elected, crowned, recognized as the Emperor of the French and not as Emperor of Rome."[42]

Napoleon did not take this well. On January 21, 1808, he ordered the occupation of Rome. The Pope took refuge in the Quirinal Palace with his trusted advisor Cardinal Bartolomeo Pacca (1756–1844), a zealous champion of the Pope's temporal and spiritual powers. On May 17, 1809, Napoleon formally annexed the Papal States to his European-wide dominions.

Virtual prisoners in the Quirinal Palace, Pacca and Pius drew up *Quam memorandum* (June 10, 1809), which excommunicated Napoleon and the French invaders. They knew this would spell trouble. "*Consumatum est*," they said to one another on this day, according to Pacca's memoirs.[43] "By the authority of almighty God," read the letter of excommunication, "by that of the holy apostles Peter and Paul and by our own, we declare that all those who, after the invasion of Rome and the ecclesiastical territories, after the sacrilegious violation of the Patrimony of St. Peter by the French forces, have committed in Rome and in the Papal States, against ecclesiastical immunity, against even the temporal rights of the Church and the Holy See…have incurred major excommunication." Pius went on to compare Napoleon to the wicked King Ahab taking the vineyard of Naboth as recorded in the Hebrew Scriptures. The letter was pasted in broad daylight on the major basilicas of Rome. When he got wind of this, Napoleon responded to Murat: "He's a raving lunatic, he should be locked up!"[44]

Actions followed words. During the night of July 5, French forces attacked the Quirinal Palace, descending from the roof to overwhelm the Swiss Guards. The Pope was apprehended and forced to leave Rome the following day for an unknown destination with only Cardinal Pacca accompanying him. Taken to Grenoble, the Pope was later brought to Savona on the Ligurian coast, arriving on August 17, 1808. There he remained a prisoner of the French under house arrest for nearly three years, until June of 1812. The sad spectacle of the captivity of Pius VI seemed to be repeating itself with Pius VII. During this time, the Pope refused many of the creature comforts and income offered to him by the French. A Benedictine monk used to solitude, he chose to live simply, praying, reading, taking walks, and enjoying pinches of snuff. He even did his own washing and mending. The image of the lonely monk, the "martyr Pope," at the mercy of a power-hungry, modern Caesar awakened sympathy for the papacy from across Catholic Europe, and this in turn contributing powerfully to currents of Catholic revival and ultramontanism.[45] Pius VII's "prisons and bonds" created a "halo" around him for future generations, as Cardinal Nicholas Wiseman later recorded.[46]

During this time, with the help of bullied and compromising clerics, Napoleon ham-fistedly sought to reorganize the Church. He appointed an ecclesiastical commission and attempted to drag many of the institutions of the papacy to France. Cardinals not dismissed for intransigence, along with heads of many religious orders, were prodded to come to Paris. The Vatican archives followed.[47] In the Papal States, the Inquisition was abolished, Jews released from the ghetto, French law was introduced, papal troops were conscripted into the French civic guard, and archeological excavations of the Roman Forum were begun. (Napoleon was always keen to associate his own power with that of ancient Rome.[48])

Furthermore, the French launched in Rome what one historian has called a "war against God."[49] Numerous monasteries and convents were closed; those religious who resisted were harassed and sometimes thrown into the street. Reminiscent of the Constitutional oath of 1791, a new oath of loyalty to the Emperor was required of all clergy. A sizable minority (nine bishops and 500 priests) refused to accept this. Those who dissented were dismissed and often imprisoned in the Castel Sant'Angelo; hard cases were shipped off to camps in Corsica or to fortresses in Calabria. For many, this period appeared as if the days of Nero and Diocletian had returned. One priest locked up in Castel Sant'Angelo composed a prayer for daily recitation: "My God, if Napoleon makes me die of privation and fatigue I will be patient. I am here for love of you, but I promise you that I will absolutely refuse to die of feeling sorry for myself."[50] But presumably many did feel sorry for themselves and the atmosphere in Rome was thick with resentment against Napoleon and nostalgia for former times.

With Rome bereft of the papacy and in the clutches of French power, Napoleon was not yet finished with Pius VII. On June 9, 1812 the Emperor moved the abstemious Pope from Savona, allegedly to prevent his escape by an English war vessel. Under cover of darkness he was unceremoniously carted off to Fontainebleau, arriving on June 19 and retained there until January 1814. Napoleon implausibly attempted to portray his captivity as the lengthy visit of an honored guest. Pius did not go along with this, continued to refuse privileges offered to him and preferred to live a simple, devout life—something that, again, contributed to his aura as a martyr of the Revolution in the eyes of the faithful and in subsequent ultramontane recollection.[51] On January 19, 1812, Napoleon paid a personal visit to the Pope at Fontainebleau; rumors circulated that he physically threatened the aging pontiff. Thereafter, Napoleon had his ministers draw up "the Concordat of Fontainebleau," an effort to ameliorate the enduring Church–state conflict, but with Rome, not surprisingly, as the lesser partner. At first the weakened Pope consented, but later sent Napoleon a letter of retraction. Napoleon was incensed.

But the Emperor's days of rule were numbered. After the "Battle of Nations" near Leipzig in October 1813, Napoleon's troops were in retreat, withdrawing to the west. On January 1, 1814 Prussian forces crossed the Rhine. Shortly thereafter, fearing the Pope would be liberated by advancing allies, Napoleon ordered his return to Savona. Desperate and outraged by the betrayal of his brother-in-law Murat, Napoleon's puppet in Rome, who had gone over to the allies, Napoleon decided to release the Pope to return to Rome, restoring him to sovereignty over his states and encouraging him to return to the Eternal City. Shortly after Napoleon abdicated, Pius VII returned to Rome on May 24, 1814, entering with lavish fanfare through the Porta del Popolo (Figure 1.2).[52] His return marked the end of a momentous, disruptive period in the Church's history that had begun in 1789. For the faithful, Pius's homecoming, combined with Napoleon's abdication, signified the triumph of the spirit over the sword, Christ over Caesar. Once in Rome, Pius discovered that someone had a made a large sculpture, showing the Pope on his throne and Napoleon naked in the dust at his feet.[53]

The story of Pius VII was not lost on the young Döllinger in distant German lands. "The impression made upon him by the character of that pope [Pius], and his resistance to Napoleon," Lord Acton once wrote, "had much to do with his [Döllinger's] resolution to become a priest."[54]

*   *   *

After the Restoration of 1815, it became commonplace among devout Catholics to produce "martyrologies" of those who had died at the hands of the Revolution and Napoleon. "A Martyrology of the Clergy of France during the Revolution," for example, appeared in Paris in 1840. Dedicated to "all pious souls," it offered an alphabetical list of clergy and religious "who died for the Catholic religion during the turmoil of the Revolution [*tourmente révolutionnaire*]."[55] This is a small but revealing example of how the trauma of 1789–1815 was remembered and commemorated in the nineteenth century. The unstated goal of such commemorations was to shore up Catholic, and specifically ultramontane, identity, by etching in memory the agony of the Church, and thereby emboldening the faithful and encouraging vigilance against "the disastrous principles of 1789."[56]

But in fact this had begun much earlier. The aforementioned triumphal entry of Pius VII to Rome on May 24, 1814 offered strong indication of the

Figure 1.2. Pope Pius VII's triumphal return to Rome, May 24, 1814.

Source: Engraving by Giovanni Botta, Italy, *c*.1850. Reproduced with permission from Getty Images.

ultramontane resurgence of the coming decades. "The triumph of divine compassion," Pius wrote from Cesena shortly before his arrival in Rome, "has now been accomplished on our person, torn by an extraordinary act of violence from our peaceful seat.... The pride of the madman [Napoleon] who set himself up as equal of the Most High has [now] been humbled and our deliverance ... followed."[57] The artist Luigi Ademollo (1764–1849) sought to convey the theological significance of the occasion in his "The Triumph of the Church and Pius VII," which showed Pius VII on a chariot accompanied by angelic hosts and the Virgin Mary and led by the iconographic symbols of the Four Gospels (Lion, Eagle, Bull, and Angel). The evil forces of the spirit of the age were portrayed being trampled underneath the chariot.[58] This papal homecoming was a frequent reference point in the ensuing decades, an indication that God would provide even against seemingly overwhelming opposition. The event was commemorated lavishly at its centenary by Pius X in 1914, at which time Catholics were reminded that two important little boys were actually eyewitnesses to the event: the future popes Pius IX and Leo XIII.[59]

The lessons from the era taken by the papacy and its defenders will be spelled out more fully later, but for now three points should be highlighted. First, the turmoil after 1789 appeared to make clear that without firm authority, not least churchly authority, anarchy would be loosed upon the world, the spirit of Antichrist would reign.[60] The "true source of all the evils" of the present age, Pope Leo XII (r. 1823–9) indicated in his letter *Ubi primum* of

1824 is "a stubborn contempt for the Church's authority." The first step in acquiring an antidote for the problem, he wrote, referencing Pope Leo the Great, is to accept "Peter in Peter's See, and in the person of the Roman Pontiff who is Peter's Successor."[61] Advocated by many others, the forceful assertion of papal authority and primacy gained momentum in the coming decades, culminating in the decrees of the Vatican Council. The second major lesson drawn from the Revolution's nationalization of ecclesiastical land and the kidnapping of two popes was that in order to have a secure spiritual voice the Pope must maintain an inviolate temporal possession. "[T]he events of the present time," Pius VII averred, "show how necessary is this temporal power to assure to the supreme Head of the Church the free and certain exercise of the [spiritual] power over the world which has been divinely committed to him."[62] Finally, "the bitterness of the times in which Catholicism now finds itself," as Pope Gregory XVI put it, was not simply a product of fleeting political unrest, but of a much deeper intellectual perfidy rooted in the "rationalist" thought of the previous century, which was often traced back to Protestantism or its wily, intra-Catholic cousin, Jansenism.[63]

Together, these lessons helped fashion a thoroughly anti-modern synoptic through which the nineteenth-century papacy viewed the emerging "modern age." In light of the despoliation and persecution that the Church had experienced, it should be emphasized, these were far from unreasonable conclusions to draw. Accommodation with modernity simply did not appear like a workable option; it was the task of the Church, in fact, to double down: to pit papal supremacy against the revolutionary era's challenge to authority, to defend the temporal powers of the papacy as a safeguard for its spiritual function, and to promote constant vigilance against ideas rooted in the eighteenth-century Enlightenment and its offspring, "the godless Revolution." Such trains of thought helped turn the trauma of the Revolution into the combative ultramontanism of the nineteenth century, which Döllinger at first embraced and then, after mid-century, forsook.

ULTRAMONTANISM AND HISTORICISM, OR *THE POPE* AND *THE POPES*

Among the most famous lines in Giuseppe di Lampedusa's *The Leopard* come when Tancredi, the nephew of the protagonist Prince Don Fabrizio, opines to his uncle: "Unless we ourselves take a hand now they'll foist a republic on us. *If we want things to stay as they are, things will have to change.*"[64] The second sentence, in particular, captures much about the post-1815 order in Europe and about the papacy's place therein. It also speaks to the enduring sense of disorientation and transition that many felt during this time, despite the best efforts of Rome and the monarchical powers of Europe to prevent the volcano of Revolution from erupting again.

Two intellectual forces came into their own during this period that impinged strongly on Döllinger's intellectual formation and sense of vocation: *ultramontanism* and *historicism*. Promoters of the first, already referenced many times now, championed the centralization of the papacy and the Pope's (infallible) authority and saw the Roman Church (both in its temporal and spiritual power) as a bedrock of order and a bulwark against revolutionary zeal. Representatives of the second, historicism, turned to history to explain the momentous changes of the recent past and sought in historical scholarship a key to human understanding in general—including understanding of sacred texts and church history. Historicism, Friedrich Meinecke wrote in 1936, represents "one of the greatest intellectual revolutions that have ever taken place in Western thought."[65] These two forces are well illustrated in two important works from the period, both focusing on the papacy: respectively Joseph de Maistre's *The Pope* (1819) and Leopold von Ranke's *History of the Popes* (1834–6). Knowledge of their broader context and content, in turn, provides a window on to the intellectual environment that both Döllinger and Pius IX inherited in the middle decades of the nineteenth century.

The immediately relevant context, of course, is the post-1815 Restoration order. After Pius VII had returned to Rome and with the downfall of Napoleon underway, the question of reorganizing Europe presented itself with great urgency. The European powers that met at the Congress of Vienna in 1814 and 1815, led by Austria's redoubtable Count Metternich, presided over the dismembering of Napoleon's Empire and reinstating "legitimate" rulers on the thrones of Europe. The oft-used phrase "turning back the clock before 1789" applies here, but it is important to keep in mind that, indeed, for things to stay the same, some things had to change. Put differently, the revolutionary upheaval of the past two decades could not simply be scuttled into oblivion; some ideas and developments were around to stay, now to be amalgamated, complexly and often fatefully, with resuscitated elements of the Old Regime.[66]

Not only a monarchical and aristocratic, but also a religious, even mystical, ethos pervaded the Congress of Vienna. Numerous statesmen and churchmen were convinced that the attack on "throne and altar"—led by the "Corsican Anti-Christ"—had amounted to an attack on God himself and accordingly conceived of their duties in profoundly spiritual terms. This was achingly true, for example, of Russia's Tsar Alexander I (r. 1801–25), who traveled to Vienna to attend the Congress himself. Under the influence of the German mystic Baroness Juliane von Krüdener (1764–1824), the Tsar had conceived the idea for a so-called Holy Alliance—eventually signed by Russia, Austria, and Prussia—designed to stanch any recrudescence of the spirit of secularism and anti-monarchicalism that had come bundled with the Revolution. But this was only one part of a more complex diplomatic system of alliances—the so-called "Congress System"—that would constitute the framework of European power relations for the next half century.[67]

The fate of the Papal States hung in the balance in 1814–15. The European monarchies tended to regard the Pope as one of their own, a fellow monarch and victim of Napoleonic aggression, and saw in him a valuable ally against future unrest. This sympathy gave the papal diplomat Cardinal Consalvi a strong hand at Vienna and allowed him to negotiate for virtually the full restoration of the Pope's lands in Italy, if not the French papal enclaves. A prudent, compromising reactionary, however, Consalvi recognized that the re-establishment of the largest "prince-bishopric" of the *ancien régime* did not come without risks and complexities, in part because a younger generation in central Italy had become accustomed to the laws, liberties, and more efficient governance administered during the Napoleonic period. Consalvi's caution and spirit of moderation, in fact, often brought him into conflict with the ultra-conservative elements of the papal Curia—the so-called *zelanti*—who did not want to concede an iota to the revolutionary interlude.[68]

While Pius VII had regained control around Rome upon his return in May 1814, a fully restored Papal States became a reality only at the close of the Congress of Vienna in June 1815. At this time, and against some Austrian hesitations, the Pope gained control of the Legations in the North and the Marches on the Adriatic Coast. Regaining the Legations proved fateful, because these regions, while the wealthiest, contained many "Jacobin," anti-papal elements and would prove a thorn in the side of the papacy until the revolutions of 1848 and beyond. The younger generation in these areas, Consalvi wrote Cardinal Pacca, "have never known the Pope's government and have a very low opinion of what it is like. They resent being ruled by priests.... Most of the people's minds are not on our side."[69]

The restored lands of the Papal States—Umbria, the Legations, and the Marches—were officially joined under a single government by a *motu propio* of July 6, 1816. The result was a jumble. Many elements of the French system were retained: the land was divided into seventeen delegations rule by clerical delegates, who were advised by local consultative bodies whose members were selected by the Papal Secretary of State. Laymen were banned from holding the highest posts of government, while lower lay members of the civil service were required to wear priestly cassocks to identify themselves with the clerical regime—a peculiarity that often struck travelers, including Döllinger and Lord Acton when they traveled together in the Papal States in 1857. Many of the older local rights of the Old Regime—feudal privileges, baronial exemptions, and municipal customs—had been attenuated or swept away during the Revolution, so the new clerical regime inherited a more direct, "Bonapartist" relationship with the people than had been the case before the Revolution. In times of scarcity and crisis, this meant that the people focused their ire all the more on the priestly caste which ruled them.

But the priests, including the Pope at the top of the system, were generally more interested in things of the spirit than in attending to the mundane affairs of revenue, roads, bridges, and law. This fact was the basic dilemma of the Papal States. The problem was presciently recognized by Cardinal Giuseppe Sala (1762–1839), who submitted a memorandum, "The Defects of our System," to the Pope shortly after 1815. The spiritual function of the papacy is essential to its nature, he wrote, employing Aristotelian categories; but the temporal function is only accidental and accessory. The system often confused the sacred and the profane and it would be better if the temporal and the spiritual were separated. (Döllinger would make a similar argument in 1861.) But for the time being, Sala nonetheless conceded, the Pope required the accidental temporal power so that he could exercise the essential spiritual power. "God is free to work miracles at His will but, in the ordinary way, the Pope will not be able to act as Pope if he has no State to enable him freely to exercise his authority and to command that respect and that obedience which all the faithful owe him."[70] *Zelanti* in the Curia and ultramontanes across Europe dispensed with looking for any miracle, and argued straight-forwardly for the necessary relationship between the temporal and spiritual power. Age-old custom appeared to support this arrangement and the lessons from the revolutionary era trauma reinforced it. As Eamon Duffy has nicely summed up: "The restoration of the Papal States is the single most important fact about the nineteenth-century papacy.... If the Pope did not remain a temporal king, then it seemed he could no longer be the Church's chief bishop. That perception colored the response of all the nineteenth-century popes to the modern world."[71]

In addition to the restoration of the Papal States, the post-1815 order witnessed the return of many institutions and practices that liberals deemed anachronistic, "medieval." The Inquisition and the Index of Forbidden Books made a come-back.[72] Divorce was rendered illegal again; mixed marriages between Catholics and Protestants were forbidden. Jews were required to return to the ghetto and attend mandatory masses. Jansenist ideas, Freemasonry, and various "secret societies" harboring subversive, "Jacobin" views (especially among the *carbonari*) were routinely and repeatedly condemned—in papal encyclicals and in conservative literature more generally.[73] Censorship and a general spirit of anti-modern suspicion became the order of the day.

Of great moment for the future of ultramontanism, the Society of Jesus (the Jesuits) was reconstituted as a religious order, having been suppressed in 1773 by Pope Clement XIV. Pius VII's *Sollicitudo omniam Ecclesiam* (1814) snatched the Jesuits from the sidelines of history, where liberals would have preferred they remained. On August 7, 1814, an elaborate ceremony marked the occasion in Rome's Church of the *Gesù*, which housed Ignatius Loyola's bodily remains. Hereafter, the Jesuits grew rapidly, spreading across Europe and beyond. Owing their new lease on life to Pius VII, and once again taking their traditional "fourth vow" of special obedience to the Pope, Jesuits soon numbered among the most ardent defenders of the Pope and his prerogatives, temporal and spiritual. Widely reviled by liberals and Protestants ("Jesuitism" became a catch-all term denoting ultramontane polemics), Jesuits gave as good as they got, utilizing the expansion of the press and transportation in the nineteenth century as effective means of spreading ultramontane opinions.[74] From their ranks emerged some of Döllinger's fiercest opponents and he, in turn, came to view the Jesuits' ascendancy—and the "Romanism" or "Vaticanism" that he felt they stood for—as a hindrance to the Church Universal and their understanding of the papacy as misguided from the standpoint of theological and historical scholarship.

*   *   *

But what exactly was the Pope in this new, uncertain, nostalgic modern age?

The voice that gave the most influential treatment of this question from an ultramontane perspective did not come from the Jesuits. Rather, it came from the lay (albeit Jesuit-educated) French-speaking Savoyard philosopher and statesman, Joseph de Maistre (1753–1821), author of *The Pope* (1819). With this book, de Maistre put the question of papal authority squarely on the agenda of post-1789 Catholic thought; it would culminate in the formal declaration of Infallibility in 1870. As we have seen, the Revolution had greatly destabilized the claims of hereditary and churchly authority. The weakening of time-tested authorities, Restoration thinkers not irrationally had concluded, had only led to bloodshed, confusion, war, and a tyranny (in the form of Napoleon) worse than in ages past. The grand ideals of liberty, equality, and fraternity, despite enjoying pockets of clerical support, became firmly associated with the guillotining of priests and the plundering of monasteries. The task of the present, it followed, was to restore the former foundations of legitimate authority—political authority, to be sure, but even more importantly the religious authority of Christianity upon which political authority had traditionally derived its claims.

Exalting the importance of religious authority pervades the writings of "Romantic" writers such as Count Louis Bonald (1754–1840), René de Chateaubriand (1768–1848), Friedrich Schlegel (1772–1829), Rafael de Vélez (1777–1850), Adam Müller (1779–1829), and Joseph Görres (1776–1848), among many others. But a rightly ordered society could not arise from just any religious authority. Catholicism had served as the social glue of Western Europe for centuries, and it was to Rome that these authors looked for ascertaining right belief and assuring social stability. Protestantism (and putatively "Protestant" movements such as Jansenism) was not up to the task, because it had originated as a challenge to Rome's authority, and as such had anticipated the more extensive challenge of the Revolution. One of the most common Catholic historical tropes of the era held the Reformation and the Revolution (and their kinship) as a kind of pernicious one–two punch against right thinking and social propriety.[75]

The work that most pointedly anticipated de Maistre's was the aforementioned *Triumph of the Holy See and the Church against the Attacks of the Innovators* (1799) written by the monk Bartolomeo Cappellari (later Pope Gregory XVI). Blaming Jansenism, especially the thought of the Italian Jansenist Pietro Tamburini (1737–1827), for the "godlessness" of the present age, Cappellari made the case for the indefectibility of the Church, the Infallibility of the Pope, and the essential "unchangeableness of the government of the church," including the theocratic government of the Pope's temporal holdings on the Italian peninsula. Published at a nadir in the history of the modern papacy, the book, seen in hindsight, evinces remarkable chutzpah and prescience. "It is easier to extinguish the light of the sun," Cappellari wrote quoting the Church Father John Chrysostom, "than to destroy the church." The key to the Church's invincibility, he argued, was the Pope's Infallibility, the immunity of his magisterial authority from the vicissitudes of the spirit of any age. The day for this dogma, long latent and ripening in the bosom of the Church, had finally come, according to Cappellari. The Revolution, a calamity and judgment upon the pride of man, had served providentially as its unwitting midwife.[76]

De Maistre sang a similar tune.[77] Although he initially expressed sympathy for the reformist impulses that led to 1789, the course of events after the fall of the Bastille, and especially the years of the Terror, turned him into an anti-revolutionary of strict observance. In September 1792, the French army invaded his native Savoy, forcing him to flee with his wife and children to Piedmont and later to Switzerland where he began to make his name as a counterrevolutionary publicist. In 1797, he published *Considérations sur la France*, in which he attributed world-historical significance to the French Revolution—an event not unlike the Babylonian captivity of Israel, at once a judgment on a derelict people and a preparing of the way for a higher development. Many of the woes of modern times, he held, could be traced back to Protestantism and its toxic children: Jansenism, Freemasonry, and the rationalist philosophy of the eighteenth century (*philosophisme*).[78] In the "satanic" excesses of the Revolution, these destructive ideas finally reaped the whirlwind, the desolating power of which made clear the long-suffering, redeeming necessity of throne and altar—and the Infallibility of the Pope.[79]

While de Maistre was concerned about "throne"—political sovereignty which could maintain social stability—he felt that political power possessed legitimacy only insofar as it reflected "altar"—the divine sanction of the Church. The problem with the modern age was that all forms of authority had been undermined by the "inexplicable delirium" and "blind impetuosity" of the French Revolution.[80] To restore political authority, one first had to make clear the prior necessity of legitimate religious authority.

And this is precisely what de Maistre sought to do in *The Pope*. Interestingly, he does not rest his arguments primarily on Scripture or Church tradition, but on the basis of what he called a "severe logic" applied to "the problem of sovereignty."[81] Given the natural predilections of human nature—where avarice, self-interest, and cupidity reign supreme—there had to exist in his view a countervailing power to establish order and right conduct. In any enduring form of government, de Maistre reasoned, there must be a "supreme tribunal" where binding decisions are made—whether king, president, council, or parliamentary body. Paradoxically, this authority at once stands above the law and is the law. Without such an authority, all laws would be contested, resulting in social anarchy.

What was true of political sovereignty also applies to spiritual authority. Authority was even more important in the sacred realm, because in de Maistre's view all forms of sovereignty ultimately rested on a religious basis. For Christianity to make sense, God must have left the Church with a "supreme tribunal"; otherwise disunity would have no end in the Church and moral disorder would reign in society. In his judgment, the Revolution and its bloody aftermath had confirmed this; the Reformation and the ensuing wars of religion did the same two centuries earlier. As de Maistre impressively connected the dots in his thinking: "[There can be] no public morals nor national character without religion, no European religion without Christianity, no true Christianity without Catholicism, no Catholicism without the Pope, no Pope without the supremacy which belongs to him."[82]

De Maistre came down especially hard on Protestantism. Its attack on authority and exaltation of "private judgment" lay behind practically every misfortune of the modern age. Luther and Calvin, in his view, were men characterized by "sectarian pride, plebian acrimony, and the fanaticism peculiar to taverns."[83] "The sixteenth century," he wrote, "enkindled a mortal hatred of the pontiff, and the incredulity of our own age, eldest daughter of the Reformation, could not fail to espouse all the passions of its mother."[84] Or, again: "Protestantism...and a thousand other sects...[are] in agitation and labor, ashamed of themselves, and seek with indescribable convulsive energy to make headway against the torrent of errors, after having abandoned themselves to them with the systematic blindness of pride."[85]

Against, this "torrent of errors"—which, with Protestantism, de Maistre also included Eastern Orthodoxy, Anglicanism, Gallicanism, Febronianism, Josephism, Jansenism, and more—de Maistre offered one solution: find one's way back to Rome, recognize the supremacy of the Pope, and submit. "The Sovereign Pontiff is the necessary, the only, the exclusive basis of Christianity. To him belong the promises; without him disappears unity—in other the words, the Church."[86]

But the Pope cannot fulfill his role under just any conditions. With the post-1789 trauma fresh in mind, de Maistre made the case for the necessity of the

Pope's temporal authority and temporal possessions. Without them, the Pope could not exercise his spiritual function freely, but would be compromised by having to live under the sovereignty of a secular prince or, worse still, "the will of the people." De Maistre knew his history well enough to recognize that popes were not always in possession of a state; but he saw the emergence of the Papal States during the Middle Ages—acquired largely by donation, not plunder, he stressed—not as an accidental, but a providential development. The kidnapping and captivity of Pius VII illustrated for de Maistre the fate of a pope stripped of temporal authority.[87]

With the Pope secure in his temporal possessions, the main *spiritual* prerogative of the Pope was infallibility. De Maistre admitted that this teaching had not always been sufficiently recognized. For this, he placed much blame on Gallicanism, which sought to grant the French episcopacy and monarchy considerable leeway to dilute papal authority. Gallicanism taught, moreover, that conciliar authority stood higher than papal authority. De Maistre pointedly disagreed: "all appeals to councils are only inventions of the spirit of revolt."[88] In fact, those eager to invoke conciliar authority, in his judgment, understand neither human nature nor the nature of deliberative bodies: "Those who believe that by multiplying deliberative bodies doubt is diminished, know little of human nature, and have never sat in the midst of a deliberative body."[89]

Authority, instead, ought to reside exclusively in the office of the Pope; for only strict obedience to papal authority promised to check the sectarian and revolutionary spirit that had poisoned the modern mind. Repeatedly, however, de Maistre stressed that his argument was not only supported by theological reasoning, but by deductive logic applied to the general question of sovereignty:

> No human society can exist without government, nor government without sovereignty, nor sovereignty without infallibility; and this last privilege is so completely necessary, that we must suppose infallibility even in temporal sovereignties (where it does not apply) on pain of beholding society dissolved. The Church requires nothing more than of other sovereignties, although it possesses an immense superiority over them, inasmuch as infallibility is on the one hand humanly supposed [*humaninement supposée*] and on the other divinely promised [*divinement promisé*].[90]

Put differently, while de Maistre certainly felt that Papal Infallibility possessed theological legitimacy, he also believed that it was socially and politically necessary. Final authority must rest in a single locus. Otherwise, anarchy enjoys free rein. The wrangling of councils, the fragmentation of Protestantism, the bloodshed of revolution—all pointed, in de Maistre's judgment, to the necessity of the papacy as the final guarantor of theological truth and social order. "This indispensable supremacy [*suprématie indispensable*] can only be exercised by one organ [the Holy See]; to divide it is to destroy it."[91]

To be sure, de Maistre did not invent the idea of Papal Infallibility from whole cloth nor was he alone in advocating for it.[92] Its complex origins stretch back deep into the Middle Ages, and its advocates, in de Maistre's time and now, would see its development in the nineteenth century as the necessary and providential outworking of still more venerable theological verities—above all, the need to maintain right doctrine and fraternal unity among Christians as the writings of the Gospels, Paul's epistles, and the Church Fathers all appeared to call for.[93] Biblical passages, such as Matthew 16:18, John 21:17, John 16:13, Luke 22:32, and Acts 15:28, and later authorities such as Thomas Aquinas and Robert Bellarmine, were especially important for the Infallibilist position.[94]

If not without antecedents, de Maistre's work of 1819 forcefully put the question of Infallibility on the agenda of modern Catholic thought, even if the teaching would attract more subtle (and many not-so-subtle) defenders in the following decades. The ultramontane imagination of the nineteenth century, as Robert McClory has argued, received its "most powerful boost" from de Maistre's *Du Pape*.[95] Or, as Klaus Schatz has written, "Through his work the topic [of Papal Infallibility] suddenly became enormously explosive even in the political and social order, because according to him the papacy and papal infallibility were the only guarantees of social order and stability in a world that had run off the tracks."[96] De Maistre's general influence, furthermore, "formed the spearhead of the counter-revolution in the early nineteenth century in Europe," according to Isaiah Berlin.[97] Döllinger himself felt the extent of this influence during the years of his early professorship in Munich, especially through the mediation of the philosopher Franz von Baader (1765–1841), a staunch admirer of de Maistre.[98] Several of Döllinger's early works—including his three-volume *Die Reformation* (1846–8)—evince pointedly ultramontane strains of thought, de Maistrean in tendency if not necessarily in direct influence.[99]

But if ultramontanism represented one pole of attraction and influence for a German Catholic scholar coming into his own in the 1820s and 1830s, historicism represented another.[100] Historicism is a notoriously difficult concept to get a handle on, in part no doubt because scholars have used it as shorthand to signify such a massive and multifaceted shift in modern Western thought. Its emergence—or what Thomas Nipperdey has called "one of the greatest intellectual revolutions of the modern era"—is generally associated with German academic culture in the late eighteenth and early nineteenth centuries. Its representatives looked primarily to the past and to the category of "development" (*Entwicklung*) to understand any human phenomena—not least the French Revolution, which had given practically all Europeans an acute sense of historical rupture and change.[101] To grasp anything relevant about the present, in other words, one must explore the past, try to grasp its manifold contingencies, and seek to divine therein the principal processes of development that had led from "then" to "now." As Maurice Mandelbaum has nicely summed up, "Historicism is the belief that an adequate understanding of the nature of any phenomenon and an adequate assessment of its value are to be gained through considering it in terms of the place it occupied and the role which it played in the process of development."[102]

Defined as such, historicism applies, *mutatis mutandis*, to a wide range of thinkers in the early nineteenth century: the philosopher Hegel, philologists such as Friedrich August Wölf (1759–1854) and August Böckh (1785–1867), jurists such as Friedrich Karl von Savigny (1779–1861) and Karl Friedrich Eichhorn (1781–1854), biblical scholars such as W. M. L. de Wette (1780–1849) and Ferdinand Christian Baur (1792–1860), among many others. The historical-critical outlook of such scholars and the pervasive historicist academic milieu of the era left a lasting influence on Döllinger;[103] his assessment of and struggles with developments in the Catholic Church of his own day were profoundly shaped by his preoccupation with church history and by the broader Mediterranean and European histories within which church history was nested. Since his outlook in this respect often bore witness to imported ideas from German Protestant academic circles, Döllinger later in life sometimes received the accusation of being a crypto-Protestant.[104]

Perhaps no figure epitomized the ethos of historicism in the early nineteenth century better than Leopold von Ranke (1798–1886), widely considered the founding father of modern academic historiography.[105] In the preface to his 1824 work, *Histories of the Latin and Germanic Nations from 1494 to 1514*, he penned words still invoked by historians today. The goal of history, the young Ranke began, "has been assigned the high office of judging the past, of instructing the present for the benefit of future ages. To such high offices this work does not aspire: it wants only to show what actually happened [*wie es eigentlich gewesen*]." Instead of selectively mining the past for examples of virtuous conduct (*historia magistra vitae* in the Ciceronian adage), the goal of modern academic historical writing was to try to comprehend the past in its own terms, to allow past facts, personalities, and milieux to speak for themselves. "The strict presentation of the facts, contingent and unattractive though they may be," Ranke wrote, "is the supreme law."[106] This could not be accomplished by imposing sweeping philosophical or theological speculations and systems on to the past, Ranke repeatedly insisted; instead the historian had a duty to examine the particulars of the past, shorn of speculative evaluation; pursue exhaustive research; engage in criticism of authentic sources; and then, and only cautiously, hazard interpretations.

Over a decade after de Maistre's *Du Pape* appeared, Ranke published the first volume of his *History of the Popes* in 1834. Volumes two and three appeared in 1836. The author took advantage of its many subsequent printings to enlarge its scope, which extended from the sixteenth century through the revolutionary and Napoleonic eras, to the time of the First Vatican Council. (Early editions bore the title, *The History of the Popes: The Church and State in the Sixteenth and Seventeenth Centuries*; later versions became *The History of the Popes during the Last Four Centuries*.) While de Maistre sought to make a normative argument about the need for papal authority, Ranke sought through "scientific history" (*wissenschaftliche Historie*) to understand the personalities and politics of the Holy See from what he called a "worldly point of view" (*weltliche Betrachtung*), and to place the papacy within the broader context of the European state system as it had developed since the early modern era.[107]

Ranke felt that not being a Catholic gave him greater impartiality and insight into the topic. "[A] Catholic would enter on the subject in a spirit very different from mine," he wrote; one that might result in "indulging in expressions of personal veneration." "[O]ur position affords us different, and, if I am not mistaken, purer and less partial views of history." Exhibiting a fairly common anti-Catholic prejudice that the papacy had become an historical anachronism, he elaborated: "For what is there in the present day that can make the history of papal power of importance to us? Not its particular relation to ourselves; for it no longer exercises any essential influence, nor does it create in us solicitude of any kind; the times are past in which we had anything to fear; we now feel ourselves perfectly secure. Popery can now inspire us with no other interest than what results from the development of its history and former influence."[108]

While some Catholics (such as Lord Acton) esteemed Ranke's work, ultramontane Catholics and the Roman Curia were not impressed by its subtle anti-Catholicism and, in fact, its occasional forthright identification with Protestant Christianity: the German Reformation, Ranke wrote, "[had] the undying merit of having restored Christianity to a purer form[,]... of having rediscovered the true religion."[109] Because of such statements, the work found itself on the Index in 1841.[110]

Although Döllinger obviously did not share Ranke's religious standpoint, he held him in high regard and felt that the type of scholarship that he and his disciples exemplified in Protestant universities ought to be embraced by Catholic scholars as well.[111] In fact, in an address on universities, in language suffused with nationalism, Döllinger once opined that German universities with their distinctive "German historical sense" had no rivals in the world:

I venture to assert that we [Germans] possess it [capacity of historical understanding] in a more eminent degree than any other nation. This power, this impulse to withdraw our minds from the dominion of habit, to break through the atmosphere which the present draws arounds us, to penetrate through clouds of prejudice to the knowledge of the spirit and hidden nature of remote times and foreign nations—is doubtless one of the highest and noblest gifts which God can bestow on man. And it is only given to those who are penetrated by a spirit of restless striving, of indefatigable research in pursuit of truth...; who are not content with surface observations or with the exploitation [*Ausbeutung*] of what has already been discovered but [who want to] advance to the very core and bottom of things.

Mentioning numerous books from other nations influenced by German historical scholarship, Döllinger concluded this address by remarking that historical inquiry amounted to our "vocation in the world" (*Weltberuf*), a universal gift to other nations but one mediated through the particular spirit and genius of the German people.[112]

As we shall see more fully later, Döllinger felt that historical inquiry had a place within the sacred precincts of Catholic theology—a place much larger than ultramontane scholars were willing to grant.[113] On numerous occasions, his historicist sensibilities led him into conflict with his ultramontane colleagues, who felt that a re-engagement with the thought of Thomas Aquinas and other scholastic thinkers remained the surest foundation for the "queen of the sciences" against the ideologies of the age.[114] Revealingly (and if I may briefly get ahead of the story), when Döllinger challenged the validity of Papal Infallibility on "historical" grounds, he received numerous reproving responses, from clergy and laity, arguing that he had set historical knowledge above the Church when in fact, as Archbishop Manning of Westminster asserted, the Church stood antecedent to history; she interprets and judges history's course, not vice versa.[115]

"WORSE THAN ATTILA": THE AGONY OF PETER'S CHAIR, 1820s TO 1860s

> Is it to be wondered that the Pope should be at war with modern civilization, if modern civilization insists upon altering the fundamental relations of society, and if the rebuilding of the social edifice rejects God as the corner stone?[116]
>
> —E. S. Purcell, *Dublin Review* (1862)

From the time of the appearance of de Maistre's *Du Pape* in 1819 until the publication of the later editions of Ranke's *History of the Popes*, the papacy faced a deluge of challenges. Textbook treatments of this period remain beholden to a "Whig" view of history, ritualistically treating the papacy as a hapless roadblock to modernity, a bumbling institution kicking and screaming as forces of liberalism and nationalism inexorably advanced. To be sure, this view is not altogether beside the point, for this period easily ranks among the papacy's most doggedly anti-modern. But too often it fails to engage seriously the standpoint of Rome itself, to make efforts to see developments of the century from the perspective of the papacy's long institutional memory. From this standpoint, the nineteenth century was anything but one of progress: it was the tragic, confusing twilight of Christendom; the sometimes sudden, sometimes gradual fraying of a way of ordering society that had endured for over a millennium. The French Revolution, as we have seen, had given birth to unprecedented anticlericalism, bloodshed, and destruction. In Napoleon Bonaparte a new, callous, and calculating Caesarism had reared its head, the likes of which had not been seen since the persecution of Christians during the Roman Empire. While the settlement at Vienna had restored a measure of stability, the papacy and its ultramontane supporters throughout Europe still felt themselves under siege, determined to resist the sinister apostasy that seemed to lurk just below the surface, crouched and ready to strike again.

To better understand Döllinger's conflict with Pius IX, three aspects of this modern "apostate" spirit ought to be spelled out. First, pontiffs from Pius VII onward recognized that the reconstituted Papal States in central Italy elicited deep-seated hostility within liberal and nationalist circles. The drive toward Italian unification, the *Risorgimento*, gained steam with the establishment of the so-called "Young Italy" (*Giovanne Italia*) movement founded by Giuseppe Mazzini (1805–82) in 1831. As this movement developed in the following decades, it became increasingly apparent that the creation of Italy as a modern nation-state (whether as a republic as Mazzini desired or as a constitutional monarchy) and the continuation of the Papal States as a political entity were likely mutually exclusive historical outcomes. The fact that Mazzini and his followers openly spoke of the founding of Italy and the demise of the Papal States in deeply religious, even mystical, terms as "God's will" only inflamed tensions between Rome and the *Risorgimento*.[117] Instead of making concessions to liberals and nationalists, the tendency of the papacy was to double down against them, denouncing critics of Rome's temporal power for their perfidy, pride, and political opportunism.[118]

Second, the danger of the modern age presented itself to Rome not only as a political threat, but as an intellectual challenge as well. This was a multifaceted challenge, but it had several dominant strands. The philosophy of the eighteenth-century Enlightenment had appeared to elevate the autonomous role of human reason far higher than what was acceptable from the standpoint of traditional Catholic philosophy, pitting modern reason against the Church. Descartes, Hume, Kant, Hegel, and a host of lesser lights had given birth to congeries of tendencies in modern thought generally designated by the popes as "rationalism" (*rationalismo* or sometimes *philosophismo*). Unlike Aristotelianism, which Catholic thought had mostly baptized and incorporated into its own bosom in the Middle Ages, this modern species of rationalism was perceived as both hubristic and anticlerical. Instead of seeking to reconcile it to the faith, it should be refuted, root and branch, and the time-tested authority of scholasticism, embodied most exquisitely in Thomas Aquinas, reasserted. As Pius IX put it in *Qui pluribus* (November 9, 1846): "For although faith is above reason, no real disagreement can ever be found between them; this is because both come from the same greatest source of unchanging truth, God."[119] The reassertion of what became known as neo-Thomism or neo-scholasticism happened only in fits and starts in the middle decades of the nineteenth century, but it received a powerful boost in Vatican I's Dogmatic Constitution *Dei Filius* (1870) and by Leo XIII's landmark encyclical, *Aeterni Patris* (1879), which sought to restore a "genuine Christian philosophy" against the intellectual spirit of the modern age.[120]

Another intellectual challenge to the papacy came in the form of religious liberty. The American and French revolutions, if in different ways, had put forward this principle as a way of defusing religious tensions in society and severing the long-standing tie between Church and state, which on the Continent traced its origins back to the Peace of Westphalia (1648) and its well-known formula of *cuius regio, eius religio*.[121] Pontiffs throughout the nineteenth century were unanimous in rejecting religious liberty. In fact, they did not see it as a liberty at all, but as heartless apathy on the part of the state toward the well-being of its citizens' eternal souls. The lackadaisical mind-set that gave birth to this "liberty" was often labeled "indifferentism" (*indifferentismo*) and regarded as one of the most pestilential of modern errors, condemned in the "Syllabus of Errors" (1864) and in several prior encyclicals.[122]

Finally, and perhaps most appallingly of all from the standpoint of Rome, modern ideas deemed inimical to the Church appeared to be capturing the hearts and minds of well-meaning Catholics, such as the Frenchman Felicité de Lamennais (who advocated for religious liberty) or the Italian Jesuit Carlo Passaglia (who came out against the Church's temporal power).[123] It was one thing for Protestants, Jansenists, Freemasons, and anticlericals to espouse dangerous ideas. It was another thing entirely for those who professed themselves to be faithful Catholics to do so. The former represented a disease of the skin, the latter of the heart. A problem of this magnitude required stiff medicine and in heavy doses. This conviction, that the Catholic faithful themselves were falling prey to and even championing misguided modern ideas, is essential to keep in mind when encountering the strident tone and uncompromising rhetoric of nineteenth-century papal statements. The popes did not share the judgment of posterity that they were anachronistic naysayers to modernity; they saw themselves as faithful, embattled shepherds trying to protect the flock in a time of grave crisis and unprecedented apostasy, in a time when the Church faced threats that, according to one prelate, were "worse than Attila."[124]

*   *   *

On July 6, 1823, at the age of eighty-one, Pius VII slipped and fell at the Quirinal Palace in Rome, severely injuring his thigh. He never recovered, but died several weeks later. After an elaborate funeral in St. Peter's, the Conclave of Cardinals met and elected his successor Annibale della Genga as Pope Leo XII (r. 1824–9). While Pius had followed the moderate lead of his minister Consalvi, Leo was more beholden to the ultra-conservative *zelanti* in the Curia. Shortly after his election, in fact, Leo sacked Consalvi as secretary of state—payback, many presumed, for Consalvi's prior dismissal of him from the papal diplomatic service in 1814.[125]

A man of keen intelligence and a rigid moralist, Leo wanted the restored Papal States to serve as a moral example to the world—a godly alternative to revolutionary excesses. And he was quite willing to use law and force to effect his will. The sale of wine was restricted. Taverns, cafés, and the theatres were closed during Lent. Encores and ovations were forbidden when the theatre was open. He decreed stricter regulations on female dress, and males who walked too close behind women were subject to fines and imprisonment. A new jail was opened in Rome under his watch, and quickly filled up with heretics and criminals. Jews were once again forbidden to own property and required to attend mass regularly, without the benefit of proxies.[126] Leo also strengthened the hand of the Jesuits in 1826, by putting them back in charge of the Collegio Romano, their traditional center of education going back to the sixteenth century. A year earlier, in 1825, he proclaimed the first Jubilee of the nineteenth century, an act which attracted thousands of pilgrims to Rome, contributing to currents of popular ultramontanism.[127]

In his first encyclical, *Ubi primum* (May 5, 1824), Leo condemned dechristianization, indifferentism, toleration, Bible societies, and Freemasonry, tracing many of the problems of the modern world to willful contempt for the Church.[128] "[I]f any one wishes to search out the true source of all the evils which We have already lamented ... he will surely find that from the start it has ever been dogged contempt for the Church's authority." As would be the case with his successors, Leo was particularly agitated about indifferentism, a lax attitude toward various worldviews that disguises itself "under the gentle appearance of piety and liberality." "Of course this error [indifferentism] is not new, but in Our days it rages with a new rashness against the constancy and integrity of the Catholic Faith." The "true philosophy" of the Church was needed now more than effort to vanquish the manifold falsehoods of the day.[129]

The death of Leo XII on February 10, 1829 paved the way for the election of the slightly more moderate Francesco Saverio Castiglioni, who became Pope Pius VIII (r. 1829–30), identifying his papacy by name with the persecuted papacies of Pius VI and Pius VII. Elected in a state of precarious health, he lasted in office only twenty months. Under his reign, some of the more severe laws governing the Papal States were relaxed. But his attitude toward the modern age remained thoroughly critical. In *Traditi humilitati* (May 24, 1829), he condemned those who relied too heavily on natural reason, those who interpreted the Bible apart from the magisterium, those who denigrated the sanctity of marriage, and those who joined secret societies (e.g., Free-masons). As he sized up the times, wrong opinions seemed to be enjoying a field day: "The heretics have disseminated pestilential books everywhere by which the teachings of the impious spread, much as cancer." "To counteract this most deadly pest," bishops and priests should "spare no labor."[130]

Pius VIII's death on November 30, 1830 allowed for the election of arguably the most reactionary pope of the nineteenth century: the austere and learned Bartolmeo Alberto Cappellari, who became Gregory XVI (r. 1831–46). As a young man in 1783, Cappellari had joined the Camaldolese Order, which rigidly kept a reformed version of the Benedictine Rule.[131] He rose to become abbot of the Monastery of San Gregorio on the Caelian Hill in Rome. During the Napoleonic occupation, he was expelled from his post and forced to flee Rome due to his intense opposition to French rule. This experience left a lasting impression, contributing to his unyielding opposition to revolutionary ideologies during his pontificate. What is more, by temperament, he distrusted practically all innovations. The Industrial Revolution and the economic liberalism advocated by Adam Smith, David Ricardo, and others received his censure, as did the socialist ideas of Charles Fourier and Saint-Simon. Trains to him were "infernal machines" and he refused their admittance into the Papal States.[132] Prior to his election as Pope, he had been named Cardinal in 1826 and served as the prefect to the Congregation of the Propagation of the Faith. After his election as Pope, he continued the abstemious life of a monk, living simply and eating frugally.[133]

Cappellari's election took place against the backdrop of the revolutionary tremblings that shook Europe in 1830, toppling in France the Bourbon monarchy of Charles X and replacing it with the "bourgeois monarchy" of Louis Philippe.[134] The Italian peninsula was also affected by the revolutionary spirit. As mentioned earlier, Mazzini's "Young Italy" came to life in 1831. By the summer of 1831, much of central Italy found itself in revolt, seeking the withdrawal of foreign powers and the establishment of a unified Italian state. Anticlericalism and anti-papalism freely mingled with the language of liberalism and nationalism.[135] Gregory had to rely on the assistance of Austria, which gladly helped suppress these revolts. But the events of 1830–1 left their mark on his papacy, convincing him ever more firmly that only the alliance of throne and altar could prevent anarchy. In 1832, he published a *Catechism on Revolution*. "Does the holy law of God permit rebellion against the legitimate temporal sovereign?" the *Catechism* asked, and answered: "No, never because the temporal powers come from God."[136]

Cappellari's election invigorated the cause of Papal Infallibility. His aforementioned book, *The Triumph of the Holy See and the Church against the Assault of the Innovators* (1799)—which made the case for extensive papal authority against conciliarists, Gallicans, Jansenists, and Josephists alike—was translated into several languages and received fresh attention in the 1830s. In his encyclicals, Gregory regularly rejected an idea that Döllinger championed after mid-century: that there could be "national churches" functioning in partial independence from Rome. In *Commissum divinitus* (May 17, 1835), he made his view clear that God had "granted to Peter alone... the keys of heaven and entrusted to him the office of feeding the lambs and sheep and confirming his brethren... It is an article of faith that the Roman Pontiff, successor of Blessed Peter the Prince of the Apostles, not only has a primacy of honor, but also of authority and jurisdiction over the universal church, and that, consequently, the bishops, too, are under his authority."[137] "On all sides," he therefore lamented in a letter from September 17, 1833, "the infallibility of the Church is attacked [and] efforts are being made to weaken in every possible way the divine rights of the Apostolic Chair in which resides the stability of ecclesiastical unity."[138]

Gregory proved an unflappable obstacle to liberal Catholics, who wanted the Church to move away from Restoration principles toward some acceptance of political liberalism. The best-known example of this came in Gregory's conflict with the French priest and scholar Felicité de Lamennais. A frequent contributor to reactionary journals, Lamennais gradually shifted his opinion, moved in large part by the harsh actions of "legitimate" rulers against Catholics in Ireland, Belgium, and Poland.[139] In *Progress and Revolution* (1828), he argued that the Church stood to benefit from separation from the state. In 1830, he founded the "agency for the defense of religious freedom" and the periodical *l'Avenir* (the Future), whose contributors advocated the Church's embrace of the principles of freedom of thought, freedom of conscience, and freedom of the press.[140]

In 1831, Lamennais traveled to Rome, hoping to bring Gregory closer to his view. This did not happen. After a long wait in the Eternal City, the meeting between the two men was brief and chilly and the topic of the Church and liberalism never came up. It seemed that Gregory had already made up his mind. In the encyclical, *Mirari vos* (August 15, 1832), Gregory condemned religious freedom as a consequence of the error of "indifferentism." "From the shameful source of indifferentism, or rather from that insanity [*deliramentum*]," he wrote, "comes the absurd and erroneous position that claims that liberty of conscience must be maintained for everyone. It spreads ruin in sacred and civil affairs."[141] Such misguided thinking he traced back to the wanton freedoms desired by Martin Luther and championed in his own time by various sects and secret societies. But the deeper sources derived from the very pit of hell, belching smoke to obscure the sun and locusts to blight the earth. From indifferentism came "the transformation of minds, corruption of youth, contempt of sacred things and holy laws—in other words a pestilence more deadly to the state than any other."[142] In *Singulari nos* (June 25, 1834), he focused on Lamennais by name, deploring "the fatal contamination of the people by indifferentism."[143]

If indifferentism was one manifestation of the modern world's sick soul, overconfidence in human reason—"rationalism"—was another. The prime example of this, as manifested within the Church, is seen in the career of the German scholar Georg Hermes (1775–1831) and his many "Hermesian" disciples—a school of thought Gregory condemned in 1835 (more on this later).[144] What is more, the aforementioned movement of neo-Thomism or neo-scholasticism slowly began stirring to life during Gregory's pontificate and with his approval. In basic terms, the movement sought to recover the thought of Thomas Aquinas along with some of his more influential commentators during the Tridentine era as a means of putting the hubris of modern rationalism in its place. At the same time, its representatives desired to accord human reason a limited but important role in the divine scheme of things. In emphasizing a modest role for reason, neo-Thomists also saw themselves combating Jansenism and various forms of Protestantism, which had gone too far in emphasizing sin's deleterious effects on human reason. With the approval and support of Gregory, the Dominican and Jesuit orders led the way in reviving Thomism. The cities of Perugia, Piacenza, Modena, and Naples were some of its early centers, as well as the Collegio Romano. At Naples, the eighteenth-century Neapolitan Dominican Salvatore Roselli had left a remarkable legacy, embodied in his six-volume *Summa philosophiae ad mentem Angelici Doctoris Thomae Aquinatis* (1777–83). Key scholars building on this legacy during Gregory's pontificate included Serafino Sordi, Carlo Maria Curci, and Luigi d'Azeglio Taparelli, among others. Their voices later coalesced around the Jesuit-run journal *La Civiltà Cattolica*, founded in Naples in 1850, and this quickly emerged as a leading organ of ultramontane and neo-scholastic thought.[145] Not surprisingly, Döllinger often found himself *persona non grata* in its pages, while the Jesuit "Italian" or "Roman" scholastics running the journal received some of his most scathing criticism.[146]

*   *   *

At the time of Gregory XVI's death in 1846, some churchmen thought that his intransigence had gone too far. When the Conclave of Cardinals met in June 1846, an unlikely "compromise" choice emerged from their brief (three-day) deliberations: Cardinal Giovanni Maria Mastai-Ferreti, Bishop of Imola, who took the name Pius IX (r. 1846–78) (Figure 1.3). The decision for him was something of a gamble. At the age of 54, Mastai-Ferreti was young by papal standards and not that well known outside of elite clerical circles. Affable, pious, and charismatic, he also had been known to sympathize with some Italian political aspirations and to criticize aspects of Gregory XVI's rule.[147] Hopes of the Pope as "the protector of the well-being of the Italian people were awakened from Sicily to the Alps," as Döllinger later wrote.[148] When as one of Pius's first acts he declared a general amnesty for former revolutionaries in the Papal States, onlookers wondered if the world was witnessing the birth of a liberal pontificate.[149]

Things turned out quite differently.

Figure 1.3. Pope Pius IX shortly after his election in 1846.

Source: Engraving by Karl Benzinger, in George White, *His Holiness Pope Pius IX*, 3rd ed. (London: R. Washborne, 1878). Image courtesy of Wikimedia Commons.

The story of "Pio Nono" in the 1840s and 1850s continues to fascinate, and it aptly illustrates the trauma experienced by the nineteenth-century papacy as a whole. In these years, and in the decade to follow, the stand-off between "the papacy" and "the revolution" reached a new level of intensity with lasting consequences for the future of Europe and the future of Catholicism—and for the shaping of Döllinger's outlook.

Pius IX's early liberalism did not stop with the amnesty for some revolutionaries. He set up a commission to allow for trains in the Papal States, had gas street lights installed in Rome, set up an agricultural institute to improve crop production, permitted pontifical subjects to attend annual scientific congresses, and introduced tariff reforms to improve trade. In 1847, he relaxed censorship laws and introduced a consultative assembly that included laymen to help with the governance of the Papal States. In 1848, Jews were released from the ghetto, and in theory they could live wherever they liked.[150] When Austrian troops occupied Ferrara, he threatened Metternich with excommunication, conveying publicly the sentiment that Austria's presence in northern Italy (a key gripe of Italian nationalists) had all along been problematic. For these actions and others, he gained international popularity and esteem. The "neo-Guelf" idea championed by Vincenzo Gioberti—that the Pope himself might preside politically over a unified Italian state—began to look improbably plausible. Wherever the Pope went, crowds yelled "Viva Italia, Viva Pio Nono"; some showered his coach with flowers from balconies; others knelt in reverence as he passed by.[151] Letters and cards of approval and congratulations were sent to the Vatican from leaders across Europe and North America—and even from Constantinople. In 1847, US President James Polk recommended in an address to Congress that diplomatic relations should be commenced with Rome.[152]

But all of this would not last. As is well known, the revolutionary year, 1848, brought about an abrupt change in the course of Pius's papacy. In this year, the demand for the expulsion of Austria from northern Italy reached a fevered pitch; nationalists and liberals began to call on the Pope to use his popularity to summon an army to oust Austria. But having the Pope turn against a Catholic monarchy threatened the whole Metternichian system that had been in place since 1815. Pius IX found himself in a bind and, at first, he vacillated. But then on April 29, he gave a speech, indicating that under no circumstances could he go to war against Austria, that he could not support a federal Italy, and that it remained in the interest of all subjects to remain loyal to their legitimate leaders. In short, he made clear that, despite the wishes projected on him after his election, he was going to toe the same line as his predecessors in matters of foreign policy.

Disillusion quickly set in. Support for him among liberals and nationalists turned to disgust and a sense that they had been betrayed. Practically overnight, Pius went from being among the most beloved of public figures in Italy to the most reviled. By the late summer and fall of 1848, the Papal States and the city of Rome bristled with discontent and a spirit of agitation. Anticlerical revolutionaries seized the moment to foment protests. By early November, the situation seemed to be careening out of control. Pius's lay Prime Minister, Pellegrino Rossi (1787–1848), was murdered, stabbed in the neck in the middle of the day by an unhinged protester. Shortly thereafter, one of Pius's secretaries, while standing next to the Pope at a window in the Quirinal Palace, was shot and killed. Shut up in the Quirinal Palace and panic-stricken at the course of events, Pius became scared for his own life and decided to flee Rome. Disguised in the cassock of an ordinary priest and wearing tinted glasses, he left the Eternal City on November 24, 1848, making his way to refuge in Gaeta, a Neapolitan territory, where he set up his papal court in exile under the protection of Ferdinand II, ruler of the Kingdom of the Two Sicilies. Ultramontanes quickly likened his situation to the exiles of Pius VI and Pius VII as well as to that of popes persecuted in the more distant past. The "Revolution" had struck again; memories of the bloodshed and desecrations after 1789 returned in full force.[153]

With the Pope in exile, revolutionaries in Rome pressed ahead. An assembly was elected that drafted a Constitution for a new "Roman Republic," worded so that it could extend to all of Italy if national unification came about. The Assembly pronounced that the temporal power of the papacy had ended for ever and made provision in Rome for an intermediate ruling triumvirate, consisting of Aurelio Saffi, Carlo Armellini, and Giuseppe Mazzini, who came to be part of the dramatic events from his exile in London.[154] "After the Rome of the Emperors, after the Rome of the Popes," Mazzini proclaimed before the Assembly, "comes the Rome of the People."[155]

The Constitution that the Assembly drafted in 1849 ranks as among the most liberal that Europe to that point had produced. Echoing language from 1789, the ideals of equality, liberty, and fraternity were boldly proclaimed. Freedom of speech and the press, freedom of association, and freedom of worship were all spelled out. Titles of nobility or privileges based on birth gave way to the equal rights of all before the law. The Constitution was the first in the world to abolish capital punishment. Concerning the Pope, it stipulated the end of his temporal power, but made provision for his return to the city on the condition that only his spiritual power (*potere spirituale*) would be recognized.[156]

Meanwhile, in exile, the Pope had a choice to make: he could baptize liberal ideas (along the lines that Lamennais had desired); he could try to work out some *modus vivideni* with the new republic; or he could condemn the republic and its principles entirely and try to rally Catholic powers in Europe to come to his aid. He chose condemnation. From Gaeta, Pius judged the actions of the Assembly as illegal and vowed to excommunicate the wrongdoers. Already in November 1848 he had begun to make appeal to the Catholic monarchs of Europe to come to his rescue. Turning from liberal counselors such as Antonio Rosmini (1797–1857), Pius increasingly relied on the judgment and advice of his new Secretary of State, Cardinal Giacomo Antonelli (1806–76), the so-called "Italian Richelieu," who emerged from this period as the Pope's highly influential political advisor for the remainder of his papacy and someone who took a keen interest in the Döllinger affair.[157] Together, Antonelli and Pius were horrified by events in Rome and given to believe even the most outrageous rumors of priests being slaughtered and churches desecrated.[158] Pius summed up his attitude in an allocution of April 20, 1849: "Rome has been turned into a forest of wild animals—and apostates and heretics. . . . [H]aters of the faith flock in and teach their diseased errors and pervert minds."[159] Antonelli put it blunter still: "*casca il mondo*," the world is collapsing.[160]

As the Pope awaited news from Gaeta, Austrian forces under generals Durando and Radetzsky began to subdue the northern territories of the Papal States. Keen to limit Habsburg influence on the peninsula, France's new president, Louis Napoleon, deployed French troops to assist the Pope, even though Louis sympathized with republican principles. Under the leadership of General Charles Oudinot, French forces landed at Civitavecchia on the Tyrrhenian coast on April 23, 1849. Confronted by fierce resistance, from the likes of Giuseppe Garibaldi and his battle-hardened followers, the French did not succeed in taking Rome until July 3, 1849. The republic held out longer than anyone expected, and when French troops finally marched into the city they were received with more scowls than smiles. As Rome fell, the revolutionaries dispersed. Mazzini returned to London; Garibaldi scuttled away to Tangier. A few lingering firebrands were captured and imprisoned.[161]

The Pope remained in exile for several more months, but returned to Rome on April 12, 1850.[162] En route back, he made it a point to stop at the Cistercian monastery at Fossanova, and prayed in a cell before a crucifix that was said to have spoken to Thomas Aquinas.[163] Upon entering Rome, he was greeted by prepared ceremonies, and respectful though not ecstatic applause from spectators. *Te Deums* were dutifully sung. But an air of uncertainty and disquiet hung over the city. "Although the Restoration satisfied the aristocracy," Raffaele de Cesare has written, "the recollection of the republic continued to disturb them, and, fearing public reprisals, they did not evince too much enthusiasm for the resumption of the Pontifical government."[164] What is more, it was blatantly clear that the restored rule of the Pope would not have happened without the military intervention of Austria and France. Pius's temporal power, in other words, was rescued and propped up by two armies made up of non-Italians. In an age of nationalism, this did not bode well. It suggested that the Restoration of the 1850s would be a fragile one; and with the benefit of hindsight, we know that the Papal States' millennium-long existence had entered its twilight. This fact was not lost on the Piedmontese government in Turin, which from this point on—under the leadership of its Prime Minister, Count Camillo Cavour (1810–61)—would spearhead efforts toward Italian national unification under a constitutional monarchy, advocating all the while for a *"libera chiesa in libero stato,"* a free church in a free state.[165]

In the 1850s, then, a tenuous and uncertain Restoration ensued, one much resented by large portions of the people and deemed intolerable by liberals and nationalists, at home and abroad. Caricatures of the Papal States as a misbegotten, misgoverned, "medieval" anachronism—torturing heretics and burning books—abounded in anticlerical literature. The British magazine *Punch* would soon portray the papacy as a hapless Humpty Dumpty (complete with a tiara) teetering on a wall, ready to fall and smash to pieces (Figure 1.4).[166] The Papal States, as one French visitor noted, appeared as "a land where the future is the very humble servant of the past."[167] The Pope's government, the traveling American Charles Eliot Norton wrote, appeared to stand in "direct opposition to the most precious of human rights, to the most sacred human hopes."[168]

Pius IX of course saw matters differently. Chastened by the experience of flight and exile, and increasingly relying on Antonelli's advice, Pius came to the conclusion that no concord could exist between the Holy See and liberal principles; the Church simply found itself in a zero-sum game. Even if all of Europe underwent a liberal transformation, Antonelli reasoned, the Papal States ought to be treated as an exceptional case because of its unique history and its supranational (and supernatural) vocation. Without a temporal kingdom, the Pope could not possess the independence necessary for him to perform his spiritual function as Vicar of Christ. Pius was given to call the Papal States "the seamless robe of Jesus Christ" on earth and he prepared to

HUMPTY DUMPTY.

Figure 1.4. The papacy portrayed as Humpty Dumpty about to fall.

Source: Artist unknown, *Punch* 37 (July–December 1859): 203. Reproduced with permission from the Lincoln Financial Foundation Collection, courtesy of the Indiana State Museum and Allen County Public Library.

defend it, if necessary, by martyrdom. Pius "returned [to Rome] a changed man," as Döllinger later laconically put it.[169]

* * *

Shortly after fleeing Rome, Pius had expressed his views on the dangers of the age in an encyclical *Nostis et nobiscum* (December 8, 1949), sent to all bishops and archbishops in Italy. "Venerable Brothers," he began,

> You know as We do... the recent wrongdoing which has strengthened some
> wretched enemies of truth, justice, and honor, who strive openly and deceitfully
> with plots of every sort to spread their disorders everywhere among the faithful
> people of Italy. These disorders include the unbridled license of thinking, speak-
> ing, and hearing every impious matter. They spread these like the foaming waves
> of a savage sea, and they exert themselves not only to shake the Catholic religion
> in Italy itself, but if possible to utterly destroy it.[170]

Significantly, the same encyclical hinted at two theological matters that would
later come to define Pius's papacy: one concerning papal authority; the other,
the Immaculate Conception of the Virgin Mary. "Let them [the faithful] recall
that Christ the Lord placed the impregnable foundation of his Church in the
See of Peter.... [T]he successor of Peter, the Roman Pontiff, holds a primacy
over the whole world and is the true Vicar of Christ, head of the whole Church
and father and teacher of all Christians."[171] And the encyclical closed by
invoking the "Mother of God, the Virgin Mary Immaculate, who by her
powerful patronage with God obtains what she asks for and who cannot be
denied."[172]

After 1850, Pius increasingly focused on spiritual matters, relying on Antonelli to administer his temporal power.[173] But, again, the two powers were
deeply interrelated in Pius's mind. And both were necessary to survive in the
zero-sum game of the age, as he conceptualized it: the epic struggle of the
forces of light (led by the Holy See) against the forces of darkness (now led by
Cavour and the Piedmontese). To extend the light in such dark times, Pius
sought to exert his spiritual influence internationally. He restored the Catholic
hierarchy in two countries that had been lost to Rome during the Reformation:
England in 1850 and the Netherlands in 1853. In both cases, Pius ultimately
prevailed, but victories came only after much rancor and opposition. In
England, members of the press, Parliament, and clergy alike clamored "No
Popery" and several effigies of the Pope were burned. Resistance also occurred
in the Netherlands.[174]

But the spiritual matter that most preoccupied Pius in the early 1850s was
defining the dogma of the Immaculate Conception. In the Latin West, the idea
that Mary was preserved from the taint of Original Sin as a prerequisite for
bearing the sinless Christ had ancient roots, traceable to the teachings of a
number of Church Fathers, notably Ambrose of Milan.[175] Many subsequent
theologians—not least theological titans such as Bernard of Clairvaux and
Thomas Aquinas—strongly demurred, contending that the idea might be
countenanced but only as a "pious opinion" (*sententia pia*) for the unlearned
masses but not as an official teaching of the Church.[176]

But the nineteenth century was an age of the masses and Marian piety had
surged in tandem with the persecution of the Church since 1789. The middle
decades of the century were in fact the great age of Marian apparitions.[177]
In 1830, Catherine Labouré of France experienced a vision of Mary crowned

with stars; her experiences were popularized by the minting of so-called "Miraculous Medals," which bore the inscription: "O Mary Conceived without Original Sin, Pray for us who have recourse to thee." Apparitions were said to have appeared to two children at La Salette, France in 1846, and still later, came the famous sightings of the Virgin at Lourdes, which remains to this day the most popular Marian shrine in the world.[178] From Rome, Gregory XVI had actively encouraged devotion to the Immaculate Conception during his papacy. Pio Nono did the same; he attributed his childhood recovery from epilepsy to the intervention of the Virgin.[179]

Pius looked to Mary again when calamity befell the Papal States in 1848. At one of the most critical junctures of this year, he appointed a commission of twenty theologians, led by the Jesuit Carlo Passaglia, to study the question of defining the dogma of the Immaculate Conception. From exile in Gaeta, the Pope issued the encyclical *Ubi primum* (February 2, 1849), asking bishops worldwide to weigh in on the matter, noting that the "maternal heart" of Mary stood ready to help deliver the Church from "the sad and grief-laden troubles" of the present.[180] Of some six hundred replies, only two responded that the dogma was indefensible; several more regarded defining it as inopportune at the present time; a number did not reply—an action that customarily signaled opposition. After the Restoration of 1850, Pius continued to mull over the matter, soliciting the feedback of Passaglia and his fellow Jesuit Giovanni Perrone (1794–1876) in particular. At this time, the plea to define it as dogma became insistent and widespread in ultramontane circles.[181]

And then on December 8, 1854 with the bull *Ineffabilis Deus*, Pius acted, declaring that "the doctrine which holds that the Most Blessed Virgin Mary was preserved from all stain of Original Sin in the first instant of her conception, by a singular grace and privilege of Almighty God, in consideration of the merits of Jesus Christ, Savior of the human race, has been revealed by God and must, therefore, firmly and constantly be believed by all the faithful."[182] The Pope was said to have wept when he first read the bull aloud in St. Peter's Basilica. Subsequently, he commissioned a room in the Vatican to be dedicated to the teaching, the frescoed walls of which explaining its history and theological significance.[183] To commemorate the event in 1857, Pius had a large column erected in the Piazza di Spagna in Rome, surmounted by a statue of the Virgin, crushing the head of the Serpent.[184] On the Feast of the Immaculate Conception, December 8, popes ever since have traditionally honored the Virgin by placing a wreath at this site. (Incidentally, both the issuing of the "Syllabus of Errors" and the calling of the First Vatican Council took place on this date.)

Following *Ineffabilis Deus*, rejoicing took place across the Catholic world; ultramontanes, in particular, saw the bull as signifying a special blessing on their outlook and reward for their loyalty to Rome.[185]

But many had reservations—some with the dogma itself, others with the manner in which it was defined. Although Pius had consulted bishops and theologians, the dogma was pronounced exclusively on the basis of his authority and not in conjunction with an ecumenical church council—a novum in the history of the Church. More than a few German-speaking theologians, bishops, and priests regretted this development, regarding the dogma as an impairment to the hope of Christian unity. Some even dismissed it as "the invention of the Jesuits."[186]

Döllinger found himself among the questioners, although he did not react to the dogma immediately after its promulgation in 1854.[187] Later, he regretted this. Several years after the First Vatican Council, he looked back and judged that the Immaculate Conception had cleared the path for the Vatican Decrees of 1870. "[T]he Pope's dogmatic definition of it undoubtedly was made with the object of preparing the way for the definition of Papal Infallibility," he asserted; "the teaching [of the Immaculate Conception] has become for us a *fons et origo malorum*," the source and origin of our miseries.[188] "The dogma of 1854 was not merely a feeler," Alfred Plummer recorded Döllinger as saying in 1874; "it virtually included the dogma of 1870. If the Pope, without a Council, could make the Immaculate Conception an article of faith, he was already infallible.... Those who allowed him to act in 1854 supplied the premises for the conclusion drawn in 1870."[189]

2

Between Munich and Rome

The Formation of a German Catholic Scholar

> It is known to the Holy See that the question of the relation of faith and reason is agitated among the Catholic theologians of Germany.
>
> —From the notes of Curial Cardinal August von Reisach (1863)

As a boy, Döllinger once watched Napoleon review his troops in the streets of Würzburg; his family at this time had no choice but to quarter several French soldiers in their home.[1] In his lifetime, Döllinger saw the rise and fall of several French regimes. And of course, he witnessed the birth of modern Italy and Germany prior to his death in 1890, two years after Wilhelm II (r. 1888–1918) ascended the throne and led the German Empire toward the abyss of the Great War. Witnessing as well early processes of industrialization, Döllinger provides an extraordinary window on to the "long" nineteenth century and the making of modern Europe.

But, again, "modern" emphatically does not necessarily mean "secular." For the century witnessed the remarkable perdurability, even revival, of Christianity in Western Europe. As many have noted, past scholarship has grossly exaggerated rumors of "God's death" and the "crisis of faith" motif in the nineteenth century.[2] On the Continent, the confessional divisions between Catholic and Protestants, established at the Peace of Westphalia (1648), remained, more or less, in place during Döllinger's life. The interesting, complicating factor about central Europe, of course, was that the Catholic–Protestant divide cut through "Germany," leaving the "belated nation" rent by religious divisions; the German Confederation (established at the Congress of Vienna) and, later, the Empire formed in 1871 remained largely Protestant in the north and largely Catholic in the south, in Silesia, and in areas around the Rhine.[3] Besides the weighty consequences that this held for German nationhood, it also carried implications for Döllinger's vocational path. In his younger years, he felt the tug of ultramontanism, lacing his scholarship with anti-Protestant invective and defending the prerogatives of Rome against the ambitions of modern states.[4] But in his mature years, he arrived at the view that since German lands had split the Church in the sixteenth century, it was the special calling of German theologians, both Catholic and Protestant, to help reunite it in the nineteenth. What is more, Döllinger came to believe that Catholic scholars had much to learn from Protestant scholarship, emanating from world-class universities such as Berlin, Jena, Halle, Tübingen, and Göttingen, among others.[5]

But his "ecumenical" sensibilities developed fully only after mid-century. In his early years, the thick, embattled Catholic milieu of Southern Germany colored his sense of self and world, and led him on the path toward the Catholic priesthood. Born in Bamberg (in Franconia) on February 28, 1799 and baptized shortly thereafter at St. Martin's Church, Döllinger had the good fortune of descending from a highly educated family. His father, Ignaz Christoph Döllinger (1770–1841) made a noteworthy career as a professor of medicine and anatomy, and is considered a founding father in the field of modern embryology.[6] His mother, Theresa Schuster, also came from a learned background; she was the more pious member of the couple—a disposition that rubbed off on her son. The oldest of ten children, Döllinger *fils* received an excellent education, both formally and informally. He learned French by conversing with Napoleon's soldiers quartered in his home after his family had been forced to move from Bamberg to Würzburg when the secularizing decrees of 1803 (the so-called *Reichsdeputationshauptschluß*) eliminated the bishopric of Bamberg and the city's university, where his father taught.[7] While in Würzburg, Döllinger had regular contact with some nearby Scottish monks, who taught him English—a skill that later gave him access into English-speaking and Anglican circles. To the classical languages, Greek and Latin, learned by all educated young men in the *Gymnasium*, he later mastered Italian and Spanish. Practically all who came in contact with the mature Döllinger remarked on his uncanny mastery of languages.[8]

At 16, Döllinger commenced university studies at Würzburg, where he soon gravitated toward theology against the wishes of his father that he study law. In November 1820, he returned to a seminary in Bamberg, where he was ordained a priest on April 22, 1822. Toward the end of 1822, he took a position as a parish priest in Marktscheinfeld (also in Franconia). A year later he accepted a teaching position at a newly established *lyceum* in Aschaffenburg. While teaching church history and dogmatics there, he completed his dissertation, *The Doctrine of the Eucharist in the First Three Centuries: A Historical and Theological Treatment* (1826), a spirited historical defense of Catholic teaching on the Real Presence of the Eucharist against Protestant detractors.[9] All the while during his formal education, he immersed himself independently in diverse areas of church history and other subjects.[10]

The University of Landshut awarded him the doctorate in 1826, but that university (originally seated in Ingolstadt) was in the process of relocating to Munich and expanding its curriculum. This proved favorable for Döllinger because shortly thereafter he was offered a position at the relocated university, assuming the title on October 3, 1826 of extraordinary professor (*außerordentlicher Professor*) of canon law and church history.[11] A year before, King Ludwig I (r. 1825–48) had ascended the Wittelsbach throne in Bavaria. A Romantic by temperament, the king desired to turn Munich into the center of a resurgent, assertive Catholicism, the influence of which—in counterpoint to Protestant, Prussian Berlin—would radiate throughout all of Europe.[12] In this heady environment, Döllinger's early scholarly vocation took shape. Except for his many travels, he remained in Munich until his death, sometimes augmenting his salary by taking in young (often English) Catholic boarders, the most famous of which being Lord Acton.[13]

Against the backdrop of revolutionary-era and nineteenth-century Southern German Catholicism, this chapter focuses attention on the early "ultramontane" period of Döllinger's career before exploring in more depth his growing criticism of Rome under Pius IX. Two addresses given in the 1860s are particularly significant for understanding his drift from Rome: the first given in two parts in 1861 called for the Church to prepare to abandon its claims of temporal power in central Italy; the second, delivered in 1863 at a Congress of German Catholic scholars in Munich, proposed that *historical* scholarship be granted a more expansive role in guiding the Church than "Roman" theologians, keen on revitalizing scholasticism, were willing to countenance. In conjunction with other events and developments, these two addresses are pertinent for understanding Pius IX's "Syllabus of Errors" (1864), among the most remarkable events of the century, Döllinger once opined, and one that helps explain his continued drift from Rome in the late 1860s as well as his excommunication in 1871 after the Vatican Council.

was 72 year old

THE WORLD OF SOUTHERN GERMAN CATHOLICISM

The year of Döllinger's birth, 1799, found Europe and the Catholic Church caught up in an extraordinary period of tumult and transition. As we have seen in Chapter 1, Pius VI, presumed by some to be the "last Pope," died in involuntary exile in this year. With Rome occupied, the College of Cardinals was forced to meet near Venice, where they elected Pius VII, whom Döllinger always admired. Meanwhile, Napoleon aggressively consolidated his power to the north. In the coming years, his military exploits and eventual downfall carried enormous consequences for central Europe. The events of this era, of course, also held considerable implications for Döllinger's own path in life. But before following that path, it is important to glance back at the previous century if we are to understand the complex world of Southern German Catholicism, which shaped Döllinger's life and which he, in turn, sought to shape.

In the late eighteenth century, the religio-political situation of Catholic Germany remained in large part formed by the legacy of the Council of Trent (1545–63), the Peace of Westphalia (1648), the sumptuous excess of Baroque piety and decorum, and the age-old structures of the Holy Roman Empire. In the bosom of the Empire stood the Imperial Church (*Reichskirche*). Like the Empire itself, it presented a bewildering complexity of institutions, offices, legal coda, individuals, and influences. At the top the "system" (if we may call it that) stood the three historic archbishoprics of Mainz, Trier, and Cologne—powerful not only religiously but politically since occupants of these offices served as imperial electors. Since the fifteenth century, however, the title of Emperor had essentially been a hereditary privilege of the Habsburgs in Vienna. In addition to the great electorates of the Rhineland were numerous smaller bishoprics, abbeys, and cathedral colleges. In these, prince-bishops and prince-abbots (*Fürstbischöfe* and *Fürstäbte*) served both as temporal and spiritual rulers. The abundance of these smaller, often quite wealthy ecclesiastical principalities—essentially versions of the Papal States writ small—meant a practical limitation on the power of secular princes even as, symbolically, they reflected the "universal" dimensions of Empire and Church, under which they directly stood. As expressions of the corporate and cloistered world of feudalism, enlightened thinkers—including a number of "enlightened" Catholics—regularly bemoaned their existence, and by century's end they were widely targeted for reform or outright elimination.[14]

From Rome, popes had tried to exercise greater control over the *Reichskirche* in the late eighteenth century, but their efforts regularly met stiff resistance. In 1785, Pius VI managed to establish a papal nuncio in Munich at the behest of the Wittelsbach Elector Karl Theodor (r. 1777–90), ruler of Bavaria and the Palatinate, in his struggles against the local bishops. A long-standing desire of the throne had been to establish a unified diocese for all of its territories. Several different bishops wielded authority in Bavaria, but nowhere did diocesan boundaries coincide with political ones. In this case, the Roman Curia worked directly with the crown to attempt to bring about this unity. Such meddling from Rome, however, perturbed many bishops, including the Rhineland electors, who felt that the previously established nunciatures in Vienna, Cologne, and Lucerne constituted a sufficient papal presence north of the Alps.[15]

For many central European princes, keen to imitate the enlightened absolutism of the major powers, Catholicism was too important a domestic matter to be left to Rome or to the unpredictable behavior of local bishops. In the late eighteenth century, Austria set the general template of state supervision of the Church. Under the rule of Maria Theresa (r. 1740–80) and her son and co-regent, Joseph II (r. 1765–90), the state's virtual take-over of the Church was begun, culminating in a series of far-reaching reforms under Joseph's exclusive rule in the 1780s. In this system of state-churchism (*Staatskirchentum*)

or "Josephinism," as it has come to be called, the state sought to curtail "superstitious" and "impractical" manifestations of the faith in order to emphasize those practical from the standpoint of a modernizing absolutist state.[16] Among other things, Maria Theresa instituted commissions to administer church lands, limited the promulgation of papal bulls, ended the legal privilege of sanctuary in churches, diminished the number of feast days and processions, took over the administration of universities and schools, and compelled the clergy to read state decrees from the pulpit. In 1781 under Joseph, bishops were made to swear an oath of allegiance to the throne; papal correspondence with prelates became subject to state oversight; only six state-approved seminaries were set up to train clergymen; and, in addition to being a holy sacrament, marriage was made into a civil contract. Joseph also targeted feast days for elimination, deeming them seedbeds of laziness and drunkenness, detractors from the commonweal. Perhaps most infamously, Joseph's Edict on Idle Institutes suppressed the "idle" contemplative orders, dissolving over one-third of the monasteries in Habsburg lands and confiscating huge tracts of property.[17] The revenue from the abolished orders went to poor relief and education. Furthermore, Joseph's commission on Church affairs sought to prescribe rules for even the smallest details of worship and popular piety. It forbade processions unless approved by the government, sought to reduce the number of relics, restricted the number of votive candles around an altar, insisted that holy pictures could be touched but not kissed, and regulated the number of side chapels in a church. He even sought to save money on the burial of his subjects by proscribing that the Church use sacks, instead of coffins! Many of these edicts—numbering 6,000 in all—proved hugely unpopular among his subjects.[18]

They also attracted the anxious attention of the Pope and the Curia in Rome. The Church's long institutional memory kept in mind the ancient conflict between the Pope and the Holy Roman Emperor, and interpreted Joseph's actions as the latest flare-up of a much older reality. In 1781, Pius VI proposed a trip to Vienna, which he made good on in 1782, to take stock of the situation. No pope had visited German lands since 1415, the year of the Council of Constance. But this trip achieved no "Canossa," where Emperor Henry IV in 1077 famously prostrated himself in the snow as an act of contrition to Pope Gregory VII.

Instead, it cast unflattering light on an enfeebled and embattled papacy. Joseph II met the Pope at Neunkirchen outside of Vienna and they then traveled together to the city followed by adoring and curious crowds. Residing at the Hofburg in Vienna for a month, the Pope conducted masses, held private meetings, and visited churches and tombs, among other activities. He and Joseph had ample time to talk about the state of the Church. The Pope made clear his concerns, but Joseph proved irenically unyielding—making promises he never kept—and in fact he had no strong motive to yield. Having recently been forced to suppress the Jesuit Order and with other looming crises on the horizon, the papacy stood in a much weakened position.[19] And so Pius's time in Vienna proved, in the final analysis, a formal accomplishment but a substantive defeat. He finished his travels by visiting Munich, where the "Josephinist" example of the Habsburgs was not lost on the House of Wittelsbach.[20]

In addition to the challenge posed by Josephinism, an intellectual development—one markedly anticipating Döllinger's mature views—emanating from German lands also sought to curtail the authority of the Pope. This challenge became known as "Febronianism" derived from the pseudonym—Justinus Febronius—of the author of a celebrated, controversial book.[21] The author's actual name was Johann Nikolaus von Hontheim (1701–90), a canon lawyer, theologian, and the suffragan Bishop of Trier after 1749; and the title of the work, published in 1763, was *De statu Ecclesia et de potestate legitima Romani Pontificis liber singularis ad reunidos dissenters in religione christiana compositus* (*On the State of the Church and the Lawful Power of the Pope, written to Reunite Christians who Differ in Religion*). Although drawing extensively on pre-existing ideas, the influence of this work on educated German Catholic opinion in the late eighteenth and nineteenth centuries cannot be overstated.[22] It is often considered a chief expression of the "Catholic Enlightenment" and a German counterpart to Gallicanism, "the foremost formulation of arguments against papal absolutism in Germany."[23] "Reviving the errors of Febronius" was a charge Döllinger sometimes heard from his critics.

Indeed, several of Döllinger's theological emphases from the 1860s and 1870s are adumbrated in Hontheim's work.[24] First, Hontheim sought to show that some of the more extravagant claims of papal supremacy and infallibility in circulation at the time were misguided; they were late, spurious developments in the history of the Church. The See of Rome was one among several in the ancient world and its bishop should be seen as a first among equals; this was a legitimate role and as such Rome could serve as symbol and center of unity (*centrum unitatis*) for all Christians. One could even accept the idea of infallibility, but this applied to the Church Universal and its ecumenical councils, not to the Bishop of Rome alone. Second, Hontheim sought to show that historical scholarship could and should serve as a guide to the Church. "Scholars," he wrote, "ought to be the natural defenders of both church and state."[25] But defending the Church *historically* meant exposing erroneous opinions of it, and in practice this often meant preference for the earlier apostolic and patristic periods of the Church (the *ecclesia primativa*) over later, medieval "accretions." Accordingly, through historical scholarship Hontheim sought to debunk the origins of exaggerated claims of a "papal monarchy" and press the Church to take a more moderate course than that advocated by those keen to expand papal power. A significant focus of his argument concerns the so-called False Decretals of Isidore, a medieval collection of documents which had been employed to promote papal supremacy. In

Hontheim's view, many of these documents were forgeries—as subsequent scholarship has largely confirmed.[26] He also sought to show how self-interested canon lawyers played a key role in spreading the idea of papal supremacy. Historical scholarship for Hontheim meant, too, sound scriptural exegesis; he felt that papal absolutists misinterpreted a number of key passages in support of their claims. For example, Jesus' admonition in John 21 to "feed my sheep" had been read by papalists to have been addressed to Peter alone, when in fact, according to Hontheim's exegesis, it was addressed to all disciples and hence—in accordance with the teaching of Apostolic Succession—to the entire Catholic episcopate, not to the Pope in isolation. Finally, Hontheim expressed a heartfelt—if perhaps naïve—view that reconciliation between Protestants and Catholics in Germany could come about if the Church followed the prescriptions laid out in his book. A national German Catholic Church, connected but not fettered to Rome and one that included Protestants returning to the fold, could lead the Universal Church forward into a felicitous future, away from the divisions and polemics of the Tridentine era.[27]

This was an inspirational idea—not least later for Döllinger—and Hontheim's work had a sensational and lasting impact. Princes, both powerful and weak, eagerly endorsed his views, as they could be enlisted to support the idea of national churches and limit the reach of Rome. Jansenist and Gallican theologians in France applauded, for in fact Hontheim had borrowed numerous ideas and arguments from French scholars such as Fénelon and Bossuet. Manuals of theology and canon law in the lands of the leading dynasties—whether Habsburg, Wittelsbach, or Wettin—became almost universally Febronian in the course of the late eighteenth century.[28]

But Rome demurred. On February 27, 1764 Febronius was placed on the Index—an act that effectively amplified his popularity. The Jesuit scholar Francesco Antonio Zaccaria (1714–95) assailed Hontheim's work in his massive *Anti-Febronius* (1767). Influential voices in the Curia fretted that a "new Luther" had arisen in German lands. The search for the identity of the book's author led nowhere at first, but eventually a special papal envoy outed Hontheim. Hontheim initially refused to recant, but when his superior, the Elector of Trier, thought it judicious for him to do so, he reluctantly agreed, signing a recantation on November 1, 1778. Three years later, however, he felt the need to explain himself, publishing a *Commentary on the Recantation of Febronius* (1781), which set forth his views again in highly elliptical language that seemed to contradict his recantation. "I have recanted like Fénelon," he wrote, "to avoid quarreling and unpleasantness. But my recantation hurts neither the world nor the Catholic religion, and will never profit the Curia of Rome. The world has read, examined, and accepted my book. My recantation will move intelligent men as little as the various refutations by monks and papal flatterers."[29]

Publication of this *Commentary* widened the influence of Febronianism. In 1785, the Elector Karl Theodor of Bavaria sought to bring German bishops to heel by the appointment of a papal nuncio in Munich—an office that would play a significant role in Döllinger's conflicts with Rome. Drawing from Febronian precepts, the electors of Trier, Cologne, and Mainz, along with the Archbishop of Salzburg, vigorously protested the nuncio's appointment as a challenge to their authority and called for a special meeting of the German hierarchy at Ems near Koblenz.[30] The resulting so-called Punctuation of Ems (1786), consisting of twenty-three articles, upheld the Febronian critique of the Pseudo-Isidorian Decretals as valid and thereby sought to limit the powers of Rome and elevate those of the German episcopate. "The Roman pope," the Punctuation sets out,

> is and remains the principal overseer and primate of the whole Church and the center of its unity, and is furnished by God with the jurisdiction required thereby; to him all Catholics must always give canonical obedience and full deference. All the other privileges and reservations not associated with this primacy in the first centuries, but accruing to it from the later Isidorean decretals to the clear detriment of the bishops, cannot be attributed to the scope of that jurisdiction now that the forgery and falsity of those [decretals] have been adequately demonstrated and is universally recognized. They belong rather to the class of manipulations (*Eingriffe*) on the part of the Roman Curia, and *the bishops ... are authorized to restore themselves to the exercise of the authority granted to them by God, under the supreme protection of His Imperial Majesty.*[31]

Even though the Punctuation did not receive the universal support of the German episcopate, and some, under pressure from Rome, later withdrew their support, it represented the most extreme statement of episcopalism and anti-papalism then produced and led for a period to a virtual schism in the German Church.[32]

By the time of the French Revolution, Febronian ideas permeated the German Empire. "Hontheim's 'single book'," as Michael Printy has summed up, "more than any other work galvanized a generation of educated German Catholics.... Febronianism as an ideology took on a scope far broader than the actual issues raised by Hontheim's book."[33] Or, as Owen Chadwick has written, "What he [Hontheim] began continued as a key issue within German Catholicism until the first Vatican Council of 1870, which tried to kill the debate, and thought that it succeeded, but was later proved wrong"—not least by Döllinger's offensive against the Council and by the emergence of German "Old Catholicism."[34]

Significantly, it was in reaction to the spread of Febronianism in central Europe that the word "ultramontane" first gained its modern meaning as someone oriented toward Rome and committed to the universal authority of the Pope. Hontheim himself used the term in this sense as a chapter heading. By the early nineteenth century, it had developed into common usage.[35]

*   *   *

A central complaint of German clergymen sympathetic to Febronian ideas was that the Pope and the Roman Curia "over the Alps" did not understand the specific conditions of the *Reichskirche* in the late eighteenth century. Little did these prelates, or the Pope, know that the centuries-old *Reichskirche*, a central pillar of "Christendom," would cease to exist in the early nineteenth century, a casualty of the train of events set in motion by the French Revolution and Napoleonic wars. Its demise was not a violent, bloody affair, like the anticlerical outbursts in France, but rather a swift legal burial, begun in the Congress of Rastatt (1797), and the treaties of Campo Formio (1799) and Lunéville (1801), and completed by the *Reichsdeputationshauptschluß* (1803) and by the expiration of the Empire itself in 1806. Nor was it a completely discontinuous affair, for the massive secularization of church lands by lay rulers at this time had clear precedents in the Josephinist policies of the eighteenth century. Even so, the world of Southern German Catholicism underwent sudden, profound, and lasting changes at the beginning of the nineteenth century.[36]

By the end of 1794, France's armies had reversed earlier losses against the powers of Europe and overran the Rhineland. The Treaty of Campo Formio (1797) recognized France's occupation of the left bank of the Rhine, including within its expanded borders the historic archbishoprics of Mainz, Cologne, and Trier, along with numerous smaller territories, ecclesiastical and secular. The subsequent defeat of the Second Coalition and the resulting Treaty of Lunéville (1801) produced further French gains in central Europe, essentially creating the conditions for the collapse of the Holy Roman Empire and with it the Imperial Church.[37] Wherever the French went, properties of the Church were expropriated, monastic orders shut down, revolutionary ideals spread into society. Liberty trees were planted; a goddess of Reason paraded down the streets of Bonn.[38]

After 1801, the question of how to compensate German princes who had lost lands west of the Rhine became a pressing matter. The issue was left up to a special "imperial committee" (*Reichsdeputation*). The final recess of this committee or the so-called *Reichsdeputationshauptschluß* (February 25, 1803) was ratified by the Imperial Diet in March of 1803 and approved by the Emperor, Francis II, the following month. The plan combined two processes: the absorption or *mediatization* of numerous small secular principalities by larger states and the *secularization* of ecclesiastical principalities.[39] Delegates focused primarily on the fate of the secular domains, but several clauses, added at the eleventh hour, created the conditions for the demise of the *Reichskirche*. "All the property of the endowed foundations, abbeys and monasteries, in the old as well as new estates," the key clause read, "shall be left at the free and full disposition of the respective sovereigns [*zur freien und vollen Disposition der respectiven Landesherrn*], whether for the support of worship, education or other social purposes, or to ease their financial problems." The only qualifications added were that cathedrals had to be maintained and pensions had to be paid to clergy whose institutions had been suppressed.[40]

In a word, the larger states (such as Bavaria) suddenly acquired the legal prerogative of confiscating practically all of the lands of the bishoprics and monasteries within their borders. "What had begun," Derek Beales nicely sums up, "as a proposal to compensate a few rulers for relatively small losses to France on the left bank had developed into a total reorganization of the map of Germany; and the suggestion that the compensation should come from the ecclesiastical states had turned into a general secularization and sale of all church lands." And while the French Revolution and the Napoleonic armies had occasioned the situation, it is noteworthy that the final impetus came from German lay rulers themselves (including Catholics), many of whom had long advocated for the modernizing value of state sovereignty and regarded priestly rule as anachronistic. "It was part of a final *putsch*," Beales continues, "by the lay rulers of Germany to establish their sovereignty and destroy the *Reich*."[41]

In Rome, Pius VII was grief-stricken. Catholic rulers seemed to be cannibalizing their own. In a letter to Emperor Francis II, the titular *Defensor ecclesiae* within the Empire, Pius lamented:

> Words, sighs and tears do not suffice . . . to express the bitterness of the wounds and the depth and breadth of so much pain. What can I say? The lawful superintendents of your lands and possessions are threatened; churches, chapters, collegiate endowments, abbeys, and monasteries will be abolished; and your possessions are handed over to secular and non-Catholic rulers. Dioceses are left to an arbitrary fate, the entire clergy is abandoned to scorn, the authority of the Holy See is . . . stomped upon, the Church has been robbed of its freedom and bound in chains."[42]

But confronted with the Napoleonic juggernaut and the appetite of lay rulers for wealth, what could Francis do? He recognized that the Empire lay on its deathbed.

Death arrived on August 6, 1806. From the balcony of the Baroque Church of Nine Choirs of Angels in Vienna, Francis announced that by God's grace he remained the King of Austria, but he had decided to lay down the imperial crown. An epoch of Western civilization ended with a whimper. When Napoleon finally met defeat a decade later, the Congress of Vienna (1814–15) hardly considered the restoration of prince-bishoprics and monasteries in Germany. They had already begun to fade into the distant past of a lost imperial world.[43]

After 1803, the situation in Bavaria is especially instructive. The world the young Döllinger inherited saw Bavaria transformed from an exclusively Catholic electorate in the Empire to an enlarged modern nation-state, the Kingdom of Bavaria, one that allowed a measure of toleration for religious minorities. These changes were in large part attributable to the aggressive statesmanship of one man: Count Maximilian von Montgelas (1759–1838), the leading official in the government of Elector Maximilian IV Joseph (r. 1799–1825). Part Savoyard, a student of the French Enlightenment, and profoundly Josephinist in his religious views, Montgelas found his moment in the historical spotlight: Napoleon's ascendancy and the crumbling Empire created a climate open to far-reaching reforms. The dispossessed church properties provided the key for Montgelas to finance his reforms and he thus pursued an aggressive policy of secularization. Already, in a memorandum from 1789 he had made clear his position of state sovereignty over the Church: "The teaching of two powers [ecclesiastical and secular] is a monstrous chimera of priestly ambition. The Church is in the state and not the state in the church."[44] Complaints against Montgelas by dissenting clergy fell on deaf ears.[45]

Beginning already in 1802 and gaining steam in 1803, the monasteries and convents in Bavaria were dissolved, nationalized, and sold off.[46] A special commission for monasteries (*Spezialkommission in Klostersachen*) was set up to administer the often messy and confusing process. Collectively, monasteries owned more than half of the land and controlled 56 percent of the farms, so their break-up meant a massive windfall for the state. Libraries, archives, and art treasures were confiscated and sold. So-called "central monasteries" were set up to house many of the dispossessed and aging monks. Religious from foreign countries were frequently sent home.[47] As monasteries went, so did the wealthy bishoprics within Bavaria; their lands and goods were sold off; dioceses found themselves at the hands of the state bureaucracy. The calamity of the situation from a traditionalist standpoint prompted Joseph Görres to exclaim that the Church must now don "a narrow slim tailored habit instead of the royal purple garment; a simple staff instead of the scepter of lost princeliness, a crown of thorns for an indentured servant. *Ecce Ecclesia Germanica*."[48] As the historian Thomas Nipperdey has described the changes: "The storming of the monasteries and the demise of the old clerical institutions are deeply engraved on the consciousness of the Bavarian people. Secularization had crucial consequences for the state, for society and for the church itself. The demise of the monasteries removed the strongest bastions of pre-modern, non-state power in the south and west. This enabled the state to establish full sovereignty and to begin to constitute itself in modern form."[49]

The winds of change that toppled the monasteries also brought measures of religious toleration, a key ideal for Montgelas. Shortly after Maximilian IV Joseph became prince-elector of Bavaria in 1799, he allowed for the establishment of a private court chapel, in which the chaplain of the electress (the Protestant Caroline of Baden) might hold Protestant religious services. The government permitted other Protestants in Munich to take part in these services, so long as it was done behind closed doors. Non-Catholic clergy were still compelled to appear in the street in civil dress.[50] A more generous measure of freedom came in a decree of August 26, 1801; it stipulated that non-Catholics should no longer be excluded from settling in the territories of the Elector. The rationale articulated was that those who professed different faiths could nonetheless contribute to the commonweal through agriculture and industry, and that Bavaria would do well to imitate the example of "progressive states."[51] More generous edicts and decrees came in the following years, abetted by the fact that Bavaria's territorial acquisitions under Napoleonic hegemony entailed a significant increase in Protestant and Jewish subjects.

The downfall of Napoleon, as one might imagine, threw many of Montgelas's reforms into question. But in religious matters there would be no returning to the *Reichskirche*. The Constitution of the German Confederation (1815), of which Bavaria was a member, stipulated that civil and political rights could not be denied to members of the three recognized Christian religions: Catholic, Lutheran, and Reformed. In principle, they were to have legal "parity" throughout the lands of the Confederation. Similar stipulations were delineated in the Bavarian Constitution of 1818.[52] Jews and Anabaptists faced a much more precarious situation.

At the Congress of Vienna, only one prince-bishopric was restored in Europe: the Papal States. In Bavaria, the lands and temporal power of bishoprics and monasteries were gone for good. The imperial office of "elector," whether ecclesiastical or secular, was also a thing of the past. The erstwhile elector Maximilian IV was henceforth simply Maximilian I, the first ruler of the modern Kingdom of Bavaria. In his lifetime, Döllinger would live under four more Wittelsbach kings: Ludwig I (r. 1825–48), the son of Maximilian I; Maximilian II (r. 1848–64), the son of Ludwig I; the so-called Fairy Tale King, Ludwig II (r. 1864–86), whom Döllinger tutored as a young prince; and, finally, Otto I (r. 1886–1913), king at the time of Döllinger's death.[53] These rulers inherited a Josephist and Febronian legacy that fostered a guarded disposition to Rome; in imitation of France's Gallican rulers, Ludwig II once spoke of Döllinger as "my Bossuet."

After 1815, the papacy pursued a policy of making "concordats" with the states.[54] Coming on the heels of decades of warfare and turmoil, these helped legally and administratively to normalize the new ecclesiastical situation. Pius VII's Concordat with Napoleon 1801 provided the general model, although the concordats varied significantly from country to country. In the Restoration climate, the Pope, working through a newly created Congregation for Extraordinary Ecclesiastical Affairs (est. 1814) and with the aid of the savvy Cardinal Consalvi, had a strong hand, but, again, the ecclesiastical arrangements of the Old Regime had vanished for good. The Bavarian Concordat of 1817 (which fully went into effect only in 1821) conceded to Rome the freedom to communicate with bishops, the right to reopen a number of suppressed monasteries, the ability of the Church to censor books, and the placement of a seminary in each diocese, among other things. Concerning dioceses, the bishopric of Freising (established in 739) was transferred to Munich at this time and elevated to the level of archbishopric; its boundaries stayed the same, so it henceforth was called the archbishopric of Munich and Freising.[55] Under its authority stood the suffragan bishops of Augsburg, Passau, and Regensburg. Bavaria's other archbishopric was seated in Bamberg, Döllinger's birthplace, and under it stood the suffragan bishops of Würzburg, Eichstätt, and Speyer.[56] In the Concordat, the king had the right to nominate archbishops and bishops, but Rome had the right to invest them in their office. Importantly for the Döllinger case, bishops and archbishops were granted extensive authority to employ church censures—including excommunication—to clergy deemed deserving of punishment according to canon law without interference from the monarchy.[57] The first archbishop of the newly created diocese of Munich-Freising was Lothar Anselm Freiherr von Gebsattel (r. 1821–46); followed by Karl-August von Reisach (r. 1846–56), who later was called to the Curia and became Döllinger's *bête noire* in Rome. Reisach was then followed by Gregor von Scherr, O.S.B. (r. 1856–77), under whom the excommunication of Döllinger was carried out in April 1871.

PROFESSOR AT MUNICH AND THE CLIMATE OF CATHOLIC THOUGHT

The same forces that toppled the Holy Roman Empire and the Imperial Church ushered in a period of creative destruction for universities in German lands. Leaving Protestant institutions aside, ten Catholic universities were forced to close their doors at this time—some for a period, some for good. Cologne was the first to go in 1794, then the universities of Mainz and Trier in 1798, Bamberg in 1803, Dillingen in 1804, Paderborn in 1808, Fulda in 1809, Breslau in 1811, and Münster in 1818. The venerable Bavarian university of Ingolstadt (founded in 1476) was first transplanted to Landshut in 1802 and finally to Munich in 1826.[58]

The revolutionary-Napoleonic age also brought tremendous forces of reform and renewal to higher education. Under the leadership of Wilhelm von Humboldt and Friedrich Schleiermacher, the epochal University of Berlin opened its doors in 1810. The first German university founded under purely (Prussian) nationalist auspices, with the imprimatur of neither Emperor nor Pope, Berlin's university was conceived to be a different sort of institution, one committed to the high-minded ideals of *Wissenschaft*, scholarship for scholarship's sake, and *Bildung*, the holistic formation of the young. Berlin quickly played host to luminaries such as Fichte, Hegel, Ranke, Phillipp Marheineke, August Neander, and W. M. L de Wette, among others. The influence of the "Berlin model," and not least its example of rigorous philological and historical scholarship, radiated across Germany and abroad, affecting both Protestant and Catholic institutions.[59]

Because of the territorial and demographic reconfigurations of this period, Protestants and Catholics in German lands were drawn into closer proximity.

The creation of the German Confederation at the Congress of Vienna diluted the Westphalian model of confessional states and created several states with mixed populations. To accommodate these shifts, a number of universities emerged from this period as "parity universities" (*Paritäts-Universitäten*)— schools, that is, housing both a Protestant and Catholic theological faculty to reflect the two largest religious constituencies of the state. The universities of Tübingen, Breslau, and Bonn (a new foundation in 1818) are among the best-known examples of this arrangement. Catholic scholars in these schools experienced a much closer proximity to Protestant ideas than their co-religionist peers in, say, Italy or Spain.[60] Of course, quite apart from institutional nearness, the reality of a shared language meant that the line between Catholic and Protestant thought became more blurred in German-speaking areas north of the Alps. This is crucial to keep in mind when assessing Döllinger's conflicts with Rome.

Döllinger was officially called to Munich in the summer of 1826. Bavaria's Minister of Ecclesiastical and Educational Affairs, Eduard von Schenk (1788–1841), had been impressed by the "extensive erudition" demonstrated by Döllinger's early work. Joining several other professors transferred from Landshut, Döllinger quickly rose to become one of the university's leading lights.[61] The devout, ambitious new king, Ludwig I, and Minister Schenk— consulting regularly with the highly esteemed Bavarian theologian Johann Michael Sailer (1751–1832)—desired that the new university in Munich help transform the city into a center of Catholic thought and culture that would rival other Catholic strongholds such as Mainz, Vienna, Münster, and Freiburg im Breisgau.[62]

By and large, they succeeded; Munich in the late 1820s and 1830s has been described by Georg Schwaiger as "the living center of the Catholic Restoration in Germany."[63] Two figures in particular shaped the climate of thought in the Bavarian capital at this time and left a lasting impression on the younger Döllinger: Joseph Görres (1776–1848) and Franz von Baader (1765–1841). An erstwhile revolutionary, an intimate of Romantic circles in Heidelberg, and the founding editor of the fiery *Der rheinische Merkur*, Görres cut a larger-than-life path in the early nineteenth century. Because of his impassioned journalistic attacks against France, Napoleon in a fit of exasperation once dubbed him *la cinquième puissance* (the fifth power) in Europe. After 1815, Görres tilted in a decidedly ultramontane direction, at every opportunity defending the freedom of the Church against states' interests and ambitions. His most sensational intervention in public affairs came with the publication of *Athanasius* (1837), a spirited defense of the conscience of Archbishop of Cologne, Clemens August von Drost-Vischering (1773–1845), who had been imprisoned by the Prussian government for refusing to sanction the marriage of Protestants and Catholics in an episode that came be known as the "Cologne Troubles" (*Kölner Wirren*).[64] This episode and Görres's involvement in it catalyzed German Catholics into political awareness, presaging in many respects the *Kulturkampf* of the 1870s. A decade prior to the appearance of *Athanasius*, Ludwig I had called Görres to Munich to establish a sphere of influence. There, energetic and captivating, he held forth on all manner of subjects to a group of scholars and publicists, who collectively were dubbed the "Görres Circle." Döllinger became an intimate in this elite group.[65]

A native of Munich, Franz von Baader was another figure whose impact Döllinger felt. An ambitious polymath and a harsh critic of modern (especially Kantian) philosophy, Baader developed a Romantic speculative theology, indebted to the Protestant mystic Jakob Böhme (1575–1624), which, among other things, offered a blueprint for the reunification of the Eastern and Western churches into a "higher whole." This organic, ecumenical vision (and particularly the idea that the Western Church had much to learn from the East) impressed Döllinger and helps in part account for his interest in Christian unity that came to full expression in his mature years.[66]

Görres, von Baader, Döllinger, and several others—including the historian Ernst von Lasaulx; the medical professor, Johann Nepomuk Ringseis; and the jurist George Phillips—met regularly at the "Round Table" at Görres's house on the Schönfeldstraße in Munich. Their heated discussions, often lasting long into the night, became legendary; outsiders referred to the group as "the Congregation." Their intellectual ferment found a public outlet in the short-lived journal *Eos* (1823–32), which treated topics of both contemporary and perennial importance. Döllinger became a regular contributor.[67] While the group not without reason is sometimes characterized as "Romantic" and "ultramontane," there are limits to these descriptions, for the topics *Eos*'s contributors entertained reveal a wide spectrum of positions and interests, which cannot be tidily captured with a single adjective.[68] An early awareness of what became known as the "social question" is manifest, for instance, in the number of essays that dealt with economic issues. Liberal ideas were also voiced. On his way back from Rome in 1832, the French intellectual Felicité de Lamennais visited the Munich circle, creating links between Döllinger and French Catholicism that would be kept alive for decades. Charles René de Montalembert paid a visit as well. To the end of his life, Montalembert corresponded with Döllinger and other members of the "*Eos* circle."[69]

But, in the final analysis, ultramontanism triumphed over liberalism among the Munich intellectuals, who, eventually, settled on another outlet of expression: *Die historisch-politischen Blätter für das katholische Deutschland*. Founded and edited by Karl Ernst Jarcke, Guido Görres (Joseph's son), and George Phillips, this journal proved widely influential from its inception in 1838 until it ceased publication in 1923. Joining ranks with *Der Katholik* (f. 1821) in Mainz, it became a leading voice of a combative, engaged, Rome-oriented "public theology," which helped Catholics stay informed about such dramatic events as the revolutions of 1848, the loss of the Papal States, the *Kulturkampf* in Germany, and more.[70] "The journal was not only a conduit for bringing news about international affairs into Germany," Richard Schae-fer has written, "it was equally a conduit for German Catholics to appear to themselves as participants in processes affecting the world Church."[71] The "Roman Question," i.e., the future of the Papal States, was a frequent topic in the *Blätter* in the years around Döllinger's 1861 address on the subject, in which, as we shall see, he came out in favor of the cessation of the Pope's temporal authority.[72]

∗   ∗   ∗

But beyond the heady political events that roiled German Catholicism in the middle decades of the nineteenth century, there lurked deeper, foundational intellectual quandaries. The challenge of the Enlightenment or *Aufklärung* (mediated in German lands by the likes of Christian Wolff, Lessing, and Kant, among others) had created a body of discourse that sought to untether philosophy from its age-old subordination to theology and to cham-pion the independent role of human reason. Still other voices, transmitters of the so-called "Radical Enlightenment," sought to eradicate theology altogether, regarding it as a straw house built on sophistry and superstition.[73] Furthermore, the reorganization of Europe after 1815 had been favorable to (Protestant) Prussia for its role in defeating Napoleon. Prussian scholars were quick, therefore, to champion the putatively onward-and-upward spirit of Protestantism as the basis of a possible, future German nation-state, contrasting it with the "backward" and "medieval" spirit of Catholicism weighing down Austria and the German Confederation's southern states. "The form of the [modern] World Spirit," as the philosopher Hegel had bluntly put it, "is the principle of the North, and, from a religious perspective, Protestantism."[74]

Not surprisingly then, in the aftermath of the Enlightenment and revolu-tionary age, Catholic scholars such as Döllinger found themselves wrestling with some fundamental questions: <u>what direction should Catholic thought take now in this supposedly Protestant-inspired modern age?</u> Was Catholic theology compatible with the *Aufklärung* and the potent academic ideal of *Wissenschaft* or not? Should Catholic theology regard the historicist modes of thought emanating from Northern German universities as friend or foe? And what of the role of human reason more generally? Should it have a more capacious role in human affairs as enlightened voices championed? Was it hopelessly mired in pride and vanity as the more confessional Lutherans, Calvinists, and Jansenists claimed? Or in its better moments, was reason, finally, complementary to revelation, as the "Angelic Doctor," Thomas Aquinas, and his numerous epigoni had long insisted?

Such questions invigorated the Munich academic scene. Even as a young scholar, Döllinger took up some of them with vigor and gusto in the pages of *Eos* and elsewhere.[75] But to understand the dominant schools of thought among Catholic scholars with respect to these questions, it is necessary to turn to two other seats of learning: Tübingen and Mainz.

The "Catholic Tübingen School" offered up a more organic, historicist theology, one significantly indebted to German Protestant universities, while Mainz emerged as a stronghold of neo-Thomist or neo-scholastic thought—or what its critics often labeled "Roman" theology. In a field dominated by these two general tendencies of thought, German Catholic theology took shape in the middle decades of the nineteenth century. Not surprisingly, the Vatican favored the Rome-oriented theologians at Mainz, while worrying about the excesses of "German" scholarship at Tübingen and other universities sympathetic to Tübingen—not least Munich. Furthermore, in the decades leading up to the "Syllabus of Errors" and the Vatican Council, some of the Church's most high-profile condemnations were directed against German scholars: Georg Hermes (1775–1831), Anton Günther (1783–1863), and Jakob Frohschammer (1821–93).[76] Taking a closer look at the directions in theology typified by Tübingen and Mainz, alongside these three condemnations, helps situate the course of Döllinger's thought in the 1850s and 1860s and beyond.

To understand the Catholic Tübingen School permit me to invoke the shopworn metaphor of an acorn becoming a mighty oak tree. This organic image—derived from the Romantic milieu in general and the thought of the philosopher Schelling in particular—helps explain how Tübingen's theologians sought to understand the Church and its history.[77] Like a growing tree, the Church had developed and matured from its obscure origins in ancient Palestine, becoming something quite different from the original "acorn." At the same time, it did not develop haphazardly, but according to certain principles present in its inception. Unlike the tree, however, members of the Church (and human beings generally) possess both free will and fallibility; and while divine providence superintends the Church's growth at one level, human beings have the freedom to work in concert with the Church or to mess things up. The job of theologians was to make sure that the Church was on track, becoming what it essentially was and is, and not embarking on a false path. To distinguish between legitimate growth and deviation, Catholic scholars were obliged to know history; they had to bring scholarly historical knowledge, as pioneered and employed by their Protestant colleagues, to the task of theology, but enlist this knowledge in the service of the Catholic Church.

Such ideas radiated from the small university town of Tübingen, a parity university since 1817, housing both Protestant and Catholic theological faculties after the Catholic seminary at Ellwangen was transferred to Tübingen as part of the educational reorganization of the Kingdom of Württemberg. The ideas of Tübingen's leading theologians were expressed in numerous lectures and publications, but especially in the *Tübinger Theologische Quartalschrift* (established in 1819), one of the longest running theological journals in German history.[78]

Among the several learned scholars at Tübingen, two stand out: Johann Sebastian Drey (1777–1853) and Johann Adam Möhler (1796–1838). Widely considered the *paterfamilias* of the "Catholic Tübingen School," Drey came from a poor background, but his piety and intellectual promise afforded him opportunities for education. Ordained a priest in 1801, he began teaching dogmatics and apologetics in 1812 at the Catholic seminary at Ellwangen, transferring to Tübingen when the seminary moved there in 1817. Through the influence of Protestant colleagues and his own reading, he became familiar with many of the leading thinkers of the day: Schelling, Schleiermacher, Kant, Fichte, Lessing, and the brothers Schlegel, among others. Schelling's influence was particularly important, especially with respect to the Romantic philosopher's ideas on education and his notion that all things developed toward organic unity pervaded by the "Absolute Spirit" (i.e., God).[79] But Drey did not indiscriminately absorb contemporary ideas. Rather, he employed them for his own Catholic purposes, frequently wielding the tools of his Protestant colleagues against them. In this sense, we might even liken him to scholastic thinkers, who borrowed heavily from Aristotle and other classical thinkers, but enlisted them toward distinctively Christian ends.

But Drey has little use for the actual scholasticism as it was practiced in his day. "[T]heology [in our time]," he wrote, "has been freed from the fruitless bickering and frivolous wordplay of the era dominated by Aristotelian scholasticism, [and] we have seen a rigorous development of the historical and exegetical disciplines." Scholasticism of old, he opined, was made up of "useless, niggling speculation, ineffectual haggling and squabbling, and [a] barbaric vocabulary."[80] In its place, Drey wanted "historical competence," the key prerequisite for genuine theological scholarship; it gave one the ability to examine faith against the historical background of its formulation. Such advocacy of history Drey advanced in a number of publications, perhaps most influentially in his *Brief Introduction to the Study of Theology* (1819). Historical competence, as Drey understood it, could be put in the service of the Church, preventing it from ossifying into a lifeless form fixated nostalgically on the past. Instead, as an organic unity the Church could and should confidently advance into the future, keeping alive the doctrinal achievements of the past, but engaging, criticizing, and (when appropriate) embracing more recent ideas and developments in human history. The acorn, in short, should not shrink from its noble vocation of becoming a tree.

The problem with Protestantism, in Drey's view, was that it wanted the Church to stay an acorn. By advocating the primacy of Scripture over tradition and the apostolic era over later periods of Church history, Protestants, despite their many recent scholarly merits, advanced a fundamentally mistaken ecclesiology. In his view, Protestants could give no account of the Church as a living, breathing historical organism, a vital tradition, developing over time under the guidance of the Holy Spirit. The teaching of *Sola scriptura* was especially problematic in his view, for it seemed to imply that each theologian, apart from the collective wisdom of tradition, had the duty to interpret Scripture correctly through the narrow pipe stem of his own subjective judgment.[81]

This idea of church history as a living, developing tradition, understood but not undermined by contemporary historical *Wissenschaft*, was the principal legacy that Drey left to the next generation of theologians at Tübingen, including his ablest protégé, Johann Adam Möhler. In 1815 as a 19-year-old, Möhler had studied under Drey at the Catholic seminary in Ellwangen, following Drey to Tübingen when the seminary relocated there. After further studies, ordination as a priest, and a period serving a rural parish, Möhler received a call to return to Tübingen when a position opened there in 1822. Before assuming his duties, he was provided a stipend by the government to undertake a "literary journey" to acquaint himself with the best minds and methods for teaching church history and historical theology—the fields that he had been tapped to teach at Tübingen. In the fall of 1822 he set off on a trip that would take him to Jena, Würzburg, Halle, Göttingen, Berlin, and other centers of learning. Attending lectures and making many friends and professional contacts, he rubbed shoulders with some of Germany's leading scholars, Catholic and Protestant.[82]

Once back in Tübingen in 1823, Möhler launched an intense if brief career (he died in 1838 at the age of 41), publishing widely and achieving renown. Among his best-known books are *The Unity in the Church or the Principle of Catholicism Presented in the Spirit of the Church Fathers of the First Three Centuries* (1825) and *Symbolism: Exposition of the Doctrinal Differences between Catholics and Protestants as Evidenced in their Confessional Writings* (1832). Like Drey, Möhler borrowed heavily from Protestant tools of learning, and he too fashioned these tools into a critique of Protestantism and a defense of a vision of Catholicism that would exert tremendous influence.[83] Most of his writings have a polemical edge. In *Symbolism*, he set out to refute Hegel's notion that Catholicism was the "religion of unfreedom,"[84] while his earlier *Unity in the Church* challenged his Protestant colleague at Tübingen, Ferdinand Christian Baur, over the appropriate interpretation of the first centuries of Christianity's expansion.[85]

Defining the Church—or ecclesiology—stood at the center of Möhler's thought. In his view, Protestants lacked a theology for understanding the Church as something that, while remaining faithful to its founding, developed and matured over time; they remained too fixed on the founding itself. This much Möhler had learned from Drey. But Catholics had their own problems, according to Möhler. Since the Council of Trent, they had over-emphasized the institutional and juridical aspects of the Church; and more recently, ultramontanes had become too preoccupied with the individual role of the Pope, separating his function from those of the broader community of the faithful (bishops, priests, councils, religious, laity). Through his own engagement with the writings of the Church Fathers, Möhler sought to recover an understanding of the Church as an interlocking community, a living tradition, which the Holy Spirit guides in all its parts over time into the fullness of truth. To be sure, in his view, the Church certainly possessed a "visible, human" dimension—an outward, institutional form—and the intellectual exertions of individuals were not beside the point for grasping truth. But both individual and institution must take a backseat to the mysterious communal nature of the Church and the superintending role of the Holy Spirit in the Church's sojourn through the ages. "The message [of the Church]," as one scholar has summarized Möhler, "was never given and received as something immediately understood, but rather as *something to be pondered and fathomed gradually.* This was never, even in apostolic times, the task of the individual; it was the community concern of the entire Church. It is this community, spreading horizontally across the world and vertically across the ages, that is possessed of the Spirit, and is protected—the individual is not—from distorting or losing any of Christ's teaching."[86]

Möhler's criticism of both Protestantism and Tridentine Catholicism earned him numerous critics. As previously mentioned, he found himself in a protracted polemical struggle with his Protestant colleague Baur, while the Archbishop of Cologne, Ferdinand August von Spiegel, spoke out against Möhler receiving a chair at Bonn, contending that Möhler's *Unity in the Church* was "insufficiently Catholic" and potentially "heterodox."[87]

But not everyone demurred. The theological faculty at Munich was receptive to the work of Tübingen's scholars. Döllinger in particular praised the work of Möhler, fondly remembering in his later years "the warmth and interiority that wafted from his book [Möhler's *Unity in the Church*]; the spirit-filled image of the Church, drawn up from the spirit of the Church Fathers, enchanted us young men. From the detritus and overgrowth of later times, we believed that Möhler had discovered a fresh, living Christianity. The ideal of the Christian Church appeared suddenly before our eyes."[88] Correspondence between Döllinger and Möhler, beginning in the 1820s, ripened into a friendship by the early 1830s. Fed up with the rancor at Tübingen, Möhler reached out to Döllinger in 1834 to help him obtain a post at Munich. This transpired in 1835 when Möhler transferred to Munich to teach historical and exegetical theology.[89] Here he finished his career, becoming sick and dying in 1838. Shortly thereafter Döllinger edited and published two volumes of Möhler's shorter writings and addresses.[90] In an address on the occasion of the 400th anniversary of the University of Munich, Döllinger exclaimed that for a short period in the 1830s we had among us "the first among the living theologians."[91]

Rome saw matters differently. Indeed, little affection existed between Tübingen and Rome in the middle decades of the nineteenth century. The Roman Curia and the Jesuit Order in particular looked frowningly upon the "academic theology" being produced in Germany's state universities, especially those under a Protestant (Tübingen) or a Josephist-Catholic monarch (Munich), and contrasted these unfavorably to Bishops' seminaries, which harkened back to the Council of Trent and stood under more direct Church control.[92] Tübingen's professors readily returned the disapprobation. "People in Rome are totally uninstructed about the needs of our churches," Möhler once opined; "they evaluate everything by the situation in Italy.... From Rome... come attitudes, judgments, and decrees which seem to emanate from another world, and an ancient one at that."[93]

But Rome found an intellectual outpost to its liking at Mainz, the seat of Germany's first bishopric under St. Boniface and an electorate during the Holy Roman Empire. In contrast to the historically-oriented "German" scholarship taking place at Tübingen and Munich, Mainz's theologians tracked much closer to Italian, "Roman" scholars in seeking to revive the thought of Thomas Aquinas and scholasticism more generally. As noted earlier, this revival had its roots in the early nineteenth century among Italian scholars such as Luigi D'Azeglio Taparelli (1793–1862), Serafino Sordi (1793–1865), Carlo Maria Curcia (1810–91), Matteo Liberatore (1810–92), and Vincenzo Gioacchino Pecci (1810–1903). It was Pecci, the future Pope Leo XIII, who issued in 1879 *Aeterni Patris*, the encyclical generally held to signal the victory of neo-Thomism as a quasi-official Catholic philosophy, which deeply shaped Catholic thought until the Second Vatican Council (1962–5) and beyond.[94] As recently as 1998, John Paul II in the encyclical *Fides et Ratio* referred to Thomas Aquinas as "a master of thought and a model of the right way to do theology."[95]

At Mainz, the thought of Aquinas and his latter-day disciples found strong resonance in the early nineteenth century. The journal *Der Katholik*, established by Andreas Räß (1794–1887) and Nikolaus Weis (1796–1869) in 1821, became the principal organ for the dissemination of German neo-scholasticism—and ultramontane ecclesiology (the two regularly went hand in hand). As a fledgling scholar at nearby Aschaffenburg, Döllinger came into contact with the "Mainz circle," which also included the notable Alsatian theologian Franz Bruno Liebermann (1759–1844).[96] For a period, Döllinger even planned to collaborate with them to produce a new Catholic theological encyclopedia. But this never transpired, and Döllinger and the Mainz circle eventually went their separate paths.[97] "The theologians at Mainz," as Franz Schnabel has summed up, "held fast to neo-scholasticism and were oriented to the [Roman] Curia in all questions pertaining to ecclesiastical affairs and politics."[98] Their defensive posture is well-captured in the subtitle of the journal *Der Katholik*: a "religious magazine of instruction and warning" (*zur Belehrung und Warnung*).[99]

Arguably the ablest contributor to *Der Katholik* was actually not located at Mainz, but wrote from Rome, where he lived since 1843 and taught at the Collegium Germanicum, a Jesuit seminary for German-speaking students.[100] This figure is the Jesuit Joseph Kleutgen (1811–83), among the most significant neo-Thomist thinkers of the nineteenth century, even if he is little known today. Leo XIII called him the "prince of philosophers"; his peers dubbed him "Thomas redivivus."[101] It was Kleutgen who prepared the first draft of *Aeterni Patris* (1879). A decade earlier, he had played a leading role in drafting the first schema of *Dei Filius* (1870), the Vatican Council's constitution delineating the proper relationship between faith and reason—a document often obscured by the greater attention given to *Pastor aeternus* (1870), the constitution on Papal primacy and Infallibility. In addition to his many shorter writings, Kleutgen produced two massive multi-volume works: *Die Theologie der Vorzeit* (5 vols., 1853–70) and *Die Philosophie der Vorzeit* (2 vols., 1863, 1870).[102]

Since Kleutgen and Döllinger found themselves moving in opposite directions intellectually, we should consider the former's outlook. We might begin by asking the question: why at this time did a host of Catholic thinkers point to Thomas Aquinas and the scholastic heritage as a means of understanding and intellectually confronting the "modern age" (*Neuzeit*)? This "modern age," as we have seen, possessed a heady political aspect: the arc of ideas and agitation stretching from the French Revolution to the *Risorgimento* unfolding on the Italian peninsula. This alarmed ultramontanes such as Kleutgen, to be sure. But the "modern age," as discussed earlier, was also held to have a much deeper, pervasive intellectual dimension, stretching all the way back to thinkers such as René Descartes and, closer to home, Immanuel Kant, the likes of whom, according to neo-Thomists, had fundamentally misconstrued the proper relationship between faith and reason, between theology and philosophy.[103] What is more, their misconstruals were regarded as having a sophisticated and beguiling quality, one capable of captivating prominent Catholic scholars such as Georg Hermes, Anton Günther, and Jakob Frohschammer—all of whom we shall return to in a moment—and through them leading young seminarians, priests, and the lay faithful astray.

In rudimentary terms, neo-Thomists sought to confront modernity's overvaluation of human reason and/or the tendency of a host of post-Enlightenment thinkers to pit reason against faith, science (*Wissenschaft*) against Christianity. To be sure, the holy mysteries of faith stood above reason, but reason, a gift from God and still present in the created order despite human sinfulness, had the capacity, if properly trained and motivated, to lead one to the doorstep of faith—if not a bit farther, just as in the *Divine Comedy* the pagan Virgil (symbolizing human reason) had guided Dante to the very cusp of heavenly bliss. Such considerations, frequently taking the form of arguments about the proper relationship of philosophy to theology in educational contexts, permeated Catholic thought in the middle decades of the nineteenth century.[104] It should come as no surprise, then, that Pius IX's first encyclical, *Qui pluribus*

(1846), dealt with the matter. Lashing out against "bitter enemies of the Christian name," Pius exclaimed:

> They feel as if philosophy, which is wholly concerned with the search for truth in nature, ought to reject those truths which God Himself, the supreme and merciful creator of nature, has deigned to make plain to men as a special gift. With these truths, mankind can gain true happiness and salvation. So, by … [a] specious kind of argumentation, these enemies never stop invoking the power and excellence of human reason; they raise it up against the most holy faith of Christ, and they blather with great foolhardiness that this faith is opposed to human reason.

Pius sought to propose a better way:

> [A]lthough faith is above reason, no real disagreement or opposition can ever be found between them; this is because both of them come from the same greatest source of unchanging and eternal truth, God. They give such reciprocal help to each other that true reason shows, maintains and protects the truth of faith, while faith frees reason from all errors and wondrously enlightens, strengthens and perfects reason with the knowledge of divine matters.[105]

In the early stages of Pius's pontificate, Joseph Kleutgen became absorbed by these same concerns. From his standpoint, grave philosophical and theological errors abounded in the "modern age." They needed to be exposed and refuted by returning Catholic theology (and philosophy) to the more salutary intellectual currents of an earlier age (*Vorzeit*) embodied in the scholastic doctors.[106] Against the Tübingen theologians, whose metaphysics, as we have seen, owed a significant debt to the organic philosophy of Schelling, Kleutgen proposed reviving Aristotelian realism, which had served as the bedrock of medieval scholastic thought. The organic, historicist elements of the Tübingen School seemed especially alarming to Kleutgen as they appeared to submit Christian morality and doctrine to the capricious winds of change and the subjective judgment of scholars. What is more, Kleutgen felt that many of the leading lights at Tübingen (and elsewhere, including Munich) simply lacked a sufficient grasp of scholasticism, understanding it only in caricature. Although well-meaning, they had drunk too deeply from the wells of German Protestant thought and thereby forfeited familiarity with surer, more dependable sources—sources present, dormant, but recoverable within Catholicism's own intellectual storehouse.[107]

But it was not simply Catholic theologians' deficit of knowledge about scholasticism that troubled Kleutgen. He felt much thornier problems resided in the intellectual architecture of the "modern age." The majority of these could be traced to René Descartes and those subsequently, including Catholic theologians, who accepted Cartesian presuppositions. Indeed, for Kleutgen, Descartes was *the* great, alarming hinge-figure in modern thought. "At the end of the seventeenth century," Kleutgen wrote, "the great transformation in philosophy—which [since] has been taken in different directions—was carried out by Descartes."[108] Kleutgen deprecated Descartes's subjective starting point for philosophy, his theory of certainty, his belief in innate rationality, his mathematical deductivism, and his famous methodical skepticism. In fact, Kleutgen's entire body of work might be construed as a relentless attack on Cartesian philosophy and its consequences for theology, and a concomitant appeal to the *status quo ante* before the *cogito ergo sum*.[109] At the same time, Kleutgen had no desire to return to scholasticism simply in the spirit of nostalgia. Far from it. He earnestly believed, and made quite trenchant arguments for, the perennial value of scholastic metaphysics over Cartesianism as a means of ensuring a properly Catholic understanding of the relationship between faith and reason, theology and philosophy, nature and grace.

Particularly troubling to Kleutgen was Descartes's exacting benchmark for achieving certainty—whether of the physical or the metaphysical. Extrapolating from Aquinas, Kleutgen asserted that knowledge of divine things simply cannot be apprehended with anything approaching mathematical certainty or through an empirical method. Limited, fallible human beings know them only by analogy, by inference, and, even then, they required a community of fellow inquirers and interlocutors—committed to *traditio*, a "handing down" to the next generation—to keep this knowledge alive. What is more, the deeper mysteries of faith—the Incarnation, the Trinity, and so on—entailed a wholly different order of knowledge; rightly cultivated reason could lead one to the threshold of this knowledge and perhaps even suggest the necessity of an act of faith. But, finally, only the gift of divine grace, accepted by one's volition, could lead one through the door.[110]

By making absolute certainty the benchmark of metaphysics, Descartes, according to Kleutgen, had created a pernicious dilemma for subsequent theologians who took seriously his premises. One could embrace Cartesianism fully and assert that practically everything—even the mysteries of the Christian faith—were accessible with the right employment of reason. In other words, one could invite Descartes fully into the holy precincts of theology. Or, following the path taken by Immanuel Kant, one could posit a radical divide between the *phenomenal* world—the world of things which we can know with certainty—and the *noumenal* world—the impenetrable (non-rational?) reality beyond our knowledge, access to which might well entail an act of faith pure and simple. For Kleutgen, if a theologian embraced Cartesianism fully, hubristic rationalism was the likely result and the necessity of faith and grace diminished. But if one leaned in Kant's direction, blind, fideism shorn of intelligible content was a likely outcome. Both of these routes in Kleutgen's mind were essentially mistaken, because they distorted a proper understanding of reason and faith, whereby, again, the former could lead to the latter and prepare one for the assistance of divine grace. For Kleutgen, scholastics of an earlier era (*Vorzeit*) had quite simply gotten this issue right: reason "walks before faith" (*praeambula fidei*) in the classic locution.[111] Catholic theology in his time, therefore, had a dramatic either/or choice to make. And the right choice, to quote Gerald McCool, was for "Catholic theology...to go back to St. Thomas and begin its work anew, using a sound method based on Thomas' epistemology and metaphysics."[112]

The implications of a "return to Thomas" was exhaustively laid out in Kleutgen's major works and articles, including those appearing in Mainz's *Der Katholik*. Since he was a key architect of Vatican I's *Dei Filius* (1870), the fruit of such a return is more succinctly presented in this document:

> Even though faith is above reason, there can never be any real disagreement between faith and reason, since it is the same God who reveals the mysteries and infuses faith, and who has endowed the human mind with the light of reason. God cannot deny himself, nor can truth ever be in opposition to truth. The appearance of this kind of specious contradiction is chiefly due to the fact that either the dogmas of faith are not understood and explained in accordance with the mind of the Church, or unsound views are mistaken for the conclusions of reason. Therefore we define that every assertion contrary to the truth of enlightened faith is totally false. Furthermore the Church which, together with its apostolic office of teaching, has received the charge of preserving the deposit of faith, has by divine appointment the right and duty of condemning what wrongly passes for knowledge, lest anyone be led astray by philosophy and empty deceit. Hence all faithful Christians are forbidden to defend as the legitimate conclusions of science those opinions which are known to be contrary to the doctrine of faith, particularly if they have been condemned by the Church; and furthermore they are absolutely bound to hold them to be errors which wear the deceptive appearance of truth.[113]

In the decades prior to *Dei Filius*, Germany's Catholic universities were seen by Rome as particularly hospitable laboratories for perverse opinions, especially those pertaining to faith and reason. Shielded politically by the enduring mists of Febronianism, too close for comfort to the hazardous ideas of Protestant theologians, these institutions were prone to receive persistent glances of suspicion and admonishment from "across the Alps."[114] At this time, it became more and more a commonplace to speak of "Roman" (read: correct and neo-scholastic) and "German" (read: errant and rationalist and/or historicist) directions in theology.[115] From the standpoint of Rome, Mainz and, to a degree, the University of Würzburg could be trusted perhaps, but the others, with Tübingen and Munich leading the way, evinced deficiencies. Behind the scenes as a "German expert" for the Congregation of the Index, Kleutgen himself played no small role in alerting the Curia and the Pope of the dangerous theological pathways of his countrymen. This climate of suspicion is essential for understanding Döllinger's relations to Rome after mid-century, not to mention his excommunication in 1871. In this period, a "massive Roman intervention in theology" took place according to McCool, the likes of which had not been seen in the modern era.[116] For our purposes, three official condemnations—those of the aforementioned Hermes, Günther, and Frohschammer—stand out in significance; together, these condemnations helped fashion a synoptic of profound wariness, through which Rome viewed German university theology in general and the thought of Döllinger in particular.

The first condemnation returns us to the 1830s and the pontificate of Gregory XVI. Around the time of Gregory's election, Georg Hermes ranked among the most accomplished and influential Catholic thinkers in Germany. His engagement with the philosophy of Kant and Fichte had pushed him to the brink of skepticism, but eventually, selectively borrowing aspects of Kant's thought and wedding them to a process of methodical doubt, Hermes worked out a system that purported to "demonstrate" rationally (according to *Vernunft*) the verities of the Catholic faith. His theological rationalism or "Hermesianism" spread like wildfire. Receiving praise and honor from many universities, even Protestant ones, he was appointed "Rector Magnificus" of the University of Bonn. Professors at Bonn, Cologne, Breslau, Münster, and elsewhere identified with his name as a badge of honor, for he had appeared to trump the Enlightenment on its own terms. Even the Archbishop of Cologne, Ferdinand August von Spiegel, looked favorably upon him.[117]

But in Rome Hermes attracted many critics. The chief concern was that this "German" theologian, seduced by Protestant and modern sophistry, had blurred the line between faith and reason by unwarrantedly magnifying the role of the latter in ascertaining theological truths. His system seemed to have left little room for divine grace. No action was brought against him during his lifetime, but after his death in 1831 a concerted effort by his opponents led to his condemnation and the placing of a number of his books on the Index. Because of his popularity, this led to an uproar among many German scholars and even by the Prussian government, since the University of Bonn stood under its authority. But Gregory XVI, who took a keen personal interest in the matter, had no intention of backing down. The verdict against Hermes in *Dum acerbissimas* (September 26, 1835) rang out loud and clear: Hermes and his followers had "adulterated the most sacred deposit of faith, while boasting that they are protecting it." Recognizing his "almost universal reputation throughout Germany," Hermes was nonetheless censured "as one who boldly left the royal path that universal tradition and the most Holy Fathers have marked out in explaining and vindicating the truths of the faith; . . . [producing instead] a dark way to error of all kinds on positive doubt as a basis for all theological inquiry."[118]

The condemnation of Hermes reverberated in the following decades and contributed to a growing suspicion among theologians in Rome about German universities. The year 1857 witnessed the condemnation of Anton Günther of Vienna. Criticizing scholasticism, Günther embraced Hegel's philosophy to produce a Christianized Hegelianism that purported to prove the transcendence of God, the Trinity, Creation *ex nihilo*, and other doctrinal verities, which the Church insisted were only accessible by faith with the assistance of grace. Like Hermes before him, Günther attracted a large following, counting devotees of his thought in Munich, Bonn, Breslau, Salzburg, Prague, Graz, Trier, Tübingen, and elsewhere. (Later, many German "Old Catholics" came from the ranks of Günther's supporters.[119]) But not in Rome. The Vatican, now under Pius IX, sought to stem this tide of error in *Eximiam tuam* (June 15, 1857), charging that "Günther's books rashly attribute the rights of a master both to human reason and philosophy, whereas they should be wholly handmaids, not masters [*non dominari, sed ancillari*] in religious matters." Günther's outlook, furthermore, had "disturbed that which should remain stable, not only with respect to the distinction between science and faith, but also concerning the eternal immutability of faith, which is always one and the same, while philosophy and humanistic studies are not always consistent, and subject to a variety of errors."[120]

In 1862 another condemnation followed. This one struck close to home for Döllinger as it was against his colleague at the university, the philosopher Jacob Frohschammer.[121] Deeply influenced by German idealist philosophy, Frohschammer had been suspect for some time. In 1857, his book *On the Generation of Human Souls* (1854) had been placed on the Index. Joseph Kleutgen had written polemically against him in his *Die Philosophie der Neuzeit*.[122] The situation became so delicate that Döllinger even felt the need to distance himself from his younger colleague, which he did publicly in the *Allgemeine Zeitung* and in his university lectures, and privately in a memorandum prepared for King Maximilian II of Bavaria.[123]

Rome's criticisms of Frohschammer were not unlike those raised against Hermes and Günther; Frohschammer had been beguiled by recent trends in modern thought and, however well-meaning his intentions, had forsaken Catholicism's own intellectual patrimony. He had placed reason on the same footing as revelation, natural knowledge of God on par with supernatural knowledge. What was especially worrisome about Frohschammer's case, however, was the Munich scholar's expansive view of academic freedom. In *On the Freedom of Science* (1861), Frohschammer argued that scholars should have "unrestricted" (*ungehinderte*) liberty to discuss and publish their views, to follow truth wherever it might lead, without worrying about the interference or condemnation of an external (religious) authority.[124]

But a condemnation against him came nonetheless. In *Gravissimas inter* (December 11, 1862), Pius IX accused Frohschammer of a twofold violation of magisterial teaching: "the first...because the author attributes to human reason such powers that in no way belong to reason itself; and the second, because he grants to the same reason such liberty of judging all things, and of always daring anything whatsoever that the rights, office, and authority of the

Church herself are completely abolished." In the final analysis, it was not liberty that Frohschammer advocated, but "unbridled license." Despite his good intentions, therefore, Frohschammer amounted to yet another scholar "in various regions of Germany" who had "betray[ed] sacred theology as well as philosophy" and thereby contributed to "the great restlessness and iniquity of these times."[125] Günther had recanted his views; Frohschammer did not, and later found himself excommunicated in 1871, the same year as Döllinger.

As a trusted advisor to the Congregation of the Index, Joseph Kleutgen played a significant role in Rome in the condemnations of Günther and Frohschammer.[126] But another figure, Karl August von Reisach (1800–69), began to assume increasing prominence during this time in advising the Church on German affairs.[127] A scholar of significant learning, Reisach had served as Archbishop of Munich and Freising since 1847, as has been mentioned. In 1855, after a tussle with the Bavarian crown, he was made a cardinal and summoned to join the Curia in Rome, where he promptly exacerbated anxieties about the direction of German university theology. When Döllinger and several colleagues called for a major congress of German Catholic scholars to take place in Munich in 1863, Reisach made explicit his fears in a memorandum. It is worth quoting him at some length as his words give evidence of how Rome viewed German universities in the early 1860s:

> It is known to the Holy See that the question of the relations of faith and reason is agitated among the Catholic theologians of Germany with great animosity, and it is also known that the various opinions on this matter which divide German theologians and philosophers derive from their having in fact abandoned the principles of the ancient and traditional philosophy and theology of the [scholastic] schools and put in its [sic] place the various principles of modern philosophy which are substantially and essentially opposed to the older philosophy and therefore opposed to the teaching received and approved by the church not only in method but also on many important points of theological doctrine. The fact of Frohschammer is not an isolated one; the doctrine taught by other professors of the University of Munich and especially by those of Tübingen, not to speak of those professors who have imbibed more or less the systems of Günther and of Hermes, shows many traces of the influence of modern philosophical systems and on that account…are opposed to the teaching of the church.
>
> This influence, while admitting divine revelation and even the authority of the church to preserve it in its integrity, attributes, however, to philosophy…a certain independence and freedom in explaining the meaning, the coherence, and the principles of revealed truth. While it refuses to recognize direction by ecclesiastical authority, it is ready to explain dogmas in a sense foreign to the definitions and the common teaching of the church. It is ready in the end to destroy the character and the nature of supernatural truths by attributing to reason the ability and the power to deduce them from the principles of natural reason and thus to arrive at a perfect scientific knowledge of the truths taught by faith.[128]

While Döllinger, too, expressed concern about the case of his colleague Frohschammer, he also worried that Rome might overreact and imperil German scholarship and academic freedom. In significant measure, this is what motivated him, working with others, to convene a Congress of Catholic Scholars in 1863, to which we shall come shortly. If the climate of suspicion from Rome did not improve, Döllinger wrote his former pupil Joseph Edmund Jörg in 1862, then Catholic scholarship had little hope, for "fear of the Index hovers over the heads of [German] Catholic authors like the sword of Damocles."[129]

DRIFTING FROM ROME

When the Chair of Peter passed from Gregory XVI to Pius IX in 1846, Döllinger had every reason to consider himself a faithful servant of the Church, championing from Munich its causes against Protestant critics and against various depredations of the modern age. By the late 1860s, this had changed. A large and growing cleft had opened up between Döllinger and Rome. What explains the shift?

To answer the question, one must highlight some of Döllinger's experiences in the late 1840s and the 1850s, leading up to the previously mentioned lectures that he gave in 1861 and 1863, respectively on the Papal States and on the state of Catholic theology. During these decades, Döllinger increasingly associated his vocation with his national identity as a German, his scholarly identity as a historian, and his religious identity as a champion of the cause of Christian unity. These vocational emphases developed gradually and during a time when Rome, as we have seen, was doubling down on ultramontane ecclesiology, which spurned national Catholic identities, and on neo-scholasticism, which had scant room for historical scholarship in its theological house. And so, eventually, the cleft appeared, widening into a chasm at the time of the Council.

During the 1840s, much of Döllinger's writing appeared in the *Historisch-politische Blätter für das katholische Deutschland*. While many of his articles treated historical topics, he also weighed in on contemporary affairs.[130] In the anti-Prussian, anti-Protestant milieu in Catholic Germany provoked by the "Cologne Troubles," Döllinger came out strongly in favor of Protestant soldiers in Bavaria having to genuflect to the Eucharist in church processions. He also defended the Archbishop of Cologne's stance against confessionally mixed marriages in a short treatise on the subject. What is more, he penned two works on Protestantism—*The Reformation* (3 vols., 1846–8) and a much shorter *Luther* (1851)—in which he expressed highly critical views, especially of the Protestant teaching on justification, in an effort to controvert Prussian historians' interpretation of the Reformation as a highpoint of the German past.[131]

Recognition and reward accompanied Döllinger's scholarly accomplishments. The prestigious Bavarian Academy of Science welcomed him as a member in 1843. In 1844/45 he served as the rector of the University of Munich. He received the Knight's Cross of the Rider (*Ritterkreuz*) award in 1845. In 1847, he was made a royal chaplain and installed as the Provost (*Stiftspropst*) of the Order of St. Cajetan. A trusted advisor to the Bavarian Minister of Culture, Karl von Abel, in educational and religious matters, Döllinger represented the university in the Bavarian Parliament on two occasions, in 1845–7 and 1849–51.[132] In 1850, Rome made its approbation known by considering Döllinger as a candidate to serve as the Archbishop of Salzburg.[133] In short, by mid-century Döllinger had become, in the words of the papal nuncio in Munich, "the most luminous, the most pious, and . . . the most distinguished [professor] at the University of Munich."[134]

But all was not smooth sailing. The mid-century years also witnessed political scandal in Munich and Döllinger's involvement in pan-German national affairs as a consequence of the revolutions that shook Europe in 1848. The scandal was the so-called "Lola Montez affair," a curious episode in Bavaria's history. Since the beginning of his reign in 1825, Ludwig I had proven himself an able leader, protector, and promoter of Bavaria's interests. But his infatuation in the 1840s with the actress Lola Montez (1821–61) and the suspicion that she was exercising undue behind-the-scenes influence led to a rancorous atmosphere of mistrust and accusation. Protests from members of the university in 1847 led the crown to halt its operations, sending many professors into involuntary "retirement." This fate befell Döllinger in August 1847 when he was given "emeritus" status, effectively suspending his duties. But large-scale, public opposition in 1848 against the crown's actions forced Ludwig's abdication and the accession to the throne of his oldest son, Maximilian. This calmed the situation and in 1849 Döllinger returned to his position.[135]

The interruption of his teaching duties gave Döllinger a freer hand to participate in the German Parliament at Frankfurt am Main when he was named as representative in 1848. Serving from May 1848 to May 1849, and delivering a major speech before the assembly in August 1848, Döllinger showed particular concern for Church–state matters and for the situation of Catholicism in the emerging German nation-state.[136] With the benefit of hindsight, we know that the establishment of nationhood did not occur in 1848, but in 1871 and then under the militaristic hand of (Protestant) Prussia—resulting, among other things, in the *Kulturkampf* against Catholics in the 1870s. But in the late 1840s, the situation looked very different for Catholics, at once more hopeful if uncertain. In 1848, most Catholics, Döllinger included, leaned toward the "Greater Germany" (*Großdeutschland*) solution, a federal national identity that would encompass Austria as well.[137] In this heady atmosphere. Döllinger, evincing both lingering Febronian sentiments and pointedly nationalist ones, began to diverge from the centralizing tendencies of Pius IX's Rome and its ultramontane backers.[138] During this time, it should be remembered, Pius was forced to flee Rome for Gaeta, and his opinion of the ideologies of nationalism and liberalism had reached a nadir, where it would stay for the remainder of his pontificate. In short, and this should be emphasized, Döllinger and the Pope had different experiences during, and drew different lessons from, 1848–9.

In the speech before the Parliament at Frankfurt and in an anonymously published essay of the same year, Döllinger made the case not for the "separation" of Church and state but for the "independence" of the Church, whether Protestant or Catholic, from the "bureaucratic police state." The arrangement of the Church functioning as a "tool" of the government had prevailed across central European states since the Restoration of 1815, enforced coercively in German lands since the Karlsbad Decrees of 1819. But the time for this arrangement had passed, according to Döllinger. "What we have longed for, the freedom of the churches, is finally at hand.... Now... either the current of political life in Germany will gradually go back to the old way of life, or the emancipation of the churches is only a matter of time; it belongs, not to the present, but certainly to the future." What Döllinger had in mind was an ecclesiastical analog to the political currents that were weakening local states' structures in favor of a grand "national German state." Would it not be appropriate at this time, he reasoned, for German Catholics to come together, too, to form a "national German Church," replete with a "national synod" and a "head."[139] To be sure, this national church would be linked to Rome in a spirit of unity and loyalty, but not in fearful subservience.[140] In making such arguments, Döllinger was especially keen to rebut those Protestant critics who regarded the Catholic Church as incapable of reform and as compromising German national identity, since Catholics, so the accusation went, were necessarily beholden to an "Italian" monarch in Rome.

The ideas Döllinger voiced at Frankfurt made their way into specifically ecclesiastical settings in these same turbulent years. In early October 1848, the first General Assembly of Catholic Societies (*Vereine*) of Germany met in Mainz.[141] Döllinger addressed the assembly, reprising aspects of his speech before the Frankfurt Parliament. Parrying the charge that Germany and Catholicism were incompatible, Döllinger laid out the case for unifying all the German bishops under one national Church. In the sixteenth century, he assayed, the Reformation had destroyed the ecclesiastical unity of Germany in the old Reich; it was now the duty of Catholics to come together in a unified front, to quiet Protestant detractors, but also to demonstrate an attractive unity that might bring Protestants back to the fold. The events of 1848 in general and the meeting of Catholic societies in particular, he felt, had been prepared by "divine providence" to function as "a powerful tool, a means for the establishment of a united Catholic Church in Germany."[142]

The first conference of German bishops took place in Würzburg in late October 1848. Döllinger was invited to give an address. The calling of the conference in the first place can in part be attributed to Döllinger, who lobbied for the meeting and its agenda to Archbishop Johannes von Geissel (1796–1864) of Cologne, who officially requested that the bishops gather.[143] In making his case for a national German Church before this audience, Döllinger evinced great circumspection, knowing that the bishops had to be of one mind about such a project. Döllinger recognized, too, that Rome's experiences with "national churches"—whether of the Anglican, Gallican, Josephist, or Febronian variety—had left a bitter legacy. Still, he argued that national distinctions were part of the divine scheme of things, and "the German nation belongs undoubtedly to those nations who play a world-historical role, who are...special instruments in the hands of Providence."[144] The events of 1848, according to Döllinger, offered providential direction for German identity to be wedded to Catholic identity: "The [Catholic] part of the nation actually bears and represents German nationality, as it stands in unbroken continuity with the entire great past of the German people." Anticipating criticism from Rome, Döllinger went to great lengths to assert that he had no intention of advocating a break-away movement from the Universal Church. Rather, Germanness and Catholicism should go together, hand in hand, the particular manifestation of the German Church being an integral facet of the Church Universal.[145]

In the long run, we might say that Döllinger was successful; or at least the Conference of German Bishops later became an important vehicle for organizing the Catholic hierarchy in Germany. But he did not succeed in the short term. Opposition came from Döllinger's home turf. The then papal nuncio in Munich, Carlo Sacconi (1808–89) and the Archbishop of Munich, Karl August von Reisach derided the idea of a national church as compromising the jurisdiction of Rome. They made known their worries to the Curia and Pius IX, who mistrusted the gathering as the rekindling of the "Febronian" problem.[146] Döllinger's speech, Sacconi wrote to Rome, "confirmed in me the suspicions" that the Munich scholar wanted to introduce among the bishops "a spirit of novelty, of democracy and of general revolution and reform."[147]

Döllinger continued to make the case for a German national church at two subsequent gatherings: at the General Assembly of Catholic Societies at Regensburg in October 1849 and at the same Assembly's meeting at Linz in September 1850. In both of these addresses, Döllinger repeated arguments first made in 1848, insisting that the time had come for a German national church and that such a development in no way compromised the Church's universal identity and mission; rather each particular national church made up a vital part of the greater "catholic" whole.

Looking at Döllinger's addresses together from this period and in light of his address before the Frankfurt Parliament (which disbanded under political pressure in the spring of 1849), several things stand out. First, the "imagined community" of the nation, nationalism, played a strong role in Döllinger's mind, informing both his politics and ecclesiology. Second, the many appeals to history in his address implicitly suggest that he felt the vocation of the historian ought to play an important role in guiding the Church in the direction of its true interests. Finally, he regarded the events of 1848 as having world-historical significance; the job of scholars—and the clergy—in this momentous time was to steer the Church prudently, embracing the salutary currents of thought of the times, expunging the detrimental.

The experience of nationalism and liberalism from the standpoint of Rome, it should be reiterated, diverged widely from Döllinger's experience. In the short-lived Roman Republic (1848–9), nationalism had been wedded to aggressive anticlericalism and political radicalism. As we have seen, Pius IX and his Curia felt that nothing short of a diabolical assault on the Church had taken place. The pervasive skepticism that colored their outlook toward nationalism and liberalism did not accord with Döllinger's limited embrace of them. No major rift occurred at this time, but we might at least hazard that some of the seeds of the later conflict between Döllinger and the Church were sown in the revolutionary years of mid-century.

In many respects, the 1850s witnessed a return to the status quo prior to 1848. But in other respects, it did not. Although the monarchs of Europe reasserted their prerogatives in this period, the flames of revolution and nationalist fervor were not fully snuffed out.[148] They would flair up mightily in the establishment of the Italian nation-state in 1859–61 and, *mutatis mutandis*, in the creation of Germany between 1866 and 1871. The 1850s for Döllinger were years of significant scholarly work, the carrying out of his duties as professor and priest in Munich, and the making or deepening of friendships that would play an important role later in his life. He also had opportunities for travel, such as his trip in 1857 to Rome, his first and only to the Eternal City, which he made with his new apprentice, soon fast friend, Lord Acton.

In the 1850s, Döllinger came into his own as scholar. With the turmoil of 1848–9 behind him, he devoted himself to realizing what he later called "the German historical sense," the national gift of "break[ing] through the atmosphere which the present draws around us, penetrat[ing] through the clouds of prejudice to the knowledge of the spirit and hidden nature of remote times."[149] This historical sense bore fruit in a number of his publications. In 1853, he published *Hippolytus and Kallistus*, a work occasioned by the discovery in 1842 of a manuscript in Greece, the so-called "Philosophumena," the disputed authorship of which had created a scholarly sensation. Weighing carefully the investigations of others, Döllinger attributed the manuscript to the Roman presbyter and anti-pope, Hippolytus, who died in 235, perhaps reconciled to the Church in Rome, but beforehand having opposed the teachings of Pope

Zephyrinus (r. 198–217) and Pope Callistus (r. 217–22). While we need not belabor the details of this debate, what is important about this work is Döllinger's insistence that in scholarship on such contested topics, one thing alone is important: historical veracity.[150] More broadly, we see a turn in this work from Döllinger the confessional polemicist of his earlier works on the Eucharist and the Reformation to Döllinger the historian's historian, intent— at least in his rhetoric if not always in practice—on following the facts wherever they might lead. For this, he received praise from both admirers and critics. The book "exhibits," according to one reviewer, "all the profound and various erudition of which he [Döllinger] is so distinguished a master, with the acuteness, sagacity, and moderation, which have placed him at the very head of the critical historians of modern Germany."[151]

More scholarship followed. *The Gentile and the Jew in the Courts of the Temple of Christ* appeared in 1857, followed by *The First Age of Christianity and the Church* in 1860.[152] The first was a survey of the ancient world, in which both Judaism and pagan thought (particularly Greek philosophy) had functioned, according to Döllinger, as a *praeparatio evangelica*, a preparing of the way for the advent of Christianity. In the second book, Döllinger surveyed the earliest decades of Christianity in the context of the Roman Empire. Several passages in this book are instructive for understanding Döllinger's later conflict with Rome. In the preface, for example, he argued that while the Church develops and matures over time, apostolic Christianity functions as a normative benchmark. Although the development of Christianity through the ages might surpass "the simple outlines and primitive forms of thought and life in the Apostolic age," it can never "transcend . . . the original fullness of its being," but must develop according to an "internal law," set in place at the beginning.[153] Or, again, from a chapter on "Scripture and Tradition":

> [T]here is no point of Christian doctrine which is not attested to and laid down in the apostolic writings. The Church cannot and dare not receive any teaching which does not find its justification in the Bible, and is not contained somewhere in the New Testament, in a more or less developed form, or at least indicated and implied in the premises of which it is the logical sequel, and thus shown to fit into the harmony and organic whole of Christian doctrine.[154]

One might glimpse the influence of the Catholic Tübingen School's organicism in this passage and infer reasons why Döllinger later felt that Papal Infallibility violated the laws of appropriate development.

But, in truth, the 1850s provide evidence both for and against Döllinger's break with Rome. On the one hand, it appears the Church continued to hold him in high regard. As mentioned earlier, in 1850 he had been considered as a candidate for Archbishop of Salzburg. In 1855 he was elected as a member of the prestigious *Academia di Religione Cattolica* in Rome.[155] Three years earlier in 1852, we know from archival evidence, when Pius IX first commissioned preparation for what would eventually become the "Syllabus of Errors" that Döllinger was considered as a possible commission member. But in this, we also see intimations of a future cleft. For when the nuncio in Munich, Sacconi, was asked about the suitability of Döllinger for this responsibility, he responded, to the Curial Cardinal Raffaele Fornari, that while Döllinger "surpassed all others in Germany with respect to erudition and instruction in the diverse areas of knowledge he was not a profound theologian, did not have appropriate ideas on papal primacy; and his views on papal infallibility were both wrong and worthy of censure." What is more, Sacconi held that Döllinger came across as "conceited and proud."[156] Furthermore, from Döllinger's own lips, we see evidence of a fissure with Rome, or at least with ultramontanism, as early as 1850. In his talk to the General Assembly of Catholic Societies at Linz (September 26, 1850), Döllinger, making the case for a German national church, noted that "ultramontanism" stood as a potential obstacle. For him, "ultramontanism" meant an attempt by some to "impose...what another nation [Italy presumably] according to its own traits in religious matters had formed and developed and then, like an ill-fitting coat, sought cumbersomely to make the German people wear." To be sure, the German people should be "in harmony with the spirit of the Catholic Church," but this harmony need not compromise national developments in the name of a coerced international unity.[157] This sentiment grew in Döllinger's thinking in the coming decades.

The 1850s witnessed Döllinger deepening old or making new friendships that would be important to him in the years between the "Syllabus of Errors" and the Vatican Council and beyond. Of particular significance, in 1850, the young Acton (aged 16) showed up in Munich at Döllinger's address, Frühlingstraße 11, prepared to embark on an academic apprenticeship under "the Professor" as well as lodge in his home. As mentioned in the introduction, Döllinger had made extensive contacts with the English-speaking world—particularly with English Catholics and with Anglicans involved in the Oxford Movement, about which Döllinger took great interest.[158] In 1845 the future British Prime Minister William Gladstone (1809–98) paid a visit to Döllinger in Munich. Captivated by the Professor's erudition and eloquence, Gladstone wrote his wife: "I have lost my heart to him."[159] Shortly after his conversion to Catholicism, John Henry Newman (1801–90) came knocking, in December of 1847, on a return trip from Rome, later seeking (unsuccessfully) to lure Döllinger to teach at the newly-founded Catholic University in Dublin.[160] Through personal contact and correspondence, Döllinger also stood on friendly terms with E. B. Pusey (1800–82), a key leader of the Oxford Movement; Cardinal Nicholas Wiseman (1802–65), the Archbishop of Westminster after the Restoration of the Catholic hierarchy to England in 1850; Henry Nutcombe Oxenham (1829–88), another notable Anglican convert to Catholicism; and Alfred Plummer (1841–1926), an Anglican theologian and historian.[161] Many other English scholars and divines came to know (and often correspond with)

Döllinger through his scholarship, some of which began to be translated into English at this time.[162] Plummer visited Döllinger regularly after the excommunication and left written records of their conversations.[163]

But Döllinger's relationship with Acton was of a different order than the others. The mentor–pupil relationship begun in 1850 matured into a full-blown friendship by the 1860s. "No one in the whole world knows me better than Acton and knows more about me," Döllinger wrote to the writer Charlotte Lady Blennerhassett (1843–1917), with whom he confided frequently in the latter half of his life.[164] Shortly after arriving in Munich, Acton in a letter to his mother recorded impressions of his new mentor that would long persist: "The Professor speaks English well and talks to me never in another language. . . . I like him immensely. His knowledge of the history and literature of all countries is just extensive."[165] Polyglots both, men of serious faith and immense learning, the two kept alive their friendship—albeit not without some tensions and differences of opinion—through correspondence and visits until Döllinger's death in 1890.[166]

A topic of particular interest for professor and pupil alike was the state of Catholicism in general and the situation of the papacy in Italy in particular—or what was generally referred to as the "Roman Question." Acton arrived in Munich roughly two months after Pius IX had returned to Rome from exile in Gaeta. The situation on the Italian peninsula remained fraught with tension and uncertainty. As we have seen, Pius returned to Rome a changed man, pivoting sharply from his former liberalism to a course of reaction and Roman centralization, convinced that anticlericalism and general rapacity constituted the heart of the revolutionary spirit. As Acton later reflected on the matter to Döllinger: "It seems to me that when he [Pius IX] lost his crown on the field of liberty, he became easily convinced that it was to be regained only in the opposite direction, and so he went over to the [ultramontane] Jesuits who were able to exploit his changed circumstances the more easily for their purposes, as the fulfillment of their teaching aims also involved an increase in papal power."[167] One can only surmise that the topic of the papacy engaged Acton and Döllinger frequently in the early 1850s.

In the spring of 1857 Döllinger and Acton embarked on an extended trip to Italy with Rome as their destination. Traveling by coach first to Milan and then Bologna, the learned travelers arrived in Rome by the end of April. During the trip, Acton kept a journal.[168] Toward the end of their lives, both men reflected back on the trip—Acton in notes for a projected biography of his mentor and Döllinger in occasional letters and conversations to friends. Combined, the evidence from these sources suggests that the trip left a strong impression on them both, with respect to their attitude toward Pius IX, to their views on ecclesiastical authority generally, and to their outlook on the Pope's temporal government in this final, troubled period of its existence.[169]

At many points, Acton's journal records Döllinger as being more preoccupied by his historical investigations (which were copious) than by the present situation of the papacy. "When I was in Rome in 1857," Döllinger himself recollected in 1870, "I gave myself to historical pursuits and artistic enjoyments with an untroubled mind. I hadn't the faintest hint that the events of 1869 were coming"[170] Acton once humorously opined that Döllinger was "not a good traveler. Too thoughtful to be observant."[171] Döllinger spent many hours in the archives of the Dominicans near the Pantheon, perusing manuscripts of medieval heresies, or on a more limited basis in the Vatican Archives, where the German Oratorian Father, Augustin Theiner (1804–74), an admirer of Döllinger's work, served as archivist and prefect. Wherever his mentor went, Acton recorded Döllinger as saying, he was received with "kindness and liberality."[172]

Even so, the trip widened the crevice between both men and the papacy. Both evinced particular concern over the Holy See's captivity to "Roman" customs and habits of mind. Acton observed, for instance, that compared to German *Wissenschaft*, the quality of contemporary Roman scholarship greatly displeased Döllinger: "1857 made him indifferent to Roman scholarship."[173] While walking from the Coliseum, Acton recorded that, while discussing the temporal power, he asked Döllinger "How long will all this last?," to which Döllinger responded: "As long as it is felt to be beneficial to religion, and no longer." In his notes for a biography, Acton remarked that the 1857 trip "destroyed the halo [of Rome]" for Döllinger, even if it "did not [yet] produce any strong sense of condemnation." At one point, Acton posed to himself the question: "How did that [trip] set him [Döllinger] to thinking?"; while also scribbling: "Experience of Rome. Luther not so wrong after all."[174] In an essay, "Döllinger's Historical Work," Acton later remarked that "Döllinger used to commemorate his visit to Rome in 1857 as an epoch of emancipation."[175]

In late April, Acton and Döllinger, with Theiner present, had an audience with Pius IX. This was the only time that Döllinger and Pius met, face to face. They spoke French, although Acton observed that the Pope had not quite mastered the language. Interestingly, Acton recorded that the Pope "had expected the professor for some time." At the meeting, Pius offered some pleasantries about the significance of ecclesiastical literature in Germany and the necessity of unity in the Church. Theiner chimed in that the late Johann Adam Möhler and Döllinger were the ablest scholars in Germany. In his journal, Acton commented on the ultramontane direction of the papacy and Pius's unfamiliarity with the political and religious situation outside of Italy. After observing that Pius wondered whether the Bavarian King Maximilian had been "injured by his protestant mother," Acton noted that Pius "said that the Holy See is the head and chief of all authority and all other authority attacked in it, wh[at] many princes do not see . . . . He knew like all Italians nothing of other countries." What is more, reflecting back on the Revolution of 1848, Acton averred that the temporal authority of the Pope "at that time failed so completely that he [Pius IX] has in reality abdicated all political power and authority, and leaves all that completely in [Cardinal] Antonelli's hands."[176]

Döllinger's own account of visiting the papal court is recorded in a series of conversations with Luise von Kobell (1828–1901), who published *Memories of Dr. Döllinger* in 1891 shortly after the Professor's death. While one ought to keep in mind that the sentiments reflected in this work came after Döllinger's excommunication and that they are reconstructed from memory by Kobell, they nonetheless suggest the negative effects of the 1857 trip on Döllinger's attitude toward Rome. "Did I ever tell you," von Kobell records Döllinger asking,

> the resolution I came to during my interview with the Pope? I formed a fixed determination not to present myself a second time. The ceremonial itself was highly displeasing to me. I was received in the audience with Theiner [and Acton] and, in common with every other priest, we had to kneel three times. First in the ante-chamber, then in the middle of the audience room, and finally before the Pope, who extended his foot, encased in a white and gold embroidered slipper, towards us to be kissed. We then rose, and Pio Nono addressed us in a somewhat commonplace fashion, to the effect that the Pope was the supreme authority over all, and that only when the world had learned to bow before the Apostolic Chair would the welfare of mankind be assured. He then asked us a few unimportant questions.... On this occasion I observed immediately on our entrance a peculiar expression... as though [the Pope] were thinking, "How will the German pedant [*der deutsche Pedant*] comport himself, and how will he stand our ceremonies?"[177]

According to Kobell, Döllinger in fact did look askance at a number of Vatican ceremonies, such as the "preposterous and unworthy custom" of seating newly elected popes on the altar of St. Peter's. "There are two little words all powerful in Rome," von Kobell attributed to Döllinger, "and by the help of which most matters are once for all decided—and these are '*è l'uso*' [it is customary]."[178]

The customs of the Inquisition especially aggrieved Döllinger. During his time in Rome, the cases against Günther and Frohschammer were underway. The Pope had requested that Döllinger be asked about the matter. When queried about Frohschammer by the Secretary of the Inquisition, Angelo Vincenzo Modena (1796–1870), Döllinger responded by asking whether anyone knew German well enough to condemn his work.[179] Modena responded that "there are only a few who understand that tongue. However it is sufficient if a person high in the opinion of the Vatican denounces the book, and translates the offensive passages ... and the book comes on the Index on the proposal of the Referent." "The Referent who does not know German?" Döllinger replied, apparently nonplussed, adding that "passages torn out and taken from their context often have a different meaning put into them and in this way a very wrong judgment may be made." "*Sono le nostre regole*" (these are our rules), responded Modena.[180] In retrospect, we know that both Frohschammer and Günther were condemned, but during his stay in Rome, as Acton later recorded, Döllinger "strove unsuccessfully to prevent the condemnation of two of his colleagues by the Index."[181]

While the evidence perhaps suggests more than it reveals, one, finally, cannot help but imagine that during their trip Acton and Döllinger discussed the temporal authority of the Pope. One passage from Acton's journal in particular adumbrates language that Döllinger offered in his 1861 address on the temporal authority. As this passage might, then, reflect some of Döllinger's own musings from 1857, permit a lengthy quote from Acton's journal:

> The pontifical states can never be well governed according to modern ideas because it [sic] has not gone through that which has influenced other states. Many things are not done by the government because it has not acquired the power of doing it. The people besides have no *Trieb* [German for "drive"] like the English for municipal self government. No great ends have caused all the powers of the state to be united for any common purpose. Besides men can do only one thing well—and one or the other must suffer. The spiritual government has never been injured by the temporal power. If it came ever to be considered as an impediment then the last hour of the papal state would have been sounded. The Church was 700 years without territory, and might be so again for 7000 years.[182]

A final item of interest comes in the fact that Döllinger departed Rome in the summer of 1857 without the customary conferral upon someone of his stature with the office of *cameriere segreto sopranummerario*, which granted one the right to the title "monsignor." Once back in Munich, Rome did extend to him this honor. But as it was also then conferred upon a priest of little distinction, some interpreted this as a slight against him. Once Döllinger received the news, he dutifully notified the appropriate authorities, royal and ecclesiastical. He was told by the palace that he could wear prelate's dress, but not at Church functions, when he should wear the vestments of *Stiftspropst* (provost). Döllinger never made use of the title "monsignor."[183]

TURNING POINTS: 1861, 1863

The crack opening up between Döllinger and Rome widened in the 1860s. As has been mentioned already, two key turning points in the making of this chasm came in the form of lectures that Döllinger delivered in 1861 and 1863—respectively on the condition of the Papal States and on the state of Catholic theology. The latter was given in the context of a major congress of leading German Catholic scholars in Munich. Some of the positions staked out at this conference, not least those by Döllinger, were censured by the Pope in the letter *Tuas libenter* (December 21, 1863) to Archbishop Scherr of Munich. This letter helped set the stage for the more consequential "Syllabus of Errors" of 1864.

On April 5 and 9, 1861 Döllinger lectured at the Odeon theatre in Munich. His talks were part of a public lecture series in which he participated with his colleagues Daniel Bonifaz Haneberg (1816–76), a biblical scholar and abbot of the Saint Boniface Benedictine monastery in Munich, and Martin Deutinger (1815–64), the chaplain at the University of Munich. Initially, Döllinger had intended to offer a survey of the present situation of "the great religions" of the world. But as the date approached, he changed his topic to one of the most pressing and vexing issues of the day for Catholics: the "Roman Question," the fate of the temporal power of the papacy confronted, as it was, by the juggernaut of Italian unification.[184]

At the time of Döllinger's lectures (Figure 2.1), modern Italy was experiencing its birth pangs. On October 26, 1860, the revolutionary firebrand Giuseppe Garibaldi had met Victor Emmanuel II for the famous "handshake of Teano," near Naples, where Garibaldi surrendered the Southern provinces of Italy to

Figure 2.1. Photograph of Döllinger *c*.1860.

Source: Photograph by Franz Seraph Hanfstaengl, Germany, *c*.1860. Image courtesy of Wikimedia Commons.

unite the peninsula under the leadership of the house of Piedmont-Sardinia. Roughly one month before, on September 18, 1860, the Pope's meager volunteer forces had been routed by Piedmontese troops near Castelfidardo. Thereafter, the majority of church lands were absorbed into the budding Italian nation-state, which was officially proclaimed on March 17, 1861. Only a rump, the so-called the "Patrimony of St. Peter," remained around Rome, and that was only made possible by the continued presence of French troops kept there at the insistence of Napoleon III, though he harbored ambivalent feelings about the continuance of the Papal States.[185] As these dramatic events played out, the Piedmontese, employing several liberal clerics, such as Carlo Passaglia, tried to convince Pius IX and Cardinal Antonelli of the benefits of Count Cavour's dictum of a "free church in a free state", of relinquishing the temporal power for the spiritual power alone.[186]

Pius would have none of it. "We never make pacts with burglars," Antonelli once asserted.[187] Insisting that maintaining the temporal power was a matter of both duty and necessity, Pius indicated that he was prepared to suffer martyrdom if necessary. In the encyclical *Nullis certe verbis* (January 19, 1860), he made clear his intransigence: "Without fear, we will leave nothing untried in fighting bravely for the cause of religion and for preserving the civil dominion of the Roman Church and its temporal possessions and rights [*temporales possessiones ac iura*]. Intact and inviolate, these pertain to the entire Catholic world." God himself, Pius continued, "gave the civil power to the Roman Pontiff, so that he, never subject to any power, might exercise in full liberty and without impediment the supreme task of the apostolic ministry divinely committed to him by Christ our Lord."[188]

Meanwhile, Döllinger had arrived at a different conclusion. The situation of the beleaguered papacy propped up by French bayonets presented to him a sad spectacle; and the time might in fact be at hand, he reasoned, when the Pope's temporal power ought to be relinquished. Drawing from his historical scholarship, Döllinger set forth in 1861 that the Church had existed for 700 years without the Papal States and could exist without them in the future. "Will the Papal State maintain itself or vanish?" as he posed the question. "Will the Head of the Church remain a sovereign prince, or has the time arrived when the temporal power of the Pope separate itself from the spiritual?" Depicting the situation on the Italian peninsula as "tragic" and attributing an "impious Machiavellianism" to Italian nationalists, Döllinger contended nonetheless that it was likely in the Church's best interest to prepare for the cessation of temporal authority—come what may.[189]

In Döllinger's mind, the reasons for this were numerous, but several factors stand out. The poor administration of the Papal States since their reconstitution after 1815 had become an "intolerable burden" to the people of central Italy, where "deep discontent and dissatisfaction" prevailed. The situation had become an embarrassment to Catholics worldwide, who were more inclined to regard the Pope as a "head shepherd of the church" (*Oberhirten der Kirche*) than as a "temporal prince" (*Landesfürst*). What is more, citing the authority of the great theologian Cardinal Robert Bellarmine, Döllinger argued that the temporal authority was neither an "advantage" nor a "perfection" in the life of the Church, but a "necessity" that had arisen because of contingent historical conditions, the days of which were numbered.[190]

That the Church could resist the tide of revolution at all in the nineteenth century, Döllinger emphasized, had been due to the support of Austria and France. But this arrangement spelled potential favoritism toward these two countries, and how could the Church be truly universal, he asked, if it owed fealty to particular nation-states—"a double prop of foreign states and their bayonets"? In the final analysis, Döllinger felt it "indisputably better and more dignified if [the Church] not be welded to the ponderous, helpless burden of a secular kingdom that she could not maintain . . . against the thronging billows of revolution."[191]

What would follow the demise of the Papal States was less clear in Döllinger's mind (Map 2.1). "The Church has truly the promise that the gates of Hell shall not prevail against her," he observed in a theological register, "but she has no promise that the successor of St. Peter should always remain monarch of a temporal kingdom." He sketched (without endorsing) several possible future scenarios. These ranged from Austria reasserting its power over Italy, to the papacy removing itself from Rome to France, to the convening of an international "Congress of Catholic Powers" to deliberate about the matter. Whatever the course of the future, he indicated that Catholics the world over would "willfully, joyfully, abundantly contribute to alleviate the situation of our common Head and Father, and to furnish him with the means of free and vigorous action." He closed the second lecture, reflecting on the Greek myth of Apollo: the island of Delos was said to have arisen from the sea miraculously to be his birthplace. Without knowing the particulars of the future, Döllinger analogized, "we will in confidence expect that a new Delos shall not be wanting for the Chair of St. Peter, should it have to arise from the depth of the sea."[192]

Döllinger's lectures caused an immediate sensation.[193] The then papal nuncio in Munich, Flavio Chigi (1810–85), in fact had ostentatiously walked out of the theatre in protest during Döllinger's first lecture, complaining to Cardinal Antonelli in Rome of Döllinger's "inappropriate, insulting, calumnious" words.[194] Napoleon III insisted that the French ambassador in Munich telegraph him the content of the second lecture immediately. A flood of commentary on the lectures soon appeared in the European press—some positive, some negative, but all noting the high significance of such a prominent Catholic scholar coming out against the temporal power at this moment of crisis. In May, Acton conveyed to Döllinger that his lectures "for the

Map 2.1. Map of central Italy/the Papal States in 1859 prior to Italian national unification.

Source: William Shepherd, *Historical Atlas* (New York: Henry Holt and Company, 1911). Image courtesy of Wikimedia Commons.

Church, against the Church State" had been the talk of England; "Just as throughout the Catholic world, so has your deed made a strong impression here."[195] "Not too long from now," the publisher Benjamin Herder of Freiburg im Breisgau opined approvingly, "Catholics will rejoice in what you have said, even if it hurts at the moment." From France, Guillaume-René Meignan, a former student of Döllinger, praised his mentor's "act of courage, the wisdom of which history would prove."[196]

But ultramontanes across Europe were dismayed. Ferdinand Walter, a law professor at the University of Bonn, in collaboration with other like-minded scholars even felt a need to pen a solidarity address to the Pope. The Würzburg church historian, Joseph Hergenröther (1824–90), who emerged as one of Döllinger's most implacable critics in the coming years, penned a reply to Döllinger in the journal *Der Katholik*, denouncing Döllinger for wounding "Catholic feeling" by his "inopportune" words.[197] "The storm that you have conjured up through your lectures," added Ernst von Moy of Innsbruck, "is on the rise. Major signs of protest against you are spreading."[198] Criticism and vituperation also flowed from Italy and France in ultramontane organs such as *La Civiltà Cattolica* and Louis Veuillot's, Paris-based *L'Univers*.[199] Writing in the *The Dublin Review*, E. S. Purcell opined that "[Döllinger] came forth as the champion of the necessity of Papal independence, and in spite of himself, he ended in becoming its greatest enemy . . . . [He] had the Papacy for his subject, and Europe for his audience, and he insulted the friends of the Church and flattered its enemies."[200]

Shaken but hopeful about the debate he had ignited, Döllinger sought to clarify his position in a hurriedly-written book, *The Church and the Churches: The Papacy and the Papal States: A Historical and Political Survey* (October, 1861), to which he appended the two lectures. In the book, he elaborated on ideas in his lectures, placing them in a broader theological and historical framework. He also emphasized several points, implicit but not fully articulated in the lectures—points that would take on increasing importance for him in the coming years. First, he called attention to the apologetic and ecumenical significance of the Church divesting itself of temporal authority. "The Roman states are the heel of Achilles of the Catholic Church," he wrote; it is "the standing reproach for adversaries throughout the world, and a stumbling block for thousands."[201] He recognized, of course, that this did not constitute the only matter separating Catholics from Protestants; still, the divestment of temporal power might prove a significant step toward "the reconciliation of the Churches, and of the true unity of Germany."[202]

Second, Döllinger expressed his hope that the lectures and the book would awaken "enlightened public opinion in the Church," to guide it into the future amid the dangers and uncertainties of the modern age. Appealing to church history, he argued that often in the past "a firmly-compacted class, like an impenetrable hedge of thorns" prevented necessary ecclesiastical reforms. The antidote to such an entrenched, reactionary faction—presumably he meant the Roman Curia—was, again, the influence of informed, Catholic public opinion: "Only when public opinion—even in Italy, and in Rome itself—had been awakened, cleansed and strengthened; and when the cry for reform resounded imperatively on every side, only then was it possible for popes to overcome resistance in the inferior spheres, and gradually, and step by step, to open the way for a healthier condition. May, therefore, a powerful, salubrious, unanimous public opinion in Catholic Europe come to the aid of Pius IX!"[203]

Finally, to those "inferior spheres," convinced that it was God's will to maintain the Papal States, Döllinger asserted "that God's knowledge and power reach farther than ours, and we must not presume to set bounds to the Divine Wisdom and Omnipotence and cry out to it—'this way, and not otherwise'." Such presumption, Döllinger opined, even risked imperiling one's faith if the course of history took a contrary route. Speaking "as an historian," therefore, Döllinger underscored the promise of his outlook: "Let no one lose faith in the Church, if the temporal principality of the Papacy should vanish.... It is not essence, but accident; not end, but means; it began late; it was formerly something quite different from what it is now.... [I]t is possible to conceive of a political condition of Europe in which it would be superfluous, and then it would only be a confining burden."[204]

Far from stemming the controversy over the lectures, Döllinger's book exacerbated it. Within one month, the first printing of 5,000 copies, sold out. English and French translations soon followed. A handful of supporters took up the pen to defend Döllinger, but many detractors did the same to criticize. Not surprisingly, Acton wrote a glowing review in *The Rambler*, indicating that Döllinger had ably weighed in on "the most difficult and complicated question of our time." He regretted the "silence of the minority who agree with Döllinger." "The same influences which deprive Döllinger of the open support of these natural allies will impede the success of the work, until events have outstripped ideas, and until men awaken to the discovery that what they refused to anticipate or to prepare for, is already accomplished."[205] William Gladstone wrote Döllinger: "In a calm, clear, and truthful narrative, you have exhibited the gradual departure of the Government of the States of the Church from all those conditions which made it tolerable to the sense and reason of mankind." "I am far from presuming," Gladstone continued, "to identify your views with my own; but I confess...they are substantially akin to one another."[206]

Alarmed by the escalating controversy, Döllinger wrote the Vatican archivist, Augustin Theiner, who then had the confidence of the Pope. This letter is revealing, for it gives indication of Döllinger's conviction that *German* historical scholarship should play a more prominent role in serving the Church. In truth, he wrote Theiner, the book is "a defense of the papacy from beginning to end," adding:

> But [it is] a defense of a particular type, completely different from what a [Roman] theologian...might write; it is much more the work of a German of the nineteenth century, who has a historical conscience [*historiches Gewissen*],

and knows that he must not show any scholarly [*wissenschaftlich*] weakness to the dominance of Protestantism. The internal ailments of the Papal States, the defects in its administration, I have not concealed.... But I have also spoken with full recognition and even with enthusiasm for the noble Pius IX and for the many good things that he has accomplished.[207]

Apparently, Theiner had prepared some sort of a report on the book for the Pope, which for the time seemed to allay any concerns.[208] Döllinger took it as a hopeful sign that the book was not placed on the Index.[209]

But among many in Rome and in ultramontane circles throughout Europe, misgivings about Döllinger began to mount. Some ultramontane German scholars referred to Döllinger as "befouler of the nest" (*Nestbeschmutzer*). Cardinal Antonelli praised the action of the nuncio in Munich, Chigi, and requested that he monitor the controversy. Joseph Edmund Jörg ran critical views of the book in the pages of the *Historisch-politische Blätter für das katholische Deutschland*, which he edited.[210] Döllinger's former secretary, Jörg, in fact confessed in a letter that he now found his views "diametrically opposed" to those of Döllinger.[211] Joseph Hergenröther published an anonymous review in the *Der Katholik*, charging that the book was "miscarried, one-sided, and garbled."[212] Döllinger responded to such charges and others by insisting that he "only wanted to speak as a historian" and as such "write a defense of the Church, nothing more and nothing less."[213]

*   *   *

But the controversy surrounding Döllinger did not subside. In fact, an entirely new chapter opened after a major congress of Catholic scholars took place in Munich in September 1863. A couple of years earlier, Döllinger had felt that a special assembly of Catholic scholars might help bridge the growing differences between the so-called "Roman" (neo-scholastic) and "German" (historical) schools of theology—again, respectively symbolized by the universities of Mainz and Tübingen (with Munich tracking closely with the latter). What is more, alongside the debates generated by the condemnations of Günther and Frohschammer, a raging feud over the publication of a book by the theologian Jakob Clemens (who sought to subordinate philosophy entirely to theology in universities) had brought into sharp relief the two schools.[214] At issue in all of these conflicts was the larger question of what direction Catholic theology should take and how one ought to construe the relationship of scholars (committed to open inquiry) and the episcopacy (committed to guarding the deposit of faith). Such questions were not only being discussed in Germany, but across Europe. In the summer of 1863, a high-profile conference took place in Malines, Belgium, for example, where the celebrated French scholar Charles René de Montalembert had come out strongly in favor of freedom of conscience despite worries and opposition from Rome about this teaching.[215]

1863

In the same year, Döllinger and others felt the time was ripe for a conference in Germany. Working closely with two colleagues in particular, Haneberg of Munich and Johann Baptist Alzog (1808–78) of Freiburg im Breisgau, Döllinger spearheaded the preparations, which were underway in the summer of 1863. Despite persistent wariness from the papal nuncio in Munich (then, Matteo Eustachio Gonella, who had replaced Chigi), the conference planners secured sufficient backing to set their plans in motion, although support from German bishops came relatively late—a fact that later provoked concern in Rome.[216]

In late summer, a letter of invitation went out to leading Catholic scholars (primarily theologians and philosophers) across Germany, Switzerland, and Austria, inviting them to attend the Congress in Munich. The letter indicated that in a time of "transition," such as the present, when the enemies of Catholicism bristled with disdain, it was necessary for them to come together "for scholarly discussion conducted in a spirit of conciliation and Christian love." "The foes of Catholic science [*katholische Wissenschaft*] are numerous and strong," the letter continued, "[and therefore] it is of the highest significance that it not splinter its own strength, or isolate or weaken itself, but rather it should unite all of its forces and strengths and encourage itself by a guarantee of mutual support."[217]

84

Toward these high-minded ends, eighty-four leading Catholics scholars, the majority being priests, came together on the morning of September 28, 1863 at the Benedictine Abbey of St. Boniface in Munich.[218] After the celebration of mass by Archbishop Scherr, the abbot of the monastery, Haneberg, welcomed the assembly, exhorting them "to overcome not only difficulties from outside, but from within [their] own ranks." Cordial greetings were then read aloud, sent from the Archbishop of Freiburg im Breisgau and the bishops of Augsburg, Speyer, Limburg, St. Plöten, and St. Gallen. Thereafter, those gathered stood and recited the Tridentine profession of faith.[219] "Many a man," as Acton later memorably described the scene, "found himself on that day for the first time, in the presence of writers whose works had deeply influenced his mind, or whose fame had long excited curiosity, without knowing their features.... Since the fifteenth century Germany has never beheld so numerous an assembly of her ecclesiastical notables."[220]

After the opening ceremonies, Döllinger was selected president of the assembly by near unanimous acclamation. (Only two participants, both "Roman" theologians from Würzburg, voted against him: Franz Seraph Hettinger and Joseph Hergenröther.) At this point, Döllinger rose to deliver a speech that he had prepared for the occasion—a speech that Acton later called "the dawn of a new era" in Catholic thought, "the most distinct and pregnant exposition its author ever made of the spirit of theology."[221] It bore the straightforward title, "On the Past and Present of Catholic Theology."[222]

What precisely did the Professor have to say on the topic and how was his message received?

Döllinger opened with a broad historical overview of Christian theology, suggesting that it had two points of origin in antiquity: the more speculative school at Alexandria and the more biblical "Anatolian" school that traced its origins to Antioch. After Augustine and the collapse of the Roman Empire, theology in the West went into a "winter sleep," he held, not to be fully revived until Anselm came onto the scene in the twelfth century. But Anselm carried forward largely the Alexandrian strand of theology, which bore fruit in the scholastic theology of the high Middle Ages. With the University of Paris as its principal seat, this theology had many merits (particularly its moral teachings); indeed it represented for Döllinger an "immense building of human thought." Nonetheless, it was essentially "one-eyed," for it lacked the exegetical-historical character of the Antiochian–Anatolian school—represented in antiquity by figures such as Gregory of Nazianzus and Gregory of Nyssa—and it relied too heavily on Aristotelian metaphysical foundations.[223]

Accordingly, a backlash occurred in the fifteenth and sixteenth centuries as humanist scholars, typified by Erasmus, attempted to recover a more exegetical theology to counterbalance scholasticism. However, in the German-speaking lands of the Empire, this backlash—taking the form of the Protestant Reformation—soon found itself regrettably operating outside of the precincts of the Church. The ensuing split of the Church amounted to a great tragedy, in Döllinger's view, but (moderating his earlier views on the Reformation) he credited the Protestant side for its scholarship and for its recognition that theology must be undertaken exegetically and historically, not just speculatively.[224]

In Catholic lands, in reaction to Protestantism, theology reverted to a one-eyed scholastic enterprise, often enforced by the Inquisition. Spain and Italy in particular, in Döllinger's interpretation, became a barren zone for sound theology in the seventeenth and eighteenth centuries—nothing there but "scholasticism devoid of history and criticism" (*geschichts- und kritiklosen Scholastik*).[225] Only in France did one see glimmers of hope. In Bishop Bossuet, the Church again gained a genuine "church father," able to combine the best of scholasticism with patristic studies and a historical consciousness. But this did not last. Intellectual and political currents antagonistic to the old European Christian order waxed ascendant in France in the eighteenth century, leading up to the great maelstrom of 1789. The revolutionary-Napoleonic era felled two of the great pillars of Christendom: the *imperium* (with the demise of the Holy Roman Empire in 1806) and *studium* (with the closing of the Sorbonne and the statist reorganization of French higher education).[226]

The current age, therefore, was one of transition and renewal, according to Döllinger. Catholic theology was searching for an appropriate future. Unfortunately, as Döllinger surveyed the scene, that future was not materializing—particularly in traditional Catholic lands. On the Italian peninsula, in reaction to the anticlerical and liberalizing currents of the *Risorgimento*, Catholic theology had become "obscurantist and sychophantical" to the Roman

Curia. France's rich theological heritage had been despoiled by Napoleon, who severed the relationship between the "queen of the sciences" and the university by having theological education removed to seminaries where it took on a more practical mien.[227]

But in Germany the university model of education had been preserved: "We Germans have to thank God that universities have continued among us and that theology takes place within them." Accordingly, Germans had a special role to play in shaping the future of Catholic theology. "In our time, the light of the theological sciences...has finally come to the German nation." In fruitful dialogue with their Protestant colleagues, Catholic theologians, such as Johann Sebastian Drey and Johann Adam Möhler at Tübingen, were already preparing the soil of a "new, great development of progressive [*fortschreitenden*] theology." Indeed, for Döllinger, Germany was destined to be "the future homeland of Catholic theology."[228]

The path forward for Döllinger was threefold. First, Catholic theology must focus on the task of Christian unity—what in contemporary parlance we would call ecumenism. Since German lands had painfully felt the sixteenth-century split in the Church, they had a special role to play in the Church's reunification (*Wiedervereinigung*).[229] To accomplish this, however, Catholic theology must not fear the insights and truths possessed by "separated communities" (*getrennten Genossenschaften*), but instead treat them as her "own possessions" and seek to integrate them into a higher, "organic" totality. This should not be done in a spirit of arrogance, but with humility, brotherly love, self-denial, and also by accepting what is true and good in others. To be sure, Protestants still erred in many ways, but cannot the true theologian derive honey even from poisonous plants, Döllinger asked with rhetorical savvy?[230]

Second, theologians must recognize that they often have a "prophetic" role to play, especially when forces of inertia thwarted necessary development. Döllinger anticipated that many in the Church would countenance neither his criticism of scholasticism nor his call for a more conciliatory theology. In response, prophetic resistance from theologians was necessary; and the appropriate arena for doing so was in the court of public opinion:

> Just as the prophets in ancient Israel stood next to the ordained priesthood, there is in the church an exceptional force [*außerordentliche Gewalt*] that stands next to the ordinary forces [*ordentlichen Gewalten*], and that is public opinion [*öffentliche Meinung*]. Through it, theological scholarship exercises its proper power, which in the long run cannot be denied.[231]

Third, German theology ought to restore "two eyes" to theology. Since the Council of Trent, Döllinger felt that the Church had relied uncritically on the heritage of Thomas Aquinas and medieval speculative philosophy. It had done so at the expense of developing an exegetical-historical theology, which, again, he traced back to the Anatolian school in antiquity and which Protestant-humanists had developed since the sixteenth century, marrying it in more recent times to the spirit of modern scholarly inquiry (*Wissenschaft*), which Döllinger greatly valued. Scholastic theology was not without abiding value, he made clear, but its exponents were limited by their Aristotelian-philosophical method; without embracing biblical criticism and historical scholarship they possessed only one eye of theology, when in fact two were necessary for the task at hand. For Catholic theology to have a future, "the two eyes of theology, history and philosophy" must both be "cared for with attentiveness, love, and thoroughness."[232]

Döllinger recognized that a critical theology indifferent to the Church posed problems of a different sort. He stressed therefore that for "believing theologians" even "the most severe criticism receives its validity when it [attempts] to correctly understand church teaching." Theologians ought to combine "fidelity to the church ... with the free independence of scholarly inquiry." But for that to happen, time and patience were needed. Intellectual errors should be met by sound scholarship and good philosophy, and not by the abrupt intervention of Church authority, as had been the case in recent memory when, as we have seen, the works of Hermes, Günther, and Frohschammer were placed on the Index.[233] "The faults of science must be met with the arms of science, for the Church cannot exist without a progressive theology. That in theology it is only through error that truth is attained, is a law which will be as valid in the future as it has been universal in the past." If the Church recognized this, then theology would realize its "inner active life-giving force" and achieve "development" (*Entwicklung*). Otherwise, it would become "narrow and deformed" (*eng und krüppelhaft*).[234]

Four days of robust, often acrimonious discussion followed Döllinger's address.[235] The "Roman" parties, particularly the attendees from Mainz and Würzburg, felt that Döllinger had come down unfairly on theology as it was practiced in "the capital of Christendom," Rome. Too smitten with "Protestant science," Döllinger had undervalued the intellectual patrimony of the Catholic Church. Such reservations made their way into a brief statement of protest, drafted and signed by eight "representatives of a strictly churchly position," as Hergenröther put it, and read aloud by Christoph Moufang (1817–97) of Mainz.[236] The signatories were especially keen to note that Döllinger's address ought not be taken as a programmatic agenda of the Congress as a whole.[237] This statement made its way into the hands of the nuncio, Gonella, and from him, was sent to Rome.[238] In short, despite Döllinger's best intentions, the reaction to his talk suggested that the divisions within German Catholic theology were not going to be mended any time soon. With the benefit of hindsight, we know that the Congress likely exacerbated them.

Even so, a fragile spirit of comity prevailed among the participants, who, to a man, believed that their efforts, disagreements notwithstanding, were serving the Church. On the final day (October 1), Döllinger offered some closing reflections, in which he underscored the reality of "two different theological directions in Germany." To overcome the "bitter tone" that often prevailed between the two, he said, the "Christian virtues of humility and charity" were needed now more than ever. Allowing the status quo to persist was at once "un-German" and "un-Catholic," in violation of the Gospels' injunctions and ignoring the peaceable example of the early Church.[239]

On the evening of the last day, a festive dinner was held in the refectory of the Benedictine Abbey. The bishops of nearby Augsburg and Bamberg graced the event with their presence. In the course of the evening, toasts of goodwill to the Pope, the Church, and the King of Bavaria were offered, beginning with one by Döllinger, in which he proclaimed his "love" and "respect" for "the Holy Father of all Catholics."[240] What is more, arrangements had earlier been made to send a telegram to Pius IX, in which those gathered expressed their firm loyalty and duty to serve the Church with the fruit of their scholarship.[241] On October 2, the Pope responded, by telegram, giving his blessing to the Congress, encouraging those who gathered to "carry forward their genuinely Catholic work."[242]

And yet—and yet. Behind the scenes, misgivings about the Congress in general and Döllinger in particular were becoming apparent in Rome. These misgivings, in fact, pre-date the actual Congress, so it is necessary to turn back the clock a bit to see what was going on.

Once plans to hold a congress were made known in the summer of 1863, the nuncio in Munich, Gonella, sent a letter, dated August 21, to Rome, in which he expressed concern that the future gathering might play fast and loose with the proper boundaries of science and faith and that it might not treat the Church's teaching authority with sufficient respect. Gonella did not stop there; he worried that the bishops in Germany too often evinced indifference when it came to matters of scholarship and ecclesiastical authority. "They [the Congress organizers] know very well that the diocesan church authority in Germany does not generally show itself very vigilant in such matters, at least in what regard measures to be taken against pernicious books and their authors."[243] Something ought to be done about the situation, Gonella felt:

> I allow myself to observe, with due submission, how necessary it seems to me that the Holy Father take some opportunity to remind the bishops of Germany to be more vigilant over the tendencies of many professors in these [German] universities, who elevate themselves to the status of judges and custodians of true Catholic doctrine and of the way it is to be propagated, while the bishops, who are the real depositories of doctrine, remain silent and permit the younger clergy to imbibe such principles.[244]

Gonella's letter of August 21 resulted in a flurry of activity in Rome, leading eventually to a reply sent to him on September 9. Taking a personal interest in the matter, the Pope looked to his secretary of state, Antonelli, and Cardinal

Reisach to get a handle on what was going on in Munich.[245] A native German speaker and Vatican loyalist, Reisach had emerged by this time, along with Kleutgen, as the Vatican's resident expert on German affairs; the archives from the Vatican's secretary of state give clear indication that the response to Gonella was dictated largely by Reisach.[246] In his notes, Reisach singled out Döllinger as an especially difficult and delicate case, and the driving force behind the Munich Congress:

> Döllinger obviously must maintain for the public the figure of a real Catholic and even of a promoter and defender of the Holy See. Together with great vanity and professorial hauteur Döllinger possesses a character that is not very decisive but is very fearful. For that reason he will not attempt to press too much further when he comes to realize that Rome knows the tendencies that could manifest themselves at the meeting and that necessarily they would have to be disapproved, even publicly, by the Holy See.[247]

What is more, to his colleagues in the Curia, Reisach felt it important to call attention to the fact that Döllinger had just published *Fables Respecting the Popes of the Middle Ages*, which seemed bent on pointing out "that the authority of the Church has not always shown itself favorable to the progress of science." (This book will be treated in the following chapter.) Finally, Reisach seconded the opinion of Gonella that the bishops of Germany should be more vigilant: "I believe it very useful and even necessary that the Holy See stimulate them to this end with *some papal act*. But perhaps it is necessary to wait for the results of the meeting."[248]

With substantial input from Reisach, Rome's official response to Gonella came on September 9 from the office of the secretary of state, Antonelli. In the letter, Antonelli indicated that the Pope "manifested for a time deep disquiet over the character and development that the discussions in such a meeting could take on and no less for the outcome of the agreements and deliberations that could perhaps be adopted there." The disquiet stemmed particularly from the worry that the Congress would prove injurious to the purity of the faith and demonstrate insufficient respect toward the teaching authority of the Church. "[O]ne certainly did not overlook the fact," Antonelli added, in somewhat garbled language, "that the personal circumstances of one or other of the signers [Döllinger appears to be in mind here], the writing, sometimes obscure and sometimes equivocal, of several articles from the program and above all the lack of initiative and agreement of the Catholic episcopate, to whom alone it belongs by native right [*per nativo diritto*] to direct and supervise theological teaching, do not presage an outcome fully conforming to the true interests and to the real advantage of the Catholic Church."[249] Antonelli furthermore instructed Gonella to convey the sentiments of the Pope to Archbishop Scherr and the other bishops. Toward this end, Gonella wrote Scherr on September 11 and received a reply on September

14, in which Scherr indicated that he had spoken with one of the Congress's convenors, Haneberg, about the worries in Rome. Döllinger, too, was informed by Haneberg of Rome's reaction—something that perhaps helps explain his laudatory toast to the Pope at the conclusion of the Congress.[250] In a letter dated September 18, Gonella replied to Antonelli that the instructions given to him had been carried out.[251]

What is noteworthy about the exchanges between Gonella and Rome is that they give indication that some sort of admonition ("some papal act," as Reisach phrased it) might have been considered even before the Congress began. It is of note, too, that while Rome had worries about the conference's outcome, equal concern was directed at the German bishops for their putative lax oversight of universities. One must also keep in mind that the whole episode in Munich played out as a more sweeping condemnation of modernity, in the form of the "Syllabus of Errors," was being prepared.[252] In the final analysis, then, despite the apparent papal approbation at the conclusion of the Congress, the behind-the-scene exchanges, and worries about the effects of Döllinger's lecture particularly, had led to the right conditions, in the eyes of Rome, to intervene and issue a pastoral letter of concern.

The intervention came several months after the Congress in the form of the apostolic letter, *Tuas libenter* (December 21, 1863), addressed from the Pope to Archbishop Scherr.[253] Three items in the letter merit underscoring. First, Pius made the general point that overconfidence in human reason and the development of science carries the risk of denigrating the teaching authority of the Church as the guardian of revelation. He warned therefore against scholars "miserably deceived" and "trusting too much in the powers of the human mind," who withhold "due obedience to the teaching authority of the Church." Pius expressed gratitude to the "men of this assembly [in Munich]" for their expressed desire to respect the "revealed truths which the Catholic Church teaches." But, again, without proper vigilance, even good men, if too confident in the "progress of science," might find themselves "profess[ing] those things ... opposed to the infallible truth of things which have been revealed by God."[254]

Second, Pius expressed concern that some German scholars—and Döllinger seems in mind here—had become too enamored with modern forms of learning at the expense of the tried-and-true Doctors of the Church, in particular scholastic theologians. "We are not ignorant that in Germany," the letter reads, "there prevails a false opinion against the old school [*falsam invaluisse opinionem adversus veterem scholam*] and against the teaching of those supreme doctors, whom the universal Church venerates because of their admirable wisdom and sanctity of life."[255]

Finally, *Tuas libenter* broached the topic of the Church's infallibility. In doing so, the letter makes a noteworthy distinction. Catholic scholars, the letter assays, should be bound not only by "what the infallible judgment of the

Church sets forth as dogmas of faith to be believed by all," but obedience should also "be extended to those matters transmitted as divinely revealed by the ordinary magisterium [*magisterium ordinarium*] of the Church dispersed throughout the world" and held by "universal and constant consensus." In the development of Catholic teaching authority, this statement breaks new ground, making a distinction between an infallible magisterium and an ordinary magisterium.[256] While some subsequent scholars have argued for a gulf between the two, this was not Pius's intent. Worried that the seeds of liberalism were taking root among German scholars, the Pope and the Curia sought to defend and extend the reach of the Church's teaching authority. Importantly for our purposes, the letter appeals to the "conscience" (*conscientia*) of Catholic scholars: they are duty-bound not only to obey the most deeply sanctioned doctrines of the Church; "it is also necessary [that they] subject themselves to the decisions pertaining to doctrine that are issued by the Pontifical Congregations, and also to those points of doctrine that are held by common and constant consent of Catholics as theological truths and conclusions." Failure to adhere to this "second-tier" order of teachings risked embracing ideas and principles that "although they cannot be called heretical, nevertheless deserve some other theological censure."[257]

Once knowledge of *Tuas libenter* became public, Döllinger sent a copy of it to Lord Acton. Unfortunately, Döllinger's accompanying letter is lost. Acton's response, however, suggests a portentous future: "You see exactly how you are feared [in Rome], and how far they dare go against you.... It is the effect of a revenge long cherished, the existence of which you must have been aware of."[258] To his friend Richard Simpson, Acton called the papal letter a "direct attack on Döllinger."[259]

* * *

Tuas libenter was not the final word on theological matters in Germany. It was followed by a papal edict of July 5 that regulated the nature of theological conferences, mandating stricter supervision from the hierarchy and the vetting of participants to ensure orthodoxy.[260] And then, on December 8, 1864—the Feast Day of the Immaculate Conception—the "Syllabus of Errors" was issued— one of the signature events of the nineteenth century.

The cascading effect of these pronouncements from Rome roiled Catholic intellectual life in Germany, and weighed heavily on Döllinger in particular.[261] At first, Archbishop Scherr of Munich balked at *Tuas libenter*'s charge that the Congress had proven injurious to ecclesiastical authority. At the request of the nuncio Gonella, however, he accepted the more stringent guidelines for regulating theological conferences in the future.[262] Others delighted in the Pope's intervention, rejoicing in the fact that Döllinger appeared to be getting his comeuppance. The theologian Franz Xaver Lierheimer (1826–1900), for example, praised "the excellent letter of the Holy Father concerning the scholarly congress." "A second gathering, which could only [now] be a private matter of Döllinger's . . . is hardly going to take place . . . . [The Pope's voice] is mightier than the goose quill of a German professor."[263] Other papal loyalists made their opinion heard in ultramontane publications. In Rome's *La Civiltà Cattolica*, for example, the journal's chief editor, the Jesuit Carlo Maria Curci, pointed a wagging finger at Döllinger, charging that the Professor's "long-winded speech" had over-valued the place of "history" in Catholic theology and arrogantly asserted "the scholarly primacy of the Germans."[264]

As the Munich Congress closed, plans had been hatched for a sequel in Würzburg the following year. But the papal intervention worked against this. As Döllinger explained the situation to Augsburg's Bishop Dinkel: "The writing of the Pope [*Tuas libenter*] breathes of such a deep mistrust of German theologians, of such a bitter, hostile attitude against the last gathering [in Munich] that it has created a general sensation." Our efforts, he continued, "seem therefore already to have failed. We should wait until this storm of accusations, suspicion and fears subsides somewhat, and a less intense atmosphere takes its place." Furthermore, Döllinger complained of ultramontanes' "unholy desire to centralize" (*unselige Centralismussucht*) theological inquiry and the prevailing "Italian antipathy against all things German." "So long as the Jesuits have their hands on the Index . . . ," he concluded, "our situation in Germany is unhealthy, unnatural, and [another] scholarly conference is a sticky issue [*mißliche Sache*], for every word spoken would simultaneously supply material for denunciations and suspicions."[265]

When the boom of the "Syllabus of Errors" was lowered in December of 1864, the memory of the Munich Congress and *Tuas libenter* remained fresh in memory. In fact, the "Syllabus," which amounted to a compendium of previous condemnations, cited *Tuas libenter* directly in articles 9–14, which focused on errors of "moderate rationalism," and in articles 22 and 33, which focused on "errors concerning the Church and her rights." Articles 11, 12, and 13 appeared aimed directly against Döllinger and the Munich Congress; they condemned the following errors:

> 11. The Church must not only abstain from any interference with philosophy; she must also tolerate the errors of philosophy and leave it to philosophy to correct itself.

> 12. The decrees of the Apostolic See and of the Roman congregations hinder the free progress of science.

> 13. The method and principles according to which the old Scholastic Doctors treated theology are by no means suitable to the necessities of our times and to the progress of the sciences.[266]

As one might imagine, Döllinger was dismayed by the papal intervention. The same person once considered by the Vatican to collaborate on the

"Syllabus" project in the 1850s proclaimed that the "Syllabus," issued by an "obstinate" Pope, amounted to Rome "declaring war on the entire thinking and educated world."[267] Indeed, the middle years of the 1860s mark a crucial turning point in Döllinger's outlook. Until this time, he held out the hope that reconciliation between "German" and "Roman" theologians could be achieved with enough effort and determination. After 1864, however, he grew increasingly skeptical that this could happen, and began to polemicize more stridently against the "ultramontane takeover" of the Church, led especially by the Jesuits in Italy and their supporters over the Alps—and not least by the theologians at Mainz and Würzburg, with whom he had sought conciliation in 1863. "The year 1864 modified his views!," as Lord Acton later tersely put it.[268]

Another flashpoint arose in 1865 when papal loyalists in Germany sought to assert more influence over theological education in Bavaria; they aimed to shift it from Protestant- and state-influenced universities to Roman-influenced seminaries.[269] If this came about, Döllinger lamented, future priests would wind up deformed by a narrow scholastic education, for which Italy was "notorious." Behind the scenes, Döllinger espied an ultramontane plot. "Ultramontanism," he blasted in 1865, "is no longer a fiction, no mere imaginary thing, but rather a real and aggressively advancing power, waging war with all the weapons available to it to achieve discord within the ecclesiastical body."[270] What is more, he felt that the ultramontane party did not harbor moderate goals, but aimed for "the absolute rule of Rome in the Church and in all branches of life connected to the Church. The ecclesiastical goal of the ultramontanes is the Romanization of all individual churches and the most extreme suppression of national particularities in ecclesiastical life."[271]

Döllinger went on the offensive again two years later when, amid a rising chorus of calls for the dogmatic definition of Papal Infallibility, Rome initiated the canonization of the Spanish inquisitor Pedro de Arbués (1441–85), a symbol of strong clerical authority who led the offensive against Jews and heretics in Spain.[272] Döllinger anonymously penned several articles against the canonization that appeared in the *Allgemeine Zeitung* and in Vienna's *Freie Presse*. A deeper motive behind such a questionable canonization, Döllinger reasoned, "is the principal tendency within the interior of the organism [the Church] of establishing Papal Infallibility, [and] to sanction anew the old hierarchical claims [of the Church] over and against the State."[273]

Döllinger's words did not go unanswered. In fact, ultramontanes gave as good as they got, branding Döllinger the ringleader of the "Munich school," which sought to use "science" and especially "history" as tools to undermine the authority of Rome.[274] In Rome, the historian Johannes Janssen (1829–91) observed that while Döllinger might well be considered the "first doctor of

Germany" (*primus doctor Germaniae*) his reputation in the inner circles of the Holy See had plummeted.[275] According to the Swiss prelate Gaspard Mermillod (1824–92), the Pope held Döllinger to be a "church historian of first rank" but he "lacked the good [scholastic] tradition of the Italian schools."[276] The two most implacable opponents of Döllinger in Rome, however, remained Joseph Kleutgen and Cardinal Reisach—particularly the latter, as we have seen. In 1865 Lord Acton recounted a story of Cardinal Girolamo d'Andrea who when suggesting that Döllinger might be "the greatest of the Catholic theologians" received the quick response from Reisach: "a cardinal should not be allowed to utter his [Döllinger's] name."[277] After a conversation in Rome about the Munich Congress, Janssen reported to a correspondent in 1863 that "the mood against Döllinger is growing in these [Curial] circles, and the Cardinal [Reisach] said with resolution after a long discussion 'we must bring an end to this activity'."[278]

In 1864, Döllinger received confirmation that Reisach's opinion of him was winning out in Rome. Abbot Haneberg, with whom Döllinger had collaborated on the Congress of 1863, received a private audience with the Pope on May 23, 1864. At that meeting, Pius made it clear to Haneberg that he was unsettled by some of Döllinger's recent writings, but that he would gladly receive Döllinger at any time for a private audience. Haneberg also conveyed that the Pope had refused his request to bestow on Döllinger "a special apostolic blessing."[279] Acton too had an audience with the Pope and later expressed to Döllinger that the Pope indicated that he could not help it if Döllinger or anyone else had a different opinion from that expressed by the "Syllabus." Döllinger made mention of another possible trip to Rome, but this never came about. Aware of his "tarnished reputation," he stayed put in Munich, never traveling to Rome again.[280]

As Döllinger's reputation was falling in Rome, world-historical events were occurring in Europe. In the summer of 1866, a rising Protestant Prussia under the leadership of Otto von Bismarck routed Austria in the so-called Seven Weeks War, awakening the sleeping giant of pan-German nationalism. The outcome of the war proved unsettling to the Kingdom of Bavaria, which had traditionally looked to Catholic Vienna for support.[281] Around the same time, back in Rome, still reeling from the proclamation of Italian statehood, rumors of a new ecumenical Council began to circulate alongside a furtive ultramontane campaign in favor of a dogmatic pronouncement on Papal Infallibility.

Both the larger historical dramas and his personal scholarly ones had shaken Döllinger greatly. For a period after the "Syllabus" was released, he ceased corresponding entirely, as he told Anna Gramich in 1865. "Ours is a most unedifying time," he confided to her, noting that the conditions within the Church left him with "bleak moods."[282] In 1867 he made his anguish known to a former pupil and future Old Catholic theologian, Franz Heinrich

Reusch (1823–1900): "It seems to me that the entanglements inside the Church are only growing and the *odium theologicum* is becoming only more intense—Arbués and the canonization of the Inquisition, Papal Infallibility beside a Council, the fruit of the Syllabus [of Errors]—and add to this the growing political power of Protestantism. What conditions and events are we up against? In this labyrinth, I have no thread of Ariadne's."[283]

3

Conscience and Authority

The Vatican Council and Excommunication

I had not the slightest clue [when I was younger] ... that I would achieve a world-wide reputation as the opponent of the Pope. This weighs heavily upon me.

—Ignaz von Döllinger, 1871

These theologians [at Vatican II] exercise a true magisterium. This is what Pius IX [at Vatican I] would have wished to avoid, at the risk of highlighting Döllinger I presume!

—Yves Congar, *My Journal of the Council*, 1962

The doors of St. Peter's Basilica opened early on the morning of July 18, 1870. Because of the inclement weather, the crowd that had gathered was scantier than that at the opening of the Vatican Council on December 8, 1869. Around 9:00 a.m. a service got underway with a simple votive Mass of the Holy Spirit. At the conclusion of the mass, Pius IX received the Constitution on Infallibility, *Pastor aeternus*, and read it aloud, concluding with this paragraph:

Immaculata conception 1854 pius IX

> Therefore, faithfully adhering to the tradition received from the beginning of the Christian faith, to the glory of God our savior, for the exaltation of the Catholic religion and for the salvation of the Christian people, with the approval of the Sacred Council, we teach and define as a divinely revealed dogma that when the Roman Pontiff speaks *ex cathedra*, that is, when, in the exercise of his office as shepherd and teacher of all Christians, in virtue of his supreme apostolic authority, he defines a doctrine concerning faith or morals to be held by the whole Church, he possesses, by the divine assistance promised to him in blessed Peter, that Infallibility which the divine Redeemer willed his Church to enjoy in defining doctrine concerning faith or morals. Therefore, such definitions of the Roman Pontiff are of themselves, and not by the consent of the Church, irreformable [*ex sese, non autem ex consensu Ecclesiae irreformabiles esse*]. Now if anyone, God forbid, shall presume to contradict our definition, let him be anathema.[1]

Thereafter, the weather having shifted from the inclement to the ominous, the roll call of bishops and the voting began. The "minority bishops," the sixty or so who had voiced concerns about Papal Infallibility, had already left Rome in quiet protest, so the vote carried by an overwhelming majority: 533 (*placet*) to two (*non placet*).[2]

As lightning and thunder roiled the sky outside St. Peter's, the thick cloud cover darkened the interior of the basilica. At the conclusion of the vote, a candle had to be brought to the Pope so he could see to read: "These things which have been read, We define and We confirm by apostolic authority, with the approbation of the Council." Pius then led those gathered in a *Te Deum*, the grand anthem of the Church, before addressing the assembly with some final words: "The supreme authority of the Roman Pontiff, venerable Brothers, does not destroy but builds up, confirms in dignity, unites in charity and strengthens and protects the rights of the Brethren, the Bishops. Therefore, let those who now are judging [us] in commotion of mind know that the Lord is not in commotion. May God enlighten minds and hearts . . . that all may come to the bosom of their Father, Christ's unworthy Vicar on earth."[3]

By the next day, the storm in Rome had subsided, but the storms of war in Europe had just begun. France declared war on Prussia on July 19, beginning the Franco-Prussian War, which resulted in 1871 in the establishment of the Second German Empire. The outbreak of the war led France to withdraw its troops protecting the last remnant of the Papal States around Rome. The forces of the Piedmontese King Victor Emmanuel, long eager to take the Eternal City, now had the chance to unify all of Italy and make Rome its capital. The king's troops breached the city's walls on September 20, 1870 at the Porta Pia. The take-over of the city effectively extinguished the Papal States as a political entity, leading one liberal newspaper to exclaim: "The light of civil liberty . . . arising in France in 1789 . . . now shines as well in the Eternal City. For Rome it is only today that the Middle Ages is over."[4] For his part, Pius proclaimed himself a "Prisoner of the Vatican," the precincts of which neither he nor his successors left until the Lateran treaties of 1929.[5] The rapidity of events also led the Pope to suspend the Council indefinitely; it was not officially closed until 1960 to make way for the Second Vatican Council.

Thus, the summer of 1870 was a momentous one in European history and in the history of the Catholic Church. The Pope's temporal power abruptly ended. Forces were set in motion that would complete the national unification of both Germany and Italy. And, not least, Papal Infallibility—among the most controversial teachings in church history—was officially defined along with the Pope's universal jurisdiction, his incontestable primacy over all other bishops.

The facts are clear enough. Interpreting the facts is of course another matter. From the perspective of champions of Infallibility, the Council's outcome appeared a clear victory, the triumph of sound theology and divine providence over Rome's many detractors, both inside and outside the Church—even if, in point of fact, the language of the decree was more moderate than what some of the diehard Infallibilists had desired. Beyond Rome and outside of ultramontane circles, matters looked quite differently. As we know, Döllinger dissented before, during, and after the Vatican decrees of 1870. Finding the decrees "notorious," he worried about a deepening rift between Rome and Eastern Orthodox and Protestant Christians.[6] The putatively unhistorical character of the decrees, in his view, would also alienate educated people from the faith. "The rent that the Vatican Council has produced...," he wrote in 1875, "is such as has not been known in the whole history of the church." It *Döllinger* amounted to nothing less than a "great revolution"; Pius IX had presided over the establishment of a new "Vatican Church" that stood in uneasy tension with "the one, holy, catholic, and apostolic Church" as set forth in the ancient creeds.[7] Emotionally spent, Döllinger confided to Acton shortly after the Council that he was at a loss of exactly what to do, although he anticipated excommunication, likely coming sooner rather than later.[8]

In this chapter, the events and ideas that precipitated the First Vatican Council and the course of the Council will be examined in closer detail. This was the first council of the Catholic Church since the Council of Trent (1545–63) and the first one in the modern age. Various questions present themselves. In the late 1860s, how did Döllinger and Vatican loyalists find themselves on theological pathways that with the benefit of hindsight seemed bound to collide? How did Döllinger—working in close alliance with Lord Acton and in the spirit of the "minority" bishops—seek to influence the Council's outcome while it was in session? What are we to make of the turbulent months after the Council and Döllinger's excommunication on April 17, 1871? Finally, how did Döllinger, his supporters, and his critics respond to this momentous event? At age 72, we must bear in mind, Döllinger stood out as among the most recognized Catholic scholars in all of Europe and beyond. His "cruel trial," as Newman phrased it, elicited sympathies, denunciations, and, perhaps above all, fascination.[9]

PETER'S CHAIR IN THE 1860s: BETWEEN THEOLOGY AND HISTORY

The Gospel of Matthew records the following exchange between Jesus and Peter: "'But who do you say that I am?' Simon Peter replied, 'You are the Christ, the Son of the living God.' And Jesus answered him, 'Blessed are you, Simon Bar-Jona! For flesh and blood has not revealed this to you, but

My Father in heaven. And I tell you, you are Peter, and on this rock I will build My church, and the powers of death shall not prevail against it. I will give you the keys of the kingdom of heaven, and whatever you bind on earth shall be bound in heaven, and whatever you loose on earth shall be loosed in heaven'" (Matthew: 16:15–19, RSV). This passage constitutes the heart of the Catholic Petrine doctrine, the teaching that the Roman Pontiff, successor to St. Peter who was martyred in Rome, holds "[the] office as the Vicar of Christ, and as pastor of the entire Church has full, supreme, and universal power over the whole Church, a power which he can always exercise unhindered," as the *Catechism of the Catholic Church* puts it.[10]

To say that the extent of papal authority has produced controversy in the history of Christianity is to state the obvious. We have already seen how Döllinger in 1861 involved himself in debates about the temporal power of the Pope. But it was not just the temporal power that caused commotion at this time; it was the spiritual power as well. What rights and responsibilities did the Bishop of Rome possess in relation to other bishops and to the worldwide faithful? Was the Pope in fact infallible as authorities such as Thomas Aquinas, Caesar Baronius, and Robert Bellarmine appeared to hold? If so, in what sense ought Infallibility to be understood? On the eve of the First Vatican Council, debates over these questions within the Catholic Church became intense and acrimonious. Through his historical inquiries in the 1860s, Döllinger found himself coming to profoundly different conclusions about papal authority than his ultramontane and Curial co-religionists. By the time of the Council, this growing divide had widened into an unbridgeable chasm.

To the modern liberal and Protestant imagination, it is tempting to deride those who subscribed to Infallibility—the Infallibilists. But derision is no substitute for understanding. To understand how the teaching on Infallibility came bursting to the forefront of theological conversations in the late 1860s, one must take into consideration the severe threat that the papacy experienced by forces of Italian unification and the fact that Papal Infallibility was not without significant—if certainly contested—sanction in the Catholic intellectual tradition. What is more, supporters of Infallibility were blessed with determined and articulate champions for their cause, particularly a group of Jesuit scholars connected to the journal *La Civiltà Cattolicà* in Rome; (the future Cardinal) Henry Edward Manning, Archbishop of Westminster after 1865; and Bishop Ignaz von Senestrey of Regensburg. What is more, the Infallibilist position enjoyed broad international support in such journals as the *Dublin Review*, *Der Katholik* in Germany, and in France's *L'Univers*, edited by the pungent pen of Louis Veuillot.

In the turbulent 1860s, when anticlericals such as Giuseppe Garibaldi denounced the Pope as "the vampire of the Vatican," momentum built on the ultramontane-Catholic side to fight back; and the doctrine of Papal

Infallibility became not only the desired instrument of a counter-offensive, but also simply the right and proper theological thing to do. The combination of theological propriety and historical timeliness, undergirded by widespread popular support, one must add, proved compelling enough for this doctrine to become among the central issues at the time of the Vatican Council. Defining the teaching as an official dogma to many seemed "opportune," to use the language of the time.

On March 17, 1861, the new Italian parliament (meeting in Turin) proclaimed Victor Emmanuel II of the House of Savoy the first king of Italy. The entire peninsula was now under Piedmontese control, except for Lombardy-Venetia (still held by Austria until 1866) and a rump of the former Papal States around Rome. Before his death in June 1861, Count Cavour, Italy's first Prime Minister, advocated passionately for a "free church in a free state" if Rome would give up its temporal power, convinced that this would be the best course for both Church and state. From inside the Church, Carlo Passaglia, as we have seen, gave voice to a similar position.[11] But Pius, reading events through his traumatic experience in 1848–9, would have none of it and refused to recognize the new Kingdom. In fact, in 1860 he had summarily excommunicated "all usurpers of the Papal States, all those who carry out their orders, all those who advise them or support them." In 1862 he excommunicated Passaglia and his supporters.[12]

Some actions of the new Kingdom seemed to confirm Pius's worst fears. Legislation was introduced to secularize marriage, for example. Measures were also introduced to decrease church influence in education and increase the role of the state to help achieve a "national" consciousness. What is more, because of the massive debts encumbered in the process of unification, politicians in Jacobin style turned to ecclesiastical properties as a source of income. In 1866–7, 2,000 religious congregations were deprived of legal status and 25,000 ecclesiastical bodies suppressed. (In the course of the next fifteen years, over a million hectares of church lands were sold off, often to already wealthy landowners, to replenish the state's coffers.)[13] Traumatic memories of Napoleon's prior despoliation painfully returned, and all efforts to achieve a *modus vivendi* between "Italy" and "Rome" faltered.[14]

And then there was the loose cannon Garibaldi, whose animosity toward the Pope and the Catholic Church seemingly knew no bounds. In 1862 under the banner "Rome or Death" (*Roma o morte*) he mustered an army of volunteers and set out from southern Italy to stir agitation and threaten the Papal States. At Aspromonte in Calabria, the mismanaged endeavor fell apart at the hand of Italian regulars, and Garibaldi was wounded in the process. Undeterred, he assembled another brigade of "Garibaldini" and tried again in 1867. This time, a French division was hurriedly dispatched from their garrison by the sea to aid the Papal Zouaves, and the Garibaldini were defeated at Monterotondo and Mentana.[15] While Garibaldi himself managed to escape, the papal government captured two other ringleaders, Giuseppe Monti and Geatano Tognetti, who were later tried and executed by the guillotine in Rome.[16]

Further details could be marshaled, but the general point should be clear. The founding of the Italian state, the apparent defection of priests like Passaglia, the suppression of religious orders and confiscation of church properties, and the threat of anticlericals such as Garibaldi came together in the late 1860s to make it seem as if in fact the very "gates of hell" sought to prevail over the Holy See. A papal encyclical from October 27, 1867 "On the Afflictions of the Church" makes clear Rome's embattled posture: "Here [in Italy] triumphant impiety rears her ugly head. We grieve to see all kinds of injustice, evil and destruction.... Like ravening wolves panting after prey, they [the Church's foes] spill blood and destroy souls with their grievous scandal. They seek the unjust gain of their own malice and seize the property of others." Again, this was not happening in some faraway place, but on the Church's historic lands and in the vicinity of the Eternal City itself: "At present We are surrounded by evil men of this sort, men entirely animated by a diabolical spirit. They plan to raise the standard of lies in this beloved city of Ours, before the very Chair of Peter, the center of Catholic truth and unity."[17]

In this fevered atmosphere, long-incubating ideas about Papal Infallibility rose in prominence. But two points are in order here. First, the spiritual authority signified by Infallibility, many felt, was necessarily connected to the maintenance of the Church as a temporal power; the Pope required a state, so the argument went, in order that he could freely—without the permission of another secular sovereign—exercise the spiritual power, including Infallibility. Second, because of the Pope's plight, ultramontanes in Italy and across Europe came to sympathize with Pius all the more; a veritable cult of veneration for the persecuted Pope developed—as it had for Pius VII earlier in the century.[18] What Alexis de Tocqueville wrote about ultramontanism in 1856 applies even more in the 1860s: "The pope is driven more by the faithful to become absolute ruler of the Church than they are impelled by him to submit to his rule. Rome's attitude is more an effect than a cause."[19] In the New Testament, followers of Christ were promised that they would likely suffer persecution from a hostile "world."[20] The Pope's embattled situation seemed to confirm the veracity of this promise even as it also justified Pius's intransigence. Paradoxically, then, precisely because of the Pope's predicament did confidence in his charisma and authority grow. As Klaus Schatz has written: "We cannot regard ultramontanism as purely an anxious reaction and a defensive posture. It had an essentially dynamic, missionary and conquering character, a unique liberating function, drawing people out of every provincial self-satisfaction and state–Church narrowness."[21]

This embattled, assertive stance evinced itself in spades in the pages of the *La Civiltà Cattolica*, the ultramontane organ on the Italian peninsula par excellence and frequently the *bête noire* of Döllinger. An article from 1867 by the Jesuit Luigi Tosi entitled "A Threefold Tribute to Saint Peter" richly illustrates the point. "We have reached a point today," Tosi began,

> when the war of the godless against the Catholic Church is completely concentrated in attacking the papacy, assaulting both its spiritual and secular prerogatives. We may even rejoice in this rather than lamenting it, because in this way, it is revealed that this [the papacy] is the unconquerable rock.... But because the supreme interest of every Catholic lies herein it is also our highest duty to bind ourselves as much as possible to this central point, and this contest involving all in the unity of faith, hope, and reverence for protection of the see of Peter must be the salvation of and the boast of all Catholic Christianity.

Tosi continued by indicating that beyond the tribute of wealth (Peter's pence) and blood (volunteering to defend Rome from its enemies), the faithful owed another "tribute of the intellect" (*tributo dell'intelletto*). This tribute was nothing less than recognizing "Papal Infallibility," and defending this teaching if necessary even to the point of martyrdom.[22] To drive home the point, *La Civiltà Cattolica* also published in 1867 a short vow that the faithful supportive of Infallibility could recite.

Two key bishops, Bishop Ignaz von Senestrey of Regensburg and Archbishop Henry Edward Manning of Westminster, took the pledge. In Rome on June 28, 1867, under the direction of Matteo Liberatore, editor of *La Civiltà Cattolica*, they made the pledge at the tomb of St. Peter on the eve of the 1,800th anniversary of the martyrdom of Saints Peter and Paul.[23] Celebrating this event had brought them, along with hundreds of other prelates, to Rome in the first place. The great lesson of this holy festival, Manning summed up afterwards, was "a reaffirmation of faith in the supremacy of the prerogatives of the prince of the apostles," the recognition of "the perpetual office and action of Peter as the source of unity and Infallibility." What is more, already in 1865, when asked by the Vatican for agenda items for an upcoming Council, Manning had replied that in order to "extirpate the errors of this time" that "it is to be expected that the dogma of the Infallibility of the Church will be equally [as with the previous Immaculate Conception] defined."[24] For his part, Senestrey was hands-down the most resolute Infallibilist among the German bishops. Not only was he a loquacious defender of the doctrine, he was also an able organizer of the "majority" at the time of the Council; his residence in Rome, in fact, emerged as the unofficial headquarters of the Infallibilists.[25]

Neither Manning nor Senestrey had much regard for Döllinger. Manning had long voiced criticism of Lord Acton's liberal *Home and Foreign Review*, where Döllinger was sometimes published in translation. In a review of

Döllinger's *pseudonymously* written *The Pope and the Council* of 1869 (more about this work shortly), Manning wrote that the book illustrated history at its worst, "an elaborate attempt ... [to] destroy, by profuse misrepresentations of history, the authority of the Pope and to create animosity against the future Council."[26] Bishop Senestrey, disquieted by the Munich Congress of 1863, had forbidden his theology students from attending lectures given by Döllinger—an action praised by Pius IX.[27]

Beyond the support offered by *La Civiltà Cattolica* and by high-ranking clergy such as Manning and Senestrey, Papal Infallibility, it merits reiterating, could hardly have succeeded if it did not enjoy broad international support from the lay faithful. Recall Britain's *Dublin Review*, edited by William George Ward, an Anglican converted to Catholicism. Critical of Döllinger since 1861, this journal enjoyed enormous support among English-speaking Catholics. Its attitude toward Infallibility is captured in Ward's famous quip that he desired nothing more than to have an infallible encyclical delivered every morning with his breakfast and *The Times*![28] France's *L'Univers*, edited by the redoubtable Louis Veuillot, was a veritable hammer against centrist and liberal Catholicism and a loud advocate of Infallibility understood in maximal terms. Veuillot was known for never pulling punches and throwing quite a few below the belt; he regularly attacked neo-Gallican bishops such as Bishop Félix Dupanloup of Orleans and Archbishop Georges Darboy of Paris, both leading Anti-Infallibilists at the Council. Veuillot reserved some of his most stinging blows, however, for the liberal critic Montalembert, a kindred spirit to Lamennais and friend of Döllinger. In the pages of *L'Univers* and in his many books, Veuillot argued that a definition of Infallibility did not need a long conciliar discussion; instead it ought to pass by simple acclamation, "made effective by the Holy Spirit." "The Infallibility of the Pope," he wrote, "is the Infallibility of Jesus Christ himself" and "when the Pope thinks it is God who is thinking in him."[29] On the eve of the Vatican Council, Pius IX made it unambiguously clear that he and Veuillot were of the same mind. Veuillot moved his residence to Rome during the Council, cheering on the Infallibilists, rebuking their opponents. "The Vatican Council marked the peak of Veuillot's influence," as Waldemar Gurian has summed up.[30]

Finally, it is important to underscore the fact that Infallibility was not cooked up by ultramontane polemicists or the Pope in a time of political crisis; it possessed much deeper sanction in the Catholic intellectual tradition—although Döllinger and others certainly contested this sanction. The crisis of the Papal States in the 1860s and the idea's considerable intellectual pedigree combined to help make the Council appear a fortuitous moment for its definition. At the time of the Council, supporters particularly invoked the authority of Robert Bellarmine, the great Jesuit Cardinal and scholar of the sixteenth and seventeenth century. Writing against Protestants and Gallicans, Bellarmine insisted that the Pope must be accepted by Catholics as the infallible teacher of the faith.

related ancient church of Gaul.
peak in 17th → freedom of Roman catholic church in France

"The Roman Pontiff," asserted Bellarmine, "when he teaches the whole Church on a matter of faith, cannot in any case make a mistake."[31] Appeals were also made to the authority of Thomas Aquinas, whose thought was enjoying a renaissance in the 1860s, as we have seen. In his *Quaestiones quodlibetales*, seeking to parry the objection that some canonized saints might in fact be in hell, the Angelic Doctor argued, "on the contrary," that "the Holy Spirit directs His Church" in these matters and "he does not err." In the here-below, moreover, it is "the Pope, to whom belongs the prerogative to determine the nature of faith." By deduction, therefore, "Divine providence preserves the Church in such matters so that she might not be deceived by the witness of fallible men."[32] Finally, one could find earlier rudiments of teachings on Infallibility in the writings of Church Fathers such as Irenaeus, Ambrose, Leo the Great, and Gregory the Great, all of whom were cited in *Pastor aeternus* (1870). And this is to say nothing of the Petrine passages in the New Testament and the extensive commentary traditions on them.[33] *advocating supreme papal authority in matter of faith and discipline*

*   *   *

As ultramontane thinkers and the Curia, agitated by the times, were increasingly coming to the *theological* conclusion for the necessity of Papal Infallibility, Döllinger found himself coming to the *historical* conclusion against it—and against many other aspects of the modern papacy. Indeed, at the heart of the controversy over Döllinger is a conflict between theological and historical ways of knowing and, particularly, about the status of historical inquiry as an arbiter of religious verities. We have already seen an aspect of this conflict rear its head in Döllinger's lectures of 1861 and 1863 and in the responses to them. The precedence of history manifested itself even more so in his thinking from the mid- to late 1860s—the time, according to Acton, when Döllinger most clearly turned from his ultramontane past to become the leading *historical critic* of the direction of the papacy at this pivotal and tumultuous moment in the Church's history.[34]

At the time of the Munich Congress in 1863, Döllinger was at work on a number of historical works, some having to do with the papacy. He had told Acton of a desire to write a multi-volume history of the papacy. We do not possess Döllinger's letter to Acton, but we do have Acton's enthusiastic response, which gives some idea of the scope of the project: "A whole history of the papacy! But one in several volumes and as popular in style as learned in research. That would be a great undertaking. Almost every, not purely dogmatic, controversial question could be treated [in such a work]—Infallibility, the development of Gallicanism, canon law, national identity...the influence of the Church on science, politics, and art.... I believe you really can offer an extraordinary treasure of theological and historical insight."[35]

Döllinger's interest in the papacy stemmed from at least two sources. First, as we have seen, after the unification of Italy in 1860, practically all of Europe was agitated about the "Roman Question" and curious about the future of the papacy in the modern age. But another reason derived from Döllinger's growing interest in questions of Church unity. It was not lost on him that the office of the papacy represented among the most vexing obstacles to reunion for both Orthodox and Protestant Christians. He began to feel that it was in his scholarly reach to demonstrate that some papal powers and prerogatives were historically unwarranted, thereby instructing the Church about its own past, cleansing it of abuses and errors, while also lowering the bar for possible reunion with non-Catholics. "He felt that sincere history," as Acton later put it, "was the royal road to religious reunion and [he] specifically cultivated those [Protestants and Catholics] who saw both sides.... [C]onciliation was always in his thoughts."[36]

A trial-run of a potentially larger study first appeared in 1863 in the aforementioned *Fables of the Popes in the Middle Ages*. A French translation appeared in 1865, an Italian one in 1866, followed later by one in English.[37] At the same time as ultramontanes were rallying behind a beleaguered Pope and making a case for Papal Infallibility, arguably Germany's leading Catholic historian published a work that sought to puncture many papal claims by *demonstrating historically* that they rested on falsified documents and erroneous understandings of the past.[38]

In the book's introduction, Döllinger indicates that what follows was the first fruit of "a larger work, intended to embrace the history of the Papacy."[39] He felt it expedient to publish some materials because various "fables and inventions" concerning the Pope's office had "a marked influence on the whole aspect of the Middle Ages,... on its theology and jurisprudence." Although he withheld the blunt charge that much of this theology and jurisprudence had persisted to the present, the astute reader might easily connect the dots.[40]

In the book, Döllinger takes up many topics that would be familiar to students of Late Antiquity and the Middle Ages: the legend of the female Pope Joan, the baptism of Emperor Constantine by Pope Sylvester I, Pope Marcellinus and the legendary synod of Sineussa, the Donation of Constantine, the fall from grace of Pope Liberius Anastasius II, and the case of Pope Honorius. The erudition required for such a study was formidable. With respect to method, Döllinger follows a similar pattern with each case. He provides, first, an overview of what had been said about a topic for centuries; he then attempts to disclose through philological and historical analysis how accepted knowledge often harbored errors or at least begged questions; and, finally, he attempts to offer a more compelling historical contextualization, often revealing, as the title suggests, that many beliefs about the papacy were in fact based on fables—and, what is more, that these fables, subsequently embedded in tradition, had distorted the Church's knowledge of its own past and hence its ability to theologize properly.

Döllinger's treatment of Marcellinus and the legendary synod of Sineussa, the Donation of Constantine, and the case of Pope Honorius will serve to illustrate Döllinger's general purpose.

The story of Marcellinus and the synod of Sineussa held direct implications for the scope of papal authority. Döllinger begins by outlining the accepted story. At the time of the Diocletian persecutions, Roman authorities persuaded then Pope Marcellinus to offer incense to the pagan gods. Once news of this spread, the scandal of a pope committing apostasy drew some three hundred bishops from across the Empire to Rome to remonstrate with the Pope. They met first in a cavern near Sineussa, but later in Rome itself. Yet since the bishops, with putative faithfulness to tradition, subscribed to the view that the Pope can only be judged by himself, not by another or by a council, they realized that they had no means to depose him. Fortunately, as the story goes, Marcellinus felt the sting of his own guilt and deposed himself, vindicating the faith and demonstrating the exclusive power of the Pope in a single act.[41]

Since earlier historical records lacked any mention of a "Council of Sineussa," Döllinger felt that the story could be explained in the so-called "Symmachian Forgeries," a number of forged documents from the pontificate of Symmachus (r. 498–514) that exalted papal authority and which had been absorbed into canon law.[42] During this time, two aristocratic families struggled for the papal mantle: those supportive of Symmachus and those supportive of the "Anti-Pope" Laurentius. The latter's supporters had accused Symmachus of several crimes and had called on the Ostrogothic King Theodoric to force the Pope to attend a synod where he could be tried. Symmachus's supporters, conversely, appealed to the "Symmachian Forgeries"—containing the *Synod of Sinuessa* and the *Constitutum Silvestri*—and, on their authority, made the case that precedent had established that no earthly tribunal had the right to try a pope. "The acts of this pretended synod," Döllinger concludes, "are clearly fabricated [*erdichtet*] to provide historical support for the principle that *a pope can be judged by no man* . . . . By this means, the laity are taught not to venture to come forward as accusers of the clergy, and the lower clergy that they must not do the like against their superiors"—and not least against the Pope.[43] Döllinger resists making heavy-handed connections to the present, but he does note laconically "in later times the fable was used for . . . different purposes."[44]

Döllinger also commented on the well-known Donation of Constantine, famously exposed as a forgery by the humanist scholar Lorenzo Valla in the fifteenth century.[45] Among other things, this forgery stated that Constantine had transferred authority and extensive lands to the papacy before taking up residence in Constantinople, the New Rome. "Where and when was this document forged?" asks Döllinger. "Without a doubt," he answers, "[it] was composed in the West, in Italy, in Rome, and by a Roman clergyman. The date at which it was composed may be placed with overwhelming probability in those years…from about 752 to the year 777, during which time Pope Hadrian first mentions the gift of Constantine."[46] Particular historical conditions in Italy then helped explain the forgery according to Döllinger. In the era prior to the rise of the Frankish kings, central Italy stood at the mercy of the Lombards and the lingering power of the Byzantine Greeks in the north around Ravenna. The forgery helped the Pope form a confederation to defend against adversaries and demonstrate that the papacy as a landed power "was the normal condition of things, planned long ago by the first Christian emperor."[47]

Döllinger rued the fact that the "donation," while long exposed, lived on in Roman theology and canon law. In the ninth century, it had been incorporated in the Pseudo-Isidorian Decretals, and thereby helped legitimize papal claims.[48] While most scholars, including ultramontanes, admitted the falsehood of the Donation by the nineteenth century (though interpretations of its origins varied), they were not ready to dispense with its long-standing juridical and theological implications. That was Döllinger's view too until the 1860s. But that was changing. As Bradford Whitner has nicely summed up: "Whereas in 1861 Döllinger had been prepared to accept as valid the papacy's claim to temporal rule over the Papal States [even if he advised relinquishing it]…, after his work on [the Donation]…he became convinced that the entire claim was based on deliberate falsehood in the name of the Church. In short, the papal claim to temporal rule over the Papal States [what Pius IX was willing to die for in the 1860s] was based on persistent, ongoing error in the Church."[49] The only remedy to such error was an appeal to sound historical scholarship, no matter how bitter the pill; and Döllinger saw himself as administering the painful, healing medicine.

Finally, Döllinger examined the controversy over Pope Honorius I (r. 625–38) and his so-called "monotheletism," the belief that Christ possessed only "one will" (namely, the divine will) and "one divine power of action," and not a twofold will (namely, divine and human) as orthodoxy had affirmed. In his letters to Patriarch Sergius of Constantinople from 634, Pope Honorius appeared to embrace the "one will" teaching as a possible avenue of reunion with the so-called "Miaphysite" Christians, those churches who had rejected the Council of Chalcedon. For holding this view, Honorius was later declared a heretic and pronounced anathema by the Third Council of Constantinople (680–1), a recognized ecumenical Council. In Döllinger's treatment, the episode presented an unavoidable lose–lose scenario for advocates of Papal Infallibility. Either Honorius was a heretic and rightly condemned as such by a recognized Council, and thus could not be infallible, or else the bishops gathered at Constantinople had disproved Infallibility by omission; that is, they knew of no such doctrine evidenced by their lack of scruples in condemning a pope. After examining the case in some detail, Döllinger criticizes papal loyalists in later centuries for either suppressing the story or constructing evasive loopholes to avoid the vexing questions that it presented. But for Döllinger one question rang out: "Has the Church, represented by a full ecumenical Council, declared the dogmatic writings of a pope heretical and thus acknowledged the fallibility of popes?"[50] The condemnation of Honorius, he declared, was "irreconcilable" with the "system" of Baronius, Bellarmine, and other advocates of Papal Infallibility.[51] The controversy over Honorius surfaced again at the Vatican Council.[52]

Belief in the therapeutic power of historical knowledge to purify the Church from errors and misconceptions grew in Döllinger's mind as his *Fables of the Popes* gained recognition (and notoriety) in the 1860s. Acton, who stood in close contact with Döllinger at this time, provides a fuller picture of what was going on in the Professor's mind. After the publication of the *Fables of the Popes*, Döllinger with Acton spent the summer months of 1864 in the libraries of Venice and Vienna, among other places. Because of Italy's revolution, numerous libraries and archives on the peninsula had been opened to scholars for the first time. At Vienna, Döllinger was shown sheets of works containing 247 Carolingian acts unknown to J. F. Böhmer (1795–1863), the recently deceased leading expert on Carolingian imperial charters.[53] From Rome, his friend Augustin Theiner conveyed to him information about documents held in the Vatican's *Archivio Segreto*; others had sent him manuscripts from Trent and Bergamo. Because of Döllinger's scholarly reputation, Acton once noted, "[even] strangers ministered to his requirements, and huge quantities of transcripts came to him from many countries."[54]

The joint effect of his own historical inquiries and the fresh outpouring of archival and library materials made available to him in the 1860s had, according to Acton, a transformative effect on Döllinger's mind.[55] He recognized at a deeper level the sheer volume of unknown materials and their potential to shape historical understanding, not least of the Catholic Church's understanding of its own past. As Acton later described his mentor's state of mind prior to the Council:

> As many things remote from current knowledge grew to be certainties, he became more confident, more independent, more isolated. The [ultramontane] ecclesiastical history of his youth went to pieces, against the revolution of the unknown ... that began on a very large scale in 1864.... Whenever some local occasion called upon him to speak, he spoke of the independence and authority of history. In cases of collision with the Church, he said that a man should seek error in himself; but he spoke of the doctrine of the Universal Church, and it did not appear that he thought of any living voice or present instructor. He claimed no immunity from philosophy, but history, he affirmed, left to itself and pursued disinterestedly, will heal the ills it causes; *and it was said of him that he set the university in the place of the hierarchy.*[56]

Acton's last line should be underscored, because Döllinger's historical work increasingly elicited harsh treatment from ultramontane critics. One theological journal received no less than twenty-one hostile reviews of his *Fables of the Popes.*[57] He was accused of being arrogant and one-sided, inflating the sordid in the history of the Church at the expense of even-handedness. A reviewer of the book in the *Dublin Review* esteemed the work's "enormous and astonishing learning," but accused the author of pitting "historical dogmatism" against the Holy See.[58]

Such criticisms stung, but did not deter Döllinger from further inquiries. But, again, these were no commonplace inquiries. At a time of assertive ultramontanism, quickened in 1867 by the announcement of a coming general Council, Döllinger intensified his interest in the embarrassing and controversial aspects of papal history, collecting manuscripts, making notes, writing to archivists and librarians. This was the path toward his undoing in the eyes of Rome, as Acton later reflected: "Döllinger began to be absorbed in the long train of hierarchical fictions, which had deceived men like Gregory VII, St. Thomas Aquinas, and Cardinal Bellarmine.... These studies became the chief occupation of his life; they led to his excommunication in 1871, and carried him away from his earlier [ultramontane] system.... The history of Church government was the influence which so powerfully altered his position."[59] But it was not only the Church's government that interested him; he planned to bundle with this project some of his ecumenical interests (particularly a history of efforts to mend the Great Schism of 1054) and also the history of censorship within the Church.[60]

In 1868 two developments strengthened Döllinger's resolve. In September he met in Munich with Henri-Louis Charles Maret, a kindred spirit and dean of the Sorbonne's theological faculty. Maret was hard at work on the second volume of his *Du concile général et de la paix religieuse*, a neo-Gallican plea for conciliarism in the spirit of Bossuet and a critique of papal absolutism. Döllinger instructed his secretary, Anna Gramich, to undertake a German translation.[61] Furthermore, on November 19, 1868, Döllinger was made a life-long Privy Councilor of the Bavarian Crown. Prior to this honor, he had harbored worries that a critical work on the papacy might imperil his position on the theological faculty at the University of Munich. But this high recognition from King Ludwig II, who scorned ultramontanism, and the sphere of authority and influence it opened to him, along with the stimulus of Maret's work, encouraged Döllinger in his plans.[62]

On the eve of the Council, Döllinger referred to his scholarly project simply as the "Cathedra Romana" or "Cathedra Petri," describing it as an "impartial history of the papacy" from its beginnings to the present. He desired that the unsparing light of scholarship shine on the good as well as the bad, so that "no one will be able to reproach me for only showing the dark side of things, or only the evil that took place." Nonetheless, he was prepared to bring out the dark side of the Church in a way that no Catholic scholar had attempted before. He recognized that resistance would come from papal loyalists, but he strove to see it through—come what may. As he wrote Acton in 1868: "The most questionable and enraging things, and the things that will shake the favorite opinions of the Ultramontanes, will be the discussions of the almost unbroken continuous fictions and falsifications.... They have already received a few teaspoons of this bitter medicine in my *Fables of the Popes*, and with it a mere foretaste; now they will receive that medicine with tablespoons, which will likely give them belly aches."[63] For a period, he even considered publishing the work anonymously because of the opposition that he anticipated; but given his venerable age, he hoped that others might concede that the work was undertaken only "in the service of scholarship and the interest of truth" (*im Dienste der Wissenschaft und im Interesse der Wahrheit*).[64] In their exchanges about the project in 1868, Acton and Döllinger both agreed that such a work was timely and necessary, particularly because it would help set the Church on a more ecumenical, less "Romanized" path. At one point, Acton even exclaimed that the project held the potential to bring about a "deep, total revolution" in an understanding of the Church.[65]

But history intervened in 1869 to complicate Döllinger's plans. In February of that year, an article appeared in the *La Civiltà Cattolica*, calling attention to the impending Vatican Council, which had been in the works for several years even if its specific agenda remained unclear. Claiming to express the voice of the faithful in France, the author made a distinction between "liberal Catholics" (*cattolici liberali*) and "actual Catholics" (*cattolici semplicemente*). Liberals were presumed to want the Council to step away from the earlier "Syllabus of Errors." Genuine Catholics, by welcomed contrast, saw the Council as an opportunity to double down on the message of the "Syllabus" and on the temporal power of the Pope. Furthermore, the Council could and should proclaim both Papal Infallibility and the Assumption of the Virgin Mary as dogmatic teachings.[66] In our present-day, colloquial parlance, such actions were presented as "no-brainers," at least for the authentically faithful. In pointed language, the Council was called on to define as true what the faithful held to be genuinely true, while exposing liberals within the Church as unwitting minions of the godless *Zeitgeist*.[67]

Critics of Rome were dismayed by the article, for they knew that anything published in *La Civiltà Cattolica* likely enjoyed support at the highest levels of the Church. Döllinger too was deeply distressed, increasingly worried that the Council might do irreparable harm to the faith and undermine the authority of those theologians and clergy less inclined toward Rome—to say nothing of further alienating Protestant and Orthodox Christians. He set scholarship aside, therefore, and began to focus single-mindedly on what he might do in a more practical register to prevent the triumph of "the ultramontane party" at the Council.

THE EVE OF THE COUNCIL

Since the Council of Trent, a universal council of the Catholic Church had not met. This was the longest period in the history of the Church without a council since the beginning of the conciliar era at Nicaea (323). Pius IX desired a Council. He first entertained the idea during his forced exile at Gaeta in 1849, but it lay dormant until the 1860s when rumors of a general council began to circulate.[68] Pius spoke openly about it at the celebration of the 1,800th anniversary of the martyrdoms of Saints Peter and Paul in 1867. In the bull *Aeterni Patris* of June 29, 1868, he officially called for it, scheduling its start in December 1869.[69]

Initial reactions varied. The Roman Curia harbored fears of hundreds of bishops descending upon Rome. Liberal and moderate bishops initially hoped that such a gathering might moderate the spirit of the "Syllabus of Errors" and make overtures of conciliation toward Christians not in communion with Rome. Bishops such as Dupanloup of Orléans and Darboy of Paris were strongly inclined in this direction; they held out the additional hope that a Council might revive older currents of Gallican conciliarism to counter ultramontanism. The majority of German bishops were skeptics of Infallibility, including Archbishop Scherr of Munich. But others regarded the Council as an opportunity to vindicate the "Syllabus" and proclaim the primacy and Infallibility of the Pope. Practically all of the Southern European bishops held this view, as did the aforementioned bishops Manning of Westminster and Senestrey of Regensburg, key players among the Infallibilists.

Invitations were sent to Eastern Orthodox bishops (September 8, 1868) and to Protestant bodies (September 13, 1868) encouraging them to return to Rome on the occasion of the Council and to the Catholic unity from which their predecessors had strayed. These pleas elicited wholly negative reactions. Furthermore, breaking sharply with historical precedent, heads of European states were not officially invited, although it was made known that they could send representatives to Rome if they liked.[70] Many did so, in an effort to keep tabs on what the Council was up to, and via proxies to engage with their bishops when the Council was not in session.

At first there was no mention of Papal Infallibility as an item for the Council. In 1867, the Pope spoke quite generally about the need for a council "in these hard times ... [to] promote the greater honor of God, the purity of the faith, the dignity of divine service, the salvation of souls, the discipline of the secular clergy, and the common peace and concord of the whole world."[71] Nonetheless, some began to suspect the topic might surface. Even before the hubbub created by the *La Civiltà Cattolica* article, Lord Acton harbored this suspicion as early as 1867, worrying about it in particular because of the worldwide influence and sympathy that Pius IX commanded.[72]

A hint of the Council's eventual direction could be glimpsed in the make-up of its six preparatory commissions.[73] Curial officials made certain that they were staffed exclusively by those from their own ranks and by ultramontane priests and theologians. The handful of Germans initially invited to participate came exclusively from the so-called "Roman," neo-scholastic camp; these included Hergenröther and Franz Hettinger of Würzburg and Willibald Apollinarius Maier (1823–74), the secretary and theological aide of Bishop Senestrey. Cardinal Friedrich Fürst von Schwarzenberg, the moderate Archbishop of Prague, complained in 1868 to Antonelli and Cardinal Prospero Caterini about the omission of those with a less ultramontane outlook. Belatedly, the "German" theologians Hefele of Tübingen (made Bishop of Rottenburg in December 1869), Johann Baptist Alzog of Freiburg, and Daniel Bonifaz von Haneberg, Döllinger's colleague at Munich, were added as consulters on the commissions. But this was mainly window dressing, as even the papal nuncio in Munich admitted, to avoid the charge of one-sidedness.[74] In 1869, Bishop Hefele, then in Rome, complained that "the longer I stay here, the more clearly I see the duplicity behind my appointment as a consulter to the council. That was just Rome's way of hoodwinking the public with an appearance of neutrality."[75] Döllinger, too, felt that this arrangement only gave the "appearance of impartiality," as he wrote to Henri-Louis Maret.[76]

Döllinger did not receive an invitation. He did not go to Rome as a consulter nor was he in Rome during the actual Council. This provoked some consternation. Hefele spoke for many in the summer of 1869 when he wrote to Schwarzenberg of Prague, asking if it was "appropriate and wise for the first theologian of Germany [Döllinger] to be made into a nemesis of Rome?"[77] Schwarzenberg had in fact asked if Döllinger could participate. But he had received evasive responses from both cardinals Catarini and Antonelli. The latter indicated that Döllinger would have been invited, but the Pope felt certain that he would not have accepted and that he would not have worked well with the other theologians.[78] Others, rightly, suspected the opposition of Cardinal Reisach as a principal, if not the only, reason that Döllinger's participation was not sought.[79] As Döllinger sized up the situation in a letter to France's Bishop Dupanloup from November 29, 1868: "I am seen in Rome as a man who is insufficiently ultramontane [*un homme trop peu ultramontain*], and, you know, this is unpardonable."[80] Later, when Montalembert implored him to go ahead and travel to Rome, Döllinger responded by asking what a single priest without an assignment was to do in Rome; it would appear comical.[81] Döllinger experienced the Council from Munich.

The aforementioned article in the *La Civiltà Cattolica* created an atmosphere of crisis after it was published in February 1869. For ultramontanes, the article had simply made explicit the appropriate course of the Council: to buttress the "Syllabus" by proclaiming Papal Infallibility. But for their opponents within the Church (not to mention for non-Catholic onlookers), the article led to disquiet, even panic. And the concerns were not strictly theological. Since the "Syllabus" strongly affirmed the temporal power of the Pope, the coming Council, many felt, would have alarming political consequences across Europe: would not Catholic citizens now have a duty to conscience to obey an infallible Pope even if his utterances contravened states' laws?[82] The anti-papalist bishops in Germany and France were particularly agitated; many communiqués to one another and to Rome were exchanged. For Döllinger, the experience of reading the article was like having a veil lifted from his eyes. "Clearly, the Jesuits have now revealed the plans they have for the Council," he wrote Charlotte von Leyden, soon to be Lady Blennerhassett on March 1, 1869.[83] He resolved to act.

Action took the form of a foray into polemical journalism. Drawing material from his "Cathedra Petri" project, Döllinger anonymously penned a series of articles in Augsburg's *Allgemeine Zeitung* from March 10 to 16, 1869. Hastily written and bristling with alarmist invective, the series, "The Council and the *Civiltà*," expressed Döllinger's agitated state of mind.[84] As such, the articles only contributed to a widening gulf between "liberals" and "ultramontanes" within the Church. Already a critic of the Jesuits, Döllinger now felt that members of this "party" were attempting to take advantage of the worldwide sympathy toward the beleaguered Pope to obtain a conciliar victory for their own theological predilections. His ongoing historical studies of papal history, as we have seen, had convinced him that these predilections rested on erroneous history and deliberate falsehoods. In his mind, the Holy See with the entire Catholic Church in tow teetered on the brink of a theological abyss. He did not mince his words:

> If the Council allows itself to be used to bind the wreath of Infallibility around the Pope's brow... [t]he Jesuits and their pupils will sing Hosanna, draw some inferences from the dogma and deploy it for their purposes; and the world will look on indifferently. But a deep antipathy against the [papacy and] the Italian priesthood will gradually grow.... In 449 a synod was held which got the name of the synod of robbers; the Council of 1869 will go down as the synod of flatterers [*Schmeichelsynode*].[85]

If Infallibility were true, his erudition and expertise in history, he claimed, had been achieved for naught: "Before I could ever inscribe this modern invention [Infallibility] on my mind, I would first have to plunge my 50 years of theological, historical, and patristic studies into the [river] Lethe and then draw them out like a blank sheet of paper."[86]

Döllinger's articles elicited both widespread praise and scorn. But he was just warming up. In the summer of 1869, he described his frustration to Acton: "The front seems to be hardening... *Consilium sine spiritu consilii* [A Council without the spirit of a Council]" appeared to be in the offing.[87] "We must do all that we can to stave off this threatening calamity [*dieses drohende Unheil*]," as he wrote to the Englishman Henry Nutcombe Oxenham.[88] To do his part, in addition to some short writings, Döllinger expanded and edited his "March articles" and published them as a book. *The Pope and the Council* by "Janus" (his chosen pseudonym) appeared in August 1869, causing now a European-wide sensation just a few months before the Council was scheduled to open in December.[89] In it, Döllinger made clear his view that the looming Council presented a possible "catastrophe" for the Church and that the doctrine of Papal Infallibility, in his scholarly estimation, could not stand up under the "light of history." "We have written under a sense of worry," as he put it,

> in the presence of a serious danger threatening primarily the internal conditions of the Catholic Church... but [it] threatens to assume much larger dimensions.... The danger does not date from yesterday and did not begin with the proclamation of the Council.... [For many years] the reactionary movement [*rückläufige Bewegung*] in the Catholic Church, which is now swollen to a powerful torrent, has made itself felt, and now is preparing like an advancing tidal surge to take possession of the whole organic life of the Church by means of this Council.[90]

Repeatedly, "Janus" assured readers that his harsh words, likening them to those of the Hebrew prophets or of Dante, emanated from his love of the Church, not from malice.[91] True piety does not conceal errors and falsehoods, he held, but seeks to expose them, especially when they threatened to disfigure the Body of Christ: "[P]iety owes its first duties to the divine institution of the Church and to the truth, and it is precisely this piety that urges us to oppose candidly and decisively every disfigurement or disturbance of the one or the other."[92]

And there were more specific worries. If the Council turned Papal Infallibility into a binding teaching, Döllinger believed that Catholic intellectual life and the search for Christian unity would be compromised if not upended altogether.

> [I]f raising the doctrine of Infallibility into an article of faith, on the one hand, must cripple all intellectual effort and scholarly activity in the Catholic Church, it would, on the other, build a new wall of separation, and the strongest and most impenetrable of all, between this [Roman Church] and the religious communities separated from her. We would have to renounce that most cherished hope that no

Christian can banish from his breast, the hope of a future reunion of the divided Churches both of the East and the West.[93]

While "Janus" clearly had the contemporary ultramontane movement in sight, the book itself is largely an act of historical inquiry. Drawing material from his *Fables of the Popes* and "Cathedra Romana," Döllinger traced the disfigurements of the papacy back to the early Middle Ages. He did not dispute the unique, chiefly pastoral role of the Roman See; it had come to function necessarily and appropriately as a *primus inter pares* and as a center point of Christian unity in the patristic era. But on both historical and theological grounds, he felt that such primacy obliged Rome to function in harmony with the collective authority of other bishops, particularly when they met together in a universal Council. The worrisome irony of the coming Council, as he expressed it to Acton and to others, was its potential to be a Council that buried forever the possibility of genuine conciliarism.[94]

The crisis afflicting the Church was not of recent making, but had deep roots in the past. It began in the medieval era, Döllinger held, when, through various turns of history, an originally salubrious papal primacy transmogrified into the "Papal System" or "Papalism" (or what he sometimes called "Vaticanism"), which was reaching dangerous proportions under ultramontane influence in his own day. Döllinger attributed particular culpability to the ninth century when Pope Nicholas I first accepted the Pseudo-Isidorian Decretals as genuine. The acceptance of these forgeries paved the way for subsequent "reforms" that unwarrantedly magnified the power of the papacy and put it on a path of slavishly imitating worldly monarchical power. The Gregorian reforms undertaken by Gregory VII, codified in the so-called *Dictatus Papae*, represented the next step down the trail of error. These documents included such papal prerogatives, Döllinger was keen to point out, as "he shall be judged by no one" and "all princes shall kiss his feet."[95]

From the Gregorian Reforms, Döllinger traced the influence of the Pseudo-Isidorian Decretals through the writings of Deusdedit, Anselm of Lucca, and Burchard of Worms to the *Decretum Gratiani*, a "most potent instrument of the new Papal system," which codified papal supremacy into law.[96] Since this work became embedded in all subsequent canon law in the West, the "papalist disease" had acquired a taken-for-granted status. Through scholastic canonists, moreover, it came to permeate the entire theological outlook of the high Middle Ages, and was later transmitted and even expanded, due to the challenge of the Protestant Reformation, by theologians such as Baronius and Bellarmine, both key authorities for ultramontane voices in the nineteenth century.[97]

In a signature intellectual maneuver, Döllinger asks the reader to envision the development of the papacy from the standpoint of the early Church, when, he felt, much healthier conditions prevailed:

If the primacy is on the one hand a source of strength to the Catholic Church, yet on the other hand it cannot be denied that, when one looks at it from the standpoint of the ancient Church—from the Apostolic age until roughly 845— the Papacy, such as it has become, presents the appearance of a disfiguring, sickly, and suffocating excrescence [*entstellender, krankhafter und athembeklemmender Auswuchs*] on the organism of the Church, hindering and subverting the action of its better vital powers, and bringing manifold diseases in its train.[98]

The only way to heal this ailment, in Döllinger's judgment, was to deliver the stinging rebukes of historical truth-telling. The crisis of the Council, he surmised, might even represent an opportunity for the Church, for what the moment called for was "a great and thorough-going reformation of the Church." Such a renewal was "necessary and unavoidable, however long it may be evaded."[99]

The press of the German edition had hardly cooled when translations of *The Pope and the Council* were underway; it appeared in Italian, French, and English before the Council began.[100] To say the work created a sensation is an understatement. Acton, who knew of Döllinger's authorship, expressed delight; he felt the book would buttress the anti-Infallibilist position at the upcoming Council.[101] Great Britain's Prime Minister Gladstone read the book, and, suspecting Döllinger's handiwork, wrote to his friend in Munich, proclaiming the book to be "one of the weightiest and most noteworthy documents that has met my eye for many a day."[102] Protestants, liberals, and anticlericals throughout Europe relished the internecine Catholic polemics.[103]

Within the Church, opposition to "Janus" came fast and furiously. Bishop Ullathorne of Birmingham described *The Pope and the Council* as "the gravest and severest attack on the Holy See and the Jesuits, and especially on the policy of Rome for a thousand years, and will [unfortunately] be a great storehouse for the adversaries of the Church."[104] Döllinger's colleague at Würzburg, Josef Hergenröther (a participant at the Munich Congress of 1863) set to work almost immediately on a lengthy rebuttal, the title of which aptly sums up the point: *Anti-Janus: An Historical-Theological Criticism of the Work Entitled "The Pope and the Council."*[105] Eager to enter the fray, *The Dublin Review*, *L'Univers*, *Der Katholik*, and the *La Civiltà Cattolica*, along with a host of other minor publications, published scathingly critical editorials and reviews.[106] The book by "Janus," as Manning later put it, was simply an attempt "to destroy by profuse misrepresentations of history...the authority of the Pope, and to create animosity against the future Council."[107] Many suspected that the book, if not by Döllinger, had been inspired by him; the smoking gun likely lay somewhere near Munich.[108] Later, during the Council, voices of opposition were sometimes dubbed simply the "Janus Party."

The February *Civiltà* article and the counter-offensive by "Janus" agitated the German-speaking world in particular. Many German bishops received hostile letters from laymen and some clergy, asking them what they planned to do about ultramontane intransigence. In the letters, the authority of "Janus" was regularly invoked. An older anti-Roman "Febronian" sensibility awakened. What is more, the matter was not just theological; it was political. If I may back up to the spring of 1869, the Prime Minister of Bavaria, Prince von Hohenlohe, issued a circular letter on April 9, drafted with the encouragement and assistance of Döllinger, to the powers of Europe, arguing that the impending Council threatened to set the Church against the governments of Europe and that this would have terrible consequences for both. Papal Infallibility understood as binding dogma, according to the letter, would commit the Church to the extreme anti-statism of the "Syllabus." Similar worries emanated from other German capitals, whether Catholic or Protestant. The Prussian government, in a communiqué that portended the coming *Kulturkampf*, made clear that the Council could drive a dangerous wedge between the Prussian government and Prussia's sizable Catholic minority.[109] Döllinger hoped that this circular would embolden political opposition to the Council, not just in German-speaking lands but across Europe.[110] But despite the worries voiced by various state chancelleries, no concerted action resulted.[111]

The persistence of concerns unsettled the German episcopate. Shortly after the appearance of *The Pope and the Council*, members of the German hierarchy decided to meet at Fulda to discuss the crisis and the coming Council. In a joint statement issued on September 6, 1869, they made clear their loyalty to Rome; they also recognized the Council as a genuinely ecumenical one and one where different voices would have the freedom to speak—thereby attempting to rebut several points that "Janus" had raised. But due in part to the widespread support of "Janus," not least among the ranks of educated German Catholics, the bishops also expressed concern about the consequences of defining Papal Infallibility for the Church in Germany—quite possibly tearing it asunder.[112] In fact, fourteen bishops at Fulda sent a clandestine (but later leaked) letter to the Pope, making clear that they thought the time "inopportune" to define Infallibility.[113] These fourteen—joined later by the likes of Bishop Dupanloup of France and Bishop Joseph Georg Strossmayer of Croatia—came to form the core of the "minority" position at the Council.[114] In addition to others, the German minority bishops included the prince-bishop of Breslau, Heinrich Förster; the Bishop of Trier, Matthias Eberhard; Bishop Pankratius von Dinkel of Augsburg; Bishop Ketteler of Mainz; Bishop-elect Hefele of Rottenburg, and, not least, the Archbishop of Munich, Gregor von Scherr, who later excommunicated Döllinger.[115]

The meeting of the bishops at Fulda heartened Döllinger. As they met, Döllinger paid a lengthy visit to his friend, Acton, at his residence, Herrnsheim, near Worms in the Rhineland. Among other things, they discussed the recently published book by the dean of the Sorbonne, Henri Louis Maret, *Du Concile général et de la paix religieuse* (1969). As Döllinger wrote to Charlotte von Leyden from Herrnsheim, the book will serve as "a rallying point for the French bishops of Dupanloup's [Anti-Infallibilist] persuasion."[116] As things turned out, Dupanloup himself, a stalwart French Anti-Infallibilist, decided to visit Acton and Döllinger at Herrnsheim in September. This represented quite a gathering: three of the leading minds in opposition to the Council, talking long into the evening, commiserating with one another about what Döllinger called "this urgent danger."[117]

Apparently, the meeting strengthened Döllinger's resolve, for soon he decided once again to take up the pen in opposition to Infallibility, this time using his own name. The opposition came in the form of a brief manifesto, *Considerations for the Bishops of the Council Respecting the Question of Infallibility* (October, 1869). Reprising some points already made by "Janus" and in his *Fables of the Popes*, these "Considerations" presented in the form of twenty-six pithy theses reasons why, in Döllinger's judgment, Papal Infallibility could not pass historical and theological muster. Drawing from Vincent of Lérins, whom he frequently invoked, Döllinger placed particular emphasis on the fact that the Church had always stressed the "unchangeableness" of its teachings; the marks of doctrinal authenticity were "universality, antiquity, and general consent" (*quod ubique, quod semper, quod ab omnibus*).[118] By contrast, Infallibility represented a novum, "altogether unknown in the Church for many centuries." He also reiterated the concern that Papal Infallibility would only further estrange Rome from Eastern Orthodox and Protestant Christians. Finally, Döllinger made a characteristic appeal to the authority of scholarship: "It may be asserted that all theologians who combine comprehensive historical knowledge [*umfassende Geschichtskenntniß*] with biblical and patristic erudition have rejected the new doctrine of papal Infallibility."[119] As bishops worldwide headed to Rome in November 1869, these "Considerations" were published in Augsburg's *Allgemeine Zeitung* and quickly translated into several languages. Those who had not read "Janus" could now receive its bitter medicine in condensed form.[120] Opponents of Infallibility "find ourselves [now] in an unprecedented, tense, and critical situation," Döllinger confided to Charlotte von Leyden (Blennerhassett) at this time.[121]

This publication intensified concerns in Rome about German theology in general and about Döllinger in particular. In November, the papal nuncio in Munich, Meglia, wrote a flurry of letters to Cardinal Antonelli in Rome, keeping him abreast of German affairs in light of the impending Council. While Meglia praised Munich's Archbishop Scherr as "a fine priest, an example of devotion," he worried about the "pestiferous teaching" (*pestifero insegnamento*) at the University of Munich, where a "hostile spirit" toward Rome prevailed. What is more, Döllinger did not appear to him simply an "inopportunist" like the German bishops; rather, his recently published "Considerations," in Meglia's view, indicated that Döllinger "directly opposes [*oppunga direttamente*] the entire teaching of Papal Infallibility."[122] Meglia's worries made their way to Pius IX. "I know," the Pope reportedly exclaimed, "that they do not think much of me in Germany. Dr. Döllinger is the Pope of the Germans."[123]

Meanwhile in Rome, the fate of "Janus" hurtled headlong toward condemnation. Only three days after the book's German publication in August 1869, nuncio Meglia had sent a copy of the book to Rome, where it was received with alarm.[124] Around the time that Döllinger published his "Considerations," Manning wrote the Secretary of the Congregation of the Inquisition, Constantino Patrizi Naro, that the author of *The Pope and the Council* was likely Döllinger and that it contained "scandalous, erroneous, and heretical" propositions.[125] Shortly thereafter it became an item on the agenda of the Congregation of the Index. In November, the book was examined by the consulters for the Index; the principal examiner, P. Hendrik Smeulders, surmised, too, that, at the very least, it must have been inspired by Döllinger.[126] On November 26, 1869, *The Pope and the Council*, "in any language" (*quocumque idiomate*), was officially placed on the Index. On the steps of St. Peter's Basilica, Pius IX approved the measure on November 30.[127]

Eight days later the Council opened.

THE COUNCIL AND "QUIRINUS"

On the rainy morning of December 8, 1869, the anniversary of Pius's declaration on the Immaculate Conception (1854) and the issuing of the "Syllabus" (1864), church bells throughout Rome alerted residents and visitors to the opening of the Council (Figure 3.1). At nine, as church bells in the city chimed and salvos of artillery fired from the Castel Sant'Angelo, the Pope in his chair of state (*sedia gestatoria*) and some 700 prelates processed toward St. Peter's Basilica. Upon entering they took their place in the northern transept. Following an opening mass, the Pope gave his benediction and received a lengthy homage from those gathered. As tradition prescribed, cardinals kissed the Pope's hand, bishops his knee, and religious superiors his foot. Afterwards, the Pope invoked divine assistance and the hymn *"Veni Sancte Spiritus"* was sung. Clergy and laity present wept. Thereafter, those gathered approved by acclamation a decree officially opening the first session of the Council. Another decree announced that the second session would convene on January 6, 1870. A *Te Deum* concluded the service, and the august assembly processed out. In all, the service lasted for seven hours.[128] "The kings of this world look grave, the statesmen sneer, the rabble gnash their teeth," editorialized the British Catholic *Tablet*, "but the Council assembles in spite of them all, because

Figure 3.1. Opening of the First Vatican Council, December 8, 1869.

Source: Engraving by Karl Benzinger, in George White, *His Holiness Pope Pius IX*, 3rd ed. (London: R. Washborne, 1878). Image courtesy of Wikimedia Commons.

God will have it so."[129] "Such an assemblage of prelates," Bishop Ullathorne of Birmingham gushed, "was never witnessed in the world before."[130]

The months ahead were filled with discussion and argument, diplomacy and intrigue, grand pageantry and whispered rumors.[131] Out of the some 1,000 bishops of the Catholic Church worldwide, over 700 made it to Rome. Most previous Church councils drew their members largely from the geographical expanse of the Old Roman Empire, later extended to the new Holy Roman Empire. By contrast, this Council drew sixty-seven bishops from North America; twenty-one from Latin America; fifteen from China, fifteen from India, and eighteen from Australia and the Pacific. Fifty bishops came from within the Ottoman Empire. While most of the overseas bishops were European in origin, this was the first council in the history of the Church where missionary bishops played a significant role. The majority of bishops—roughly one half—came from Italy or France: Italy because of its small diocesan structure and France because the French were preponderant among the missionary bishops. Roughly 10 percent of the bishops came from Germany or Austria-Hungary.[132]

From the beginning and despite its absence from the Council's official agenda, the topic of Infallibility lurked as a major issue, and the bishops were divided over it. The "majority," as they came to be designated, favored Infallibility, less because of Curial pressure to do so, as some scholars have asserted, than because of the tremendous sympathy and devotion that Pius commanded due to the ongoing crisis over the Papal States.[133] This "bloc" presented a more unified outlook, even if all supporters were not diehard Infallibilists in the mold of Manning and Senestrey. Their opposition, the "minority," arrived at the Council as a house divided. A few were committed Anti-Infallibilists, but most considered themselves "inopportunists," willing to concede that Infallibility had sufficient theological sanction to be countenanced, but that the present—with Europe in turmoil over the "Roman Question"—was not the appropriate time to define it. Leaders of the minority included the titular bishop Cardinal Hohenlohe (brother of the Bavarian Prime Minister), Bishop Hefele of Germany; Bishops Dupanloup and Darboy of France, and, not least, Bishop Strossmayer of Croatia, among the ablest orators within the minority.[134] Döllinger and Acton quickly recognized that the minority's stance of inopportunism posed problems, for it appeared to cede the high ground of theological principle to the Infallibilists. "The only invincible opponent," Acton wrote to Prime Minister Gladstone (who obsessively followed the Council), "is the man who is prepared, in extremity, to defy excommunication, that is, who is as sure of the fallibility of the Pope as of revealed truth."[135] Acton doubted that any bishop would take defiance this far, but speculated that Hefele and Strossmayer might prove to be exceptions.[136] Among the bishops, only about 150 made up the minority—an unpardonably high number in the mind of Pius IX.

Most of the German bishops leaned in the direction of the minority. The sentiments that had been expressed in September at Fulda remained valid for them as the Council began. But the German bishops' corps also illustrated the divisions within the minority. On the one hand, there was Hefele, a historian of Church councils, who had only recently been elected Bishop of Rottenburg. Among the German bishops, he stood closest to Döllinger and Lord Acton's position of outright opposition. On the other hand, Bishop Ketteler of Mainz expressed personal belief in Infallibility, but wondered if the evidence was sufficient to proclaim it as a binding dogma on all Catholics. Archbishop Scherr of Munich stood close to Ketteler's position. Both men made clear before the Council that they, and all dutiful Catholics, ought to accept the outcome of the Council irrespective of one's personal beliefs.[137]

On the evening of November 22, 1869, Scherr dined with Archbishop Deinlein of Bamberg and Bishop Dinkel of Augsburg at the bishop's palace in Munich. At ten, with their entourages, they boarded the train at the Munich station, bound for Rome. Passing through various Austrian and Italian cities, they reached the Eternal City on November 27. Before he had departed Munich, Scherr had written a pastoral letter to his diocese, warning his flock not to heed all the fearmongering in the press, for "nothing lies farther from the Church than the repeatedly-heard reproach that it desires domination."[138] Although Scherr did not emerge as a major voice at the Council, because he was Döllinger's bishop, he often stood, as his biographer put it, "in the spotlight of public interest."[139]

From the sidelines, Döllinger and Acton, professor and former pupil, played a distinctive and fascinating role during the Council. As has been mentioned, Döllinger was not invited to the Council and resigned himself to observe things from afar in Munich. But he had excellent informants, not only in Acton, but also in his colleague Johann Friedrich, Döllinger's future biographer, who gave Cardinal Hohenlohe theological advice during the Council.[140] With the admiring support of Gladstone, who had recently conferred a peerage on Acton, the young "lord" once in Rome functioned, in the words of Roland Hill, as a "Chief Whip" at the Council, seeking to bring the divided Anti-Infallibilists together in common cause. Acton was singularly prepared to play this role.[141] Because of his aristocratic lineage and international background, he had personal or family connections within many of the key national bodies represented among the bishops and among the diplomatic corps in Rome. Because of his fluency in English, German, French, and Italian, he ably bridged linguistic divides among the prelates and brought them into closer communication. Finally, owing to his formidable theological and historical erudition, owed in no small part to Döllinger, he possessed a far-ranging grasp of the topics under discussion at the Council.

In November 1869, Acton relocated his family to Rome, so he could follow the Council at close range. His spacious apartment, off the busy Corso Umberto, came to function as a kind of headquarters of the minority, where friends, bishops, and diplomats came to dine and talk, often until late into the evening, after which Acton somehow managed to sustain an enormous correspondence and keep a diary of events! It was an intoxicating experience for the 33-year-old baron.[142] Loyalists to the Pope, however, looked with great suspicion on Döllinger's former pupil; some called him "*un diable dans un bénitier*" (a devil in a holy-water stoop).[143] And Pius IX himself once called him a "rascal" (*briccone*), "who licks my feet and at the same time works with the opposition."[144]

Making full use of his many connections, and despite the vow of confidentiality made by all bishops, Acton somehow managed to obtain up-to-date news on the happenings of the Council, which he readily conveyed to Döllinger in Munich. Because of the secretive atmosphere of Rome at this time, Acton placed his letters with great care in the mail bag of the Bavarian diplomat or else he sent them to the Prussian representative in Florence, where they were then forwarded to Munich. To cover their tracks, Acton and Döllinger even devised code names for some personages at the Council. Dupanloup became "Padre Giovanni"; Manning became "Miranda," from the Catholic convert in a poem by Robert Browning who wanted to serve two masters—ease and religion; Cardinal Antonelli became "Melander"; and for himself, Acton selected "Monsignor."[145]

Working together—and, again, with the active support of their confidant, Johann Friedrich—Acton and Döllinger managed to publish sixty-nine letters from the beginning of the Council in December 1869 until July 1870, all written from the perspective of a committed and doubtlessly erudite Anti-Infallibilist. Appearing under the pseudonym "Quirinus" in the *Allgemeine Zeitung* (the same outfit that published "Janus"), these letters became the talk of the town and exerted enormous international influence not only during the Council but also on its subsequent historiography. At the conclusion of the Council, the letters were collected and published as *Letters from Rome on the Council by Quirinus*.[146]

Although not in Rome, through "Quirinus" Döllinger made his presence felt at the Council. In fact, the very conspicuousness of his absence, paradoxically, gave his voice a kind of hovering presence. The minority bishops, Acton noted in his diary, repeatedly expressed to him the wish that Döllinger would have heeded Montalembert's advice and headed to Rome. Bishop Strossmayer of Croatia, according to Acton, "regretted his absence deeply. We bishops, he said, have to govern our dioceses, and don't understand theology. We are of great want of his learning and ability."[147] What is more, Döllinger's works were often referred to by the minority bishops, who frequently asked Acton if he had received any correspondence from his former teacher. It was not uncommon for the majority bishops to pay backhanded respect to Döllinger by speaking of their opponents as captive to the "Döllinger school" or under the spell of the "Munich party."[148] One of the most flattering estimations of Döllinger came from no less a figure than Bishop Senestrey, a leading Infallibilist. Shortly after the Council opened, he expressed blinkered optimism that the impasse among the bishops could be overcome and, according to Acton, "[he] expects that a formula [for Infallibility] will be found which will satisfy Döllinger and the Pope."[149]

This did not happen. Döllinger and Acton knew that the minority bishops were divided and that the defense of "inopportunism" stood on shaky ground. "Our party," Acton wrote Döllinger, "is made up of material that has only slight resistance. It must be worked on every day, built up, the good supported and warned of cunning.... He who was yesterday convinced, wavers today."[150] To embolden the minority, Acton and Döllinger felt that the European court of "public opinion" ought to weigh in. But first it had to be awakened: the "Pius cultus" that had claimed so many Catholics and the quiet resignation that characterized European capitals had to be overcome by a heady mix of historical knowledge and truculent journalism. The perceived difficulty of their task can be measured by the bitterness of tone adopted by "Quirinus". Oscillating between narration of the Council and biting critique, "Quirinus" left no room for doubt about which side was right and which wrong. What is more, in the view of "Quirinus", the Council itself was not a free one, since the preparatory commissions had been staffed wholly by Curial papalists or their sympathizers.

Bishops could only react to what had been prepared for them, "Quirinus" charged, and not truly speak their mind. And behind the cabal of Curial loyalists stood "the Jesuit party," whose role at the Council "Quirinus" colorfully described:

> [T]he influence of this party is very powerful, and already preponderates; the whole mechanism of the Council, the order of business, the *personnel* of its officers, in short everything, is substantially in their hands, or will be placed in their hands, or will be placed at their disposal. All preparations were made in their interest, and all alternatives were foreseen. That great ecclesiastical polypus [*kirchliche Polyp*], with its thousand feelers and arms, the Jesuit Order, works for it under the earth and on the earth; *mea res agitur* [my business is done] is its watchword.[151]

For "Quirinus", the doctrine of Papal Infallibility was nothing but "moonshine" based on "forgeries and fictions," and would prove a "millstone" around the neck of the Church. Those actively promoting it were "lackeys" to the papal court, bent on a task that the ancient Church would find unimaginable: employing a Church Council to vitiate conciliar authority.[152] Citing an unnamed critic of the majority, "Quirinus" notes that "if the Pope ordered them to believe and teach four instead of three persons [are] in the Trinity, they would obey."[153]

Reflecting views characteristic of his other writings, Döllinger through "Quirinus" frequently appealed to the witness of earlier tradition and to the therapeutic power of historical knowledge to cleanse the Church from error. The "millstone of the new dogma" represented a clear breach with the views and traditions of the ancient Church, he held.[154] Elevating Infallibility into an official teaching would in fact mean the "triumph of dogma over history"—a saying of Manning's that Döllinger found scandalous. Any future Catholic who was also a "student of history...will only be able to console himself by saying, *Credo quia absurdum*," I believe because it is absurd.[155]

Through "Quirinus", Döllinger sometimes expressed an unsavory, pugilistic nationalism. "It may truly be said," he wrote "that theology is now rare, very rare, in Rome. There is, of course, no lack of theologians; the Pope himself has no less than a hundred, chiefly monks; but if they were all pounded together in a mortar into one theologian, even this one would find some difficulty in getting his claims recognized in Germany." Because so many "Roman" theologians adhered single-mindedly to the scholastic heritage and approved of Infallibility, "Quirinus" likened them to "the daughters of Phorcys, who had only one eye and one tooth, which they lended to one another by turns to use."[156] Subtlety was not "Quirinus"'s strong suit.

Already a leading newspaper in Germany, the *Allgemeine Zeitung* added thousands of subscribers largely because of the sensation of "Quirinus".[157] Once published, the letters from "Quirinus" were quickly translated into other

European languages. They were read widely in Rome during the Council, despite the best efforts of majority bishops and ultramontane journalists (such as Veuillot) to disparage them. Part of their appeal derived from the mystery of their authorship. If not Döllinger as some suspected, it was obviously someone with great erudition and intimate knowledge of the Council (despite the secrecy rules). The regular Roman correspondent of the *Allgemeine Zeitung*, an elderly, half-blind German scholar who had resided in Rome for decades, was suspected and almost expelled from Rome, only prevented by the intervention on his behalf of Carl von Tauffkirchen-Guttenberg (1826–95), the minister of the Bavarian legation in Rome.[158]

Perhaps Acton summed up the influence of "Quirinus" best, if somewhat hyperbolically, when he wrote Döllinger from Rome that "the *A[llgemeine] Z[eitung]* is a power in Rome, greater than many bishops, and much feared—greater even than many states."[159] In the preface to the post-conciliar, edited letters, Döllinger defended the work as "the best authority for the history of the Council" and an ally for those "whose ecclesiastical conscience [*kirchliches Gewissen*] protests against the imposition of dogmas effected by all kinds of crooked arts and means of force."[160] After the Council, both boosters and opponents of "Quirinus" recognized the weighty impact of the letters. The Infallibilist Hergenröther admitted that by and large they presented a reliable account of the Council, while Strossmayer could effuse that they offered the "most honest and best history of the Council."[161] Such sentiments have certainly been disputed, but whatever the case, the letters certainly exerted strong influence on post-conciliar interpretations of the Council.

In addition to "Quirinus," Döllinger entered into public controversy during the Council twice under his own name. Both instances were occasioned by developments at the Council that gave him cause for concern. The first was prompted by a petition, issued in late January 1870 and signed by 372 of the majority bishops, calling for the proclamation of an expansive definition of Papal Infallibility.[162] Furtively organized by Matteo Liberatore, Manning's theological consultant at the Council, this petition came as a surprise and caught the minority off guard, even as they soon mounted their own counter-plea. As the commotion unfolded in Rome, Döllinger could not keep silent, but decided to pen a rebuttal, which appeared in the *Allgemeine Zeitung* on January 19, 1870. If the aim of the majority's petition was realized, Döllinger opined, it would amount to nothing short of a "revolution" in the Church; "[it] would be an event unique in the history of the Church. Nothing of this kind has happened in the last eighteen centuries."[163] Döllinger took particular issue with the majority's gloss on the fifteenth-century Council of Florence, the last council to seek reunion between East and West.[164] In the majority bishops' view, the decrees of this Council demonstrated that the Greek representatives in Florence had recognized a form of papal primacy in addition to conciliar authority. But for Döllinger, the decrees were the result of later interpolations (and these resting on earlier forgeries), because the evidence suggested, in his view, that the Greeks were only prepared to consent to an understanding of Infallibility when the Roman See acted in conjunction with and, in fact, simply expressed the will of the entire Church as made known in conciliar decisions. Because the final Latin conciliar texts seemed to gainsay the Greeks' intentions, Döllinger was even willing to dispense with the Council of Florence as a recognized ecumenical council. It was one, instead, where Latin pressures and chicanery in his view ran roughshod over the more moderate hopes of Eastern Christians. Döllinger concluded his article by reiterating that Papal Infallibility was a "new article of faith," one "unknown to the Church" in earlier ages, and, hence, the aspirations of the majority bishops were misguided.[165]

Döllinger's article fell like a bombshell into the deliberations of the Council. "The article was an event," as J. B. Bury has written; "it created an uproar in the precincts of the Council. Döllinger, who bore the reputation in all lands of being the first theologian of the day—Döllinger *locutus est!*"[166] In central Europe, in what might be viewed as the early rumblings of the Old Catholic movement, statements supporting Döllinger came forth from Breslau, Braunsberg, Bonn, Prague, and Münster, signed by a total of eighty-two professors; subsequent statements of solidarity with Döllinger followed. A key mobilizer of this sentiment was professor Joseph Hubert Reinkens of Breslau, who later became the first German Old Catholic bishop.[167] Munich, too, was caught up in the agitation: who was in the right: the majority of the Council Fathers or their esteemed professor at the university?[168]

Disputing the ecumenicity of the Council of Florence was a big deal; and for it Döllinger drew fire not only from majority bishops, but from minority ones, Bishop Ketteler of Mainz foremost.[169] The former stood against him root-and-branch; the latter, while sympathetic to his Anti-Infallibilism, winced at the prospect of calling into question a widely-accepted ecumenical council. What is more, Döllinger's analysis of the Council of Florence had betrayed the fact that he had not taken into consideration some of the most recent scholarship on the topic.[170] Even Acton questioned the prudence of Döllinger's intervention.

Besides the bishops, predictable opponents assailed Döllinger. *La Civiltà Cattolica* accused Döllinger of being a "Febronian," and, worse, "the head of the liberal anti-Catholic party."[171] The papal nuncio in Munich, Meglia, communicated to Rome that the Infallibility petition and Döllinger's response were causing quite a sensation among students and citizens in Munich. Meglia also conveyed that measures were being taken in the dioceses of Munich and Augsburg to prohibit seminarians and clergy from attending Döllinger's lectures.[172] To Bavaria's Cardinal Hohenlohe, Pius IX railed about "not being able to suffer that lame priest [*magro prete*] of Munich."[173] The Pope also had encouraged the *Civiltà* to print a more thorough-going rebuttal to Döllinger. This came to fruition quickly when Matteo Liberatore published on

February 5, 1870 an essay condemning the "virulent" and "most fallacious" article of Döllinger's appearing in the "anticlerical" *Allgemeine Zeitung*. It was a sad commentary on the times, Liberatore elaborated, that "the scientific history of Döllinger" had led him to adopt positions normally associated with "schismatics and Protestants."[174] Finally, Curial pressure was brought on Scherr to discipline Döllinger. At the time, Scherr resisted, telling the Pope that Döllinger had lost some of his former prestige and that seminarians in Munich were not as captive to him as those in Rome suspected. To cover his bases, however, Scherr published a general pastoral letter, urging those in his diocese to resist actions that would exacerbate the unfolding controversy.[175]

Döllinger entered the fray once again in March 1870 with an article in the *Allgemeine Zeitung*. On February 22, a Vatican decree called for a modification in the procedural rules of the Council that were first laid down in *Multiplices inter* (November 27, 1869). The new regulations stipulated that conversation on a motion could be halted by just ten bishops and then the motion could be brought before the entire Council for a majority vote. In Döllinger's judgment, this measure vitiated the point of an authentic ecumenical council, which ought to proceed by the principle of unanimity not majority rule. What is more, not only this procedure but prior ones appeared to be foisted on the episcopate by the Vatican without their consent. He felt this impermissible. In Döllinger's words: "The present Roman synod is thus the first in the history of the Church in which instructions about the procedure have been made ... without them [the bishops] having any say-so in the matter." The regulations and their modification on February 22, appeared to Döllinger designed to make "the majority still more powerful and irresistible" and to prevent the concerns of the minority from fully developing—whereas in the past, he held, the persistent concerns of a sizable minority during a Council militated against a teaching being universally recognized. In light of these concerns, Döllinger concluded that the current Council did not allow the bishops' genuine freedom and, because of minority dissent, the teaching of Infallibility did not have the stamp of universality, whether in the past or the present.[176] On this point, practically all of the minority bishops sympathized with Döllinger's position, even as they recognized that they had nothing to gain from identifying with him publicly.

Despite their best efforts, the aims of Döllinger and Acton did not appear promising as spring arrived in Rome in 1870. The Council itself was moving at a snail's pace. Of the many drafted texts, or schemas, only a few were actually discussed. Largely written by the Jesuits Johann Baptist Franzelin and Joseph Kleutgen, the schema *De doctrina catholica* had been first discussed in December 1869. At root, it sought to flesh out the "Syllabus's" condemnations of modern "rationalism" by restating Catholic (Thomistic) principles about the proper relationship between faith and reason.[177] It was discussed again, beginning in late March, and adopted as a dogmatic constitution on April 24,

1870. The minority reluctantly gave their consent, hoping, somehow, that the *consensu unanimis* principle would in turn be applied in the case of *Pastor aeternus*, which dealt with the Church and Infallibility. But with this vote, Acton and Döllinger felt that the minority conceded too much ground. Aware that Infallibility loomed next as a topic, *Quirinus* adopted an even more strident tone: "Whoever holds the doctrine of Infallibility as a false teaching must consider the pope as an innovator. And not your usual innovator, some *Doctor privatus*, but the most dangerous and horrible enemy of the doctrine of revelation and the church... The pope is abusing the highest power, the power of loosing and binding, in order to mislead consciences and corrupt souls."[178]

With the minority's fortunes stagnant, a tone of acute distress characterized Acton and Döllinger's thinking at this time. The two discussed the possibility of Döllinger making a final, dramatic plea against Infallibility under his own name. But this idea was scuttled by the pressure of some of the minority bishops (notably Hefele) who felt another public intervention by Döllinger would produce more harm than good. Döllinger also felt that he had little left to say and that another work would only put pressure on Archbishop Scherr to discipline him—something, again, regularly gossiped about in Rome and ardently desired by the majority bishops. "For now it is better to follow Hefele's advice," Döllinger wrote Acton, "[and] 'at least temporarily pull myself back from the fight'."[179]

The only way to snatch victory from the jaws of defeat, Döllinger and Acton concluded, was if the minority bishops held firm to the principle that legitimate church councils required unanimity, not majority consent, and if the European powers could be roused to denounce the Council out of fear that its decrees would throw a wrench into Church–state relations across Europe. Acton worked especially with Bishop Dupanloup and other French Anti-Infallibilists in putting pressure, albeit unsuccessfully, on the government of Napoleon III.[180] In Bavaria, scant help came as ultramontanes in February had driven from office the liberal minister Hohenlohe—although the mercurial Ludwig II remained deeply skeptical of the Council.[181] The government of Austria wrote several menacing but inconsequential letters to the Pope. Finally, Prussia had adopted a wait-and-see attitude toward what Bismarck once referred to as "the papal insanities" taking place in Rome.[182]

Consequently, Acton and Döllinger turned from the Continent to Britain's Prime Minister Gladstone, whom they regarded as a pivotal figure who might yet rouse European capitals to action against the Council. Acton warned Gladstone that the doctrine of Infallibility, if adopted, would make Catholics, in Ireland but also across Europe, "irreconcilable enemies of civil and religious liberty. They will have to profess a false system of morality, and to repudiate literary and scientific sincerity."[183] Döllinger even enjoined the Prime Minister to see if Parliament would pass a resolution condemning the Council.[184]

Although troubled by the Council and by the person of Pius IX, whom he described as "a light-minded and hot-headed pope," Gladstone stopped short of pursuing any official action.[185] The opinion of his foreign secretary, the Earl of Clarendon, George Villiers, and that of the British diplomat in Rome, Odo Russell, proved to him more persuasive. Against the advice of Acton and Döllinger, they argued that heavy-handed political utterances about the affairs of the Church would only backfire and inflame ultramontane sentiment. In late March 1870, Villiers put the matter to Gladstone humorously and bluntly:

> Döllinger and Acton, like good Catholics as they are, feel stressed at the dangers which beset the Church from the Pope's audacious assault on human reason and they catch at every straw to save it. Far be it from me to consider you a straw or to underrate the power of your words, but I am sure that if the angel Gabriel trumpet-tongued were to rise from the treasury bench and hold the language recommended by Döllinger, it would have no more effect in arresting the car of Juggernaut at Rome than it would have in changing the East wind.[186]

Despondent about the inaction of governments, Acton complained to Gladstone on March 20, 1870 that "the governments that dislike to act now, and look forward to some mode of self protection after the Dogma is adopted, must prefer that necessity should be averted, that the Definition should be prevented before it involves them in struggles and disputes at home."[187] Although a friend of Gladstone, Döllinger grumbled to Acton that many of Europe's Protestant nations, like Protestant theologians of Germany, positively appeared to relish the unfolding *reductio ad absurdum* of Catholicism at the Council.[188]

The one Catholic scholar of international stature who might affect the outcome of the Council, Döllinger reasoned, was John Henry Newman, who had a record of doubting the Infallibilist position and a general distaste for ultramontanism.[189] Newman's reticence and equivocation about the Council had long perturbed Döllinger. On March 19, 1870, Döllinger therefore asked the future Cardinal to enter the fray. The letter (written in English) merits quoting in full:

> My Dear Dr. Newman
>
> In my opinion, and probably in yours too, the situation of the catholic Church has not been more dangerous in the last four centuries than it is at present. At such a time the true sons and friends of the church ought to be communing together. There is a Spanish proverb: *Quien no parece, perece* [a man who does not come forth is lost] .... Every one of us, who are the theologians of the church, ought to cast the weight of his testimony, whatever it may be, into the scales of the balance. Your position in the church is such a high one, that silence becomes a snare for thousands. It will be said: *qui tacet, consentit* [he who is silent, consents]. And yet it is impossible that you should be of one mind

with [Archbishop] Manning.... Among the theologians of Germany, except a few disciples of the Jesuits, there is not one man of some note who does not abhor and deprecate this new dogma of personal Infallibility, which is to be forced upon us. Of course I don't pretend to judge the reasons which you may have had to remain silent up to this moment. But I think the crisis is so near, that those reasons must now have lost their weight. Neutrality in such a case is too near akin to lukewarmness, but if you speak out, then let "the trumpet give a clear and certain sound" and believe such a splendid opportunity to do signal service to the cause of the church will not be offered again.

Totus tuus, I. Döllinger.[190]

In his response, Newman made clear his position to Döllinger: "I suppose in all Councils there has been intrigue [and] violence ... because the truth is held in earthen vessels. But God over rules [sic]."[191] Newman even conceded that the Council's current proceedings represented a "grave scandal,"[192] but he felt nonetheless that God's handiwork would appear in the final results, for "all that was divinely guaranteed in a Council was the truth of its resulting decision," not the propriety of its proceedings. Later he would hold up the third, fifth, and seventh ecumenical councils in antiquity as analogous examples of how chicanery and intrigue had nonetheless led to divinely-ordained ends.[193] In short, Döllinger did not find the ally that he hoped for in Newman.[194]

"Quirinus"'s letters from late spring and early summer of 1870 evince a spirit of profound bitterness and desperation. The Council "flatly denies the force of historical evidence, and closes with a repudiation of the necessity of moral unanimity," "Quirinus" argued.[195] Broadsides were launched at the Pope, the Curia, and the Jesuit order. Schooled in scholasticism, advocates of Infallibility were deemed by "Quirinus" immune from considering historical arguments, especially when made by German scholars: "Above all is German theology in ill repute, and the mere word 'history' in the mouth of a German acts like a red handkerchief on certain animals."[196] "Quirinus" also complained that if ultramontanes got what they sought, the Council would permanently sever Catholicism from Protestantism and Orthodoxy while emboldening anticlerical forces in Europe. Finally, there was the all-important question of conscience: a declaration of Infallibility risked causing perplexity of mind and difficulties of conscience for legions of Catholics: "The very sense of truth and error, right and wrong—in a word the conscience—[will be] thrown into confusion."[197]

But the Council proceeded apace. Already back in January, the schema on the Church (*schema de ecclesia*), drafted largely by the Jesuit Clemens Schrader, was handed out to the Council fathers; its eleventh chapter dealt with the primacy of papal jurisdiction.[198] On March 6, an additional chapter (*caput addendum*) on Papal Infallibility had been appended to it at the behest of the Pope. In late April, Pius, following the advice of key Infallibilists, had this chapter on papal authority removed from the schema on the Church in order that it might be given priority by a special deputation. This excised chapter became the *Pastor aeternus* constitution. It consisted of four sections: the institution on the primacy of Peter by Christ, the perpetuation of this primacy in the Bishop of Rome, the primacy of jurisdiction, and, not least, the Infallibility of the Pope. Heated conciliar debate on this constitution began in mid-May and was terminated by majority decision on June 6.[199] The majority and minority bishops faced off, hopelessly divided. The former tended to see Infallibility as a direct gift to the Pope from God, whereas the latter, insofar as they desired it at all, wanted the teaching firmly hitched to the witness of the Church Universal as manifest in the episcopate.[200] Lingering currents of Gallicanism, Jansenism, and Febronianism informed the minority; an assertive, post-1789 ultramontanism informed the majority. Both sides felt the weight of the moment.

In a last-ditch, memorable effort to mediate between the two sides, the Dominican Cardinal Filippo Maria Guidi of Bologna approached the Pope in mid-June, suggesting to him that the papal office did not necessarily depend on the bishops for his *authority*, but rather on their collaborating *witness* "in order to learn from them what the faith of the entire Church is and what traditions exist in the various individual Churches regarding the truth in question."[201] Pius was none too happy about the distinction and gave the now infamous response: "*La tradizione sono io*," I am the tradition.[202] Once leaked, in fairly short order this led to "Quirinus"/Döllinger's commentary: "*La tradizione son'io*—it would be impossible to give a briefer, more pregnant or more epigrammatic description of the whole system which is now to be made dominant than is contained in those few words."[203]

By June, exhausted and ill, Acton felt that he had little left to offer and decided to leave Rome with his family for his estate near Tegernsee, Bavaria. On his final day in Rome, June 10, he was paid visits by Strossmayer, Hefele, Heinrich Förster (Bishop of Breslau and a critic of Infallibility), and the Prussian minister in Rome, von Arnim.[204] Acton also visited Archbishop Scherr, who recently had had an audience with the Pope. The Bavarian diplomat Tauffkirchen indicated in a report to Ludwig II that Scherr had warned the Pope of the dangers in Germany if the Council passed the extremists' version of Infallibility. The Pope, probably with Döllinger in mind, responded: "I know those Germans; they know everything better, everyone there wants to be Pope."[205] As shall be made clear later, the German Old Catholic schism was already gaining momentum at this point.

Following an intervention by Bishop Vinzenz Gasser of Brixen (Austria) to moderate interpretations of Infallibility, a preliminary vote on *Pastor aeternus* took place on July 13.[206] Of the 601 bishops then voting, 451 accepted (*placet*), 88 rejected it (*non placet*), and 62 expressed a desire for a modification (*placet iuxta modum*). Wrangling, acrimony, and petitions to the Pope followed in anticipation of a final vote. Archbishop Darboy of Paris and Ketteler of Mainz pled for more moderate language that would connect infallible judgments made *ex cathedra*, from the Chair of Peter, more explicitly with the witness and tradition of the Church. But this language was rejected and in fact a pointed phrase was added on July 16 to the effect that solemn definitions of the Pope were to be considered valid and "irreformable of themselves without the consent of the Church" (*ex sese, non autem ex consensu Ecclesia irreformabiles esse*).[207]

With rumors in the air of war between Prussia and France, a final vote was scheduled for July 18. Persuaded in large part by France's Bishop Dupanloup, some sixty members of the minority, instead of voting, decided to make a statement by their absence and departed Rome. Leading German bishops, such as Ketteler and Scherr, were among those who left.[208] On this day, amid a massive storm of thunder and lightning, the final vote took place: 533 *placet* and 2 *non placet*.[209] Infallibilists could claim a victory, even if the eleventh-hour wrangling over the language of the Constitution portended future conflicts of interpretation. The *Times* of London reported the historic scene at St. Peter's: "The storm was at its height when the result of the voting was taken up to the Pope, and the darkness was so thick that a huge taper was necessarily brought to him and placed by his side as he read…. And again the lightning flickered around the hall, and the thunder pealed; the entire crowd fell on their knees, and the Pope blessed them in those clear sweet tones distinguishable among a thousand."[210]

Dramatic developments on the European stage ensued in the following days and weeks. On July 19, the Franco-Prussian war broke out. In fairly short order, this led Napoleon III to recall his troops from Italy, making possible the final collapse of the Papal States and the completion of Italian unification. The troops of Victor Emmanuel breached the Roman walls at Porta Pia on September 20; Rome was now destined to become the capital of the new nation, and Pius, a self-proclaimed "prisoner of the Vatican."[211] On the same day, the embattled Pope suspended the Council, *sine die*.

In the final letter of "Quirinus", Döllinger opined: "Future historians will begin a new period of Church history with July 18, 1870, as with October 31, 1517… [T]he absolute papacy celebrates its… triumph over the Church, which now lies defenseless at the feet of the Italians. It only remains to follow up the anathematized enemy, the bishops of the minority, into their lurking places, and compel each of them to bend under the Caudine yoke amid the scornful laughter of the majority."[212] On July 23, Döllinger wrote Acton, then back at Tegernsee: "I am not clear of what I am to do or let be. I often express my thoughts, and to anyone who asks, I'll say that I expect excommunication from Rome (either very soon or after pleas to recant, which will come to naught) and then certainly all theologians and priests in Germany will experience frustration and despondency."[213] Acton responded on July 25: "If one really believes the doctrine is false, then the conclusion is unavoidable that the

Pope and the majority are heretics.... ~~We are heretics if he [the Pope] is right.~~
~~He is if he is wrong.~~"[214]

"PRISONER OF THE VATICAN" AND DÖLLINGER'S EXCOMMUNICATION

The outbreak of the Franco-Prussian War compelled many remaining bishops
of the majority to leave Rome to attend to their flocks. Only a rump of 150
stayed behind. For a period, committees went on drafting and discussing
documents in an attempt to keep the Council alive. But historical events
soon overwhelmed their efforts.

As mentioned above, when Napoleon III recalled his troops from Italy in
early August 1870, Rome was rendered defenseless against Italian forces.
Uncertainty prevailed at first, for if French forces proved victorious over
Prussia, one could reasonably conjecture that France might resume its protection of Rome. This illusion was shattered on September 1–2 when Prussian
troops routed the French army at the Battle of Sedan, turning the tide of war,
creating a political crisis in France, and eventually paving the way for German
national unification.[215] Shortly afterwards, Döllinger commented cryptically
to Acton: "Isn't the Battle of Sedan a world-historical event? With it one must
mark a new beginning. There appears to me to be an inner connection
between July 18 [*Pastor aeternus*] and September 1."[216]

In Rome, many voices urged Pius to go into exile as he had done in 1848.
The French Empress Eugénie even sent a man-of-war to Civitavecchia to
evacuate the Pope if he so wished. But at the age of 78 Pius had no intention
of making a second flight. Cardinal Antonelli seconded this opinion. On
September 10, the Pope received an envoy from the Italian government who
brought the message from Victor Emmanuel that the security of Italy depended on Italian forces occupying Rome and that the Pope ought to surrender
peacefully. Pius rebuffed the request and ordered the next day a three-day
intercession before the image of the Madonna della Colonna at St. Peter's for
the protection of Rome. "If we are unable to prevent the thief from entering,"
Pius proclaimed, "let it at least be known that he enters only by means of
violence."[217]

On September 19, General Raffaele Cadorna, taking orders from the Italian
government then seated in Florence, assembled 60,000 troops outside of
Rome. The papal Zouaves and volunteers defending the city under the command of General Hermann Kanzler numbered a little over 10,000. They had
previously petitioned the Pope to be allowed to die defending the Eternal City.
On the same day, the Pope made his way to the *Scala Sancta*, the "holy stairs"

near the Basilica of St. John Lateran, climbing them on his knees to ask for the Virgin's intercession. As he left, he blessed the troops gathered on the nearby piazza and then had his coachman drive him slowly toward the Vatican through large crowds eager to glimpse the beleaguered Pope.[218]

The bombardment of the city began in the early morning of September 20. *1870* Fifty men and several horses were slain. When the wall was finally breached at the Porta Pia, General Kanzler sent a message to the Pope asking for direction. Pius ordered surrender, fearful of a massacre and large-scale destruction of the city. As previously arranged, the diplomatic corps of Rome had gathered at the Vatican with the Holy Father during this time of trouble. After a morning mass, he protested to them against the "sacrilegious" actions taking place, remarking as well: "I surrender to violence. From this moment I am the prisoner of King Victor Emmanuel."[219] The formal capitulation was signed in the afternoon of September 20 at the Villa Albani. When Father Daniel, chaplain of the papal troops, entered the Pope's presence that day, Pius found a moment of respite in gallows humor: "My dear Daniel, here we are really in the lion's den."[220]

The Italian army now controlled the Eternal City, effectively ending the oldest ecclesiastical state in Europe. King Emmanuel indicated that he would not infringe upon the grounds of the Vatican and that the Council might continue. But Pius felt that if he accepted such an offer he would confer legitimacy on what had taken place. Instead, he doubled down on the sentiment that the temporal power was necessary for the spiritual power. Bereft of the former, he finally suspended the Council on October 20, *sine die*, until a more propitious time. On November 1, he issued an encyclical condemning the "monstrous crime" that had taken place. Comparing his plight to that of Pius VII at the hands of Napoleon, Pius issued a blanket excommunication against "any who have invaded or usurped Our provinces or Our beloved City."[221] "[A]s prisoner, [he] is infinitely more glorious than His jailers in the capitol," the ultramontane *Unità Cattolica* later editorialized.[222]

Subsequent popes followed Pius's example, regarding themselves after election as a "Prisoner of the Vatican." No pope in fact left the precincts of the Vatican until 1929 when a concordat with Italy created the present-day Vatican City. And as for the Council, it never reconvened; it was formally closed only in 1960 as, a necessary item of business prior to the Second Vatican Council—a different kind of council in a different age.[33]

*   *   *

Munich's Archbishop Scherr, who had voted *non placet* on July 13, 1870 and signed the minority bishops' protest on July 17, returned to Munich on July 19.[223] Troubled by the vote on July 18, he nonetheless felt that the vows of his office obliged him to accept the outcome irrespective of personal doubts.

On July 21, he called members of Munich's theological faculty, including Döllinger, to the bishop's palace and expressed to them bluntly: "*Roma locuta est*. Gentlemen, you know what that involves. We can do nothing but submit."[224] A few days later, Scherr met Döllinger alone for a conversation that lasted several hours. According to Johann Friedrich, the meeting ended with a portentous exchange. Archbishop: "Let us now begin to work again for our Holy Church." Döllinger: "Indeed, for the Church of old." Archbishop: "There is only one Church that is neither new nor old." Döllinger: "They [at the Council] have made a new Church."[225] A few days later, the nuncio Meglia reported to Rome that Döllinger had "obstinately resisted" and that he would likely "continue to believe and teach what he had [previously] believed and taught."[226]

In a state of turmoil, Döllinger wrote Acton, expressing to him the vague hope that some future council would correct what had taken place in Rome. He also mulled over whether he should take up the pen yet again and, if so, under his own name or a pseudonym. He especially feared that the remaining German bishops, following Scherr and others such as Ketteler, would cave in and submit to the Vatican decrees, one by one. The Anglican theologian and clergyman Henry Perry Liddon visited Döllinger in late July and recorded the following in a letter to the English Catholic convert, Henry Nutcombe Oxenham: "A large amount of our conversation, of course, turned on the Council and the Definition; and he speaks with the most entire unreserve. He says that the great danger now is lest the Bishops of the minority, being separated from each other ... [,] should gradually acquiesce. Nothing would be worse for the cause of the Church in Germany than the spectacle of such submission."[227] To Friedrich von Schulte, a canon lawyer in Prague and future Old Catholic leader, Döllinger wrote that the new definition of Infallibility was "positively monstrous."[228]

The situation in Munich was especially volatile. "The spiritual confusion [*Verwirrung der Geister*]," Scherr wrote Archbishop Joseph Ritter von Rauscher of Vienna, "is much greater here than I had imagined in Rome. And I hardly know how to calm the waters. Already many people of high standing have conveyed to me in writing their exit from the Catholic Church."[229] The nuncio Meglia told Antonelli in Rome that Munich had become a breeding ground for "young people without a churchly spirit and [who were] imbued with false principles."[230]

Among Döllinger's first actions was to turn to the government, which had not withheld its support of him despite clear knowledge of his dissent from the Council. Döllinger and the Bavarian Minister of Culture, Johann Freiherr von Lutz, were in close contact during this time. To him and others, Döllinger appealed to the Bavarian Concordat of 1817 and argued that the Vatican's decrees could not become valid for Bavaria without the government's consent.[231] He also drafted a series of questions on behalf of Lutz that were then sent to theological and law faculties in Bavaria asking for feedback on the legal status and implications of the Vatican's decrees.[232]

But Döllinger's most acute concern remained the reaction of the German minority bishops. Melchers of Cologne and Ketteler of Mainz, upon leaving Rome, had indicated decisively that they were prepared to submit to the decrees. Scherr leaned in that direction, too. But some were more divided in their thinking. This was especially true of Bishop Hefele of Rottenburg, who underwent a difficult struggle of conscience. In August 1870 Döllinger and Hefele exchanged letters. To Döllinger, Hefele confided his worries about the "new dogma" and his doubts about the freedom of the Council and its lack of unanimity. "Let the Romans suspend and excommunicate me," he concluded, "and order a new administrator for the diocese. Perhaps God in his mercy before then will whisk the disturber of the Church [*Perturbator Ecclesiae*] [Pius IX] from the scene."[233] Hefele was especially upset with Ketteler and Melchers, whose submission in his judgment made them "appear to have forgotten everything that they did and said in Rome." "I gave consideration to abdicating my post," he concluded to Döllinger, "but I gave up that idea and will drink the cup before me. I know not what else to do."[234]

Taking his cue from Hefele's dilemma and the prospects of similar reactions among other minority bishops, Döllinger whipped into action, calling a meeting in Nuremberg of dissenting Catholic theologians. Fourteen professors from Munich, Bonn, Breslau, Braunsberg, and Prague—including many future Old Catholic stalwarts—showed up there on August 25, 1870 to deliberate on how they might best respond and sway the wavering bishops. Appealing to their "strictly scholarly" credentials, they penned a declaration, in which they disputed the validity of Papal Infallibility, regarding it as a "new doctrine that the Church has never before recognized" and therefore one that could not pass muster by the standards of the Vicentian canon. What is more, the Council that proclaimed the new doctrine lacked the status of a genuinely ecumenical council in their view, because dissenting voices were not given the freedom to make their case and because "moral pressure was brought to bear on its members." The Council was also compromised because its results "completely destroyed" the historic episcopacy, and promised to wreak havoc in Church–state relations by turning the Pope into a veritable oracle of God. Finally, in light of "the crisis of the church and the pressures on conscience" (*Bedrängnisse der Gewissen*) that the Council had created, the signatories of the declaration (which eventually numbered thirty-two) asked the German bishops to hold firm in their opposition "until a genuine, free, and therefore not Italian, Council, held on this side of the Alps" could moderate what had recently taken place in Rome.[235] (The nationalist element here should be duly noted.)

This so-called "Nuremberg Declaration" exacerbated an already tense situation. A writer in Mainz's *Der Katholik* proclaimed that its signatories had cut themselves off from "our common mother, the Church."[236] Many began to

speak openly of a schism. The influence of "Quirinus"'s letters on the interpretation of the Council was taking its toll. Agitation against the Council had
formed in Bonn, Breslau, Cologne, Prague, and elsewhere, sometimes expressing itself in written rebuttals.[237] Munich in particular, not least because of
Döllinger's influence, had become a hotbed of opposition, and Scherr knew
that the remaining German bishops needed to act decisively to prevent a much
larger revolt, especially among the professional and educated classes, among
whom opposition was strongest.[238] To this end, Scherr contacted Bishop
Melchers of Cologne, indicating that "there is no doubt that our holy Catholic
Church in Germany is threatened by great dangers and difficult struggles lie
ahead. To counter and put to rest these [dangers], the best and most appropriate means is a common action of the German episcopate."[239] Together with
Ketteler of Mainz, they therefore made arrangements for a meeting of bishops
to take place.

On August 30 and 31, 1870, nine minority bishops met in Fulda to discuss
the situation in Germany.[240] Together they drafted the so-called "Pastoral
Letter of Fulda," which sought to moderate the interpretation of the Vatican
decrees offered by "Quirinus" and other critics, and to demonstrate solidarity
against oppositional forces in their various flocks. While those who gathered
continued to voice concerns about the Council's procedures, the meeting
effectively ended Döllinger's hope that a defiant rump of bishops would hold
out in their opposition. Bishop Ketteler of Mainz and the German secretary at
the Council, Bishop Josef Fessler of St. Pölten in Austria, had set about
penning milder interpretations of the Council decrees, and these proved
influential.[241] Ketteler in particular played a key role at Fulda, softening
interpretations of the decrees and enjoining his colleagues to desist from any
further resistance.[242] Warning the faithful against those who might lead them
astray and rebuking as "wholly unfounded" the view that the Council lacked
ecumenicity, the Bishops' Pastoral Letter of Fulda exclaimed

> that the present Vatican Council is a legitimate General Council; and, moreover,
> that this Council as little as any other General Council has propounded or formed
> a new doctrine at variance with the ancient teaching; but that it has simply
> developed and thrown light on the old and faithfully preserved truth contained
> in the deposit of faith, and in opposition to the errors of the day it has proposed
> [this truth] expressly to the belief of all the faithful; and lastly that these decrees
> have received binding power on all the faithful due to the fact of their final
> publication by the Supreme Head of the Church in solemn form at the Public
> Session.[243]

The letter was issued in mid-September 1870 and included the signatures of
Scherr, Ketteler, Melchers, Krementz, Dinkel, and Eberhard—all erstwhile
members of the minority while at Rome. In explaining the motivation for
his submission, Bishop Dinkel of Augsburg gave expression to a common

worry: "The movement launched by Döllinger would lead directly to schism, and in such a maneuver [I] could take no part.... I now consider it my duty to protest against the misunderstandings that are being spread among the faithful on the subject of Infallibility."[244] In October, Pius IX conveyed his gratification for the letter.[245]

The final hold-outs among the German bishops—Deinlein (Bamberg), Förster (Breslau), Hefele (Rottenburg), and Beckmann (Osnabrück)—submitted, one by one, in the following months. Döllinger's friend Hefele was the last to do so, an act that came with profound turmoil of conscience several months later—on April 10, 1871.[246] He had been conspicuously absent at the meeting at Fulda, and earlier, as we have seen, complained to Döllinger of the amnesia that his peers seemed to exhibit.[247]

The submission of the bishops, not surprisingly, came as a sore disappointment to Döllinger and other dissenters. Acton, too, was greatly displeased, and even accused the bishops of "treachery" in a circular letter.[248] Similarly, an outraged Johann Friedrich charged the minority bishops with breaking their word and deceiving the faithful,[249] while Joseph Hubert Reinkens, the future, first German Old Catholic bishop, regarded the Fulda Pastoral Letter as "shameful," a document "without warmth or light, without clarity or truth."[250]

In the letter, the bishops had exhorted "divinely appointed pastors and teachers"—i.e., theologians—in particular to heed the Council decrees in order to calm "agitation ... [that] forms no small trial and danger to many souls."[251] In his diocese, Bishop Melchers of Cologne lashed out at professors in Bonn who refused to recognize the Council.[252] The ultramontane press clamored for the same to be done at universities across Germany, wherever dissent was found. The papal nuncio in Munich, Meglia, was also of this opinion. Doubtlessly, therefore, Archbishop Scherr felt pressure from many quarters to bring to heel Munich's theological faculty.

The impending start of the winter semester concentrated Scherr's mind. On October 20, 1870, he addressed a lengthy letter to Munich's theological faculty, "the pearl of my diocese."[253] Making an appeal to sentiments expressed by the bishops at Fulda and candidly recognizing his own misgivings about Infallibility prior to the Council, he made clear that it was now the duty of all teachers of theology to submit. In his own words:

> Seeing then that the situation is now undeniably clear, it is impossible for it to remain a matter of indifference to me what position the honorable theological faculty and its individual members assume in reference to it [the Council].... I cannot silently allow the sacred science [*heilige Wissenschaft*] to be taught in my diocese by someone about whom I am uncertain that he teaches, without exception and without reserve, in accord with what the Catholic Church has expressly declared a belief. It is impossible for me to let my candidates for the priesthood stand in danger of being taught in a manner that differs from the will of the Catholic Church.

In the letter, Scherr also made know that while in Rome during the Council he had put in a good word for Munich's theological faculty to Pius IX, but now "under quite different conditions, I should perhaps not be able to do so again." He concluded by asking the faculty to "keep me from the pain, which would certainly be the greatest of my episcopal office, namely, that of being obliged to employ against you the severity of my pastoral duty [*den Ernst meiner oberhirtlichen Amtspflicht*]."[254] Shortly thereafter, the nuncio Meglia approvingly informed Antonelli in Rome that Scherr had requested "a declaration of their [the faculty's] submission to the decisions of the Vatican Council, and particularly to the dogma of the Infallibility of the Pope."[255]

Scherr's letter provoked heated discussion among members of the theological faculty. In fact, they met on three separate occasions, on November 10, 17, and 25, to discuss the bishop's request and possible responses.[256] More sensationally, the senate of the university got involved, raising the question of whether the bishop's intervention violated the rights of the faculty, which stood, as many faculty members held, as an academic body exclusively under the authority of the crown.[257] In the end, on November 29, the majority of the professors submitted and made clear their adherence to the Council's decrees. These included the faculty's dean Franz Xaver Reithmayr along with Daniel Bonifaz Haneberg, Valetin Thalhofer, Alois von Schmid, Karl Wilhelm Reischl, Joseph Bach, and Joseph Schönfelder.[258] But two notable dissenters stood out: Johann Friedrich and, of course, Döllinger.

The lack of unanimity among the faculty grieved Scherr. In mid-December, Friedrich, who had voiced his determined opposition to the archbishop in a letter, was given four weeks to make a public submission.[259] In the same month, Döllinger and Hefele exchanged letters; the latter at this point had still not submitted. The Bishop of Rottenburg made clear that he, like Döllinger, stood between a rock and hard place, pressured by conviction and educated opinion to resist, but by Rome and his fellow bishops to submit. In fact, Pius IX, in a handwritten note, had personally requested from Hefele a clear declaration of submission. "My position will not hold for much longer," he wrote Döllinger, "but a schism has no chances in itself; the world is too apathetic and those in dissent are too scattered."[260] As indicated previously, Hefele submitted in April 1871.[261]

In January 1871, as Prussia's victory over France ushered in German nationhood, the Archbishop of Munich-Freising acted more boldly. On December 26, 1870 Scherr completed a lengthy pastoral letter "to the entire honorable clergy and all believers" in his diocese. Published shortly after the new year, Scherr made the case for the ecumenical character of the recent Council and for the dogmatic nature of Papal Infallibility: "From the first moment of the founding of the church until today, from Peter to Pius IX, it [Infallibility] has been uninterruptedly exercised."[262] In the final analysis, the Council's decrees now presented in Scherr's eyes an unavoidable choice for Catholics: either faithful obedience or departure from the Church. Nuncio Meglia approvingly conveyed to Rome that the erstwhile minority bishop had penned "a most excellent and learned document" (*un bellissimo ed eruditissimo Documento*).[263] Pius IX recognized Scherr's letter approvingly.[264]

Shortly after issuing the pastoral letter, Scherr sent a personal letter to Döllinger, imploring him to end his defiance and submit. The letter, dated January 4, 1871, merits lengthy quotation:

> Thus at last after long hesitation ... I now find myself compelled to request and formally challenge you to an open expression of your opinion on this subject [the Vatican decrees].
>
> I can well imagine that giving a clear declaration of your position on the matter in question to be very difficult.
>
> Your glorious past, which has been filled with meritorious deeds for the sake of Catholic scholarship, for our future Catholic clergy, [and] for Catholic public life, acts as a forceful barrier against making a breach with the Church, to which you have belonged for your whole life.
>
> On the other hand, to that movement which in Germany occasioned the well-known agitations against the Council both before and during its deliberations, and which always, whether rightly or wrongly, appealed to your name, you seem to have made concessions of such a kind that it will now cost you a severe struggle [*schweren Kampf*] to renounce them.
>
> [Please] ... take to heart the great responsibility that you will have to bear before the judgment-seat of God for all those who allow themselves to be detained still longer in their isolation by your example ...
>
> I pray and plead, therefore, that you desist from helping harm the unity and unanimity among the members of the one Church, and with an heroic resolution, by a public churchly confession, break the chains which still holds many honest Catholics in its grasp.
>
> It is still impossible for me to believe that ... you will challenge the authority of your bishop, who, nonetheless, must and will most certainly exercise his inalienable rights if hopeful patience is finally deceived.[265]

Döllinger felt cornered. He wrote Acton, telling him about both the pastoral letter and the personal letter from Scherr "asking for my submission," and he floated the idea of penning a circular letter to the archbishop that would appear after the conclusion of the war.[266] Döllinger's actual, private response to Scherr came in a letter dated January 29, 1871; it, too, merits extensive quotation:

> Conscious of the difficult position in which I find myself, and of the responsibility with which I am burdened, I have for some weeks been making the great question of the nature and scope of papal authority and its relation to the Church the subject of renewed inquiry.... Should I succeed in gaining the conviction that this doctrine [Infallibility] is the true one as warranted by the Scriptures and by tradition, and I, who have hitherto believed the opposite, as the large majority

of German theologians have done, am in error, I shall then not hesitate to confess this before the world without reservation.... Yet this is to be done only on one condition, namely that he [the one who confesses] is also actually convinced of the veracity of what he is to confess anew, and of the falseness of what he has previously taught; for without this conviction, a submission of this kind would, of course, be a grievous sin and a gross lie, and I am quite certain that your Excellence does not intend to drive me to such an extremity by your challenge. Your challenge can only bear this interpretation: "Take pains and do all that you can to procure for yourself the same conviction as I have now." According to the best of my conscience [*nach bestem Gewissen*], this is what I am doing.... [But] this is a task that requires time, and I therefore beg to you to grant it to me and to remain patient with the old man.[267]

But Scherr was near the end of his patience with the septuagenarian. On February 14 he lamented to Döllinger that his response did not contain "[a] satisfying declaration about your position on the General Vatican Council." He then added an ultimatum: Döllinger had until March 15 to declare his submission or else face "the further steps which my office as bishop requires of me."[268] On March 14, Döllinger pled to Scherr for more time "to do what your Excellence requires of me with a clear head and after a full consideration of all the consequences."[269] Scherr consented, giving Döllinger until March 31, even as he also told him that "after this date I shall not be in a position to grant any further extension."[270] On March 18, 1871 Meglia reported to Rome that Döllinger's submission "would be a great fortune for him and for religion," because it would represent "the most solemn defeat of the enemies of the Catholic Church in Germany."[271]

Looking back at this period in his life, Döllinger called it his darkest. "I have had only one sleepless night in my life," he told Louise von Kobell, "and that was when I was considering the impossibility of reconciling my conscience to the dogma of Infallibility, thinking it over and over and coming to the conclusion that I could not." "A man may go far," he also told her, "and yet come to a point where he must stop, because his conscience refuses to go further."[272] With an allusion to Martin Luther, Lady Blennerhasset (Charlotte von Leyden) described Döllinger's state of mind at this time as follows: "How... estimable is this venerable man, who in only days time will for the second time in German history say: 'Here I stand, God help me, I can do no other.' He feels the responsibility of his situation very heavily and is often sad, but nonetheless determined."[273]

The prospect of Döllinger being disciplined practically unhinged Bishop Hefele. In anguish, he wrote Döllinger on March 11, 1871: "I cannot even think about it: Döllinger—the one who for so long, so early, while others were sleeping, the protector of the Catholic Church and its interests, the greatest of all German theologians, an Ajax of Ultramontanism—must be suspended or even excommunicated by a bishop who does not have even a thousandth of Döllinger's merits. It is abmoninable."[274]

As Scherr brooded over the matter, Döllinger responded on March 28, 1871. In an open letter to Scherr, soon published in newspapers the world over, the septuagenarian made clear his refusal to submit. Reprising in abbreviated form many arguments already advanced by "Janus" and "Quirinus," Döllinger made a characteristic appeal to the arbitrating role of historical knowledge. The recent attempt to justify the Vatican decrees by the German bishops, he held, rested on "a complete misunderstanding of ecclesiastical tradition.... [It] contradicts the clearest evidence and facts." What is more, asking bishops to make a "sacrifice of the intellect" (*sacrificio dell'intelletto*) by assenting to what history disproved was not only misguided from Döllinger's standpoint, but it baptized "mental sloth" as a religiously meritorious disposition. Instead, the validity of the Vatican decrees rested on a "purely historical question." For this reason, he asked Scherr if he might form a commission, to which "[I] might be able to bring forward my case." "I should esteem it a great honor if your Excellency would be willing to preside... and set me right in reference to any errors in my quotations and exposition of evidence and facts, which, I am sure, would only redound to the advantage of truth."[275]

Furthermore, Döllinger bewailed the centralization of power in Rome and its diminution among the bishops in Germany. "As every student of history and of the Fathers will admit," he claimed, "the episcopate of the ancient Church is thus destroyed [by the Vatican decrees] in its inmost being." Bishops might "perhaps still be dignitaries of the Church, but no longer real bishops." The "new" doctrine of Papal Infallibility, he felt, also had negative implications for Church–state relations in Europe even as it also burned ecumenical bridges to non-Catholic Christians. For all these reasons and more, Döllinger concluded in thundering language: "As a Christian, as a theologian, as a historian, as a citizen, I cannot accept this doctrine." The situation from his standpoint could hardly be more dire: "Are we not now standing before a dizzy abyss that opened itself before our eyes on July 18 [1870]."[276]

The letter created a sensation. Liberals, Protestants, and dissenting Catholics immediately hailed Döllinger's "declaration" as an act of momentous courage. The liberal Bavarian minister to Florence, Wilhelm von Dönniges, called it a "historically great" event, inspiring to the educated classes throughout Europe.[277] The *Rheinischer Merkur* editorialized that Döllinger's declaration was an "incontrovertible witness to the truth, a stumbling block" for Jesuits and ultramontanes everywhere.[278] Soon, letters of support and "solidarity addresses" poured into Döllinger's residence from near and far.[279] A group of professors at the University of Rome pledged to defend him with the pen against his persecutors.[280] More than a few began to compare his actions to those of Martin Luther.[281]

Not surprisingly, those inclined toward Rome saw matters differently. Meglia reported to Antonelli of the "impious document" by the "obstinate professor," noting as well that all hopes of Döllinger's conversion had now been "disappointed."[282] Ultramontane Catholics in Germany and elsewhere clamored for the Church to discipline the Professor and his followers—or what some had begun to call "the Döllinger movement."[283] An "apostate," "the Bavarian heresiarch," and "the heretical Provost" were among the various labels given to him.[284]

Fearful of a widening schism in his diocese, Archbishop Scherr resolved to act. On April 2, 1871, he published a general pastoral letter in which he castigated Döllinger's "exceedingly deplorable" declaration and accused him of "placing historical scholarship above the Church" (*die historische Forschung über die Kirche gestellt*). Furthermore, he proclaimed that all along "the author of this declaration has been the intellectual head of the whole movement set...against the Vatican Council, which has produced so much perplexity of mind and agitation of conscience [*Verwirrung der Geister und Beunruhigung der Gewissen*]...[T]he matter has now assumed the form of a direct revolt against the Catholic Church."[285] Shortly after its publication, Antonelli conveyed to Meglia the Pope's satisfaction with Scherr's sentiments in this letter.[286]

But before disciplining Döllinger, Scherr reached out both to Rome and to the Bavarian crown, seeking approbation from the former, understanding from the latter. On March 31, at Scherr's request, nuncio Meglia sent a telegram to Antonelli informing the Curia of Döllinger's act and voicing concerns about disciplining Döllinger, particularly in light of the fact that Ludwig II appeared to support him. This telegram, extant in the Vatican archives, contains the handwritten note of the Pope, who commented: "The Act [of] Dolinger [sic] puts [him] out of the church and he certainly cannot exercise the ministry in whatever position he occupies."[287] In the official response of April 5, 1871, however, Antonelli curiously appeared to leave the matter up to Scherr, even as he subtly pressured the archbishop by letting him know, through Meglia, that he (Scherr) certainly knew his canonical duties.[288] Three days later, Antonelli ratcheted up the pressure, alluding to an open schism in the Church as a possibility due to the "disastrous consequences" of Döllinger's "deplorable act."[289] Then, on April 12, 1817, Antonelli made known the Pope's approval of Scherr's pastoral letter of April 2.[290] For his part, Scherr certainly knew of the Pope's approval of Archbishop Melchers's harsh measures against defiant professors at the University of Bonn.[291] While there is no smoking gun, all evidence suggests that Pius IX either actively encouraged or regarded approvingly the actions being taken against Döllinger. Toward the end of his life, Döllinger conveyed his own conviction that the proceedings against him came in response to an order from the Pope.[292]

The role of King Ludwig II at this time comes across as curious and contradictory. On the one hand, the young king appeared poised to play the role that Friedrich the Wise's played for Martin Luther: asserting his own sphere of authority and protecting Döllinger. During the Council in fact

Ludwig had encouraged Döllinger "not to tire in this serious and consequential fight" against "jesuitical machinations" (*jesuitische Umtriebe*). In a birthday greeting to Döllinger from February 28, 1871, Ludwig referred to Döllinger proudly as "my Bossuet"—by implication likening himself to Louis XIV and casting Döllinger as the defender of the "Gallican" privileges of his realm.[293] The king also engaged in some (ultimately unsuccessful) behind-the-scenes diplomatic intrigue to try to have Rome intervene *against* Archbishop Scherr.[294]

On the other hand, when Scherr approached the king about the matter, the king behaved more passively. On April 14, Scherr wrote Ludwig, appealing to him as "the supreme protector and shield of our holy Church" and warning that "the anti-churchly movement" inspired by Döllinger, if left unchecked, could lead to "endless trouble and unspeakable misfortune" for the Church in Bavaria.[295] The next day, Scherr met with the king in person to discuss the matter and left the meeting feeling "very comforted" that the king, although agitated about Döllinger's individual plight, recognized the high stakes and would not prove to be an obstacle.[296] This came as a great relief to Scherr and to those in Rome. Antonelli, in fact, when he learned about the meeting, exclaimed that the king's disposition was likely even more important than the submission of Hefele for calming the ecclesiastical turmoil in Germany.[297] On April 17, Scherr dutifully wrote the king, informing him of the actions being taking against Döllinger, assuring him that such extreme measures only came to him as a "most difficult duty of conscience."[298]

And the excommunication came. The ordinariate of Munich-Freising had already formally contacted Döllinger on April 3, notifying him that his defiance of the Vatican decrees amounted to opposition to established teaching and therefore his case "falls under the head of heresy." Consequently, he was to incur "the greater excommunication" (*excommunicatio major*) and that therefore "you will have to examine your conscience [*Ihr Gewissen . . . prüfen*], and see whether you have not already fallen under ecclesiastical censure."[299] With the sword of Damocles above his head, Döllinger participated in Holy Week, celebrating his last high mass on Easter Sunday, April 9, 1871, in the Royal Chapel, All Saints Church. At this service, he told those gathered that "today I have celebrated my last high mass. . . . I do not want to bring shame to the royal house; I see myself in light of what the Archbishop makes me out to be."[300] The same day, coincidentally, Newman had written him, indicating his fervent prayers because "you [must] have so overpowering an anxiety upon you."[301]

The drama's final act occurred on April 17, 1871, when the ordinariate accused Döllinger of "conscious and obstinate denial of the clear and sure decrees of the faith of the Catholic Church" and of propagating "heretical principles of faith and hurl[ing] the most malicious charges against the Church."[302] This decree was published in the diocesan newsletter (*Pastoral-blatt*) three days later and read aloud from the city's pulpits on the first Sunday after Easter, April 23, 1871.[303] "He is sad and agitated," the nuncio had earlier reported, recounting as well what a third party overheard Döllinger say about himself: "'I am the most unfortunate man in the world; if I go back I am lost, if I continue going forward, I am equally lost.'"[304]

In the spirit of Don Fabrizio in Lampedusa's novel *The Leopard*, "how deep was [Döllinger's] revulsion from the ... circumstances in which he was so inextricably involved."[305] At the age of 72, arguably the most learned Catholic scholar of the century found himself excommunicated.

4

After the Council

Renown, Christian Unity, and its Obstacles

> Behold, how good and pleasant it is when brothers dwell in unity! It is like
> the precious oil on the head, running down on the beard, on the beard of
> Aaron, running down on the collar of his robes.
>
> —Psalm 133:1–2

> All of Europe...was watching Döllinger.
>
> —C. B. Moss

According to the Gospel of John, before his crucifixion, Jesus prayed for the
unity of his disciples and their followers: "I do not pray for these only, but also
for those who believe in me through their word, *that they may all be one*; even
as thou, Father, art in me, and I in thee, that they also may be in us, so that the
world may believe that thou hast sent me. The glory which thou hast given me
I have given to them, *that they may be one even as we are one*" (John 17:20–2).[1]
This passage has long served as a touchstone for what theologians sometimes
call the "ecumenical imperative," the effort to achieve, or at least work toward,
unity among divided Christians.

For many educated Christians today, ecumenism counts as a theological
duty—even if it has proven vexingly difficult. The stubborn legacy of the
sixteenth-century breach and the splintering of Protestantism into countless
"denominations" bear much of the blame. So too do much earlier divisions,
notably those between churches in antiquity who accepted the Council of
Chalcedon (451) and those that did not—or what are sometimes referred
to as the "oriental" Orthodox churches, including those of Egypt, Syria,
Armenia, Eritrea, and Ethiopia.[2] And then, of course, the Great Schism
of 1054 drove a wedge between Eastern Orthodox Christians and their
Western, Latin counterparts.[3]

The newly founded German Empire of 1871 holds particular significance
for reflection on Christian unity. Not only did this new Empire harbor
divisions between Protestants and Catholics within its borders, but along

with Switzerland and the Austro-Hungarian Empire, it became after the Vatican Council a staging ground for the stand-off between *Old* Catholics, who dissented from the Council, and *Roman* Catholics, who accepted the Council's outcome.[4] Understanding the dynamics of these rifts is essential for understanding the *Kulturkampf,* the harassment of Germany's sizable Catholic population in the 1870s by the predominantly Protestant state.[5] Many statesmen in the Empire, Otto von Bismarck not least, saw officially recognizing Old Catholicism—sometimes spoken of in the early 1870s as "the Döllinger movement"—as a way of splitting the ranks of the Catholic clergy and thereby blunting Rome's influence in Germany.[6]

With respect to church unity, scholars often see the beginnings of the so-called "Ecumenical Movement" as a consequence of the famous Edinburgh Missionary Conference of 1910. This movement brought mainly Protestants together in common cause, albeit with considerable interest among some Orthodox Christians. Catholics largely stood on the sidelines of ecumenical discussions until the Second Vatican Council (1962–5) with its epochal Decree on Ecumenism (*Unitatis redintegratio*), which committed Rome "irrevocably" to the search for Christian unity.[7] In concentrating on the twentieth century as the formative period of modern ecumenism, however, scholars tend to relegate the nineteenth century to being mostly a "second confessional age," to quote again the title of an influential article by Olaf Blaschke.[8]

To be sure, the perduring influence of confessional divisions is apparent in the nineteenth century, but over-reliance on Blaschke's notion as an interpretative lens obscures what we might call the "pre-history" of ecumenism or *Wiedervereinigung* (reunion) to use the parlance of the time: efforts to reflect on and achieve Christian reunion *prior* to the modern Ecumenical Movement. This pre-history is in fact crucial for understanding not only the roots of twentieth-century ecumenism but religious history generally in the modern era.[9] The German Empire after 1871, again, holds particular interest, for it bore the wounds of divisions more saliently and with more historical consequences than more confessionally homogeneous nation-states such as, say, (Catholic) Spain or (Lutheran) Denmark. As mentioned previously, Döllinger felt that since Germany was the site of sixteenth-century divisions, it possessed in his own time a special obligation to help mend them.

The outcome of the First Vatican Council, not surprisingly, dealt a blow to those who longed for reunion. Nonetheless, not only did the Council engender the Old Catholic movement, but it also inspired a peculiar form of anti-Roman, episcopal ecumenism. The Bonn Reunion Conferences of 1874 and 1875—spearheaded and orchestrated largely by Döllinger—are an especially arresting case in point. These meetings brought Anglicans, Eastern Orthodox, and Old Catholics (those non-Roman Christian bodies maintaining Apostolic Succession) together to the Rhineland university of Bonn to discuss prospects for church unity and reconciliation after what all parties regarded as the theological disaster of the recent Council. Largely forgotten today, such a gathering of Eastern and Western ecclesiastics and scholars had not taken place since the Council of Florence in the fifteenth century, the last council to attempt to mend the divisions of 1054.[10]

The Bonn conferences, their origins, Döllinger's role in them, and Rome's reaction to them will be treated in due course. In leading up to these topics, several important questions merit exploring beforehand. First, what became of Döllinger immediately after his excommunication, and how was *"l'affaire Döllinger"* reported, interpreted, and often sensationalized within Germany and internationally? Second, how did the German Old Catholic movement develop and what was the new Empire's relation to it? Third, was Döllinger an "Old Catholic" or not?—a question that has divided Roman Catholics and Old Catholics until the present.[11] Finally, how did the repercussions of the Vatican Council affect the search for Christian unity in Europe after 1870? This last question, as we shall see, bears directly on Döllinger's own reflections on Christian unity in the 1870s and it helps us contextualize the Bonn Reunion Conferences. Attempting answers to these questions, in turn, will help us probe, in the book's conclusion, the broader significance of Döllinger and his conflicts with Rome within the intellectual and religious history of the nineteenth century.

L'AFFAIRE DÖLLINGER AT HOME AND ABROAD

According to the canon law of Döllinger's day, the Church possessed two forms of excommunication: minor and major. Judged by Archbishop Scherr as an unrepentant teacher of heresy, Döllinger received the latter, the harsher: *excommunicatio major*. This deprived him of the right to receive or administer sacraments, forbade him from exercising any ecclesiastical jurisdiction, prohibited intercession of the Church on his behalf, and denied him a church burial upon his death. It even enjoined fellow Catholics to shun him. The penalty did not, however, profess definitively to extend to the union of the soul with God, since that union was held to depend on the immediate effect of sanctifying grace and to be unaffected by an act of the Church.[12] Döllinger clung tenaciously to this stipulation and held to the conviction, after examining his conscience, that amid the tempest surrounding him he nonetheless remained in a state of grace.

But of course excommunication came as a bitter blow to the septuagenarian. It "stung Döllinger to the quick and wounded him in his inmost soul," recorded one of his confidantes, Louise von Kobell.[13] Toward the end of his life, Döllinger registered his bitterness in a letter to Scherr's successor, Archbishop Antonius von Steichele: "The way in which I was treated lacks any example in the history of the Church. It has never happened that an old man who, during the forty-five years that he was a public teacher, never incurred any blame or even a remonstrance from his bishop, and whose orthodoxy to that point had never been exposed even to a recorded suspicion, has been summarily... 'handed over to Satan.'"[14]

Both his excommunication in April and his earlier letter of defiance to Archbishop Scherr from March 28, 1871 captivated the religious and secular press in German-speaking lands and far beyond, making an already well-known Döllinger an intellectual celebrity with a "global reputation," as he himself put it in a letter to Lady Blennerhassett.[15] Not infrequently, commentators compared Döllinger to past critics of the Church such as John Wycliffe, Jan Hus, or especially Martin Luther.[16] Berlin's irreverent, satirical weekly *Kladderadatsch*, for example, depicted Luther happily greeting Döllinger from beyond the grave, bringing greetings from Hus as well.[17] But irrespective of one's attitude toward Döllinger's actions, practically all onlookers—journalists, scholars, clergy, and laity alike—were gripped by the seemingly momentous historical significance of the succession of events taking place in Munich in the spring and summer of 1871.

On April 12, 1871, for example, Berlin's *National-Zeitung* led with a front-page piece on "Dr. Döllinger of Munich." Referring to Döllinger as one of the true giants in the realm of scholarship, a man with "extraordinary powers of retention secured by an extraordinary capacity to work," the article commends him as the "Ajax against [Papal] Infallibility." "Flattery" and "all the tactics of temptation of the Jesuits" had failed to gain his submission to the Council, so now, the author predicted, Archbishop Scherr's efforts at ecclesiastical discipline, too, would come to naught. "At the present, Dr. Döllinger is identical with the great [Old Catholic] movement animated by opposition to Rome and Infallibility."[18]

The *Braunschweiger Volksfreund* similarly extolled Döllinger, astounded by the fact that Scherr had previously opposed Infallibility at the Council and now excommunicated the star theology professor in his diocese.[19] Meanwhile, the *Süddeutsches Telegraph* reported that Döllinger's declaration of March 28 had made clear the existence of two parties within the Church: one allied with the Pope and the Council and the other with Döllinger against the Council.[20] From Bremen, the *Norddeutsches Protestantenblatt* opined that all Protestants should recognize in Döllinger "flesh of our flesh, bone of our bone." A veteran fighter against an "ultramontanism that reduces conscience to obedience and spirit to darkness," the author opined, the Munich professor has now "burned his ships like Cortez."[21]

The *Rheinischer Merkur*, the organ of record for the budding Old Catholic movement, printed Döllinger's declaration *in toto* (as did many newspapers), commenting on it as follows: "Amid the sinful deluge of infallibilist sophistry, this declaration is an ineradicable sign for the truth, an enduring stumbling stone against the Jesuitical champions of the anti-Christly 'Kingdom of this World.'"[22] Subsequently, a writer for the *Merkur* labeled Döllinger's excommunication by Archbishop Scherr as "a gross act of ecclesiastical power."[23] Munich's satirical weekly *Punsch* criticized the Church by depicting in a cartoon Döllinger and Johann Friedrich being burned alive at the stake.[24]

In addition to the approbation of many newspapers, Döllinger received support from Catholics disenchanted with Rome in the form of letters of solidarity, often bearing many signatures. Some priests and laymen from the Rhineland, for instance, drafted and signed a letter to Döllinger, praising him for opposing "Roman novelties." Faced with excommunication, the signatories enjoined Döllinger to "be comforted. Truth does not allow itself to be chained or suppressed. From this higher tribunal . . . sooner or later your voice will be heard."[25] Similar pro-Döllinger, anti-ultramontane shows of support came from Nuremberg, Mannheim, Heidelberg, Bayreuth, and Freiburg im Breisgau, among other places.[26] A letter bearing multiple signatures from Freiburg is typical; it praised Döllinger for hanging on to the "inherited old faith" against the new "absolutism" of Rome.[27] Such supporters frequently formed the nuclei of future Old Catholic parishes.[28]

Praise for Döllinger was matched by criticism and vitriol from ultramontane quarters. An Austrian newspaper, for example, made approving reference to Pius IX's assessment of Döllinger as a "prideful" professor before concluding that Döllinger seemed to hold himself as high an authority as a general church council. "Poor Döllinger, how far has your pride led you from the path of truth."[29] Some newspapers of ultramontane persuasion fabricated letters from deceased heretics, putting in their mouth effusive praise for Döllinger's actions.[30]

Döllinger's old nemesis, Joseph Hergenröther of Würzburg, entered the fray once again, publishing a hastily written *Criticism of Döllinger's Declaration in March of 1871* shortly after the excommunication. "When a Catholic Christian makes such utterances [as Döllinger's]," Hergenröther contended, "he has already forsaken the Catholic standpoint. The Catholic is to believe all that the Church presents as a matter of faith, enjoining him to submit his private judgment to the Church's instruction [*sein Privaturtheil dem der lehrenden Kirche zu unterstellen*]. The theological virtue of faith is something supernatural, protected by Scripture and the Fathers, and not by inner convictions and research; it rests on authority, it is simple and obedient [*Einfalt und Gehorsam*]."[31] Even closer to home, the diaconate of Tegernsee released a statement, asserting that Döllinger got what he deserved because he had forfeited being a "priest of grace" (*Priester der Gnade*) to become a "priest of science" (*Priester der Wissenschaft*).[32] In Munich, a group of ultramontane priests on April 13 printed a protest against Döllinger's declaration and had it placed on shop windows throughout the city.[33]

As the welter of positive and critical opinions of Döllinger increased and intensified, Archbishop Scherr felt the need to make clear the septuagenarian's status within his diocese. He accomplished this by printing the excommunication brief in his regular *Pastoralblatt*, and by insisting in two pastoral missives that the acceptance of Infallibility did not create a conflict between one's duties to the Church and one's duties to the state, as Döllinger and his sympathizers argued, nor did it imperil the progress of Catholic scholarship.[34]

Döllinger's treatment divided the citizens of Munich. Already during the excommunication ordeal, churches in the city responded differently. Fervent prayers were offered for Döllinger at the Church of Our Lady (*Frauenkirche*), the Church of St. Francis, and the Abbey of St. Boniface, while harsh sermons thundered against him at the Jesuit Church of St. Michael and the City Church of St. Peter's.[35] The city priest and Döllinger's friend, Anton Westermayer, felt compelled to come out against Döllinger in an article in the *Allgemeine Zeitung*. Westermayer also initiated a statement of protest against Döllinger, which appeared on April 14, 1871, printed along with the bishops' earlier statement of submission to the Council. Several additional open letters by the city's clergy protesting against Döllinger appeared. At the same time, Döllinger enjoyed support from many quarters, particularly among city officials; in 1873 he was awarded honorary status (*Ehrenbürger*) as one of Munich's prized citizens.[36] His former students were often torn in their loyalties—between the Church and their beloved professor.

Döllinger's relationship to the royal house after his excommunication was a delicate matter. Waffling about Döllinger before Scherr acted, the young Ludwig II threw compliance with ecclesiastical authority to the wind after the fact and pled for Döllinger to continue in his duties as the royal chaplain. Döllinger politely declined, recognizing this would only bring the Kingdom of Bavaria into a deeper conflict with the Church. Nonetheless, the king permitted Döllinger, who voluntarily desisted from sacerdotal functions, to retain his title "Stiftspropst" and the accompanying pension for the remainder of his life.[37]

Döllinger's status among the academic elite of Munich was yet another matter. He commanded enormous respect among the university's professoriate, which had a history of chaffing against ecclesiastical meddling. This respect manifested itself on July 29, 1871 when, receiving 54 of the 63 votes cast, Döllinger found himself elected to the annual office of rector of the university, the third and last time that he would serve in this prestigious role.[38] And this was no ordinary year, but the university's 400th anniversary. The snub against Rome intended by the vote was aptly captured by a cartoon in the satirical newspaper, *Kladderadatsch*, in which a jack-in-the-box labeled "Döllinger" smacks an image of the tiara-wearing Pius IX on the nose.[39] In his rector's address, striking a nationalist note, Döllinger proclaimed that Rome's decision in favor of Papal Infallibility was in effect "a declaration of war" against "the German spirit, German scholarship."[40] What is more, Döllinger's friends, Lord Acton and Prime Minister Gladstone, were awarded honorary doctorates from the University of Munich, in significant part because of their utterances against the Council. Finally, in 1873 Döllinger was elected as President of the Bavarian Academy of Science, joining in this office, which he occupied for the remainder of his life, the ranks of the renowned philosopher Friedrich Schelling and the chemist Justus von Liebig.[41] While Döllinger might arguably have deserved all of these recognitions, they none-too-subtly also served as pointedly anti-Roman statements.

The university's theologians who had submitted to the Council at first were at a loss, not knowing exactly how to comport themselves after Döllinger and Friedrich were excommunicated. In July 1871, pressure on them was ratcheted up and they released a public statement. Making clear in it their "pain" and recognizing the "highly consequential events" taking place in their midst, they voiced strong disapproval of Döllinger's declaration of March 28, adding their hope that, somehow, "the agitation against the Vatican and its decrees will promote regeneration in the Church."[42] Within the theological faculty, an agreement was reached whereby Döllinger would cease offering lectures in ecclesiastical history (as seminarians were already banned from attending them) and give them instead simply on "the history of modern times." As a provisional measure, his colleague Isidor Silbernagl gave lectures in church history before these were taken over by Alois Knöpfler (1847–1921), who officially succeeded Döllinger upon his death in 1890.[43] Legally, however, Döllinger remained a member of the university for the remainder of his life.

Döllinger's excommunication was far more than an affair of Munich or even an affair of the German Empire. It was truly an international event, inviting opinion and commentary from numerous countries across Europe and across the Atlantic.

In France, voices on the far sides of the religio-political spectrum either praised or lamented Döllinger's treatment at the hands of his bishop. Long pilloried in Louis Veuillot's *L'Univers*, Döllinger got what he deserved according to this paper and others of ultramontane conviction. But numerous individuals sympathized with him or fretted about his situation. Montalembert's daughter, Cathérine de Montalembert, for instance, wrote a long, plaintive letter to Döllinger shortly after his excommunication, pleading for her father's friend to examine his soul and submit: "the act of submission would delight the divine heart, would comfort the whole Church, and would make you as great in character and virtue as you are in scholarship and in other work" (*grand par le caractère de la vertu que par la science et le travail*).[44] But irrespective of one's position, French *cognoscenti* followed events in Munich with fascination. One priest expressed more than a grain of truth when he exaggerated that "by the light of burning Paris [a reference to the Communard take-over of the city in 1871] men were still watching every move of the combat going on between the archbishop of Munich and Dr. Döllinger."[45]

In Italy, a variety of views on events taking place in Munich were expressed.[46] Around the time of his excommunication, Döllinger received in the mail an address of solidarity by faculty members of the University of Rome—an act that enraged Pius IX.[47] Thanking Döllinger for awakening the "moral conscience" of all Catholics, the address continued: "we hail your utterances with great hope, and offer our best wishes for the triumph of your cause, which is also ours, and that of the whole Christian civilization."[48] Similar shows of support came from the Society of Teachers (*Società degl'insegnanti*) and the Society for National Emancipation (*Società nazionale emancipatrice*), both seated in Naples. The president of the latter wrote a letter, praising Döllinger for encouraging "Christian conscience" and "radical reform" of a Church deemed badly degenerated.[49] What is more, liberal and anticlerical newspapers such as *La Nazione*, *La Libertà*, and *Il Diritto* covered affairs in Munich in some depth, praising Döllinger for his stand against Rome and associating his personal conflicts with a broader, Europe-wide struggle for freedom of conscience and knowledge against the dead hand of traditional authority.[50] Many liberals felt that the church schism portended by Döllinger's protest was the logical consequence of the Council's foolhardy embrace of Infallibility. In a cartoon from Turin's satirical *Il Fischietto*, for example, an egg labeled "Infallibility" gives birth to a multi-headed monster called "schism," one of the heads of which is labeled "the protest of Döllinger"[51] (Figure 4.1).

By contrast, Vatican loyalists in Italy blasted Döllinger for perfidy, pride, and apostasy. The ultramontane *L'Unità Cattolica*, for example, expressed indignation at what it regarded as the emerging "Döllinger church" (*la chiesa döllingeriana*) in Germany.[52] In its pages, Döllinger was branded a "heretic" biding time in this life for damnation in the next. Viewing him as the chief opponent of the Holy See, the editors opined that "it would have been better for him if he had never learned his alphabet."[53] Similarly, the strongly Roman *La Voce della Verità* weighed in against the "Döllinger movement" (*il movimento döllingeriana*), comparing the Munich professor to Martin Luther with the difference that Luther had led an actual rebellion from Wittenberg while Döllinger only presided over a pathetic comedy of dissent in Munich. Admitting the Munich professor's high scholarly credentials, the paper nonetheless contended that he had tragically abused them by his "proud and malicious opposition" to Rome.[54] Not surprisingly, *La Civiltà Cattolica* expressed indignation at Döllinger and welcomed news of his excommunication. Branding him the chief (*capo principale*) of liberal Catholic opposition to the Council and the Pope, the *Civiltà* charged him with the sin of pride (*superbia*) and with fomenting schism and sectarianism. In keeping with

Figure 4.1. A cartoon of church schism as a consequence of Papal Infallibility, indicating "the protest of Döllinger."

Source: Mario, *Il Fischietto* (May 18, 1871): 541. Image courtesy of the Harvard Widener Library.

their past criticisms of Döllinger, the editors argued that he had pitted "German science" (*scienza tedesca*)—or what they even labeled "Döllinger's science" (*scienza döllingeriana*)—against church authority, and therefore justifiably had gotten what he deserved.[55] The fact that Döllinger's stand coincided with the establishment of German nationhood, it bears mentioning, only aggravated ultramontane disquiet about German scholarship. On April 29, 1871, *Il Fischietto* aptly captured this reality in a caricature depicting an allegorized "Germania" allied with Döllinger and other Anti-Infallibilist theologians (*teologi fallibilisti*) against the denunciations of Rome.[56]

Reactions in the English-speaking world, and not least in the United States, suggest the extensive reach of interest in the Döllinger affair. Predictably negative views of Döllinger and concomitant approvals of his excommunication emanated from ultramontane sources such as the *Tablet*, which toed a line against Döllinger similar to that of Westminster's Archbishop Manning. Acutely aware of the relative novelty of their emancipation in Britain, British Catholics worried that Döllinger's stand against Rome would only revive and reinforce long-standing ridicule of "popery" by British Protestants. Such an outlook received expression by a writer in the *Dublin Review*: "He [Döllinger] who has spent a life in attacking the Reformation is hailed in his old age as a second Luther. His enormous and astonishing learning is now used as a quarry, out of which ignoble hands hew stones to cast at the religious principles in which he [as a Catholic] still believes."[57] Another writer charged that Döllinger in cahoots with kindred "theological windbags of Munich" had fashioned an "envenomed lie" against the Council's decrees.[58] From such perspectives, Döllinger's excommunication appeared simply as warranted comeuppance; and those who followed him—"Döllingerites" as Bishop Ullathorne of Birmingham branded them—did so at their peril.[59]

But not all English Catholics felt this way. Catholics wary of Rome, Lord Acton foremost, were downright outraged by the assault against Döllinger.[60] Others, such as John Henry Newman, expressed their displeasure at Döllinger's treatment with circumspection. Although Newman refused to follow Döllinger in his opposition to the Council, the future Cardinal nonetheless grieved at how the Church had dealt with Döllinger. "[M]y heart goes along with Dr. Döllinger with extreme sympathy in this cruel trial," Newman wrote Alfred Plummer. "Nay more, I will say I can hardly restrain my indignation at the reckless hardheartedness with which he and so many others have been treated by those who have been their true brethren, and of whom the least that can be said is that they know not what they do."[61] In the midst of his "cruel trial," Newman in fact had written Döllinger: "I hope I am not wrong to intrude upon you just now, when you have so overpowering an anxiety upon you. At least, in doing so, I am able to assure you that you are continually in my thoughts and my prayers. I am sure you must have many hearts, feeling and praying for you and astonished that so true a servant and son of the Catholic Church should be so tried."[62]

From the pens of British Protestants and liberals, Döllinger's letter of protest and excommunication were regarded as tell-tale events, exposing the Catholic Church as a fortress of reaction in need of reformation. Two British universities in fact—Oxford and Edinburgh, acting roughly concurrently with the Protestant German University of Marburg—conferred on Döllinger honorary degrees in the wake of his excommunication.[63] Learned Anglicans uniformly stood with Döllinger, sharing to various degrees sentiments expressed to Döllinger by the theologian Alfred Plummer: "A fight with Hydra [Rome] is not ended in a day. But you [Döllinger] are not alone. The hopes of many thousands, who you will never know in this world are centered in you."[64] A reviewer of an English translation of one of Döllinger's books gushed in *The Christian Observer*: "Like the Coriolanus of Shakespeare, he [Döllinger] stands out in simple majesty, a giant among pigmies, a hero among cravens."[65]

In a lengthy, front-page article, "The Excommunication of Dr. Döllinger," of April 26, 1871, Britain's *Guardian* weighed in on events in Munich: "Let Dr. Döllinger console himself. A dogma [Infallibility] which issues in such absurdity, pitting light for darkness and darkness for light, must go the way of all error. It is impossible that it can find a home in the bosom of the church, and Dr. Döllinger's brave attitude is already bearing fruit." Exactly what the future held, the author admitted, was unclear, but "it is certain that his excommunication has opened up questions which all the skill of the Vatican will find it hard to close."[66]

Across the Atlantic, with the exception of ultramontane venues, American journals and newspapers tended to cheer on Döllinger's defiance and rue his disciplining, while interpreting the broader revolt against Rome in Germany as a world-historical event.[67] Theological nuance was often sacrificed in efforts to interpret Döllinger as a Luther redivivus ready to chart a new course of religious reform. "[W]e consider, admire you as the second Martin Luther," wrote a group of American evangelicals from Chicago to Döllinger.[68] In July 1871 *Harper's Weekly* printed a cartoon by the famous caricaturist Thomas Nast titled "The Luther of the Nineteenth Century," depicting Döllinger, hammer in hand, reminiscent of the iconic depictions of Martin Luther, ready to smite a wall engraved with lines from the Council's *Pastor aeternus*, under which appeared the Jesuits' emblem, IHS (Figure 4.2).[69]

In a similar key, the notable American theologian John Nevin, writing in the *Mercersburg Review*, praised "the sage of Munich" for his courageous stand, elaborating that

[t]he memorable Letter of Dr. Döllinger to the Archbishop of Munich...is of special historical interest as related to the latest effort for the reformation of the Catholic Church. No man has stood higher heretofore in the confidence and admiration of his own communion; as indeed no one has been more of an ornament and credit to it in the eyes of the Christian world. His venerable age, his vast historical learning, his exemplary Christian piety, his high position, all have contributed to make his Letter an object of universal attention. Its words have gone forth to the ends of the earth, and though very calm and quiet in themselves, have fallen upon the ears of men, like thunder.... [T]his Letter of Döllinger is more than an ordinary spoken or written word; it is a grand dramatic deed, like Martin Luther's nailing of his theses on the church door in Wittenberg.

"He is a very different man [than Luther]," Nevin qualified, "but it is quite possible...that this act of his, in the years hereafter, may be looked back upon as of no less world-historical meaning than the Wittenberg act itself."[70]

From a comparable point of view, the *New York Herald* followed the controversy unfolding in Munich.[71] Esteeming Döllinger as "the greatest living historian of the Church," the *Herald* opined in April 1871 that "the menacing terms of his letter [to Scherr] bear a striking resemblance to Martin

Figure 4.2. Döllinger depicted as a new "Martin Luther" attacking Papal Infallibility and the Jesuit order.

Source: Engraving by Thomas Nast, *Harper's Weekly* (July 5, 1871): 648. Image reproduced with permission from the Graphic Arts Collections, Department of Rare Books and Special Collections, Princeton University Library.

Luther's final missive to the Holy See.... The Jesuits, who hit upon the expedient of the doctrine of Infallibility in the interest of the preservation of the unity of the Church, must take care. Often he who sowed the wind reaped the storm."[72] Shortly after his excommunication, the *Herald* editorialized that "Döllinger may prove to be a more destructive Luther. Pius the Ninth is old, and Antonelli seems to have lost his wits."[73] "Dr. Döllinger was, before and during the Council," the *Herald* went on several days later, "the soul of the anti-infallibilist party.... [He] is the one man who has stood out, and for conscience sake [sic] braved all the consequences. Loving the Catholic Church dearly, and believing that the unity of Christianity was still possible under the Catholic banner, he fought and still fights against what he considers an innovation, a wrong, a folly."[74]

The *New York Herald* was not alone. Its nearby competitor, the *New York Times*, also followed events in Munich, rooting openly for Döllinger—or at least the newspaper's interpretation of what Döllinger stood for—even if inattentive to the finer points of canon law. "The most erudite of the contemporary theologians of the Roman Catholic Church," one article set forth, "has, thus, after fifty years of single-minded devotion to its service, been formally committed to everlasting perdition because he refused to sacrifice either his intellect or his conscience to the bidding of some hundreds of Italian priests. A few triumphs like this would shatter the foundations of the Papacy more irretrievably than a new Reformation."[75]

The international magnitude of the Döllinger affair is perhaps best registered by the fact that even lower-tier American newspapers followed it closely. The *Trenton State Gazette*, for example, sized up the historical significance of events unfolding in Munich as follows: "The voice of protest, and of reform, as during the sixteenth century, again comes from Germany. Dr. Döllinger, the greatest living Catholic theologian and scholar, has assumed an attitude of open hostility to the Pope on the question of Papal Infallibility.... Dr. Döllinger is over seventy years old, but he has plenty of vitality, and will probably live to fight this out. The contest once inaugurated, its results may be far-reaching and tremendous."[76] The *Hartford Daily Courant* weighed in, speculating that "there can be schism [after Döllinger's protest]; and it may be that the German nation is now going to complete for itself the work that Luther began."[77] The *New Hampshire Sentinel*, moreover, expressed its shock about the excommunication of the man "generally regarded as the ablest and most learned Catholic divine in Europe—of tried wisdom and venerable age."[78] Finally, on America's West Coast, the *San Francisco Bulletin* noted that "the attitude assumed by Dr. Döllinger ... in denying the Infallibility dogma promulgated at the Ecumenical Council, is attracting [attention] ... throughout Europe and the Catholic world. In Germany it is thought it will result in schism."[79]

OLD CATHOLICISM, DÖLLINGER, AND GERMAN NATIONHOOD

Döllinger's excommunication and the emergence of the German Old Catholic Church coincided with the establishment and early phases of the *Kaiserreich*, the second German Empire (1871–1918). Unlike more confessionally homogeneous nations, the new Empire embraced *within* its borders sixteenth-century divisions between Protestants and Catholics. The former, typified by Chancellor Otto von Bismarck, dominated the ranks of (Prussian) political leadership, leading some to speak of a "Protestant Empire"; the latter, a large minority comprising one-third of the Empire's population, were concentrated in the Rhineland, Silesia, and, Bavaria.[80] From the start, the co-mingling of confessions was fraught with difficulties, misunderstandings, and quickly led to conflict in the well-known *Kulturkampf* of the mid-1870s. Not surprisingly, statesmen within Germany and far beyond kept a keen eye on events taking place in Munich in 1871. At the hour of Germany's rendezvous with history, many wondered whether the Catholic Church was witnessing, once again, a new schism: was Munich in fact becoming a new "Wittenberg"?

What follows is a sketch of the birth and infancy of the Old Catholic Church in Germany. What was Berlin's reaction to it? Rome's? And, front and center, what was Döllinger's relationship to the Old Catholic movement? The last question remains a delicate one, even today. Old Catholics have traditionally regarded Döllinger as a founding father, as *the* figure who more than any other inspired the movement and gave it theological legitimacy.[81] By contrast, some Roman Catholics, particularly since the Second Vatican Council, have argued that in the final analysis Döllinger remained within the Catholic fold. Enduring a questionable excommunication, he stood firm, quietly sowed seeds for future reform, never becoming a (schismatic) "Old Catholic."[82] Both sides make valid points, and I freely draw from each. But I am persuaded that Döllinger's relationship to Old Catholicism can only be described as exquisitely ambivalent. Without his impetus and intellectual authority, the German Old Catholic movement is hard to imagine. But Döllinger quickly came to stand aloof from it and criticize its direction. Insofar as he might be considered the founder of a religious movement, rarely has history witnessed a more reluctant one and one whose legacy has been more contested.

Yet Döllinger profoundly shared—and in large part was responsible for—one of the Old Catholic movement's core principles: the importance of reconciliation among divided Christians or Christian reunion (*Wiedervereinigung*). Additionally, he felt that his historical erudition could be helpfully enlisted in this crucial task—a task at once more pressing and more difficult after the Vatican Council and founding of the confessionally divided Empire.

While Munich stood out as a key center of post-conciliar Catholic dissent from Rome, opposition manifested itself elsewhere as well and almost always in connection with centers of higher learning. Sociologically speaking, German Old Catholicism was a child of the *Bildungsbürgertum*, the educated middle class, since lower classes tended to follow the lead of their bishops or remained indifferent to theological squabbles altogether.[83] As we have seen, Bonn and Breslau were strongholds of opposition. In the former, Franz Heinrich Reusch, Franz Peter Knoodt, Joseph Langen, and Bernhard Joseph Hilgers provided energy and leadership; in the latter, direction came from Johann Baptist Baltzer, Theodor Weber, and Joseph Hubert Reinkens. Braunsberg was another site of resistance, the movement there guided by Friedrich Michelis and Andreas Menzel. In addition to Germany, the movement gained traction in Switzerland, especially in Bern and Lucerne, where Eduard Herzog would provided leadership, and in the Austro-Hungarian Empire, not least in Prague, where the lay canonist Johann Friedrich von Schulte (once described as "Prague's Döllinger") led the charge, becoming among other things the first to chronicle the Old Catholic movement.[84]

But in late 1870 and 1871, all eyes focused on Munich, and not just those of churchmen and journalists, as we have seen, but those of politicians and diplomats as well. As C. B. Moss has written, "[T]he principal centre of interest was Munich. All Europe, even in the midst of the Franco-German War and the siege of Paris, was watching Döllinger."[85] On March 31, 1871, the Austrian ambassador in Munich, Karl Ludwig von Bruch, for instance, reported back to Vienna that the situation between Döllinger and Archbishop Scherr had reached a boiling point. "Since the author of this declaration [Döllinger] is of such eminence and has a large following in Catholic circles, not least among those who are inclined to take on the name 'Old Catholics', one should very much fear a schism."[86] On April 8, 1871, the liberal Bavarian ambassador in Florence, Wilhelm von Dönniges, praised Döllinger's actions as "historically great" and conveyed to Munich that the situation with Döllinger and his supporters was the talk of the town among the educated classes.[87] Furthermore, the Bavarian ambassador in Rome, Carl von Tauffkirchen-Guttenberg, who was in frequent contact with Cardinal Antonelli, repeatedly sent communiqués to Otto von Bismarck updating him on what he called "the agitation stirred by Döllinger" (*Döllingersche Agitation*) or the "Döllinger movement" (*Döllingersche Bewegung*).[88] On August 11, 1871, Tauffkirchen reported to Bismarck that in the eyes of the Roman Curia the "Old Catholics" (*Altkatholiken*) or "German Catholics" (*deutsche Katholiken*) were regarded simply as a sect, despite their claim to the mantle "Catholic," and that Döllinger was generally the one blamed in Rome for precipitating the movement.[89]

Meanwhile, in Munich, Döllinger found himself responding to and attempting to canalize powerful currents of anti-Roman hostility. With the exception of his colleagues in the theological faculty who had submitted to the

Vatican decrees, practically all other university professors supported Döllinger. And support did not stop there. On April 10 a large meeting of laymen—lawyers, school teachers, public officials—took place in Munich's Museum; this resulted in a petition, receiving eventually 12,000 signatures, to the king to use the prerogatives of the state against the "new doctrine" of Infallibility and to forbid its teaching in schools and universities. "We fear for the liberty of our conscience, for the peace of our families and of our country," the petition read. The archbishop's office responded quickly: the Sunday following the presentation of this address, a pastoral letter was read in the churches of Munich announcing that all who had taken part in the so-called "Museum Address" were *ipso facto* excommunicated.[90] This signified a new phase: a more widespead defection from Rome.

The Museum meeting preceded another, anxious conclave of German bishops, who met at Eichstätt on May 7–9, 1871 and issued two pastoral letters. In these, they reiterated their allegiance to the Council, sought to define Infallibility circumspectly, and warned against a new "state-churchism" (*Staatskirchentum*) as well as against the dangers of "German science" (*deutsche Wissenschaft*).[91] Concerning the last item, the bishops' second letter set forth (almost certainly with Döllinger in mind) that "[t]his scientific movement, which separates itself from the authority of the church and believes only in its own Infallibility, is incompatible with Catholic faith. It is a separation [*Abfall*] from the true spirit of the church."[92] Coming on the heels of these letters, Pius IX, never one to mince his words, raised the stakes in two allocutions in the early summer of 1871. In these, he blasted "liberal" Catholics dissenting from the Vatican decrees as a more deadly enemy than the French Revolution, more despicable than the Communists, "those fiends let loose from hell," who had recently set fire to Paris and lethally shot Archbishop Georges Darboy.[93]

In this agitated atmosphere, Döllinger with others convened a closed meeting of like-minded dissenters over three days, May 28–30, 1871, to discuss the situation and the road ahead. Those who met set in motion plans for a future, larger meeting in Munich in September.[94] They also drafted the so-called Munich Pentecost Declaration, sometimes regarded as the founding document of German Old Catholicism. Published in the *Rheinischer Merkur* and the *Allgemeine Zeitung*, the document concluded with thirty-one signatures—Döllinger's coming first followed by those of many future Old Catholic stalwarts such as Schulte, Reinkens, Friedrich, and Knoodt. (To their surprise, the names of Lord Acton and Sir Rowland Blennerhasset [the husband of Lady Blennerhasset] were added without their knowledge.) Its drafters sought to make a clear stand against Rome for promoting the "notorious" new teaching, contending that never in the history of the Church had the faithful been harassed for refusing to accept a "novelty" (*Neuerung*). "Who will show us the church as it was in antiquity?" the drafters plaintively asked, citing a question made famous by Bernard of Clairvaux.[95]

The Pentecost Declaration took particular aim at the German bishops. It charged them with interpreting the Council in a manner "that contradicts the clear wording of [its] Decrees," of threatening dissenters with the refusal of sacraments and excommunication, and of causing a general "perplexity of conscience" (*Verwirrung der Gewissen*) among the faithful. The declaration also set forth that the new dogma on Infallibility upset the equilibrium of Church and state, and it appealed to the latter to forbid its teaching and to protect the rights for churches that rejected it. Finally, the declaration sought, against all odds, to strike a note of hope and unity, proposing that the present unhappy circumstances might provoke "reform" in the Church that would lead to "reunion [with] separated Christian brethren."[96]

The declaration was largely Döllinger's handiwork. In the *Allgemeine Zeitung*, it even appeared under the headline: "The Declaration of Döllinger and his Associates."[97] At the same time, Döllinger had made clear at the meeting his reservations about forming a separate communion and his desire *not* to pronounce on questions of worship and sacraments. His intention was aptly captured in an earlier letter that he had written to his English friend and translator, Henry Nutcombe Oxenham: "Our position in the Church is quite plain. We abide by the old teaching, reject the innovation, discard the unfree Vatican Council, but make no separation and will not permit our right and property to be infringed.... We continue to receive the sacraments from the servants of the Church regardless of whether they are infallibilists or not. If a priest or bishop should require us to subscribe to a new dogma, we refuse."[98]

But the situation was rapidly moving beyond Döllinger's control. Matters came to a head quickly and precisely over the questions of sacraments. On June 30, Franz Xaver Zenger, an esteemed professor of law at the University of Munich, passed away. He had been an early supporter of Döllinger and a signatory to a protest of the Council. On his deathbed, Zenger requested that a Franciscan friar and longtime friend be summoned to administer the Last Rites. He and his family received the unwelcome response that Zenger's protest of the Vatican decrees, if unrepented of, disqualified him from receiving the sacraments and also from having a Catholic burial. An appeal was made to the archbishop, but Scherr remained intransigent. Deeming the situation an emergency, Döllinger's colleague and fellow excommunicated priest, Johann Friedrich, stepped into the breach and administered the Last Rights, procuring the holy oil and sacraments from the Anti-Infallibilist priest Joseph Renftle of nearby Mehring.[99] This act, which took place on June 25, 1871, represents the first instance of an excommunicated, "Old Catholic" priest performing sacerdotal functions.[100]

The denial of sacraments to a respected professor at the university created a commotion in Munich and its environs. Another petition soon circulated, receiving 18,000 signatures, calling for a revision of Church–state laws and for the usage of a church, with its furnishings and revenues, in which Old Catholics (the term was now in regular circulation) might practice their faith without accepting the Vatican decrees and its priests might officiate at recognized marriages. The petition coincided with the funeral of Professor Zenger, whose burial rites were also administered by Friedrich. Thousands of guests or curious onlookers participated in the funeral, including numerous government officials and practically all professors outfitted in full academic regalia, including Döllinger.[101] In effect, the funeral served as a large-scale public protest against Rome and the archbishop.[102] "The incidents in connection with the death of Professor Zenger," an outside observer noted, "produced the most intense excitement, and stimulated the movement [against Rome] in all parts of Bavaria."[103]

Zenger's death lingered in memory when the first Old Catholic Congress convened in Munich on September 22–24, 1871.[104] This congress had been proposed at the Pentecost meeting, out of which a "central committee" had formed.[105] Leadership of the congress fell not to Döllinger but to Schulte of Prague, who served as its chairman, and to Bernhard Windscheid of Heidelberg and Augustin Keller of Aarau in Switzerland, where a strong Anti-Infallibilist movement existed.[106] Three hundred delegates attended, coming mainly from Germany, the Austro-Hungarian Empire, and Switzerland. But sympathetic guests came from France, Spain, Brazil, and Ireland, in addition to participants from the Church of England, the American Episcopal Church, the Greek Orthodox Church, and the Dutch Church of Utrecht, later to be called the Old Catholic Church of the Netherlands (*Oud-Katholieke Kerke van Nederland*).[107] Several Anglican bishops sent letters of solidarity, assuring those gathered of their brotherly feeling and opposition to the Vatican decrees, and giving strong signs of future cooperation. In addition to the closed sessions attended only by the delegates, several open sessions witnessed as many as 8,000 lay participants. A movement was expanding.[108]

Döllinger actively participated in the congress, consenting to, even inspiring, much in the final report. But he also voiced reservations. These arose over the question of the formation of parishes (*Gemeindebildung*) and the setting up of a separate ecclesiastical jurisdiction. With others, chairman Schulte—whom some playfully called "unser Bismarck"—called attention to the spiritual difficulties and practical problems dissenting Catholics faced without recourse to parish life and the availability of the sacraments. Where would these "Old" Catholics go to baptize their children, receive communion, be married, receive the Last Rites and a proper Catholic burial? In short, Schulte contended, the severity of the situation necessitated the setting up of "regular pastoral care" (*regelmäßige Seelsorge*) and a "regular episcopal jurisdiction" (*regelmäßige bischöfliche Jurisdiktion*) for the care and consolation of those

Catholics who conscientiously felt that Rome had led them astray at the recent Council.[109]

Döllinger agreed that the situation was dire; those at the congress found themselves in an "emergency situation" (*Notstand*) as he and many others put it. He also recognized that according to canon law, not to mention simple love of neighbor, priests were duty-bound to administer the sacraments and provide other priestly services in truly extreme circumstances. But extrapolating what consequences followed from their present situation had limitations, for in Döllinger's eyes all emergency measures must be carried out *within* the Catholic Church, and one must avoid pitting "parish against parish, altar against altar" (*Gemeinde gegen Gemeinde, Altar gegen Altar*) as he, referencing a maxim of Augustine's, formulated the potential danger.[110]

During the congress, Döllinger gave two notable speeches, forcefully making the case for conceiving of the situation as a genuine emergency, but against erecting a separate ecclesiastical apparatus, as many others desired. Above all, Döllinger wanted to keep the movement—somehow—*within* the Catholic Church. In his own words:

> At present we are within the Church like good seeds, [like] the salt that prevents rot [*Fäulnis*] and which looks to the future in hope.... In this light, the principle applies: when it comes to a reform of the Church, it must take place within the Church. *Reformatio fiat intra ecclesiam* has always been the mantra of all enlightened men of the Church. From this correct insight [it merits noting] that once one steps out of the Church and finds oneself *extra ecclesiam*, then one can no longer exercise action and influence on the Church one left behind.[111]

Always keen to draw historical analogies, Döllinger looked to the past for instruction and settled on two examples. He compared the Old Catholic movement to those priests under Arian bishops in antiquity; their duty and happy legacy was to hold fast to the non-Arian (Nicene) position until the heresy ran its course in the Church's hierarchy. By contrast, the Reformation of the sixteenth century presented a case where dissenters followed a path toward "complete separation" from the Church—a reality that had produced enduringly "negative consequences" and a "hostile relationship" between the divided confessions. For Döllinger, the Old Catholic movement should emulate the long-suffering, faithful non-Arians of the fourth century and eschew the example of the reformers of the sixteenth.[112] As he concluded his second address at the congress: "We must avoid any step that would justify opponents' charge that [our actions] lead necessarily to schism."[113]

Döllinger's opinion did not win the day. The majority at Munich, while holding Döllinger in high esteem, nonetheless felt that the realities of parish life and sacramental practice in their emergency situation (about which all were agreed) led inexorably to some alternative, mission church—a church in "inner exile," not categorically snubbing but certainly protesting the

Roman Catholic Church, and one also imbued with powerful ecumenical impulses.

Three days of meetings and discussions in Munich resulted in the drafting of a report that gave expression to broadly-held resolutions. Mirroring much in the earlier Nuremberg and Pentecost Declarations, these resolutions repudiated the recent Vatican Council and the censures derived from them, and affirmed in their place the Tridentine creed of Pius IV.[114] They recognized "the primacy of the bishop of Rome as it was acknowledged... in the old undivided Christian Church," but deplored the centralization of this bishop's authority at the expense of others'.[115] The fourth and fifth resolutions called, respectively, for greater education of the clergy and loyalty to civil governments affected adversely by the "Syllabus of Errors." A subsequent resolution called for a blanket expulsion of the Jesuits while yet another demanded the right of Old Catholics to a share in the properties of the Church—something which Rome and the hierarchy vehemently forbade. The report struck an ecumenical note, calling for reunion with Eastern churches and greater rapprochement with Anglicans and other Protestants. Quite significantly, it also declared that the accusation of "Jansenism" against the Church of Utrecht was baseless and that the Munich Congress had "no dogmatic differences" with this Church.[116] The overture to the Church of Utrecht—a small communion that nonetheless possessed a line of consecrated bishops that had run afoul of Rome in the early eighteenth century—is quite important, for from this line of bishops the first German Old Catholic Bishop, J. H. Reinkens of Breslau, was ordained.[117]

In sum, the Munich Congress accomplished much, even if it found itself in a rather impossible situation, which the Old Catholic historian C. B. Moss has aptly summed up: "The purpose of the congress was not to form a schism, but to provide for the spiritual needs of those who had been excommunicated for refusing to submit to the Vatican Council. As it turned out, this was impossible without forming a schism. But the Old Catholics did not leave the Roman Communion of their own free will. They were expelled, and it was necessary, if they were to continue to live as Catholic Christians, to form an organization."[118] The sense of being involuntarily and unjustly expelled, not exiting of their own accord, has powerfully shaped the ecclesiology of Old Catholics—then and now.[119]

The movement continued to take shape in late 1871 and early 1872 in Cologne. A particularly noteworthy flashpoint came on March 20, 1872, when J. H. Reinkens gave a speech, "Conscience and the Vatican," justifying the movement's dissent from Rome. At root, the future Old Catholic bishop believed, it was a simple question of conscience. The date "18 July 1870" had vitiated "the old apostolic church order" and it was the duty of the truly faithful, he felt, to bear witness against Rome. "[T]he war we wage," he proclaimed, "is the war of conscience against compulsion in matters of religion." A faithful conscience required "the solid pillars of truth and justice," he recognized, but "[i]f the hierarchy itself breaks these pillars...then the consequence is that our conscience no longer serves as the foundation of authority, and then authority itself sinks into the ground."[120]

To restore a semblance of authority, the Second Old Catholic Congress, which took place at Cologne on September 20–22, 1872, sought to flesh out matters of church governance and ecumenical outreach to other Christian bodies. This time the tag "Old Catholic" was officially adopted for the program. (The wording has only been applied retroactively to the earlier Munich Congress.) Döllinger participated in this congress, even if its direction often proceeded against his counsel.[121] Outside interest had grown since the Munich Congress; this meeting was truly an international sensation, generating widespread news coverage in numerous countries as well as vituperative attacks in the ultramontane press. The Old Catholic movement itself had also grown, with numerous Old Catholic societies (*Vereine*) cropping up in areas where anti-Roman sentiment prevailed. Altogether, 350 delegates participated in the Cologne Congress, mostly coming from German-speaking lands. Significantly, the Archbishop of the Church of Utrecht, Henricus Loos, showed up with four of his priests. Three bishops from the Church of England—including the famously erudite Bishop Christopher Wordsworth of Lincoln—attended and twenty-two Anglican priests. The Orthodox priest Johannes Janyschev, Rector of the Theological Academy in St. Petersburg, also came along with General Alexander Kiréeff from Russia. Numerous supportive Protestants also attended.[122]

Following the precedent set at Munich, both open and closed sessions were held. Desirous not to use language indicating a separation from the Catholic Church, the Cologne Congress nonetheless settled on a few reforms for the church organism in embryo. These included the use of the vernacular in the liturgy, the abolition of mass offerings and other fees for services and devotions (*Stolgebühren*), the abrogation of indulgences, and the curtailing of excesses in the veneration of saints. It was also agreed that parishes might be organized and priests appointed, and that marriages be solemnized. But the truly momentous leap came when a committee was formed to secure a bishop to provide leadership and direction to the fledgling movement.[123]

J. F. Schulte chaired this committee and its work lasted throughout the remainder of 1872 and well into 1873. Several prospective individuals were considered for the high office, including Bishop Strossmeyer of Croatia, who at this point still had not submitted to the Vatican decrees.[124] Döllinger was also briefly considered, but he declined. Significantly, though, and an apparent breach with some of his earlier statements, he expressed the opinion that the office of a "mission bishop" might be countenanced as part of an emergency measure, for it would give the Old Catholic movement a "vital center" and check the more extreme tendencies in its ranks.[125]

And what if Döllinger had accepted the post? One contemporary at least speculated on this weighty counterfactual: "[H]ad Döllinger, with his immense reputation as a scholar, as a divine and as a man, allowed himself to be consecrated bishop of the Old Catholic Church, it is impossible to say how wide the schism would have been."[126]

Not until June 4, 1873 was the selection committee prepared to hold an official election. This occurred at St. Pantaleon's Church in Cologne. As indicated earlier, Professor Reinkens received the most votes among the candidates, and he agreed, if somewhat reluctantly, to serve in the new office.[127] The news was declared to a waiting crowd shortly thereafter. A *Te Deum* was sung and bells rung, and much weeping ensued according to eyewitnesses. It was "a most inspiring moment, such as the Church has not seen since Apostolic times," according to Schulte's recollection.[128] Earlier it had been decided that the consecration of the bishop would come from the Church of Utrecht, but as things turned out Bishop Loos died on the day of Reinkens's election—an event that many ultramontanes regarded as the rightful judgment of God. This left the Church of Utrecht with a single bishop, Herman Heykamp, Bishop of Deventer.[129] A delegation of German Old Catholics soon paid him a visit in Rotterdam and they settled on the month of August for the consecration. In the Church of St. Lawrence and St. Mary Magdalene in Rotterdam, on August 11, 1873, therefore, the Bishop of Deventer consecrated J. H. Reinkens as the first Old Catholic Bishop of Germany.[130]

From Munich, Döllinger took stock of this and other developments with some unease, but he did not mount a loud public protest. Indeed, he appeared to have one foot in the Old Catholic movement and one foot out. This, in fact, had caused more than a little friction in his relationship with Acton as is evident from their correspondence in the early 1870s. While not relinquishing his misgivings about the Vatican Council, Acton nonetheless viewed the Old Catholic movement as fundamentally schismatic and he questioned Döllinger about his involvement in it.[131] In his response, Döllinger recognized the validity of Acton's concerns, but told him that although he would rather withdraw from the public eye to scholarly solitude, his status as a professor, member of the Academy, and, not least, public official (*Reichsrath*) did not permit him the luxury of disengagement. But he also made clear to Acton his desire that the movement stay within the Church: "In order that the false teaching [Infallibility] not master the church and so that it can later be ejected, there must be some people who, repeatedly and loudly, reject and dispute [the teaching], but who *do not separate themselves from the Church*."[132] Such sentiments partially allayed Acton's concerns, even as he continued to view the Old Catholic movement and Döllinger's proximity to it with misgivings.[133]

By sharp contrast, many outside observers waxed positively jubilant about the emergence of Old Catholicism on the Continent. More than a few Eastern

Orthodox Christians recognized in it their own esteem of ancient tradition and criticism of the papacy in the movement.[134] German Protestants, too, expressed varying degrees of affection and solidarity. The Halle theologian Willibald Beyschlag, for instance, observed that in Old Catholicism Protestants should see "spirit of our spirit; in contrast to Roman Catholicism, here is an evangelical Catholicism [*evangelischer Katholicismus*] that merits our cooperation and our brotherly love."[135] Similarly, the American Reformed theologian John Nevin divined "immense meaning" and "true world-historical importance" in the Old Catholic movement. Germany, he elaborated, is "now destined, even more than in the 16th century, to lead the way in any great spiritual revolution having to do with the religion and civilization of the Christian world."[136]

Anglicans were arguably the most smitten by the movement. Members of the Anglo-Continental Society—and especially its founder and secretary, Frederick Meyrick (1827–1906), a frequent correspondent with Döllinger—perceived in the movement a tradition-minded, ecumenical ethos of the sort that they sought to cultivate.[137] John Newenham Hoare, rector of an Anglican parish in Killiskey, Ireland, expressing a more pervasive sentiment, observed that "it may be that Old Catholicism is attracting towards itself much that is great and noble in the Church of Christ" and it is therefore poised to help all Christians "reach that highest end of Christian development, the union of the now divided Christians."[138] Similarly, Bishop Wordsworth of Lincoln hailed the movement as "a great and holy cause."[139]

As Old Catholicism garnered praise in various quarters, its legal status within the German Empire was being decided. Although political developments earlier in the century had brought an end to the long-standing configurations of the Peace of Westphalia (1648), vestiges of its confessional approach to the legal status of religion persisted. In the Bismarckian Empire, this meant that most decisions about religion were ceded to the individual states, each of which had an established territorial church (*Landeskirche*), Protestant or Catholic. As indicated already, the *Kulturkampf* was heating up concurrently with the formation of the Old Catholic Church. On June 29, 1873, Schulte addressed a letter to the government of Prussia, requesting that Old Catholics enjoy full legal status as other Catholics.[140] Some Prussian statesmen felt that recognizing Old Catholicism as an official religion would help win over its adherents to the government's cause and split the ranks of the Catholic clergy. This strategy was explicitly recommended by the Prussian emissary in Munich, Georg von Werthern. "I have ... been of the opinion," he wrote to Berlin, "that the split of the church caused by the Old Catholics could be of inestimable value in [our] conflict with Rome," and for that reason the movement "would be worthy of government support.... They are our natural allies ... [and] could become even more useful to us because they dispute the [Roman Church's] hierarchy on their own turf."[141]

In Döllinger's Bavaria, no legal distinction was made between Roman and Old Catholicism, and therefore the movement sputtered in the place of its genesis, although Old Catholics gained the right not to have their tithes sent to Rome.[142] According to Minister Lutz, the Bavarian Concordat of 1817 only made provision for eight bishops and, therefore, the government could not recognize the legitimacy of Bishop Reinkens, who would bring the total to nine.[143] By contrast, the governments of Prussia, Baden, and Hesse moved quickly to confer legal recognition on Old Catholicism. Shortly after Reinkens's consecration, the Prussian government recognized its legitimacy and set aside for Reinkens 48,000 marks per annum for administrative expenses.[144] What is more, Old Catholics established a share of control over the University of Bonn's theological faculty. Finally, coming on the heels of the Prussian Anti-Catholic "May Laws," which had launched the *Kulturkampf*, a series of "Old Catholic" laws in 1874 and 1875 granted the movement a firmer legal footing. The most far-reaching example came in July 1875 when the Prussian Diet—at the instigation of the Old Catholic lawmaker Wilhelm Petri—passed measures that allocated more financial support and use of church properties to Old Catholics throughout Prussia.[145] This show of state support led one critic to opine, "The Old Catholics have found their Constantine at a very suspiciously early period in their religious development."[146]

Even with legal recognition and financial support, the Old Catholic movement never took off as the "new reformation" that some envisioned it to be nor did it split the clergy in the way government prosecutors of the *Kulturkampf* desired. At its height in the 1880s, Old Catholics in the entire German Empire reached numbers only of about 70,000 with 122 parishes, and they have maintained low numbers until the present.[147] The fact that Old Catholics received state support and tended to identify politically more with the National Union and National Liberal Party than with the (Roman) Catholic Center Party alienated them from more rank-and-file Catholics, restricting the movement to a "niche market" within the professoriate and educated middle class.[148] As Ronald J. Ross has concluded, "Although the Old Catholic Law[s] resolved the immediate question of finances, liturgical property, and church buildings, ... it did little or nothing to expand the influence or to increase the number of Old Catholic communities.... [Old Catholics were] too small to effectively challenge Rome and its followers."[149] What is more, after the ebbing of the *Kulturkampf*, the government lost considerable interest, not wanting to further antagonize Roman Catholics in the Empire. By the 1880s, as Willibald Beyschlag has written, "[t]he Old Catholics did not fit into an administrative mold which was made for only two confessions; the administration feared ... the Roman Catholic majority of the population, desiring as far as possible to please them."[150]

Old Catholics' paucity of numbers did nothing, however, to temper ultramontane and Roman hostility to them. Catholics loyal to Rome were urged to boycott Old Catholic shops and businesses and to regard their worship services as acts of desecration and sacrilege. They were denied burials in consecrated ground; their funeral processions were sometimes met with angry, mocking crowds, hooting and jeering. The Munich Congress and the Cologne Congress along with subsequent ones were regularly castigated as *faux* Church councils and the movement as a whole derided as a "schism" or "sect" seduced and nourished by the protection offered to it by governments. According to one German ultramontane, Old Catholics represented only a pitiable community of "statesmen and professors"; they were "men of German scholarship who esteem their academic arrogance more highly than they esteem the pope and the bishops."[151]

Lest any Catholic be tempted to judge differently, Pius IX weighed in with an encyclical, *Etsi multa* (November 21, 1873), shortly after the consecration of Reinkens and as the movement had begun to gain official recognition. Labeling Reinkens a "pseudo-bishop" and his followers the "sons of perdition," the encyclical set forth: "[T]he Prussian and other governments support those recent heretics who call themselves Old Catholics. Their abuse of such a name would be simply ridiculous if it were not for the fact that so many monstrous errors of this sect [*errores monstrosi istius sectae*] against the principal teachings of the Catholic faith, so many sacrileges in divine service and the administration of the sacraments, so many grave scandals, and so much ruin of souls redeemed by the blood of Christ did not force tears to Our eyes."[152]

Where, finally, did Döllinger stand vis-à-vis Old Catholicism? As Peter Neuner has perceptively noted, this question is too complicated to be answered by a simple for or against. Those who regard Döllinger as an Old Catholic can point to his fierce criticism of the Vatican decrees, to his unparalleled intellectual authority in the movement's early stages, to his involvement in Old Catholic congresses at Munich and Cologne, to his silence with respect to the consecration of an Old Catholic bishop, and (as we shall soon see) to his heavy involvement in ecumenical activities growing out of resolutions from Old Catholic congresses. Conversely, those who see him as a faithful, if excommunicated, Catholic can point to the fact that he never regularly attended Old Catholic services, that in accordance with his excommunication he did not administer or receive the sacraments, that he fiercely contested some developments within Old Catholicism, such as the decision in the late 1870s not to require the celibacy of priests, and that in his correspondence he appears to have attributed schismatic tendencies to the Old Catholic movement.[153] In short, then, the evidence about Döllinger's stance toward Old Catholicism is mixed.[154] Critics might regard this as unseemly vacillation, a dereliction of intellectual leadership, while admirers might see it as a valiant, if finally unfeasible, effort to carve out a nuanced position in a milieu rife with polarizing, difficult choices.

CHRISTIAN UNITY AND THE BONN REUNION
CONFERENCES OF 1874 AND 1875

From the time of its inception until the present, German Old Catholicism has brimmed with ecumenical impulses, conceptualizing its identity as a "bridge church" (*Brückenkirche*), an ecclesial body, repristinating the ancient faith, conceived for the purpose of restoring Christian unity in the modern era.[155] Paradoxically, this sentiment has coexisted with powerful anti-Roman sensibilities. If Rome had burned its bridges to other Christian communities after the Council in 1870, Old Catholics reasoned it was their duty to keep hopes of church reunion alive.[156]

In significant measure, Döllinger was responsible for these impulses and he followed up on their practical implications after his excommunication, working especially closely with Anglican and Eastern Orthodox Christians. As we have already seen, in his 1861 lectures on the Papal States and in his 1863 address on the state of Catholic theology, Döllinger emphasized the importance of Christian unity. Through "Janus," he contended that "the dearest hope that no Christian can banish from his heart... [is] the future reunion of divided churches, of the East and of the West."[157] What is more, in the Nuremberg Declaration of August 26, 1870, he made reference to the desire for "peaceful harmony" (*friedliches Einvernehmen*) between Catholics and those with differing convictions. And in the Pentecost Declaration of May 1871, he equated "the highest goal of Christian development" with "continually increasing the coming together [*Vereinigung*] among those Christians currently divided from one another."[158] Finally, several months after his excommunication, he expressed the hope to Alfred Plummer that despite recent events preparation must be made for "a great reunification of divided Christians."[159]

Often Döllinger spoke of Christian unity in purely theological terms, but sometimes he saw it as linked with German political unification. "We have entered a new era in the religious history of Europe," he proclaimed in his rector's address in 1871: "[I]t is evident that the narrow polemical spirit since the Reformation must give way to one of compromise and reconciliation. The restored unity of Germany points imperatively to this; for until the religious disunion has been bridged, the new empire will remain an unfinished building."[160]

While in many respects Döllinger was prescient in his ecumenical sensibilities, these sentiments did not drop from the sky during his lifetime. But recognizing their roots has arguably become more difficult lately, for scholars of the nineteenth century, as mentioned earlier, have been inclined to interpret the period as a "second confessional age," a time of renewed rivalry and hostility within "Christendom," in which different religious groups hived off into closed if proximate "milieus."[161] While such a synoptic captures much that is true about the century, it also obscures much. Therefore, permit some back-tracking and a widening of the lens to put Döllinger's ecumenical aspirations and activities—particularly his lectures on reunion from 1872 and the Bonn conferences of 1874 and 1875—into broader historical perspective.

Permit for a moment, in fact, a brief return to the age of the Reformation. Amid the prejudices, persecutions, and polemical fireworks of the sixteenth century, we should at least recognize that the reality of disunity was widely recognized as a grave theological problem—a "monstrous scandal" to the Christian Gospel, as the humanist-reformer Phillip Melanchthon had written to Martin Bucer as Wittenberg widened its breach with Rome.[162] "We must count among the worst evils of our time," John Calvin wrote, "the fact that Churches are separated from one another to the extent that a human society scarcely exists among us."[163] One of Döllinger's heroes, Erasmus, penned before he died *On Restoring Concord to the Church* (1533).

Pockets of irenicism and regret over disunity dot the intellectual landscape of the otherwise "confessionalized" religious landscape of the seventeenth and eighteenth centuries.[164] One of the notable irenic humanists of the confessional age, the Lutheran theologian Georg Calixtus (1586–1656) of the University of Helmstedt worked indefatigably to promote a vision of church unity based on the Apostles' Creed and the writings of the Church Fathers. His phrase, *consensus quinque saecularis* or "the unity of the first five centuries," was appropriated by Döllinger and later ecumenists eager to shore up consensus around a shared patristic heritage.[165] The philosophers Hugo Grotius (1583–1645) and G. W. Leibniz (1646–1716), if more in a political than a religious register, put forth grandiose plans advocating the spiritual unity of all Europe, a new *corpus Christianum* that would overcome the divisions of 1054 and 1517.[166] Striking a very different note, the Moravian Pietist Count Nikolaus Ludwig von Zinzendorf (1700–60) contended that joint service, mutual prayer, and communities dedicated to piety and worship constituted the true tools to bring down the walls that divided Christians, among whom he included (at least potentially) Roman Catholics.[167] While firmly believing in the superiority of Gallican Catholicism, Bishop Bossuet of France advocated the reunion of all churches, sympathized with Protestant concerns, and went to great lengths to distinguish between firm Catholic teaching and mere opinion, with an eye toward lowering the barrier for Protestants to return to Rome.[168] Additional examples could be offered, but, in short, the period from the "wars of religion" to the French Revolution was not bereft of notable irenic and reunionist currents.[169]

The nineteenth century, of course, ushered in new concerns and endeavors toward unity. The French Revolution and its widely perceived "godless" excesses in the 1790s stimulated ecumenical—or proto-ecumenical—thinking in a new direction, as confessional partisans often perceived a greater common enemy in the Revolution's dechristianizing elements. In a ham-fisted political key, one can see this in the so-called Holy Alliance of 1815, one of a series of alliances tied to the Congress of Vienna and the Restoration that sought to stanch any recrudescence of the spirit of 1789. Signed by (Orthodox) Tsar Alexander I of Russia, (Catholic) Francis I of Austria, and (Protestant) Friedrich Wilhelm III of Prussia, the Alliance sought to uphold general Christian principles of statecraft and thereby provide a united religious front against the revolutionary tide.[170] As revolution once again roiled Europe in 1848, it is revealing that Döllinger wrote King Maximilian II of Bavaria from the German parliament at Frankfurt, explaining that "the position of Catholics and Protestant to one another has in recent times been fundamentally altered. Both churches have now a great enemy in the anarchic-republican party."[171]

Among Catholics, besides Döllinger himself, his colleague Johann Adam Möhler, and particularly his *Unity of the Church, or the Principle of Catholicism*, merits mention as an impetus to reunion; this book left a strong impression on Döllinger.[172] In France, the church reformer and frequent correspondent of Döllinger, Eugène Michaud, stands out as another proto-ecumenical voice. In 1872, Michaud published *Program for the Reform of the Western Church*, which stimulated questions about Christian unity by calling for the West to drink more deeply from the wells of Eastern Orthodox theology.[173] Like Döllinger, Michaud regretted the outcome of the Council in 1870.

Among the Eastern Orthodox, the nineteenth century witnessed a number of important ecumenical overtures. The Society of the Friends of Religious Instruction, seated in St. Petersburg, took great interest in Western Christianity, following the Old Catholic movement closely and sending delegates to the Bonn Reunion Conferences. Although some of his schemes for reunion seem outlandish, the theologian Vladimir Solovyov (1853–1900) made mending "the broken unity" of Christendom a central pillar of his theology, expressing his ideas in a number of significant works. Throughout the nineteenth century, as Georges Florovsky has demonstrated, points of contact took place between Orthodoxy and the West heretofore unimaginable.[174]

Turning briefly to Britain's religious landscape, whether Anglican or "Nonconformist," pioneers of the ecumenical movement and advocates of pan-denominational cooperation are fairly well known. Organizations that nourished these developments included but were not limited to the Church of England's Society for Promoting Christian Knowledge (1698); the Church Missionary Society (1799), the YMCA (1845) and the YWCA (1855), the Evangelical Alliance (1846), and the Association for the Promotion of the Unity of Christendom (1857).

And all of this makes no mention of the Tractarian or Oxford Movement, which had the effect of moving the Church of England at once closer to Rome and the East through a renewed preoccupation with the early Church Councils and Fathers. This was the express goal of the aforementioned Anglo-Continental Society (1853), led by Frederick Meyrick, a frequent correspondent of Döllinger from the 1870s. E. B. Pusey also typified the priority which the Oxford Movement gave to reunion.[175] Published in the summer of 1865 in response to some of Archbishop Manning's dismissive statements about Anglicanism, Pusey's *Eirenicon* (and its sequels) sought to show that both Anglican and Catholic dogma were actually much closer than supposed; most differences, Pusey held, had to do with "quasi-authoritative" practices, especially Marian devotions.[176] After reading Pusey's book as a young man, Döllinger wrote the Tractarian leader to express his strong agreement: "I am convinced by reading your Eirenicon [sic] that inwardly we are united in our religious convictions, although externally we belong to two separated Churches. There can be no fundamental difference of opinion between us."[177]

Other harbingers of ecumenism and influences on Döllinger could be adduced, but the above should suffice to demonstrate that Döllinger, although a pioneering ecumenist in some respects, developed his thoughts on the subject in a milieu in which concerns about Christian reunion were, if not dominant, certainly not scanty.[178] Any attempt to view the age strictly through the lenses of a renewed or enduring confessionalism must reckon with these countervailing theological currents.

Döllinger's most extensive reflections on Christian unity took the form of seven lectures given between January and March 1872 at the German Museum in Munich and titled straightforwardly "The Reunion of the Christian Churches." The lectures took place under the auspices of a public lecture series on "contemporary church issues" (*kirchliche Zeitfragen*) that representatives of the Old Catholic movement had planned after the Munich Congress in 1871. Initially, Breslau's Reinkens, who actually lodged with Döllinger from December 1871 to March 1872, was slated to serve as one of the speakers. But on account of Reinkens's illness, Döllinger ended up on the roster. Published later in 1872 under the title *Lectures on the Reunion of the Churches*, these lectures served as the quasi-official basis for the Bonn Reunion Conferences held in 1874 and 1875.[179]

Citing as a touchstone scriptural passage Christ's High-Priestly prayer for his disciples in the Gospel of John (chapter 17), "that they all may be one," Döllinger made clear in the first lecture that reunion among divided churches, myriad obstacles notwithstanding, remained a theological imperative and that the mission of the Church in the modern era was gravely compromised so long as divisions persisted. "One cannot deny," he wrote, "that there is something repulsive [*Abstoßendes*] in the present shape of the Christian world, with its sharply divided and hostile churches and sects, mutually hating and incriminating one another."[180] To dramatize his point, he called attention to the fact that in the Holy Lands, where "to the shame of the Christian name, Turkish soldiers have to interfere between rival parties of Christians, who would tear one another to pieces in the holy places, and the Pasha holds the key to the Holy Sepulchre."[181]

Since Döllinger had long possessed special concern for mending the Great Schism dating from 1054, papal centralization in the West intensified by the recent actions of Pius IX especially vexed him. "The great stumbling block and real hindrance to any understanding in the eyes of the Easterners," he opined, "is the papacy, in the form which it has assumed ... according to the ultramontane theory." In addition to differences over the papacy, Döllinger felt that most divisions between East and West were more historical and cultural in origin than theological. The big exception to this, though, was the clause in the Creed concerning the procession of the Holy Spirit—or the "filioque"—which Western Christians accepted, but Eastern ones vehemently rejected. This controversy bears emphasizing because it became one of the leading topics at the Bonn conferences, especially the second one in 1875. In his lectures, Döllinger sympathized with Orthodox concerns, and, overall, he evaluated Orthodox theology favorably, regarding it as "thoroughly patristic and traditional, keeping to the writings of the Fathers up to the seventh century, and practically closing with St. John of Damascus"—a figure whose theology possessed enduring relevance, Döllinger felt, for helping bridge the East and West.[182]

The church bodies descending from the Reformation presented more difficulties in Döllinger's eyes, although he treated Protestantism in 1872 far more favorably than in his previous writings. He sympathized with the German clergy of the sixteenth century faced with the corruptions of Rome and regretted that the general "perplexity of men's minds" at that time had left so many in central Europe "utterly helpless" to make sense of the ecclesiastical situation. Even so, the abrogation of Apostolic Succession by Continental reformers had dealt a severe blow to the possibility of reunion.[183] The ancient office of "bishop" and a continuous episcopacy, Döllinger regularly insisted, following the Church Father Cyprian, ought to serve as the basis of church unity and as a mechanism against schism and heresy.[184] Nonetheless, he maintained that the original impulses of the Reformation were commendably reformist, not separatist:

> It was only a reformation that was demanded; it had been desired and demanded for centuries before. The old dwelling-house [of the Church] was thought to require repairing and cleansing, but there was no intention of pulling it down and building a new one in its place. The idea of two rival churches in Germany existing in enduring hostility to one another shocked everyone. All diets and religious conferences of the day were held on the assumption that the adherents of the new and the old religion were still members of one universal Church and that a common understanding could and ought to be reached.[185]

In seventeenth-century figures such as Calixtus, Molanus, and Leibniz, the reformist, irenic currents of the Reformation gained a new voice, Döllinger contended, but they were not heard by Catholics due to the relentless attacks and obfuscations of the Jesuits, a religious order that he presented, not surprisingly, in wholly negative terms.[186] Once Jesuits gained dominance over Catholic higher education and became "confessors and directors of the conscience" at many European Catholic courts, hopes of even modest concili-ation were lost, according to Döllinger. An important exception during this period was France's Bishop Bossuet; he stood out as a genuine, if largely unheeded, beacon of light, able to disentangle authentic Catholic teaching from Rome's "repellent" actions. What is more, to Döllinger's strong approval, Bossuet, he argued, "put aside the question of Infallibility as a mere scholastic controversy having no relation to the faith."[187]

Döllinger positively assessed the Church of England, not least because in his estimation it had preserved the historic episcopate. Despite strong sentiments against "Popery," dating especially from the time of "Bloody Mary," and despite the pointedly Protestant nature of the Thirty-Nine Articles, signs of ecumenical possibility abounded in the Church of the *via media*, according to Döllinger. He was especially inspired by the "Oxford or Anglo-Catholic school," as he called it, and believed that Pusey's *Eirenicon* (1865), as previ-ously seen, presented a workable blueprint for reunion, even as he rued the fact that "the notorious decrees of the Vatican Council" had muddied the waters.[188] "In England," as he summed up, "the friends of union are numerous and daily increasing....The whole movement of the Oxford school...is essentially, and for the most part consciously, directed to union with the Western Catholic and Eastern Churches."[189]

As he sized up the broader theological landscape, Döllinger felt that three forces worked against greater union. The first were low-church Protestant communities, especially in the Anglo-American world, which continued to regard the papacy as the "Antichrist" and Catholics as minions of the devil. The second were theological liberals, of mostly German Protestant stock, who dismissed or else radically reconstrued ancient creedal beliefs. And, finally and not surprisingly, there were the recent Vatican decrees; wrought in his view by Jesuit intrigue and Curial power, they appeared to him designed "for the express purpose of making all plans of reunion forever impossible."[190]

Nevertheless, convinced that the practically impossible should not impede the theologically necessary, Döllinger felt that efforts of reunion should forge ahead, led in particular by those churches that had maintained the historic episcopacy. Irrespective of the actions of Rome, "the Western, Eastern and English churches"—those maintaining Apostolic Succession—constituted for him the basis for "the universal church" and they should work toward greater unity. "The body of the Church," he wrote, "one in origin has in course of time, through the sin of man and by Divine permission become divided into three great branches—outwardly separated, but inwardly united—which, when the right time arrives, will grow together again into one tree, over-shadowing the world with its foliage."[191]

Germany had a special role to play in Döllinger's vision. Germany's recent political unification in his view represented only a "half measure" in need of a comparable "ecclesiastical union."[192] He justified this conviction on the basis of self-critical, irenic trends within German Protestantism and also on his belief (inaccurate as things turned out) that most German Catholics, due to the historical character of German learning, would ultimately reject the legitimacy of Papal Infallibility.[193] Furthermore, Döllinger continued to believe that as the site of sixteenth-century divisions, Germany had a special calling to mend ecclesial fences. As he put it with more than a little grandiloquence and nationalist sentiment:

> [W]e [Germans] have suffered so unspeakably from this religious division, which pierces though the body of the nation like a sharp sword, and our weakness, dismemberment, and humiliation, stand in such close relation of cause and effect to the division of our churches, that the belief is always pressing itself on every German knowledgeable of the history of his country, that where the religious split and schism started, there the reconciliation must follow, and the division must lead to a higher and better unity. That would be the tragic expiation in the great drama of our history.[194]

But the primary purpose for church reunion, according to Döllinger, tran-scended national identity: unity allowed the Church, the Bride of Christ, to fulfill her mission of bearing witness to the transcendent truths of Christianity. Unbelief or what he called "Voltaireism" was spreading, Döllinger felt, and he regarded this as an understandable response to churches' interminable bicker-ing. If churches came together, bearing witness to "[an] unbroken continuity of . . . life and doctrine," Döllinger asked, "would she [the Church] not gain in strength and authority? Would not her testimony be weightier and her power of popular attraction increased?"[195]

The Council's "folly" on July 18, 1870, Döllinger reiterated in his final lecture, presented a seemingly insurmountable obstacle. But this did not stop him from closing on a practical note, suggesting some sort of international conclave, made up of clergymen and theologians from differing churches, starting in Germany, but then spreading to other countries. Such a gathering, Döllinger speculated,

> would soon draw others . . . in rapidly increasing numbers, by the magnetic power of a work so pure and pleasing to God, and [they] would thus be brought into communication with like-minded men in other countries. The basis of their consultations would be Holy Scripture, with the three ecumenical Creeds, interpreted by the still undivided Church of the early centuries. Thus an international society of the noblest and most beneficial kind would be formed, and what began as a snowball might well become an irresistible avalanche. There would be no lack of hostility to the work; but they [its critics] would fail to overthrow it.[196]

Döllinger intuited accurately on this last point. Ultramontane critics pounced on his lectures, the contents of which, due to the renown that excommunication had brought him, were transmitted and amplified far beyond Germany's borders.[197] But others—Old Catholics, the Orthodox, irenic Protestants, and, not least, Anglicans—glimpsed in Döllinger's words an inspiring ecumenical blueprint for the future. As Alfred Plummer wrote to Döllinger shortly after the lectures: "The hopes of many thousands, whom you will never know in this world are centred in you. Many a one who has . . . long yearned for reunion as for a never-to-be-realized dream, is now looking to Munich with something like hope."[198]

* * *

In the months following his lectures, the idea to hold some form of conference to seek out Christian unity gained traction. Döllinger floated the idea to the Anglican theologian Henry Parry Liddon while strolling in Munich's English Garden, proposing to him that the two evils of unbelief and "Vaticanism" (he felt the latter inflamed the former) should encourage well-meaning Christians to come together.[199] In a similar vein, Döllinger wrote Eugène Michaud, reporting to him about his lectures on reunion and opining that "it is my sure idea that God permitted the Council with its heresy as a means to prepare the Church for a reform and as a consequence of this reform a future reunion of divided churches."[200]

Enthralled by Döllinger's lectures, William Chauncy Langdon, the founding rector of the American Episcopal parish in Rome, showed great enthusiasm for a conference. In the summer of 1872, he visited Döllinger and later sent him a lengthy public letter on "the restoration of Christian unity." Döllinger's erudite vision of church history and the composition of the Old Catholic movement, Langdon contended, made the time ripe "to take a practical step, at least in the direction of reunion."

Many other Anglican divines agreed, as did some Continental Protestants and Orthodox Christians who had been following the Old Catholic movement. All eyes began to focus on the next Old Catholic Congress at Cologne. "Rarely in the history of the Church," Langdon opined, "has there been such a need of the wisdom from above . . . as may await a wise and godly issue of this conference [at Cologne]."[201] Bishop Wordsworth of Lincoln felt the need to attend, explaining to those in his diocese that the congress had meaning for "the whole of Christendom" and was nothing less than "the cause of God."[202]

As we have seen, the 1872 Congress at Cologne launched a commission to select an Old Catholic bishop. But another commission, a Commission for Church Union (*Unions-Kommission*), was also established at Cologne. Persuaded by the correctness of Döllinger's ecumenical longings, Reinkens, Reusch, and others felt that the fragile Old Catholic movement, on grounds of principle and necessity, must immediately make overtures of unity to other churches. Echoing many of Döllinger's sentiments, Reinkens gave a forceful speech on the project: one to promote gradual unity, not coerced uniformity, among churches and to do so "on the basis of the Holy Scripture and the Ecumenical Confessions of the early Church, expounded in accordance with the doctrine of the [ancient] undivided Church."[203] Shortly thereafter, on September 21, 1871, a resolution passed, formally establishing a commission and providing it with a mandate to network with others interested in unity, to examine reasons for past divisions, and to promote reconciliation through scholarly publications and other means. Döllinger was proposed as the commission's chairman and he accepted. Other members included Johann Friedrich, J. F. von Schulte, Josef Langen, F. H. Reusch, Friedrich Michelis, J. H. Reinkens, and Eugène Michaud.[204]

Two days later on September 23, members of the commission agreed on some core principles, namely that their task should have as its theological basis: (1) the divinity of Christ; (2) the fact that Christ established the Church; (3) the authority of Holy Scripture, the teachings of the early ecumenical councils, and the instruction of the Church Fathers of the early undivided Church; (4) the abiding significance of the Vincentian canon: *quod semper, quod ubique, quod ab omnibus creditum est*; and, finally, (5) the method of historical inquiry, which should be employed to separate fact from fiction in the history of the Church.[205] In these principles, it is not difficult to detect Döllinger's fingerprints.

From this commission, the idea to hold an actual "reunion conference" took shape between September 1872 and the summer of 1874. Often the process moved slowly, as Döllinger and others had many competing obligations. What is more, the commission did not always agree on what should take place or how to describe their endeavor. For example, Michelis wanted to pick up where two previous (failed) church councils dedicated to reunion—the Second Council of Lyon (1274) and the Council of Florence (1438–45)—had left off. Döllinger tamped down such grandiose zeal, insisting that they intended no "church council" but simply a gathering of recognized experts who possessed "longing and hope" to understand and work to bridge past divisions among Christians.[206] At the third Old Catholic Congress in Constance (1873), the project received additional impetus and organization.[207] Finally, by the summer of 1874 sufficient consensus had been achieved to take concrete action, even if Döllinger at this juncture began to act sometimes in unilateral fashion.[208] Drafted largely by Döllinger, the letter of invitation was sent out in July 1874 and made public; it set as a benchmark discussion of church reunion on the basis of the consensus of the early, undivided Church. Permit the letter to be quoted in its entirety:

> We are in a position to announce that on September 14 and the following days a conference will be held at Bonn on the Rhine made up of members of different

religious communities animated by the common desire to promote the cause of ecclesiastical concord and union.

The discussions will be conducted on the basis of what was taught and believed in the ancient church, and the common ground and authoritative guides will be sought in the doctrines and institutions of Christianity, both eastern and western, and in the formulas of faith, as they existed before the great disruption which separated the eastern church from her western sister and broke up the unity of Christendom.

The aim that will be kept in view is not be the absorptive union and complete fusion [*völlige Verschmelzung*] of existing churches, but only the bringing about of ecclesiastical intercommunion and religious fraternity [*Herstellung einer kirchlichen Gemeinschaft*] on the principle of "unitas in necessariis" side by side with the liberty of individual religious bodies or national churches in regard to those peculiarities of doctrine and constitution which do not touch the substance of the faith as it was professed and taught by the undivided church.

The Committee for the Promotion of Christian Union—Döllinger.[209]

The timing of the invitation was fortuitous, for not only had Oxford Movement divines such as Pusey stimulated ecumenical thinking in the Church of England, but in Russia, the liberal era of Tsar Alexander II (r. 1855–81) allowed for an openness toward the West that had not been the case in recent memory. Vexed by the so-called "Eastern Question" and Russia's encroaching interest in the Balkans, furthermore, public officials throughout Western Europe sensed important political implications of some sort of East–West religious rapprochement. Gladstone, for example, took a keen interest in the gathering and maintained regular correspondence with Döllinger before and after the conference.[210]

In fact, Gladstone, who had recently been voted from office, visited Döllinger in Munich just prior to the opening of the conference, which they discussed. During his visit, a noteworthy occurrence took place that Gladstone later recorded in a eulogy penned for Döllinger. As the two men were walking in Munich's English Garden they came

within sight of a tall and dignified ecclesiastic—a man of striking presence.... As we met, Dr. Döllinger had, as was not unusual with him in walking, his hat in his hands behind him. The dignified personage, on his side, lifted his hat high above his head, but fixed his eyes rigidly straight forward and gave no other sign of recognizing the excommunicated professor. "Who," I said to him, "is that dignified ecclesiastic?" "That," he [Döllinger] replied, "is the Archbishop of Munich, by whom I was excommunicated."[211]

Presumably Archbishop Scherr was none too pleased with the impending gathering at Bonn.

But for many others, such a conference was a theological dream come true. Frederick Meyrick of the Anglo-Continental Society, for instance, responded to the invitation with elation, writing Döllinger that such a gathering would be "the realisation, or rather the commencement of the realisation of a hope that I began to entertain 21 years ago.... I think that there can hardly be anyone in Christendom whose heart is more with yours in it [the search for Christian unity]."[212] "I cannot refrain from saying," wrote the American minister John Lias in a similar key, "how heartily I have long desired and prayed for such a movement for union as you [Döllinger] are now inaugurating."[213]

Bonn was selected as the site for the conference, due in large part to the influence of Franz Heinrich Reusch, who then served as the Rector of the University of Bonn and because the city on the Rhine, like Munich, had been a center of Old Catholic agitation. The meetings took place on September 14, 15, and 16, Tuesday through Thursday, in the music hall (*Musik-Saal*) of the university. Döllinger arrived in Bonn by train on the morning of the thirteenth, as the *Bonner Zeitung* reported, "to open on Tuesday the reunion proceedings among leading theologians from different Christian confessions. The wizened Nestor [*der greise Nestor*] of the Old-Catholic movement... was escorted to the home of Bishop Reinkens, whose guest he will be for the duration of the conference."[214]

Over fifty additional participants showed up, including a large delegation of Old Catholics led by the recently consecrated Bishop Reinkens. Greek and Russian Orthodox theologians and ecclesiastics attended, including Johannes Janyshev, confessor to the Tsar and Rector of the prestigious Ecclesiastical Academy in St. Petersburg, and Zikos Rossis, professor at Rhizarion Seminary and the University of Athens. Many Anglicans came, including Bishop Edward Harold Browne of Winchester, Henry Parry Liddon, Alfred Plummer, Dean John Saul Howson of Chester, and Edward S. Talbot, Warden of Keble College. The Anglican delegation was joined by a number of American Episcopalians, including Bishop John Kerfoot of Pittsburgh, William Chancey Langdon of Geneva, and Robert J. Nevin, Rector of the American Episcopal Church in Rome. In addition, several Lutheran and Reformed theologians came as invited expert guests and listeners. The invitees who could not attend often sent letters of encouragement and support.[215]

The august assembly conducted its business in English and German; proceedings were taken down in both languages.[216] Döllinger presided over the sessions as the unanimously agreed-upon moderator, setting a tone of high-minded irenicism and the scholarly search for truth, although not without some heavy-handedness.[217] Conspicuously missing of course were Roman Catholics, with the single exception of Henry Nutcombe Oxenham (1829–88), a former Tractarian priest who had converted to Catholicism in 1857, but harbored misgivings about the recent Vatican Council. (He translated Döllinger's lectures on 1872 reunion into English.)

The recorded proceedings of the sessions do not make for light reading. Detailed discussions of Greek and Latin terms; meticulous scriptural exegesis; and the delicate revisiting of key events and personalities in early Church history were the order of the day. Not surprisingly, given the fact that a major goal was to help mend the breach between the Greek and Latin churches, much time went into discussing the Nicene Creed and the question of the "double procession" of the Holy Spirit or the "filioque."[218] On this point (and others), Döllinger paid great deference to Orthodox sensibilities: "the greater share of the blame rests with the West."[219] The resolution on this issue, in fact, was one of the chief accomplishments of the gathering. "We agree," a joint declaration read,

> that the way in which the "filioque" was inserted into the Nicene Creed was illegal, and that, with a view to future peace and unity, it is much to be desired that the whole church should set itself seriously to consider whether the Creed could possibly be restored to its primitive form, without sacrifice of any true doctrine expressed in the present Western form.[220]

This represented, in fact, a compromise formula proposed by Bishop Brown of Winchester; he sought to appease both Döllinger and the Orthodox delegates, who were inclined to dispense with "filioque" altogether, but also to garner support among the Anglicans and (the Catholic) Oxenham, who admitted that the "filioque" clause lacked antiquity but nonetheless stood by its theological merit.[221]

But the Anglican delegation did not think with one mind; some harbored more reservations than others about the declaration. Shortly after the conference, Liddon wrote his mentor Pusey "that the 'filioque' caused a great deal of difficulty; and I thought at one time that we should never get through it.... As there is no possibility of the Roman Catholic Church ever doing this [removing the filioque], no harm was done." Thus Liddon, as Mark Chapman has wittily observed, "proved himself an early master of the ecumenical fudge."[222]

Besides the "filioque" issue, participants discussed fourteen other articles that had been drawn up prior to the conference principally by Döllinger, but in collaboration with Frederick Meyrick, Secretary of the Anglo-Continental Society. These articles touched upon topics such as the canonicity and uses of scriptural texts, the validity of employing the vernacular in liturgy, the role of faith and love in justification, the controversial nature of indulgences, the number of sacraments, the importance of both Scripture and early tradition, the questionable nature of the Immaculate Conception, the importance of public and private confession, the invocation of the saints, prayers for the dead, and the Real Presence in the Eucharist.[223]

In many areas, participants arrived at significant consensus. But not in all cases. Differences arose between the Anglicans and the rest over the precise number of sacraments. Participants agreed that the acceptance of seven sacraments was not firmly fixed until the twelfth century and therefore beyond their scope if the focus was to remain on the early Church. All acknowledged, however, that baptism and the Eucharist occupied positions of primacy.[224] Concerning prayers for the dead, the Orthodox representatives strongly endorsed this practice, citing the Seventh Ecumenical Council in their defense.[225] Anglicans and even a few Old Catholics tended to be wary, but nonetheless recognized its ancient sanction and consented with the Orthodox to the following article: "We agree that the commemoration of the faithful departed—i.e., a calling down of an outpouring of Christ's grace for them—has come down from the Primitive Church, and should be preserved in the church."[226]

The Immaculate Conception—a topic many would have preferred to avoid—proved a more contentious matter. Liddon expressed the view, held by no less an authority than Thomas Aquinas, that the belief could be entertained as a "pious opinion" (*sententia pia*) but not as a mandatory article of faith. Döllinger opposed Liddon on this point, insisting that this teaching, even as an opinion, had been a "fons et origo malorum" in church history, and that by making it a binding dogma without convening an ecumenical council, Pius IX in 1854 had paved the way, theologically, for the Vatican's decree on Papal Infallibility. "If the Pope without a Council, could make the Immaculate Conception an article of faith, he was already infallible," as Alfred Plummer later summarized Döllinger's position.[227] Bishop Kerfoot of Pittsburgh and Dean Howson agreed with Döllinger that the teaching had no clear sanction in early tradition. From the outset, Orthodox participants had made clear their skepticism of the teaching. Despite strong opposition to the belief, whether as opinion or doctrine, Liddon proposed an amendment to allow for those who held it as an opinion. But this did not carry the day as most participants subscribed to the original article: "We reject the new Roman doctrine of the Immaculate Conception of the Blessed Virgin Mary as being contrary to the tradition of the first thirteen centuries, according to which Christ alone was conceived without sin."[228] The lone Catholic, Oxenham, voiced his displeasure at how this matter was handled.[229] He did not return to the second conference in 1875.

Concerning the article on the Real Presence in the Eucharist, the Reverend John Hunt of London asked whether it meant that the Body and Blood of Christ were received in another sense in the Eucharist from that in which they were received in all other acts of worship. He was roundly condemned on this point, and most upheld that the Eucharist was both a representation and presentation (*Darstellung* and *Vergegenwärtigung* were the German words used), and that "while the character of the Eucharist [is] in reference to the sacrifice of Christ, it is also a sacred feast, wherein the faithful, receiving the Body and Blood of our Lord, have communion one with another."[230] During the discussion of this topic, Döllinger pointedly questioned the Roman

Catholic formulation of "transubstantiation," arguing that prior to the rise of scholastic theology in the West, the term *sacramentum* (mystery), whether applied to the Eucharist or other sacraments, had been an exquisitely vague and indefinite term.[231]

One final point of discussion should be noted: the question of the validity of Anglican Orders. This issue was not discussed extensively, but as it reared its head, it threatened to derail the whole enterprise by invalidating Anglican participation. Döllinger vigorously defended Anglican Orders—and hence the validity of Apostolic Succession in the Church of England. This was seconded by Bishop Reinkens, but a few other Old Catholics expressed reserve. The Orthodox delegates indicated that they lacked sufficient knowledge to make an informed decision, but would "rejoice if further research should lead to the establishment of the validity of Anglican orders."[232] Still, others expressed doubts. For the meantime, the issue was shelved, but, as we shall see, it contributed to the unraveling of the conference's goals in the near future.

The mood among participants at the completion of the first conference was hopeful. Bishop Kerfoot of Pittsburgh expressed delight at "the brotherly concurrence" felt among those gathered.[233] The Greek Orthodox theologian Zikos Rhossis indicated that the conferences demonstrated that the search for Christian unity was more than "a product of the imagination" but a realistic enterprise.[234] Formally, the first conference closed late in the afternoon of September 16. The proceedings indicate that everyone rose from their seats and together recited in Latin the *Te Deum* and *Paster noster*. The Old Catholic Bishop Reinkens offered a brief benediction: "*Benedicat nos omnipotens et misericors Deus Pater et Filius et Spiritus Sanctus. Amen.*" "The last solemn act of the Conference," Plummer recorded, "was some evidence that a bridge, frail possibly and far from secure, had really been thrown across the abyss."[235] Amid the goodbyes, a second conference was already in the works.

Extensive press reports carried in *The Guardian*, *The Times*, the *Allgemeine Zeitung*, and elsewhere—if not always sympathetic with the aims of the conference—suggested that an historically epochal meeting had taken place.[236] In point of fact, nothing quite like this had happened in modern times; while Bonn was no "council," not since the Council of Florence had such a gathering of eminent Eastern and Western Christians taken place.

Not surprisingly, esteem for the first Bonn conference in some quarters was met by disapproval in others. The ultramontane press howled at its implicit anti-Roman attitude, seeing in it little more than an example of erstwhile foes brought together in common animosity toward Rome.[237] Many liberals, who had delighted in Döllinger's bucking of Rome's authority in 1871, seemed more diffident about his efforts at constructive theological engagement.

After the completion of the final session, Döllinger himself expressed satisfaction, pleased with the level of consensus reached and by the fact that a spirit of good will had prevailed. He communicated this satisfaction to others in his correspondence. In at least one unfortunate instance, he did so in racialist terms, and this should be documented. Writing to Lady Blennerhassett of the "Germanic orthodoxy" that had been achieved at the conference, he praised "a northern national Catholicism" that had guided the conference, which "could easily go hand in hand with racial superiority over southern [Catholic] Europeans."[238]

Some Tractarian boosters of the Bonn conference thought that John Henry Newman might have a positive word to say about Döllinger's efforts. This was not the case. As Newman wrote Plummer: "I must say frankly that what the Papers lately tell me of him [Döllinger] has filled me with dismay, and I am prepared to hear anything, however dismal, of him. He is not an Anglican getting near to the truth [possibly a reference to Plummer], but a Catholic receding from it. It is not a yearning after unity which made him turn from Rome...to Bonn."[239]

For Anglicans like Plummer or Liddon, however, Bonn only heightened the infatuation that many of their co-religionists had for the Old Catholic movement and hopes for its possible convergence with their own theology. Expressing the sentiment of many, Liddon gushed in a preface to the conference's proceedings: "Is it irrational to hope that a body such as this [Old Catholicism], uniting all that is sincere in modern inquiry, with all that is deepest and most tender in ancient... [Christian] devotion, may yet hope to win the ear of Europe, and to bring succor to the intellectual and moral ailments of our modern world?"[240]

*   *   *

Between the first conference at Bonn and the second one in August 1875, several noteworthy developments took place. In Germany, the *Kulturkampf* reached a fevered pitch, seen especially in the anti-Catholic May Laws.[241] Laws granting legal status to Old Catholics, moreover, alongside this movement's posture toward Orthodox and Anglican Christians at Bonn were having the effect of alienating Old Catholics from other Catholics in Germany being persecuted by the state for their loyalty to Rome.[242] In Rome, Pius IX proclaimed 1875 to be a year of jubilee. In the letter announcing this, he deplored the "grave calamities" that had led to the suspension of the Council and warned the faithful against "the enormous crime of blasphemy which violates everything these days."[243] In an encyclical from February 5, 1875 to Catholics in Prussia, Pius warned the faithful not "to give to Caesar what belonged to God" and lamented "these new [May] laws [that] thoroughly overturn the divine establishment of the Church and totally destroy the rights of the bishops." In a passage alluding to Old Catholics, he "advise[d] the pious faithful not to approach the holy rites of such people nor to receive the sacraments from them. They should prudently abstain from any business dealings and association with them so that the bad leaven does not corrupt the undefiled lump of dough."[244]

Several months after the first Bonn conference, Gladstone, who remained in regular correspondence with Döllinger, dramatically entered into public controversy by publishing his famous pamphlet, *The Vatican Decrees in their Bearing on Civil Allegiance* (1874). Relying strongly on Döllinger's interpretation of the Council, Gladstone argued that the Vatican decrees had thrown a wrench into Church–state relations in Britain, which he felt had been improving for decades. The Pope's Infallibility, Gladstone contended, was now "binding on the conscience" of every Catholic and "his supremacy [elevated] without any reserve of civil rights." "I submit then, that . . . England is entitled to ask, and to know, in what way the obedience required by the Pope and the Council of the Vatican is to be reconciled with the integrity of civil allegiance?"[245]

The pamphlet elicited varied responses.[246] Germany's Chancellor Bismarck praised Gladstone in a letter: "It affords me deep and hopeful gratification to see two nations, which in Europe are the champions of liberty of conscience encountering the same foe, stand henceforth shoulder to shoulder in defending the highest interests of the human race."[247] Archbishop Manning possessed an entirely different opinion, which he published in the *Times* on November 7, 1874. Appealing to Catholic notions of natural law and the biblically sanctioned limits of "Caesar," Manning argued that the "civil allegiance of no man is unlimited, and therefore the civil allegiance of all men who believe in God, or are governed by conscience, is in that sense divided . . . . The civil allegiance of every Christian man in England is limited by conscience and the law of God and the civil allegiance of Catholics is limited neither less nor more." Manning went on to praise the religious tranquillity of Britain and contrasted it with what was taking place in Germany, taking a shot at Döllinger (and his influence on Gladstone) in the process:

> The public peace of the British Empire has been consolidated in the last half century by the elimination of religious conflicts and inequalities from our laws. The Empire of Germany might have been equally peaceful and stable if its statesmen had not been tempted in an evil hour to rake the old fires of religious disunion. The hand of one man, more than any other, threw this torch of discord into the German Empire. The history of Germany will record the name of Dr. Ignatius Von Döllinger as the author of this national evil. I lament not only to read the name but to trace the arguments of Dr. Von Döllinger in the pamphlet [of Gladstone's] before me.[248]

It was in the context of this loud public debate over the loyalties owed to God, country, conscience, and Church that John Henry Newman published his well-known treatise on conscience under the title *Letter to His Grace the Duke of Norfolk* (1874). Widely recognized as a classic of rhetoric, Newman's open letter to the duke, among the highest-ranking lay Catholics in Britain, sought out a *via media* between Gladstone and Manning.[249] The essay is also relevant to Döllinger's own wrestling with conscience, offering implicit support to Döllinger's defiance that would appear to contravene some of Newman's more explicit comments on Döllinger's situation. (More on this in the conclusion.) In the work, Newman recognized that conflicts between Church and state had been frequent in history and would persist. Like all Christian citizens, Catholics possessed a "divided allegiance": they should recognize both the things that are Caesar's and the things that are not. Papal Infallibility applied narrowly to explicit pronouncements on faith and morals, in Newman's judgment, and not to matters of discipline and rule as Manning held.[250] Catholics ought to listen to the Pope just as Anglicans should to their bishops, and church authority should be given the benefit of the doubt when matters remained unclear. But in the final analysis, Newman contended that Catholic teaching upheld the inviolable role of conscience, which he famously described as "the aboriginal vicar of Christ, a prophet in its information, a monarch in its peremptoriness, a priest in its blessings and anathemas." If an individual truly and honestly felt that conscience—the very "voice of God" inside one—compelled one to dissent from church authority, so be it. For Catholics, Newman believed that such a decision should be extremely rare, but not one that was altogether inadmissible: "Unless a man is able to say to himself, as in the Presence of God, that he must not, and dare not act upon the Papal injunction, he is bound to obey it, and would commit a great sin in disobeying it." Newman ended his essay with a rhetorical flourish: "Certainly, if I am obliged to bring religion into after dinner toasts ... I shall drink,—to the Pope if you please, still to Conscience first, and to the Pope afterwards."[251]

As this debate churned in the religious press across Europe, preparations for the second conference at Bonn got underway. An international preparatory committee comprising Döllinger (Germany), Kiréeff (Russia), Rhossis (Greece), Nevin (USA), and Meyrick (Great Britain) maintained a lively correspondence between the two conferences.[252] But as the date approached, all eyes turned to Döllinger, and many felt that something momentous was at hand. For both political and religious reasons, Gladstone was especially transfixed by the prospects of some form of Anglican–Orthodox–Old Catholic rapprochement, praising his friend's "arduous and hopeful work."[253] He and Döllinger even discussed the possibility of Gladstone attending or at least paying an "unofficial" visit to the second conference. In the end, the former Prime Minister decided against this, worrying that his presence would only politicize the conference and distract from its deeper theological goals.[254]

The second "Bonn Reunion Conference" opened on August 10, 1875 and lasted for six days.[255] Döllinger saw fit to issue a general invitation open to "every one of sufficient theological knowledge who is interested in the objects of the conference."[256] The stated objectives of the second conference were two-fold: (1) to arrive at a "common confession" based on "the sum of the articles of Faith fixed by the original undivided Church in its Confessions," and (2) to promote "intercommunion" and "mutual recognition" among church bodies that led neither to "amalgamation" (*Verschmelzung*) of churches nor to the "detriment... [of] the peculiarities of national Churches." "Ambiguous phrases" were to be eschewed in favor of "thorough investigation and discussion" with an eye toward establishing "such propositions as expressed, with simplicity and precision, the substance of Scriptural doctrine and patristic tradition and for that very reason are calculated to serve as a band and guarantee of the fellowship which has been attained."[257] In a letter to professors of theology at Constantinople, Döllinger waxed quite hopeful, proposing that their efforts might "lead to the re-establishment of ecclesiastical unity, as it once existed for more than twelve centuries."[258]

Despite the open invitation, a self-selected group responded, but the attendance was higher than at the first conference.[259] Bishop Reinkens again headed up the Old Catholic delegation, which included the usual suspects such as Reusch, Langen, and Knoodt, as well as Eduard Herzog, the first Old Catholic (or *christkatholische*) Bishop of Switzerland.[260] The Orthodox presence notably increased. Janyschew, Ossinin, and Kiréeff returned, along with others, from Russia. Alexander Lykurgos, Archbishop of Syra and Tenos in Greece, cut an especially striking figure, as did Genna-dios of Argesu and Melchisedek of Dunarei-de-jom, both bishops of Romania. The patriarch of Constantinople sent two archimandrites, Philothéos Anastasiadis and Sotiri Bryennios. One Western convert to Orthodoxy, the theologian Julian Joseph Overbeck, also showed up. Charles Waldegrave Sandford, the Anglican Bishop of Gibraltar, headed the Angli-can delegation this time, which included many American Episcopalians, but no American bishop.[261] In addition to Anglican, Orthodox, and Old Catholic representation, a number of Lutheran and Reformed divines and theologians were in attendance, although they rarely participated. Oxenham did not return, hence not a single *Roman* Catholic was present. Döllinger commanded the respect of all gathered. "There was not a question as to the presidency of the meeting," the American William Stevens Perry later recalled. "Every eye was turned to the venerable theologian [Döllinger] at whose summons we had met together, and for whose lightest word one waited in profound expectation."[262] An image in the British *Graphic* ably captured Döllinger's commanding presence (Figure 4.3).

At the conference, considerable progress was made, not least with respect to the "filioque" issue, which from the outset dominated the discussions. Most knew that this was coming. "The Filioque was to be the great question," Plummer recorded prior to the beginning of the conference.[263] Various

Figure 4.3. Döllinger presiding at the second Bonn Reunion Conference (1875).
Source: Artist unknown, *The Graphic* (August 28, 1875): 204.

Anglican bishops and theologians, not to mention Gladstone, had written Döllinger prior to the conference, offering their own, often long-winded theological reflections on the topic.[264] "This time," Döllinger himself wrote in a letter to Alexander Kiréeff of St. Petersburg, "the chief subject for deliberation will... be the dogma of the Procession of the Holy Spirit."[265]

While the first conference had resulted in recognition of the problematic insertion of the "filioque" phrase into the Western Creed, the second conference sought to supply the theological rationale for the original formulation while attempting to take Western theological concerns into consideration. Long hours were filled with (sometimes) testy conversations and the marshaling of formidable theological erudition on the matter. At the first conference, Döllinger indicated a willingness to drop the "filioque" altogether; at the second he pursued a tactic of attempting to convince both parties that the disagreement was more terminological than substantive. As a matter of both diplomacy and principle, however, he showed great deference to the Eastern position. The last Father of the undivided Church, John of Damascus (*c.*655—*c.*750), Döllinger felt, provided the authority and language that could help all parties make progress.[266]

Much debate centered on the meaning of the Latin verb "to proceed" (*procedere*) and its Greek equivalent (ἐκπορεύομαι) in the Creed. For the most part, the debate moved along productively. However, at one point, Overbeck nearly derailed it by insisting that the Anglicans and Orthodox needed prior agreement on whether there were six or seven recognized, ancient councils—a matter of considerable contention.[267] Various differences of opinion also manifested themselves among the British delegates and between them and their American counterparts.[268] Yet in the end, a fragile comity prevailed and consensus was achieved and summarized in four short articles:

1. We agree in accepting the ecumenical creeds and the decisions in matters of faith of the ancient undivided church.

2. We agree in acknowledging that the addition of the "filioque" to the creed did not take place in an ecclesiastically permissible manner [*nicht in kirchlich rechtmäßiger Weise*].

3. We give our unanimous assent to the presentation of the doctrine of the Holy Spirit as taught by the Fathers of the undivided Church.

4. We reject every representation and every form of expression in which is contained the acceptance of two principles, or beginnings, or causes, of the Trinity.[269]

A special committee drew up six explanatory articles in an effort to further appease both Westerners and Easterners. Referencing particularly John of Damascus's *De fide orthodoxa*, these articles sought to ensure a single procession of the Holy Spirit (from the Father), but the indispensability of the Son as the means and the locus, but not the agency, of that procession.[270] (One might fault the discussants for some things, but not for undervaluing theological nuance!)

By the final day, August 16, a general agreement had been hammered out. Döllinger closed the conference with a nearly five-hour extempore speech (!), in German and English, summarizing the results of both conferences, defending the legitimacy of Anglican orders, canvassing recent events in church history, expressing dismay at the Vatican Council's actions in 1869–70, and waxing eloquent about the theological imperative of church unity. Frederick Meyrick left a memorable description of Döllinger's speech:

> [A]t the end [of the conference] . . . he stood up as if he had been a man of thirty-eight instead of seventy-six, and delivered a speech of five hours' length on the disastrous effect that had been wrought on Western Christendom by the Papacy, passing in review one after another Germany, France, Spain, Italy. . . . [A]nd throughout the five hours he riveted by his voice and action the attention of everyone present, and retained their interest hour after hour.[271]

In the conference's final moments, Döllinger, gratified and exhausted, concluded: "I see still more clearly than before that in reference to dogma, there really is no contradiction between us. The contradiction which exists has arisen chiefly because two different terminologies have been framed, and the difference between them has been artificially intensified."[272]

At the conclusion of his speech, he was thanked by Archbishop Lykurgos, who, representing the Orthodox churches, expressed gratitude to Döllinger "for [his] marvelous efforts in the work of reuniting the severed Churches, of bringing together again the numerous divisions of the Rock of our Redeemer." Similarly, the Anglican Bishop Sandford of Gibraltar thanked Döllinger and praised the conference for achieving "real fruit": "We have witnessed the remarkable spectacle of theologians... endeavoring to the utmost of their power to remove misapprehension and to frame propositions which all might accept as expressing the orthodox faith of all Christendom."[273] Meyrick later summarized the moment as follows: "Thus then agreement was arrived at on this grave doctrine by Eastern and Western theologians for the first time since the Eastern Church, in the time of Photius [c.810–c.893], charged the Westerners with heresy for introducing the Filioque into the Creed."[274]

Following the precedent of the first conference, the Old Catholic Bishop Reinkens led the participants in a *Te Deum* and *Pater noster*, followed by a final benediction.

The results of the conference were a sensation. As one participant noted afterwards, "[T]he aims and results of the Conference... filled the press in England, from the 'Times' and the 'Westminster Review,' down to the most obscure journals of the day."[275] The same was true in other countries, with respect to both religious periodicals and the more popular press. Much was quite positive, but criticism came from expected quarters. Austria's ultramontane *Brixener Kirchenblatt*, for example, lambasted the "Döllinger three-church idea," the impossible coming together of Anglicans, Orthodox, and Old Catholics on the basis of fraternal affection alone without a governing church structure.[276]

But Döllinger received letters of thanks and encouragement from divines in many countries. Astoundingly, from Britain, an address was sent to Döllinger that previously had been circulated, receiving the signatures of 4,170 laity, 3,838 clergy—thirty-eight bishops among them—and including churchmen from as far away as India. It "express[ed] our gratitude to those members of the Old Catholic and the Orthodox Churches who were, under Divine Providence, instruments of this important gathering, and especially to its originator and president, Dr. Von Döllinger."[277] Of comparable significance, practically all bishops of the US Episcopal Church sent a letter of thanks to Döllinger, comparing him to Moses, called by God to reform the Western Church and bring divided Christians together once again on the basis of the "primitive purity" of the faith.[278]

Döllinger, too, was pleased. "The conference proceeded happily and with general satisfaction and exceeded my expectations," he wrote to Gladstone in late August.[279] To Lord Acton, who remained leery of the Old Catholic movement, Döllinger reported that the conference had generally gone well, even as he noted that "the worst obstacles were in the mistrust of the Orientals and Russians and the fear they had for authorities back home, and in the divisions among the Anglicans."[280] Soon goals and plans for future conferences were being considered.

DISAPPOINTMENT

But the center did not hold.

A third conference failed to take place, due both to theological and political reasons. In point of fact, theologically, the goals of reunion had begun to unravel even during the second conference and with heightened intensity thereafter. The joker in the pack proved to be Julian Joseph Overbeck, a former Catholic priest, who through stints as an Anglican and a Lutheran had settled on the implacable correctness of Eastern Orthodoxy. Although he participated at the second conference, evidence suggests that all along he felt that Orthodoxy alone was the only true way—*ex oriente lux* appears frequently in his writings.[281] At the second conference, as we have seen, he had expressed pointed doubts about Anglican Orders and he felt that all present should recognize the legitimacy of the seventh ecumenical Council, which had endorsed the use of icons. He also felt that Western Christians simply had to give up on the "filioque" clause due to its lack of antiquity, and that Old Catholics should abandon any hopes of reunion with Rome, which he viewed as a fundamentally heretical church, Pius IX being its most recent great-heresiarch.[282]

In a number of pamphlets after the second conference, Overbeck turned against Döllinger and others, making the additional case that Anglicans were simply too hamstrung by Protestant principles (expressed in the Thirty-Nine Articles) to be good-faith participants in the conferences and that their tenuous claims to unbroken episcopal succession constituted an unbreachable chasm between them and their Eastern interlocutors. Overbeck also harbored feelings against Old Catholicism, which despite appearances, he held, was poisoned by Protestant elements that eventually would lead to heresy and indifferentism.[283] Such convictions motivated Overbeck to write impassioned appeals to Orthodox leaders in Russia, Greece, and Constantinople, encouraging them to look on the results of the Bonn conference with skepticism.[284] And his advice was heeded. In the final analysis, truth was more important than unity in Overbeck's eyes and the ecclesial task of the future, as he conceived it *contra* Döllinger, was not to seek some sort of convergence among churches but to labor for a "Western Orthodoxy" and entreat others to convert.

Meanwhile, on the Anglican front, the redoubtable E. B. Pusey, who had not attended the conferences even if his *Eirenicon* played a role in inspiring them, made clear that he was standing by the "filioque" clause in its Western

formulation and that the general direction of the Bonn conferences represented inadmissible concessions to the Orthodox. To Liddon, shortly after the
second conference, Pusey confided: "I do not see any occasion for any formula
in which the Greeks and we should agree .... [I] fear that they are animated by
an evil spirit of ambition; and that they are unwilling to have their battle-cry
against Rome 'You are heretics believing in two $\alpha\alpha\rho\chi\alpha\iota$ [processions] in the
God-head' taken from them."[285] If Anglicans tampered with the "filioque" in
the Western creed, Pusey also told Liddon, he would either become a Roman
Catholic, shutting his eyes to do so, or trust that God would save him as a
member of no church.[286] "Döllinger, of course, attempted an impossibility,"
Pusey wrote to Newman, "[in attempting] to squeeze the principle of our
Western Confession into the words of St. John Damascene."[287] In 1876, in a
lengthy treatise, Pusey went public with his criticism of the Bonn conference,
making plain his sympathy for Döllinger's intentions, but insisting that with
respect to the "filioque" "we could not part with what, through so many
centuries, has been the expression of our common faith."[288]

Faced with such opposition, Döllinger grew despondent about the prospects
of another conference. On a walk in the English Garden in Munich, he told
Liddon that Pusey's book had made him "very sad" as it "threw everybody
back."[289] "Several reasons have worked together" against convening another
reunion conference, Döllinger wrote Acton:

> The Russians and the Orientals desired a discussion of the seventh council (of
> Nicaea, of icon veneration, etc.) which would have ignited a fire in the English
> Church; at the same time the Bonn articles on the Holy Spirit have also not been
> received by them, and so there is a case to be made for allowing more time. In
> England, Pusey, and Overbeck and—regrettably even Liddon—have injured the
> situation which would make it quite risky to resume the meetings in August or
> September.[290]

But theological opposition alone did not obstruct another conference. The
geopolitical climate in Europe in the late 1870s also worked against their
continuance. The liberal policies and open attitude to the West of Tsar
Alexander II that had facilitated Russian participation in the first place
changed abruptly with the build-up to the Russo-Turkish War of 1877–8,
after the Turks had intervened in Bulgaria in 1876 to suppress a rebellion.
Prime Minister Disraeli's support of the (Muslim) Ottoman Empire against
(Christian) Russia outraged public opinion across the Orthodox world. Many
Slavophiles, such as Dostoevsky, regarded the moment as a chance to unite all
Orthodox nations under Russia's helm, thus fulfilling Russia's putative historic
mission. Strains between England and Russia predictably escalated over the
matter as all of Europe found itself embroiled in the "Eastern Question,"
presaging tensions between East and West that would play a role in the
coming of the Great War in 1914.[291]

In light of such developments, alongside the theological opposition, Döllinger and his Old Catholic allies—who, as we have seen, were meanwhile caught up in the cross-fire of Germany's *Kulturkampf*—decided against any future conferences. This decision was met by regret from many quarters, even if many well-wishers recognized the manifold complexities that had intervened. Frederick Meyrick spoke for many when in *The Guardian* he wrote that "we must regret the lost opportunity if we take into consideration this man's [Döllinger's] age, on whose life, understood in human terms, the success of the undertaking appeared to hang."[292] In 1878, Döllinger, almost 80 years old, briefly revived the idea of another conference in a letter to Liddon. But it never came about.[293] "I am afraid that the world is not ready for a third session of the Bonn conference," Meyrick sighed to Döllinger in 1879.[294]

And the "one holy catholic and apostolic church" persisted in its divided state.[295]

5

Conclusion

"[T]ake pains to have a clear conscience toward God and toward men."

—Acts 24:16

" ... these confused times."

—Giuseppe di Lampedusa, *The Leopard*

On February 7, 1878 Pius IX, still a "Prisoner of the Vatican," died at the age of 85. The tolling of bells in Rome's churches alerted those in Italy's new capital that history's longest reigning pope was no more. The rites of death were conducted by Cardinal Luigi Bilio of the Piedmont. For three years Pius's body rested at the Vatican. In 1881, complying with the Pope's final will and testament, it was moved to the Church of San Lorenzo outside the walls, where a small monument stood dedicated to the papal Zouaves who had died defending Rome at Pius's bidding. The Pope's desire for this particular resting spot made a posthumous statement that the old churches of Rome were still papal, when this was not the case after national unification. It also identified Pius with the popular, third-century San Lorenzo (Saint Lawrence)—the latter persecuted by ancient Caesars, the former by modern ones.[1] Beloved by the faithful the world over, the deceased Pope had many enemies close to home. On the night of July 12, 1881, during the torchlit procession of the body to San Lorenzo, a mob of angry anticlericals yelled insults and attempted to throw the coffin into the Tiber before Roman security forces intervened.[2]

Calls for "Pio Nono" to be made a saint occurred shortly after his death. These went unrealized for over a century. In 2000 however, Pope John Paul II initiated the first step toward sainthood by having him (along with Pope John XXIII), beatified.[3] On the occasion, John Paul II reflected:

> [Pope Pius IX's] lengthy pontificate was not at all easy and he had much to suffer in fulfilling his mission of service to the Gospel. He was much loved, but also hated and slandered.... However, it was precisely in these conflicts *that the light of his virtues shone most brightly* ... Sustained by ... deep conviction, he called the First Vatican Ecumenical Council, which clarified with magisterial authority certain questions disputed at the time, and confirmed the harmony of faith and

reason. During his moments of trial Pius IX found support in Mary, to whom he was very devoted. In proclaiming the *dogma of the Immaculate Conception* he reminded everyone that in the storms of human life the light of Christ shines brightly in the Blessed Virgin and is more powerful than sin and death.[4]

Shortly after Pius's death in 1878, the Conclave of Cardinals met and elected as his successor Vicenzo Gioacchino Pecci, who took the name Leo XIII (r. 1878–1903). The new Pope, *sotto voce*, regretted the handling of the Döllinger affair, even as he, like his predecessor, rued Döllinger's influence on the Old Catholic movement. During Leo's papacy, several attempts were made to reconcile Döllinger to Rome.[5]

One of the more remarkable efforts—one endorsed by the Pope himself—was spearheaded in the 1880s by the English Catholic and accomplished Egyptologist Sir Peter le Page Renouf and his wife, Maria Ludovika (*née* Brentano) Renouf. The Renoufs had developed a friendship with Döllinger and had long sympathized with his plight after the Council. In their plan for his reconciliation, they employed as collaborators members of their circle of friends, including James Augustin Campbell (rector of the Scottish College in Rome) and the Pope's own brother, the Curial Cardinal Giuseppe Pecci. When Cardinal Pecci had an audience with the Pope in 1885, he raised the prospect of Döllinger's reconciliation. According to a communiqué from Campbell, who had knowledge of the audience, to Lady Renouf, the Pope expressed displeasure at how Archbishop Scherr treated Döllinger. Subsequently, Leo indicated that while it would be out of place for the Holy See to initiate anything, he would certainly be open if Döllinger took the first steps.[6] All parties recognized what a feat it would be for the Church if such a learned voice of opposition, somehow, could die at peace with Rome. The ultramontane press not only blamed Döllinger for inciting the Old Catholic movement but also for throwing fuel on the fire of liberal and Protestant anti-Catholic sentiment generally. His submission and reconciliation might possibly curtail both.

The Renoufs tried to rouse Döllinger to act, writing him several times about the matter.[7] "Bad men, or even good but mistaken men, may forcibly cast us out of this Ark [the Church]," Peter le Page Renouf wrote, "and the sin is theirs, but no excuse can be offered if we have an opportunity of returning to its shelter and refuse to avail ourselves of it."[8] In one of Döllinger's private notebooks, one finds this tantalizing (and unfortunately undated) remark: "The Pope wants me to say: I should apply directly to him and declare only that I stand by views of the papacy that I previously [pre-1869–70?] expressed."[9] But even if this suggests that Döllinger mulled over the matter, no fruit came of it. Despite the Renoufs' best efforts, the octogenarian apparently had arrived at the conviction that the hierarchy would accept nothing less than a full repudiation of the views that he had articulated during the

Council and at the time of his excommunication. And this he simply was not prepared to do, as is clear from the responses given to others who made efforts toward his reconciliation.

Quite a few of these efforts took place, in fact, coming from lay Catholics, priests, and high-ranking prelates, including Scherr's successor as Archbishop of Munich, Antonius von Steichele (r. 1878–89); Bishop Hefele, Döllinger's friend and the last German bishop to submit; Luigi Ruffo Scilla, the papal nuncio in Munich from 1887 to 1889; and Christoph Moufang, the capitular vicar of the Diocese of Mainz. The latter, a former student of Döllinger's, audaciously, if ultimately unsuccessfully, wrote directly to the Pope, arguing that reconciliation with Döllinger would satisfy those worried about the Professor's soul, burnish the image of the Church internationally, and be in keeping with "the gentleness and mercy of the Good Shepherd."[10]

In addressing Döllinger, pleas for reconciliation often came with anxiety over the Professor's spiritual condition. Archbishop Steichele, for instance, begged Döllinger "to be reconciled to the Holy Catholic Church .... It would be a cause of rejoicing for millions of believers, joy for the choirs of the blessed, and a pledge of your own eternal salvation."[11] One correspondent, "a lady of high rank" (the Duchess Adelheid von Braganza) warned Döllinger that, spiritually considered, he stood on the ledge of an "abyss": "[B]e aware that when a priest so highly-favored, talented, and enlightened as you are, sets himself against the authority of Church, and dies in disobedience to it, he has much more terrible punishment to expect in eternity than others who had less knowledge, less grace, and hence less responsibility."[12]

In evaluating Döllinger's responses to such queries, three observations are apposite. First, he remained convinced in his own mind that historical inquiry had flatly rendered Papal Infallibility implausible as a binding teaching of the Church; the teaching simply lacked substantial support in the early tradition and in fact rested considerably on past forgeries and misrepresentations. If he recanted, he wrote one correspondent, "there would no longer be for me any such thing as historical truth and certainty; I should then have to suppose that my whole life long I had been in a world of dizzy illusion, and that in historical matters I am altogether incapable of distinguishing truth from fable and falsehood."[13] To Archbishop Steichele, he indicated that a recantation would be tantamount to admitting that "a derangement of my mind had taken place, which incapacitated me from understanding historical facts." In this case, instead of rebuking him, the Church would do better to "practice an exorcism on me."[14]

Second, Döllinger made repeated, impassioned appeals to the inviolability of conscience: recanting his views would damage his conscience, rendering him a "liar" or "perjurer" for stating something that contradicted his actual convictions. "Can you seriously exact anything of this sort [a recantation] from me?" he asked Steichele. "Am I to appear before the eternal Judge with ...

perjury on my conscience?"[15] In a few instances, Döllinger even went a step further, suggesting that those learned theologians who accepted Infallibility had in fact inflicted moral damage on themselves: "I have asked several of our equals [other theologians] how they are able to make such an act of perjury harmonize with their consciences. The answer has always been an evasive one, or an embarrassed shrug of the shoulder."[16]

Finally, Döllinger insisted on the injustice of the sentence carried out against him. To Steichele, he thundered: "In the anathema [against me] ... I can recognize only an injustice and an act of violence, for had I not offered to listen to reason and allow myself to be publicly refuted?"[17] "What crime had I committed," he plaintively asked, "that I should be subjected to the heaviest of all punishments, to a punishment which, according to the dicta of the Church, is heavier than a sentence of death?"[18] To the papal nuncio Scilla, who sought Döllinger's reconciliation in October 1887, he averred that "the crime imputed to me was an unprecedented enormity. I refused to change my faith; I refused to believe and teach a new dogma.... [And] this was enough to inflict on an old man of seventy-two, who up to that point had incurred neither reproach nor blame, a punishment which, according to the teaching of the Church, is worse than death."[19]

Such utterances suggest that Döllinger stood shoulder to shoulder with Old Catholics, such as Reusch, Friedrich, and Schulte, among whom one could find comparably resolute points of view. And there is no small amount of additional evidence to support this, as has been previously discussed. But, again, Döllinger's relation to Old Catholicism is a contested matter, and it was to the nuncio Scilla in fact that Döllinger appeared to distance himself most emphatically from the Old Catholic movement. "I do not wish to be part of a schismatic society," he wrote; "I am isolated [*je suis isolé*]. Convinced that the sentence decreed against me is unjust and legally null, I persist in regarding myself as a member of the great Catholic Church; and it is the Church herself, who, through her holy Fathers, tells me that such an excommunication cannot harm my soul."[20]

On this last point, Döllinger made implicit appeal to canon law, which recognized, as the article on excommunication from the *Catholic Encyclopedia* of 1909 summarizes, that "[s]ome persons ... may be free in the eyes of God bound in the eyes of the Church, ... for God's judgment is based on the very truth itself, whereas that of the Church is based on arguments and presumptions which are sometimes erroneous." Further: "Consequently, a person unjustly excommunicated is in the same state as the justly excommunicated sinner who has repented and recovered the grace of God; he has not forfeited internal communion with the church and God can bestow upon him all necessary spiritual help."[21]

The nuncio's letter of 1887 also focused Döllinger's mind on questions of conscience and his eternal state. To Scilla, he therefore responded that "my conscience [is] at rest and in safety" and, standing by his convictions, added that he was "in a state of inward peace and tranquillity of mind even on the threshold of eternity."[22]

NONAGENARIAN AND DEATH

Döllinger turned 90 on February 28, 1889. On the occasion, greetings poured into Munich from abroad. Both the universities of Cambridge and Oxford heaped praise on the aged professor in letters with multiple signatories. The latter applauded him for a life of "distinguished service to theological and historical learning...marked throughout by high and sustained integrity of character."[23] Similarly, the theological faculty at the University of Bern sent greetings, calling Döllinger "the authentic professor of scholarly freedom and truthfulness" and "the leading fighter for the endangered ancient Christian faith."[24]

Many journals and newspapers deemed the birthday newsworthy. In Britain's *Church Times*, for instance, Alfred Plummer praised "the life-long services which he [Döllinger] has rendered in the cause of a purified Catholicism." Keen to make a dig at Rome, the Anglican Plummer added that "[i]t is a strange commentary upon the action of the Ultramontane party that the man who lives under the ban of the Papacy should be honored by all the best intelligences of Europe and America."[25] The Old Catholic organ, the *Deutsche Merkur*, carried front-page greetings, thanking Döllinger effusively for his enduring stand against Rome, which produced "the Catholic reform movement of our time," and praising his present "undiminished intellectual energy." "More recently," the greeting continued, "we owe you the warmest thanks for reviving the idea of Christian unity...through the reunion conferences at Bonn and thereby holding before our eyes a more elevated ideal of union than the purely mechanical unity of the Roman Church."[26] Similarly, the Swiss Old Catholic (*christkatholisch*) journal, *Der Katholik*, in the context of a wide-ranging survey of the political and religious developments of the century, thanked Döllinger for his manifold services and guidance, commenting: "you are for us *Christkatholiken* more than an academic teacher; you are for us a genuine, trustworthy leader."[27]

Döllinger was grateful for the tributes—a sentiment he expressed publicly in the *Allgemeine Zeitung*.[28] But the Professor's days were numbered. At the beginning of the new year in 1890, he came down with the flu. Several days later he appeared to be on the mend only to suffer a stroke the evening of January 9. From this he did not recover, but passed away on the evening of January 10, 1890.[29]

In light of his excommunicated status—which, again, meant deprivation of the sacraments and denial of a Catholic burial—the circumstances of

Döllinger's death and funeral provoked no small commotion. In his final years, he had increasingly relied on the support of two nieces, Elizabeth and Johanna Döllinger—especially the latter. But since he had given them no clear direction of how to handle his death, many things had to be improvised. During his final days, he refused the solicitations of several Catholic priests, eager to bring about a dramatic deathbed reconciliation. This led Johanna to exclaim: "Now they come after him having ill-treated him in every possible manner throughout all these years. They shall not be allowed near him."[30] As was the case with Martin Luther at the time of his death, many rumors of Döllinger's submission circulated—rumors that had in fact occurred episodically ever since his excommunication.

As Döllinger's death neared, his former ally and Old Catholic friend, Johann Friedrich, stepped forward to administer Extreme Unction and to oversee the funeral service, indicating that Döllinger himself had previously requested that of him. Aware that her uncle had rebuffed many Catholic priests, Johanna Döllinger felt that the only options available were either to allow Friedrich's sacerdotal interventions or to forgo any ritual and let their uncle "die like a dog," according to the memory of Alfred Plummer, who was present at the time. More fully from Plummer's pen: "On the whole it was thought [by his nieces] to let their uncle without any Christian office,—die like a 'like a dog,' as his enemies would say,—would be worst of all, and Friedrich was [therefore] sent for, who administered Extreme Unction. It could do no harm; would commit him to nothing, as he could not speak; and might [make] his end more peaceful."[31] In the end, Friedrich administered the sacrament and conducted the funeral service.[32]

The funeral took place on January 13, 1890. It was a grand, solemn affair despite the fact that Roman Catholic clergy—by prescription of canon law and order of the diocese—were not present and certain typical rituals (such as the ringing of the city's church bells) were impermissible because of the excommunication.[33] But numerous other religious leaders attended: Old Catholic, Anglican, Protestant, Eastern Orthodox, and even a Jewish rabbi.[34] The new president of the Bavarian Academy of Science, the rector of the university, the university senate and representatives from all academic faculties (with the exception of theology) gathered, as did numerous political figures, including the minister president of Bavaria, Friedrich Krafft von Crailsheim (1841–1926). Furthermore, the prince-regent Luitpold of Bavaria; the German "Kaiserin" Victoria, the Grand Duke of Baden, Gladstone, and the municipalities of Munich and Bamberg sent wreaths to the gravesite and words of consolation to the bereaved.[35]

Döllinger's death triggered another round of reflections on him in private correspondence and in newspapers and journals the world over.[36] "[T]o talk to him," Lord Acton wrote his wife Mamy, "was altogether different from talking on such matters [religious topics] with any other man. The void, for me, is a very great one."[37] In another letter to her, Acton lamented: "He was a tremendous background. Now, when I don't understand, there is nobody to go to."[38] Acton set to work in the spring of 1890 on an assessment of Döllinger's historical craftsmanship, which appeared in October under the title "Döllinger's Historical Work" in the *English Historical Review.*[39] And as mentioned earlier, Acton began a biography of his friend, but this project never made it very far.

Gladstone (Figure 5.1) memorialized Döllinger in *The Speaker.* After commenting on the vigor that Döllinger exhibited in his old age (he and Gladstone went on a seven-mile walk together near Tegernsee when Döllinger was 87!) and proclaiming that the Professor's legacy should command "universal interest," the former Prime Minister eulogized:

> It is with trembling hands that I lay this trivial offering on a tomb which is one to be honoured by the human race.... This eminently peaceful and judicial man was dragged into conflict, and has become the occasion of offense.... Döllinger is to be honoured with admiration, for attainments never surpassed in their extent or as to the wonderful manner in which he held them digested and at command to use. He is be honoured yet more fervently, with reverence and love, because in him the spirit of self was down-trodden and extinct, that he might live a larger life; and because, pursuing truth as he best could see it, in the spirit of courage and of

Figure 5.1. Döllinger, Gladstone, Lord Acton, and others at the "Villa Arco" in Tegernsee, Bavaria.

Source: Photograph by Karl Hahn, Bavaria, 1886. Image courtesy of the John M. Kelly Library, University of Toronto, via the Internet Archive.

peace, he united in his aims the things most precious to mankind, and set ... [a] great example for the generations to come.[40]

Across Europe, Old Catholics lamented. Numerous parishes held special vigil services in Döllinger's memory. The *Deutscher Merkur* bemoaned the loss of "the Nestor of all Catholic theologians and all scholars in Germany." Because of his commitment to the "historical method" and recognition of the "historical character" of theology, the *Merkur* continued, making reference to Friedrich's graveside speech, Döllinger occupied "a sovereign space in theology" and, although now deceased, was to be remembered as "a truly great theologian." His knowledge brought him into conflict with Rome, and this had made him into a "martyr" for the cause of truth and reform in the Church.[41]

Britain's *Guardian* devoted no less than three full pages to Döllinger's life in a retrospective article penned by Henry Parry Liddon. Facing down both unbelief on the one hand and "Romanism" on the other, Döllinger, according to Liddon, kept his "historical and theological conscience intact." "He was far removed from the boisterous assertion of self which is observable in Luther.... Rome forced him to dissent from her by bidding him accept a novel doctrine as a term of communion." But unlike both Protestants and, to a lesser degree, Old Catholics "he did not add to the refusal of submission the proclamation of a fierce anti-Roman crusade." After 1871, "at the moment he was driven from the visible communion of the Church he expressed his confident belief that the time would come when all Christians would be united in one fold and under one Shepherd. In this sure and certain hope he lived and died." For all these reasons and more, Liddon felt remembrance of Döllinger's legacy ought to continue long into the future.[42]

Writing in the *Edinburgh Review*, the Welsh scholar-priest John Owen offered a notable assessment of Döllinger. He viewed the deceased professor as the lonely "leader of a forlorn cause." "Many men," he wrote, "have attained eminence in history by being identified with successful causes." But Döllinger was one of those "choice spirits" who embodied a "magnificent failure," namely, in his efforts to combat ultramontanism. "He gave both existence and genuine *raison d'être* to the movement [Old Catholicism] which rejected the Papal claim to infallibility, and his death robbed it of one great source of its permanent vitality." But even apart from his breach with Rome and involvement with Old Catholicism, Owen continued, Döllinger "has earned the esteem and veneration of the coming ages ... [as] the greatest Catholic theologian and the most learned Church historian in Germany during the present century."[43]

Finally, across the Atlantic, the United States' high-brow *Atlantic Monthly* featured a thirteen-page retrospective of Döllinger's life written by the American Germanist E. P. Evans. Interpreting Döllinger rather unrestrainedly as "the greatest Catholic theologian of this or perhaps any century" but one whose "ideal of the Catholic church" led him into conflict with the actual

Church, Evans went on to praise Döllinger for resisting Rome after 1870 and refusing to entertain a "Jesuitical compromise with his conscience." "[T]he infallible Pope had made a fearful blunder [in allowing his excommunication]. It was a boomerang curse which returned to smite the man who hurled it." In the final analysis, Döllinger had right on his side in the overly black-and-white picture that Evans paints of the century: Döllinger took "a firm stand" in "the eternal conflict between liberty and servitude in the social, political, moral and intellectual life of the race, of which history is merely the more or less faithful record."[44]

CONSCIENCE, CATHOLICISM, AND THE MODERN AGE

In *A Tale of Two Cities*, Charles Dickens's narrator ruminates: "A wonderful fact to reflect upon, that every human creature is constituted to be that profound secret and mystery to every other. A solemn consideration, when I enter a great city by night, that every one of those darkly clustered houses encloses its own secret; . . . that every beating heart . . . is, in some of its imaginings, a secret to the heart nearest it! Something of the awfulness, even of Death itself, is referable to this."[45]

What, finally, are we to make of the life and death, "the profound secret and mystery," of Ignaz von Döllinger (Figure 5.2) and the aggregate of these mysteries, which we might label historical experience, that he engaged during a life that spanned a century of profound change for church and society alike? Permit me to conclude by reflecting on several areas of significance.

For starters, while the particular circumstances of Döllinger's conflict with Rome certainly reflect exigencies of his own milieu, they also bear witness to a deeper—one is tempted to say archetypal—conflict between theological inquiry and ecclesiastical authority. If I may generalize: the two were largely coextensive for much of Christianity's early development, but a subtle parting of the ways occurred with the establishment of universities in the Middle Ages and with them the differentiation of the *studium* as a discrete arena of endeavor with marked independence from both the *ecclesia* and *imperium*. As the late Cardinal Avery Dulles has observed, after the founding of universities it became commonplace to distinguish between the *clavis scientiae* (the key of knowledge) and the *clavis potestatis* (the key of power) and speculate on the relationship between the two. Employing a different terminology, Thomas Aquinas wrote of the *magisterium cathedrae magistralis* (magisterium of the professor's chair) and the *magisterium cathedrae pastoralis* (magisterium of the pastoral chair). The two often dovetailed, but not infrequently came into conflict. Thomas Aquinas himself and other scholastic thinkers, it bears noting, were once condemned by the Church hierarchy for dabbling too

Figure 5.2. Döllinger in old age painted by Franz von Lenbach, undated.

Source: Painting by Franz von Lenbach, Bavaria, undated. The painting hangs today in the Bavarian Academy of Science. Image courtesy of the Bayerische Akademie der Wissenschaften.

deeply in Aristotelian philosophy.[46] Centuries later, Luther, Melanchthon, and company appealed to their university credentials, their academic *cathedrae*, to legitimize criticisms of Rome. After the Reformation, Catholic universities, and not least the insistently Gallican University of Paris, continued to claim a certain magisterial authority apart from Rome until the majority of them—the German universities being a major exception—were repressed in the wake of the French Revolution.[47] A German scholar and a knowledgeable student of the history of universities, Döllinger bore witness in his person to the persistence of the academic chair's independent claims to magisterial authority, albeit in an age of assertive ultramontanism.

If similar in some respects to antecedent cases, Döllinger's case also evinces strong differences. In contrast to the views of his medieval and early modern forebears, his outlook bore witness to the historicization of European thought in the nineteenth century and with it the ascendancy of German *Wissenschaft*. This revolution in "historicism," as previously discussed, had many intellectual and cultural implications, but it was perhaps most acutely felt in theology.[48] At an even deeper level than the specific issue of Papal Infallibility, therefore, one can see a more general conflict between historical approaches to religious verities and the more normative approaches of theology and philosophy. Put as a question, what was the proper role of history in theological discussion? As we have seen, this matter sometimes took on a nationalist dimension: the "Italian or Roman mind" being associated with (anti-historical) neo-scholasticism and the "German mind" reflecting a modern scholarly historicism.

Unlike some later critics, such as Ernst Troeltsch, who felt that historical criticism constituted an acid that dissolved all stable verities, Döllinger held on to supra-historical or transcendent truths—and he even believed them to be capable of faithful mediation in ecclesiastical tradition.[49] For him, the vocation of the *schola theologorum* (a favorite phrase of Newman's) was in fact to figure out what was true in the tradition and what was not, what merited preserving and what could be dispensed with.[50] But, as Acton put it, Döllinger regularly spoke of the "independence and authority of history" to adjudicate the truth of tradition. And in an era of papal centralization and a newly assertive scholasticism on the part of the hierarchy, it should not surprise that conflict arose: "history, he affirmed, left to itself and pursued disinterestedly," Acton wrote, "will heal the ills it causes; and it was said of him that *he set the university in the place of the hierarchy.*" Or, again: "The historian . . . prevail[ed] over the divine, and [Döllinger tended] to judge church matters by a law which was not given from the altar."[51]

If perhaps then more historian than priest, Döllinger was nonetheless a fundamentally religious thinker and a proto-ecumenist at that, someone for whom, to quote Acton again, "conciliation was always in his thoughts."[52] Although his ecumenical sensibilities preceded the Bonn Reunion Conferences of 1874 and 1875, they were most strikingly on display during these largely forgotten gatherings—"the most important ecumenical conversation of the nineteenth century," according to Franz Xaver Bischof.[53] The enormous international attention that these conferences elicited and the comparable interest in the fate of Döllinger more generally, as witnessed by the coverage of his ninetieth birthday and death, should, again, help put to rest the tired notion of "the secularization of the European mind" in the nineteenth century.[54]

But equally important, Döllinger's ecumenical sensibilities and the Bonn conferences, as I have argued, suggest the limitations of thinking about the age strictly as a time of renewed confessionalism—a "second confessional age."[55] One can find confessionalism aplenty throughout the century, to be sure. But the ecumenism—or proto-ecumenism—highlighted in this book calls attention to the efforts made to realize one of the Christian Gospel's highest, most elusive demands: unity among those who call themselves Christians. We might sum up then by recognizing Döllinger's age as neither preponderantly secular nor preponderantly confessional, but churningly religious and undeniably complex.[56]

Döllinger's historical cast of mind and his ecumenism raise a delicate question for Catholics today: to what degree was this excommunicated scholar an intellectual architect, or at least a significant harbinger, of the Second Vatican Council (1962–5), which pivoted sharply from the ethos that had shaped Vatican I?[57] Here one must be careful and distinguish between direct and indirect influence. To trace Döllinger's direct influence is difficult and rather speculative, for what reformer would gain anything by appealing explicitly to an anathematized thinker? At the same time, the manifold affinities and suggestive possibilities of indirect influence between Döllinger's thought and the currents of theology that led to the Second Vatican Council are substantial and significant.[58]

The Second Vatican Council's Dogmatic Constitution on the Church (*Lumen gentium*) and its revolutionary Decree on Ecumenism (*Unitatis redintegratio*)—not to mention John Paul II's later encyclical on ecumenism, *Ut unum sint* (1995)—represent noteworthy vindications of Döllinger's aims—aims for which he was soundly condemned by an ultramontane hierarchy during his lifetime.[59] It is more than accidental, I would submit, that two of the key ecumenists shaping Vatican II, the German Augustin Bea (1881–1968) and the French Yves Congar (1904–95), were well-versed about the Döllinger affair and the theological problems that it had left for the Church. In his native land, the former inherited a theological legacy in which ecumenical ecclesiology and historical exploration loomed large. While the German roots behind Vatican II are often attributed to Döllinger's contemporary and friend, Johann Adam Möhler, Döllinger too should not be forgotten, for Döllinger, in the words of Jerome-Michael Vereb, "identified the subject of the Church as the primary topic of the Christian vocation, and called for sharpening of the critical tools regarding Sacred Scripture, Church history, and theological exploration."[60]

Several decades after Döllinger's death, Pope Pius XI (r. 1922–39) condemned ecumenism with non-Catholics in *Mortalium animos* (January 6, 1928): "the Apostolic See cannot on any terms take part in their [ecumenical] assemblies, nor is it anyway lawful for Catholics either to support or to work for such enterprises."[61] But Vatican II largely controverted this point of view; and one could imagine Döllinger happily penning the opening lines of the Council's Decree on Ecumenism: "The restoration of unity among Christians is one of the principal concerns of the Second Vatican Council.... [D]ivision [among churches] openly contradicts the will of Christ, scandalizes the world, and damages that most holy cause, the preaching of the Gospel."[62] One can, additionally, imagine Döllinger applauding Pope John XXIII's opening address when this avuncular pope invoked "history, which is...the teacher of life" to guide the Council's work.[63]

Finally, let us turn, again, to the topic of conscience, a recurring focus of this book. The case of Döllinger raises theological, and bitingly existential,

questions about the nature and role of conscience for an individual attempting
to live faithfully within a religious tradition. If we take Döllinger at his word,
he could not subscribe to Papal Infallibility because he felt doing so would
violate his conscience; he refused to perjure his soul, as he told the papal
nuncio Scilla and many others. On this point, Döllinger finds copious
support from Catholic moral theology, which firmly ties conscience to
truth-seeking and a supra-temporal moral law and not, as modern liberal
theory holds, to the subjective rule of a sovereign self-will.[64] We have already
seen how John Henry Newman in his *Letter to the Duke of Norfolk* sought to
defend the inviolability of conscience even if, and only as a last measure, this
meant disagreement with the Church hierarchy: "Certainly, if I am obliged to
bring religion into after dinner toasts…I shall drink,—to the Pope if you
please, still to Conscience first, and to the Pope afterwards."[65] Vatican II's
Pastoral Constitution on the Church in the Modern World (*Gaudium et
spes*) buttressed Newman's point, describing conscience as that "most secret
core and sanctuary of a man. There he is alone with God, whose voices
echoes in his depths."[66]

Döllinger's actions, furthermore, accord well with Thomas Aquinas's teaching on conscience. In his *Disputed Questions on Truth*, after a lengthy definition of conscience as both a habit of the soul and an act of volition, informed
by knowledge of the moral law and guided by right reason, the Angelic Doctor
raises the question, "Does conscience always bind?" Not surprisingly, he
answers that it does: "conscience is nothing else but the application of knowledge to an act, it is obvious that conscience is said to bind by the power of a
divine precept."[67] Insofar as Döllinger acted according to conscience, he
attempted precisely this.

But, of course, what if, as his critics maintained, Döllinger was mistaken in
his judgment; what if, although acting according to his *own* conscience, his
actions were not in accord with the divine law and, implicitly, somewhere
along the line, his conscience had been misshapen? For Aquinas and moral
theologians following him, this would be regarded as the problem of an
"erroneous conscience" (*conscientia erronea*), a subject in moral theology
that has received much attention. Directly after discussing the binding nature
of conscience in the *Disputed Questions*, Aquinas asks: "does an *erroneous*
conscience bind?" He concludes that in fact it does: "conscience binds, no
matter how erroneous it may be." Although the argument offered is rather
intricate, the ultimate rationale is fairly commonsensical. As finite, concupis-
cent beings, Aquinas states, we can never have perfect knowledge of the moral
law; we can only go on the best knowledge that we are able to acquire, and this
can be distorted by ignorance, disordered desire, and other factors. Even so, in
the moment of decision, if we honestly think—even if mistakenly so—that we
are obeying conscience by doing or avoiding an action, Aquinas commends

this. He does not call such an act good, but it does mitigate the culpability of the moral actor. In his own words:

> Whoever wills to transgress a divine precept has a bad will, and thus sins. But whoever believes something to be a precept [even if false] and wills to transgress it, has the will not to serve the law; therefore he sins. One who has an erroneous conscience, whether about intrinsically evil matters or about whatever, believes that what is contrary to his conscience is contrary to the law of God. Therefore, if he wills to do it, he wills contrary to the will of God and thus sins. *Thus a conscience in whatever way it be erroneous obliges on penalty of sin.*[68]

Applied to the case of Döllinger, all indications suggest that his dissent from the Vatican decrees accorded with his conscience, at least as best as he could perceive its dictates, from 1870 until his death. It might have been a *conscientia erronea*, a mistaken conscience, to be sure. But at least according to Aquinas, Döllinger acted honorably, if not inculpably, by not *acting against* his conscience.

Of course, the vexing difficulty in assessing Döllinger's case—and this is perhaps but an instance of a difficulty embedded in the human condition—is the fact that at the Vatican Council, Pius IX and the other Council Fathers presumably thought that they, too, were acting in accordance with conscience and in the highest interests of religious truth.

As we have seen, Newman described Döllinger's situation as tragic. Historical retrospection corroborates Newman's judgment even as it adds new dimensions to it. While theologians and historians have incessantly debated whether the Second Vatican Council represented "discontinuity" or "continuity" in the history of Catholicism, practically all agree that Vatican I's prior treatment of the papacy was "one-sided," "provisional," or even "distorted" and today should only be properly understood in light of the complementary insight provided by Vatican II's aforementioned *Lumen gentium*.[69] This key Constitution of the Council defined the Church less juridically and more mystically, less exclusively and more ecumenically. It also curtailed reading any papalist overreach into *Pastor aeternus* (1870) by fleshing out the vital roles of the episcopate, councils, and, not least, the laity in the life of the Church—the *sensus fidelium*.[70] It "trim[med] the boat," as Newman, weary of ultramontane glosses on Vatican I, predicted would be required of a future Council.[71] Or, as Hans Urs von Balthasar has noted, *Lumen gentium* brought about a "reassuring satisfactory balance" between papal authority and episcopal collegiality.[72] Furthermore, *Lumen gentium* with other texts of Vatican II implicitly recognized, in the words of the philosopher Charles Taylor, that "some of the most impressive extensions of a gospel ethic depended on a breakaway from Christendom," from the temporal power of the Church and nostalgia for the political and social norms that had governed Europe's *ancien régime*.[73]

Döllinger possessed many gifts; clairvoyance was not one of them. He did
not have recourse to *Lumen gentium*, and therefore had no choice but to react
to the one-sidedness that he felt *Pastor aeternus* had presented. He belonged to
an unfortunate generation, swung between the old world and the new, a world
rife with false choices and uncompromising rhetoric, to which he with his
ultramontane critics contributed. This resulted in the Church excommunicat-
ing one of its most accomplished scholars and in Döllinger living the final
decades of his long life in forlorn exile from the Church that he loved and had
vowed to serve.

Notes

INTRODUCTION

1. Giuseppe di Lampedusa, *The Leopard*, trans. Archibald Colquhoun (New York: Pantheon Books, 2007), 180.
2. Auguste Comte, *Cours de philosophie positive*, 5th ed., vol. 6 (Paris, 1894), 277.
3. "The Suppression of the Italian Monasteries," *DR* 13 (July 1869): 76. Cf. Tim Blanning, *The Romantic Revolution: A History* (New York: Random House, 2012), ix–x.
4. On the eighteenth-century roots of anticlericalism, see Jonathan I. Israel, *Radical Enlightenment: Philosophy and the Making of Modernity, 1650–1750* (New York: Oxford University Press, 2002). This is not to say that the Revolution was bereft of religious roots, too. See Dale K. Van Kley, *The Religious Origins of the French Revolution: From Calvin to the Civil Constitution, 1560–1791* (New Haven: Yale University Press, 1996).
5. Peter Berger, Grace Davie, and Effie Fokas, *Religious America, Secular Europe? A Theme and Variations* (Aldershot: Ashgate, 2008), 26–8 and Thomas Albert Howard, *God and the Atlantic: America, Europe, and the Religious Divide* (Oxford: Oxford University Press, 2011), 2–23, 193–205.
6. René Rémond, *Religion et société en Europe: La sécularisation aux XIXe et XXe siècles* (Paris: Éditions du Seuil, 1998), 19.
7. Charles Taylor, *A Secular Age* (Cambridge, MA: The Belknap Press of Harvard University Press, 2007), 159ff.
8. Margaret Lavinia Anderson, "The Limits of Secularization: On the Problem of the Catholic Revival in Nineteenth-Century Germany," *Historical Journal* 38 (September 1995): 647–70 and Joseph A. Komonchak, "Modernity and the Construction of Roman Catholicism," *CnS* 18 (1997): 353–85.
9. Michael Burleigh, *Earthly Powers: The Clash of Religion and Politics from the French Revolution to the Great War* (New York: HarperCollins, 2005), 124. Cf. Arno J. Mayer, *The Persistence of the Old Regime: Europe to the Great War* (New York: Pantheon Books, 1981).
10. Ultramontanism, it should be noted, has much deeper roots than the early nineteenth century; and some prefer to speak of its post-1789 manifestations as "neo-ultramontanism." On this phenomenon, see Otto Weiß, "Der Ultramontanismus. Grundlagen—Vorgeschichte—Struktur," *ZBL* 41 (1978): 821–77. Cf. Jeffrey von Arx, S.J., *Varieties of Ultramontanism* (Washington, DC: Catholic University of America Press, 1998).
11. On this theme generally, see Christopher Clark and Wolfraim Kaiser, eds., *Culture Wars: Secular–Catholic Conflict in Nineteenth-Century Europe* (Cambridge: Cambridge University Press, 2003).
12. On the pontificate of Pius IX, see Owen Chadwick, *A History of the Popes, 1830–1914* (Oxford: Oxford University Press, 1998), 61ff.

13. John Micklethwait and Adrian Wooldridge, *God is Back: How the Global Revival of Faith is Changing the World* (New York: Penguin Press, 2009). Cf. Richard Wolin, "Jürgen Habermas and Post-Secular Societies," *Chronicle of Higher Education* 52.5 (September 23, 2005): B16.

14. David Blackbourn, *The Long Nineteenth Century: A History of Germany, 1780–1918* (New York: Oxford University Press, 1998), 297.

15. Friedrich Wilhelm Graf, "Ignaz von Döllinger," in Katharina Weigand, ed., *Münchner Historiker zwischen Politik und Wissenschaft* (Munich: Hervert Utz Verlag, 2010), 58.

16. Newman to Döllinger (December 15, 1853) in C. S. Dessain and Vincent Ferrer Blehl, S.J., eds., *The Letters and Diaries of John Henry Newman*, vol. 15 (London: Thomas Nelson and Sons, 1964), 506. The original is found in BSB, Döllingeriana II.

17. See the Catholic historian Johannes Janssen to Döllinger (November 22, 1864), BSB, Döllingeriana II: "Man hat Sie in Rom, was auch vorkommen, doch sehr lieb und Sie bleiben doch der *primus doctor Germaniae.*"

18. "The Life and Writings of Ignatius von Döllinger," *Edinburgh Review* 175 (1892): 49.

19. William E. Gladstone, "The Right Rev. Dr. Von Döllinger," *The Speaker: A Review of Politics, Letters, Science, and the Arts* 1 (1890): 58. Cf. M. Chandler, "The Significance of the Friendship between William E. Gladstone and Ignaz von Döllinger," *IKZ* 90 (2000): 153–67.

20. See Richard J. Blackwell, *Galileo, Bellarmine, and the Bible* (Notre Dame: University of Notre Dame Press, 1991).

21. The notes are available in Lord Acton's papers at the archives of Cambridge University Library (CUL) and have been extensively consulted for this book.

22. *GG*, 483–4.

23. Döllinger's address is found in Johann Finsterhölzl, *Ignaz von Döllinger* (Graz: Verlag Styria, 1969), 225–63.

24. Rudolf Reinhardt, "Teologia romana nella Germania de XIX secolo," *CnS* 12 (1991): 553–67.

25. *ESDD*, 2901 (translation modified). On scholastic theology in general, see Ulrich Gottfried Leinsle, *Introduction to Scholastic Theology*, trans. Michael J. Miller (Washington, DC: Catholic University of America Press, 2010).

26. Gladstone to Döllinger (February 20, 1875), BL Add. 44140/340.

27. *KGV*, vol. 3, 220ff. and Anton Landersdorfer, *Gregor von Scherr, 1804–1877* (Munich: Verlag des Vereins, 1995), 423ff.

28. Ignaz von Döllinger, *Briefe und Erklärungen über die vaticanischen Decrete, 1869–1887* (Munich: C. H. Beck, 1890), 91.

29. Döllinger, *Briefe und Erklärungen*, 96.

30. Luise von Kobell, *Ignaz von Döllinger: Erinnerungen* (Munich, 1891), 8.

31. *Aktenstücke des Ordinariates des Erzbisthums München und Freising betreffend das allgemeine Vatikanische Concil* (Regensburg, 1871), 136.

32. After his excommunication, in fact, Döllinger was elected rector of the University of Munich and served as president of the Bavarian Academy of Science—arguably the two most prestigious intellectual posts in Munich. *GG*, 485.

33. The first post-conciliar "Old Catholic" Congress was held at Munich on September 22–24, 1871. On the early history of the German Old Catholic Movement, see Urs

Küry, *Die altkatholische Kirche: Ihre Geschichte, ihre Lehre, ihr Anliegen* (Stuttgart: Evangelisches Verlagswerk, 1966), 100f. and C. B. Moss, *The Old Catholic Movement: Its Origins and History*, 2nd ed. (London: SPCK, 1964), 226–42.

34. *National-Zeitung* (April 12, 18717), BSB, Döllingeriana XXI.7.

35. See "The Dollinger Movement: Spread of the Catholic Agitation in Europe," *New York Herald* (July 28, 1872) and "The Döllingerites, Nationalists, and the Papacy," *Brownson's Quarterly Review* 1 (1873): 34–52.

36. "A New Reformation," *Trenton State Gazette* (April 29, 1871).

37. "Dr. Döllinger and the Papacy—A New Era," *New York Herald* (May 5, 1871).

38. See, e.g., William Ewart Gladstone, *The Vatican Decrees in their Bearing on Civil Authority* (New York, 1875).

39. BSB Döllingeriana I.5.

40. These were published in the *Allgemeine Zeitung* and translated into English and published as *Lectures on the Reunion of the Churches*, trans. Henry Nutcombe Oxenham (New York, 1872). Only in 1888 were they published in German as *Ueber die Wiedervereinigung der christlichen Kirchen: Sieben Vorträge gehalten zu München im Jahr 1872* (Nördlingen, 1888).

41. On the origins of these conferences, see Christian Oeyen, "Die Entstehung der Bonner Unions-Konferenzen im Jahr 1874" (Unpublished Habilitationsschrift, University of Bern, 1871).

42. On the importance of this phrase for Christian ecumenism, see D. A. Carson, *The Farewell Discourse and Final Prayer of Jesus* (Grand Rapids, MI: Baker, 1980).

43. On the Council of Florence (or, more fully, the Council of Basel-Ferrara-Florence), see Deno J. Geanakoplos, "The Council of Florence (1438–9) and the Problem of Union between the Byzantine and Latin Churches," *CH* 24 (1955): 324–46.

44. See Thomas Albert Howard, "Neither a Secular nor Confessional Age: The Bonn Reunion Conferences of 1874 and 1875," *JHS* 11 (March 2011): 59–84. On the enduring significance of Döllinger and the Bonn conferences for Old Catholics, see *Alt-katholisch-zeitgemäß: Die Geschichte einer anderen katholischen Kirche* (Nordstrand, 2009), 79ff., 95ff. See also the website of the Old Catholic diocese of Germany at <http://www.alt-katholisch.de/> (accessed July 4, 2013).

45. "The Conference at Bonn—Döllinger's Address—New Yorkers Present—A Proposed Concordat," *New York Times* (August 26, 1875).

46. "The Conference at Bonn," *The Guardian* (August 25, 1875), BAB Reusch 7.353.

47. Mark D. Chapman, *The Fantasy of Reunion: Anglicans, Catholics, and Ecumenism, 1833–1882* (Oxford: Oxford University Press, 2014), 258–62.

48. *TG*, 352ff. Cf. Hubert Wolf, "Rekonziliation Döllingers durch Johann Heinrich Floß?" *TQ* 172 (1992): 121–5.

49. Döllinger, *Briefe und Erklärungen*, 147ff.

50. BSB, Döllingeriana II.9, 11.

51. The "Old Catholic" priest and friend, Johann Friedrich, administered the Last Rites to Döllinger; see *TG*, 483–92. The circumstances of his death and burial are recounted in the conclusion.

52. E. P. Evans, "Ignatius von Döllinger," *Atlantic Monthly* 68 (October 1891): 553–65.

53. "Death of Döllinger," *The Times* (January 13, 1890).

54. Quoted in Victor Conzemius, "Der Tod Ignaz von Döllingers in Briefen der Freunde," *KJB* 8 (1968): 303–4.

55. Tony Judt, *Reappraisals: Reflections on the Forgotten Twentieth Century* (New York: Penguin Press, 2008).

56. Thomas Albert Howard, "A 'Religious Turn' in Modern European Historiography?" *Historically Speaking: The Bulletin of the Historical Society* 4 (June 2003): 24–6 and David Blackbourn, "The Catholic Church in Europe since the French Revolution: A Review Article," *CSSH* 33 (1991): 778–90.

57. Jürgen Osterhammel, *The Transformation of the World: A Global History of the Nineteenth Century*, trans. Patrick Camiller (Princeton: Princeton University Press, 2014), 873.

58. Olaf Blaschke, "Das 19. Jahrhundert: Ein zweites konfessionelles Zeitalter?" *Geschichte und Gesellschaft* 26 (2000): 38–75. Cf. Helmut Walser Smith, ed., *Protestants, Catholics, and Jews in Germany, 1800–1914* (Oxford: Berg, 2001).

59. See, for example, A. N. Wilson, *God's Funeral: The Decline of Faith in Western Civilization* (New York: W. W. Norton, 1999). On the popular durability of the "secularization thesis," see Jeffrey Cox, "Towards Eliminating the Concept of Secularisation. A Progress Report," in Callum Brown and Michael Snape, eds., *Secularisation in the Christian World* (Farnham: Ashgate Publishers, 2010), 13–26.

60. See Brian Tierney, *The Origins of Papal Infallibility, 1150–1350* (Leiden: E. J. Brill, 1972) and Mark E. Powell, *Papal Infallibility: A Protestant Evaluation of an Ecumenical Issue* (Grand Rapids, MI: Eerdmans, 2009), 20–48.

61. Alasdair MacIntyre, *Whose Justice? Which Rationality?* (Notre Dame: University of Notre Dame Press, 1988), 12. Cf. *Three Rival Forms of Moral Enquiry* (Notre Dame: University of Notre Dame Press, 1990).

62. E. P. Thompson, *The Making of the English Working Class* (New York: Vintage Books, 1963), 12.

63. Brad S. Gregory, "Can we 'See Things their Way'? Should we Try?," in Alister Chapman, John Coffey, and Brad S. Gregory, eds., *Seeing Things their Way: Intellectual History and the Return of Religion* (Notre Dame: University of Notre Dame Press, 2009), 25. For this and the preceding paragraph I recognize a debt to Gregory's work. Cf. Richard Schaefer, "Intellectual History and the Return of Religion," *Historically Speaking* 12 (April 2011): 30–1.

64. On this point, see Herbert Butterfield's classic, *The Whig Interpretation of History* (London: G. Bell, 1931).

65. On the inescapably moral nature of historical inquiry, see George Kotkin, "History's Moral Turn," *JHI* 69 (2008): 293–315.

66. See John Henry Newman, *A Letter Addressed to His Grace the Duke of Norfolk on Occasion of Mr. Gladstone's Recent Expostulation* (London: B. M. Pickering, 1875), 73.

67. Thomas Aquinas, *Summa Theologiae*, I-I.79.13.

68. See, e.g., Acts 23:1, 24:16; I Corinthians 4:2, 5:11; I Timothy 1:5, 1:19, 3:9, 4:2; Hebrews 9:9, 9:14, 10:22 (RSV). Cf. Paul Strohm, *Conscience: A Very Short Introduction* (Oxford: Oxford University Press, 2011).

69. F. X. Bischof, "John Henry Newman and Ignaz von Döllinger: Papstdogmen und Gewissen," in Mariano Delgado, ed., *Ringen um die Wahrheit: Gewissenskonflikte in der Christentumsgeschichte* (Fribourg: Academic Press, 2001), 271–86.

70. Johann Finsterhölz, ed., *Ignaz von Döllinger* (Graz: Verlag Styria, 1969), 9.

71. Walter Rauschenbusch, "The Life of Döllinger," *AJT* 7 (October 1903): 734.

72. Döllinger, *Briefe und Erklärungen*, 147ff.

73. Küry, *Die altkatholische Kirche*, 57ff.

74. On the emergence of historicism (*Historismus*), see Hans Erich Bödeker, Georg Iggers, Jonathan B. Knudsen, and Peter Hanns Reill, eds., *Aufklärung und Geschichte: Studien zur deutschen Geschichtswissenschaft im 18. Jahrhundert* (Göttingen: Vandenhoeck & Ruprecht, 1986) and Ulrich Muhlack, *Geschichtswissenschaft im Humanismus und in der Aufklärung: Die Vorgeschichte des Historismus* (Munich: C. H. Beck, 1991). Cf. Johannes Zachhuber, *Theology as a Science in Nineteenth-Century Germany* (Oxford: Oxford University Press, 2013), 5–10.

75. CUL Add. 4906/100.

76. See Bernard Lonergan, "The Transition from a Classicist World-View to Historical-Mindedness," in Lonergan, *A Second Collection: Papers* (Toronto: University of Toronto Press, 1996).

77. On the challenge of historical thought for nineteenth-century Catholic theology, see Mark Schoof, O.P., *A Survey of Catholic Theology, 1800–1970*, trans. N. D. Smith (Glen Rock, NJ: Paulist Newman Press, 1970), 14–44.

78. Manning as quoted in James Pereiro, *Cardinal Manning: From Anglican Archdeacon to Council Father at Vatican I* (Herefordshire: Gracewing, 2008), 205.

79. Von Scherr to Döllinger (April 2, 1871) in Döllinger, *Briefe und Erklärungen*, 95–6 (emphasis added).

80. On Febronianism, see *ODCC*, 602–3 and on Gallicanism, see *ODCC*, 653–64. Both will be treated more extensively in Chapter 2.

81. Steven Ozment, *The Age of Reform, 1250–1550: An Intellectual and Religious History of Late Medieval and Reformation Europe* (New Haven: Yale University Press, 1980), 245ff.

82. Newman to Lady Simeon (April 26, 1871) in Dessain and Gornall, eds., *Letters and Diaries of John Henry Newman*, vol. 25, 22.

83. On *Nouvelle théologie*, see Jürgen Mettenpenningen, *Nouvelle théologie—New Theology: Inheritor of Modernism, Precursor of Vatican II* (London: T. & T. Clark, 2010) and Hans Boersma, *Nouvelle théologie and Sacramental Ontology: A Return to Mystery* (New York: Oxford University Press, 2009). On Döllinger as harbinger of the reforms at Vatican II, see, inter alia, Peter Neuner, *Döllinger als Theologe der Ökumene* (Paderborn: Schöningh, 1979). Pope Benedict XVI's greatuncle, Georg Ratzinger (1844–99) was a key research assistant for Döllinger between 1863 and 1867. Fergus Kerr, *Twentieth-Century Catholic Theologians* (Oxford: Blackwell, 2007), 187n15.

84. For an overview of "Modernism" within the Catholic Church see Claus Arnold, *Kleine Geschichte des Modernismus* (Freiburg im Bresigau: Herder, 2007), Darrell Jodock, ed., *Catholicism Contending with Modernity: Roman Catholic Modernism and Anti-Modernism in Historical Context* (Cambridge: Cambridge University Press, 2000), and Alec Vidler, *The Modernist Movement in the Roman Church* (Cambridge: Cambridge University Press, 1934).

85. Paul Maria Baumgarten, "Johann Joseph Ignaz von Döllinger," *CE*, vol. 5 (New York: Robert Appleton Company, 1909), 94–9.

86. On Döllinger as a precursor of twentieth-century ecumenism, see Hubert Huppertz, "Döllingers Bedeutung für die ökumenische Bewegung," in Elisabeth Bach, Angela Berlis, and Siegfried J. Thuringer, eds., *Ignaz von Döllinger zum 125. Todestag: Spurensuche, Schlaglichter auf ein außergewöhnliches Leben* (Munich: Alt-Katholische Gemeinde St. Willibrord, 2015), 111–36. On Catholicism and ecumenism generally, see Henn William, "*Ut unam sint* and Catholic Involvement in Ecumenism," *ER* 52 (2000): 234–45. On Congar, see Gabriel Flynn, "Yves Cardinal Congar: un maître de théologie," *LS* 29 (2004): 239–57 and Richard McBrien, "Church and Ministry: The Achievement of Yves Congar," *Theology Digest* 32 (1985): 203–11. On Bea, see Gudrun Griesmayr, *Die eine Kirche und die eine Welt: die ökumenische Vision Kardinal Augustin Beas* (Frankfurt am Main: Peter Lang, 1997).

87. See Fergus Kerr, "Yves Congar: From Suspicion to Acclamation," *LS* 29 (2004): 273–87. On Murray, see John T. McGreevy, *Catholicism and American Freedom: A History* (New York: W. W. Norton, 2004), 189ff.

88. The phrase "handed over to Satan" comes from I Corinthians 5:5, where the Apostle Paul tells the Christian community in Corinth that "you are to deliver this [unrepentant] man to Satan for the destruction of the flesh, that his spirit may be saved in the day of the Lord Jesus" (RSV). See Artur Landgraf, "Sünde und Trennung von der Kirche in der Frühscholastik," *Scholastik* 5 (1930): 217, Alexander Murry, *Conscience and Authority in the Medieval Church* (Oxford: Oxford University Press, 2015), 172–5, Francis Edward Hyland, *Excommunication: Its Nature, Historical Development and Effects* (Washington, DC: Catholic University of America Press, 1928), 19–21, and *ODCC*, 584–5.

89. Newman to Alfred Plummer (January 5, 1871) in Dessain and Gornall, eds., *Letters and Diaries of John Henry Newman*, vol. 25, 269.

CHAPTER 1

1. E. E. Y. Hales, *Revolution and Papacy, 1769–1846* (Notre Dame: University of Notre Dame Press, 1966), 98, 101.

2. See Filippone Giustino, *Le relazioni tra lo stato pontifico e la francia: Storia diplomatica del Trattato di Tolentino*, 2 vols. (Milan: A. Giuffre Editore, 1961, 1967).

3. For a listing of all works brought from Italy to France during this time with their dates of exhibition and repatriation, see M. L. Blumer, "Catalogue des peintures transportées d'Italie en France de 1796 à 1814," *Bulletin de la Société de l'Histoire de l'Art Français* (1936): 244–348. Cf. Ernst Steinmann, "Die Plünderung Roms durch Bonaparte," *Internationale Monatsschrift für Wissenschaft, Kunst und Technik* 11 (1916–17): 641–76.

4. Charles Freeman, *The Horses of St. Mark's* (New York: Overlook Press, 2004), 1–14.

5. Quoted material taken from Owen Chadwick, *The Popes and European Revolution* (Oxford: Clarendon Press, 1982), 457, 462.

6. From the memoir of François R. J. de Pommereul as quoted in Dorothy Mackay Quynn, "The Art Confiscations of the Napoleonic Wars," *AHR* 50 (April 1945): 439.

7. Jeffrey Alexander, Ron Eyerman, Bernhard Giesen, Neil J. Smelser, and Piotr Sztompka, *Cultural Trauma: Theory and Applications* (Berkeley: University of California Press, 2004), 1.

8. Ron Eyerman, "The Past in the Present: Culture and the Transmission of Memory," *Acta Sociologica* 47 (June 2004): 161.

9. On the Catholic Revival more generally, see Michael B. Gross, *The War against Catholicism: Liberalism and the Anti-Catholic Imagination in Nineteenth-Century Germany* (Ann Arbor: University of Michigan Press, 2005), 29–73.

10. Images can be found in Timothy Tackett, *La Révolution, l'Eglise, la France* (Paris: Du Cerf, 1986), 180ff.

11. Christopher Clark and Wolfram Kaiser, eds., *Culture Wars: Secular–Catholic Conflict in Nineteenth-Century Europe* (Cambridge: Cambridge University Press, 2003).

12. The role of the clergy, especially those influenced by Jansenism, promoting the Revolution in its early stages has been the subject of fascinating research in recent years. See Dale K. Van Kley, *The Religious Origins of the French Revolution: From Calvin to the Civil Constitution, 1560–1791* (New Haven: Yale University Press, 1996) and Joseph F. Byrnes, *Priests of the Revolution: Saints and Renegades in a New Political Era* (University Park, PA: Pennsylvania University Press, 2014).

13. Prior to this, the tithe was abolished with the renunciation of feudal dues. See John McManners, *The French Revolution and the Church* (London: Harper & Row, 1969), 19ff. It should be underscored that numerous clergy willingly cooperated with nationalization at first because they felt that only by saving the state could they save the church and their own livelihoods.

14. On the reforms of Joseph II that closed down contemplative orders, see "Josephism" in *EVP*, 246–7.

15. For the rationale behind suppressions, see Joseph Marie Lequinio, *Suppression des religieux, extinction de la mendicité* (Paris, 1789). For a case study in France, see Mary Kathryn Robinson, *Regulars and the Secular Realm: The Benedictines of the Congregation of Saint-Maur during the 18th Century and the French Revolution* (Scranton, PA: University of Scranton Press, 2008). For case studies of the Napoleonic occupation of Italy, see Bruno Bertoli, *La soppressione di monasteri e conventi a Venezia dal 1797 al 1810* (Venice: Deputazione di storia patria per le Venezie, 2002).

16. Denis Diderot, *La religieuse* (Paris: Le livre de poche classique, 2000).

17. Quoted in Derek Beales, *Prosperity and Plunder: European Catholic Monasteries in the Age of Revolution, 1650–1815* (Cambridge: Cambridge University Press, 2003), 261–3.

18. On Erastianism, or the view that the state should administer the affairs of the Church, see *ODCC*, 558.

19. Augustin Theiner, ed., *Documents inédits relatifs aux affaires religieuses de la France 1790 à 1800 extraits des archives secrètes du Vatican*, vol. 1 (Paris, 1857), 32ff.

20. *PE*, vol. 1, 177–9. On the Civil Constitution and its effects, see Joseph F. Byrnes's masterly study, *Priests of the Revolution: Saints and Renegades in a New Political Era* (College Station: Penn State University Press, 2014).

21. Michael Burleigh, *Earthly Powers: The Clash of Religion and Politics from the French Revolution to the Great War* (New York: HarperCollins, 2005), 64.

22. McManners, *The French Revolution and the Church*, 64–5.

23. On the Vendée uprising and the long rebellion that followed, see Harvey Mitchell, "Resistance to the Revolution in Western France," *Past & Present* 63 (May 1974): 94–131.

24. Bruno Marguery-Melin, *La destruction de l'Abbaye de Cluny: 1789–1823* (Cluny: Centre d'études clunisiennes, 1985) and Beales, *Prosperity and Plunder*, 265–6. Cf. Louis Réau, *Histoire du vandalisme: les monuments détruits de l'art français* (Paris: R. Laffront, 1994), 364ff.

25. In all, some 30,000 priests fled abroad at this time. On this period and *déchristianisation* in general, see McManners, *The French Revolution and the Church*, 86ff., Dale K. Van Kley, "Christianity as Casualty and Chrysalis of Modernity: The Problem of Dechristianization in the French Revolution," *AHR* 108 (October 2003): 1081–104, and Charles L. Souvay, "The French Papal States during the Revolution," *CHR* 8 (1923): 485–96.

26. Hales, *Revolution and Papacy*, 113–14.

27. Denis Woronoff, *La République bourgeoise de Thermidor à Brumaire, 1794–1799* (Paris: Éditions du Seuil, 1972), 177–8.

28. Quoted in Hales, *Revolution and Papacy*, 114–15.

29. Francesco Leoni, *Storia della Controrivoluzione in Italia* (Naples: Guida, 1975), 92–6 and Tommaso Astarita, *Between Salt Water and Holy Water: A History of Southern Italy* (New York: W. W. Norton, 2005), 251, 254–5.

30. Hales, *Revolution and Papacy*, 128.

31. Quoted in Angus Heriot, *The French in Italy, 1796–1799* (London: Chatto & Windus, 1959), 174.

32. On Gregory XVI, see *ODDC*, 710.

33. Hales, *Revolution and Papacy*, 133.

34. Jean Leflon, *Pie VII: Des Abbayes bénédictines à la Papauté* (Paris: Libraire Plon, 1958), 414ff.

35. Consalvi left a fascinating memoir of this conclave. See Ercole Consalvi, "Memoire sul conclave in Venezia," in *AHP*, vol. 3 (1965): 239–308. Cf. Frank J. Coppa, *The Modern Papacy since 1789* (London: Longman, 1998), 33–5.

36. See Margot Lührs, *Napoleons Stellung zu Religion und Kirche* (Vaduz: Kraus, 1965).

37. Quoted in Chadwick, *Popes and European Revolution*, 484.

38. An exhaustive record of the negotiations over the Concordat is found in Boulay de la Meurthe, ed., *Documents sur la Négociation du Concordat*, 5 vols. (Paris, 1891). The text of the Concordat is found in Hales, *Revolution and Papacy*, 298–300.

39. Chadwick, *Popes and European Revolution*, 489.

40. Chadwick, *Popes and European Revolution*, 490.

41. Coppa, *The Modern Papacy since 1789*, 47 and Chadwick, *Popes and European Revolution*, 490–2, 494, 508ff.

42. Quoted in Chadwick, *Popes and European Revolution*, 510.

43. Noted in Robin Anderson, *Pope Pius VII (1800–23): His Life, His Times and His Struggle with Napoleon* (Rockford, IL: TAN Books, 2000), 196. On Napoleon's attitude to the Pope at this time, see his diary, *The Corsican: A Diary of Napoleon's Life in his own Words*, ed. R. M. Johnston (Boston: Houghton Mifflin, 1921), 277–9.

44. Quoted material from "Pius VII" in *PE* vol. 2, 1187. On the biblical Ahab–Naboth story, see I Kings 21.

45. Chadwick, *Popes and European Revolution*, 513.

46. Cardinal Nicholas Wiseman, *Recollections of the Last Four Popes and Rome in their Times* (London, 1858), 17.

47. 3,339 chests of archival papers were sent to France; only 2,200 returned after the downfall of Napoleon. Fragments from the archives could be bought in French bookshops until late in the nineteenth century. On the fate of the Vatican archives during this time, see Francis X. Blouin, ed., *Vatican Archives: An Inventory and Guide to Historical Documents of the Holy See* (New York: Oxford University Press, 1998), xx–xxi and Owen Chadwick, *Catholicism and History: The Opening of the Vatican Archives* (Cambridge: Cambridge University Press, 1978), 14–18.

48. The reforms and persecutions of this time are treated well in D. Menozzi, "L'orginazzazione della chiesa italiana in età napoleonica," *CnS* 14 (1993): 405–45.

49. Michael Broers, *The Politics of Religion in Napoleonic Italy: The War against God, 1801–1814* (London: Routledge, 2002).

50. Cited in Claudio Rendina, *Imperial City: Rome, Romans and Napoleon, 1796–1815* (Welwyn Garden City: Ravenhall Books, 2005), 208.

51. Wiseman, *Recollections of the Last Four Popes*, 18ff.

52. See Anon., ed., *Centenario del ritorno di Pio VII alla Sede Romana* (Rome: Cuggiani, 1914), Margaret O'Dwyer, *The Papacy in the Age of Napoleon and the Restoration: Pius VII, 1800–1823* (Lanham, MD: University Press of America, 1985), 125ff., and Donat Sampson, "Pius VII and the French Revolution," *ACQR* 35 (1910): 663–5.

53. Rendina, *Imperial City*, 223. On Döllinger's attraction to Pius VII, see Acton's notes, CUL Add. 4905/156.

54. See Lord Acton, "Döllinger's Historical Work," in J. Rufus Fears, ed., *Selected Writings of Lord Acton, vol. 2: Essays in the Study and Writing of History* (Indianapolis: Liberty Classics, 1986), 434.

55. *Martyrologe du clergé français* (Paris, 1840).

56. E. C. Pursell, "Bonapartism," *DR* 49 (1860): 104.

57. Quoted from "Pius VII" in *PE* vol. 2, 1188.

58. Luigi Ademollo, *The Triumph of the Church and Pius VII* (Rome: Gabinetto Nazionale delle Stampe, 1814). Cf. Roberta J. M. Olson, "Representations of Pius VII," *Art Bulletin* 68 (March 1986): 77–93.

59. See Anon., ed., *Centenario del ritorno di Pio VII alla Sede Romana*. Cf. "Celebrate Pope's Return: Catholics Observe Centennial of Pius VII's Arrival in Rome," *New York Times* (June 7, 1914).

60. B. Van den Herten, "La Révolution française: prélude à la fin des temps," *RHE* 89 (1994): 29–53.

61. The Benedictine Monks of Solesmes, eds., *Papal Teachings: The Church*, trans. Mother E. O'Gorman, R.S.C.J. (Boston: St. Paul's, 1962), 111. Pope Leo I or Leo the Great was a major figure in shaping claims of papal primacy and was frequently referred to in nineteenth-century debates. See W. Ullman, "Leo I and the Theme of Papal Primacy," *JTS* 11 (1960): 25–51.

62. The Benedictine Monks of Solesmes, eds., *Papal Teachings: The Church*, 105.

63. *AGP*, vol. 1 (Rome, 1901), 309. A theological movement in seventeenth-century France, Jansenism traces its origins to the writings of Otto Cornelius Jansen (1585–1638), especially his *Augustinus* (1640). In the eyes of the Church, its exponents, in their interpretations of Paul and Augustine's writings, veered dangerously close to Calvin's teaching on grace. The movement was condemned by Sorbonne in 1649 and by Pope Innocent X in 1653, and again in the papal bull *Unigenitus* (1713). Frequently persecuted but never uprooted in France, Jansenists often took refuge in the Netherlands. In 1723 Dutch Jansenists nominated a schismatic bishop. This history intersects in the nineteenth century with the story of German Old Catholicism, for from this line of bishops the first German Old Catholic bishop, J. H. Reinkens, was consecrated. This topic will be taken up in Chapter 4. On Jansenism in general, see *RPP*, 650–2 and *ODCC*, 862–3.

64. Giuseppe di Lampedusa, *The Leopard*, trans. Archibald Colquhoun (New York: Pantheon Books, 2007), 28 (emphasis added).

65. Friedrich Meinecke, *Historism: The Rise of a New Historical Outlook*, trans. J. E. Anderson (New York: Herder and Herder, 1972), liv. Cf. Thomas Albert Howard, *Religion and the Rise of Historicism* (Cambridge: Cambridge University Press, 1999), 12–17.

66. Brian E. Vick, *The Congress of Vienna: Power and Politics after Napoleon* (Cambridge, MA: Harvard University Press, 2014), 4–5, passim.

67. See T. C. W. Blanning, "The Role of Religion in European Counter-Revolution, 1789–1815," in Derek Beales and Geoffrey Best, eds., *History, Society and the Churches: Essays in Honour of Owen Chadwick* (Cambridge: Cambridge University Press, 1985), 195ff. and Burleigh, *Earthly Powers*, 119f.

68. On Consalvi's central role during this time, see Alessandro Roveri, *La Santa Sede tra Rivoluzione e Restaurazione: il Cardinal Consalvi 1813–1815* (Florence: La Nuova Italia, 1974). Cf. Vick, *Congress of Vienna*, 153ff.

69. Quoted in Chadwick, *Popes and European Revolution*, 555.

70. Cardinal Giuseppe Sala, *Scritti di Giuseppe Antonio Sala*, vol. 4 (Rome, 1888), 72–3.

71. Eamon Duffy, *Saints and Sinners: A History of the Popes* (New Haven: Yale University Press, 2006), 272–3.

72. See Hubert Wolf, ed., *Römische Inquisition und Indexkongregation: Grundlagenforschung, 1814–1917: Einleitung* (Paderborn: Schöningh, 2005), 220.

73. On the Carbonari (or "charcoal burners") and other secret societies during this period, see John Rath, "The Carbonari: Their Origins, Initiation Rites, and Aims," *AHR* 69 (January 1964): 353–70 and E. E. Y. Hales, *Mazzini and the*

Secret Societies (New York: P. J. Kenedy, 1956). Cf. Thomas Frost, *The Secret Societies of the European Revolution, 1776–1876* (London, 1867).

74. On the Jesuits during this period, see Jonathan Wright, "The Suppression and Restoration of the Jesuits," in Thomas Worcester, ed., *The Cambridge Companion to the Jesuits* (Cambridge: Cambridge University Press, 2008), 263–77 and Bartholomew Murphy, *Der Wiederaufbau der Gesellschaft Jesu in Deutschland im 19. Jahrhundert* (Frankfurt am Main: Peter Lang, 1985), 27ff.

75. Darrin M. McMahon, *Enemies of the Enlightenment: The French Counter-Enlightenment and the Making of Modernity* (Oxford: Oxford University Press, 2001), 77–8, 216–17, n.116.

76. Gregory XVI, *Il trionfo della Santa Sede e della Chiesa contro gli assalti de' novatori respinti e combattuti stesse loro armi* (Rome, 1799), 1. This work was reprinted and translated into many languages after Capellari become pope in 1831.

77. On de Maistre generally, see Carolina Armenteros, "Joseph de Maistre (1753–1821): Heir of the Enlightenment, Enemy of Revolutions, and Spiritual Progressivist," in Jeffrey D. Burson and Ulrich L. Lehner, eds., *Enlightenment and Catholic Europe: A Transnational History* (Notre Dame: University of Notre Dame Press, 2014), 125–44.

78. Joseph de Maistre, *Du Pape* (Lyons, 1836), vol. 1, xl.

79. De Maistre, *Considérations sur la France* (Paris: Garnier, 1980). Cf. his *Réflexions sur le protestantisme dans ses rapports avec la souveraineté* (1798). On his turn to ultramontanism, see Emile Perreau-Saussine, "Why Maistre became Ultramontane," in Carolina Armenteros and Richard A. Lebrun, eds., *Joseph de Maistre and the Legacy of the Enlightenment* (Oxford: Voltaire Foundation, 2011), 147–59.

80. Joseph de Maistre, *The Works of Joseph de Maistre*, trans. Jack Lively (New York: Macmillan, 1965), 70.

81. De Maistre, *Du Pape*, vol. 1, xxii.

82. Quoted in Robert McClory, *Power and the Papacy: The People and Politics behind the Doctrine of Papal Infallibility* (Liguori, MO: Triumph Press, 1997), 52.

83. De Maistre, *Du Pape*, vol. 2, 663.

84. De Maistre, *Du Pape*, vol. 1, 262–3.

85. De Maistre, *Du Pape*, vol. 1, xl–xli.

86. De Maistre, *Du Pape*, vol. 2, 594.

87. De Maistre, *Du Pape*, vol. 1, 207ff. On the origins of the Papal States, see Thomas F. X. Noble, *The Repulic of Saint Peter: The Birth of the Papal States, 680–825* (Philadelphia: University of Pennsylvania Press, 1984).

88. De Maistre, *Du Pape*, vol. 1, 194.

89. De Maistre, *Du Pape*, vol. 1, 191.

90. De Maistre, *Du Pape*, vol. 1, 194–5.

91. De Maistre, *Du Pape*, vol. 1, 195.

92. On the broader climate of opinion, see August Bernhard Hasler, *How the Pope Became Infallible: Pius IX and the Politics of Persuasion*, trans. Peter Heinegg (Garden City, NY: Doubleday, 1981), 39ff.

93. For a variety of outlooks on this topc, see Brian Tierney, "The Origins of Papal Infallibility," *JES* 8 (1971): 841–64, Klaus Schatz, *Der Päpstliche Primat: Seine*

Geschichte von den Ursprüngen bis zur Gegenwart (Würzburg: Echter Verlag, 1996), and James Heft, *John XXII and Papal Teaching Authority* (Lewiston, NY: Edwin Mellen Press, 1986).

94. Hermann Josef Pottmeyer, *Unfehlbarkeit und Souveränität: Die päpstliche Unfehlbarkeit im System der ultramontanen Ekklesiologie des. 19. Jahrhunderts* (Mainz: Matthias-Grünewald Verlag, 1975), 354–63.
95. McClory, *Power and the Papacy*, 52.
96. Schatz, *Der Päpstliche Primat*, 179.
97. See Isaiah Berlin, *The Proper Study of Mankind: An Anthology of Essays* (New York: Farrar, Straus, & Giroux, 1997), 264.
98. CUL Add. 4903/56, 102. On Baader and de Maistre, see Carla de Pascale, *Tra rivoluzione e restaurazione: la filosofia della societádi Franz von Baader* (Naples: Bibliopolis, 1982), 43, 47, passim. As Lord Acton once noted: "These conversations [with Baader about de Maistre] were the origin of Döllinger's specific ultramontanism." See Acton, "Döllinger's Historical Work," 413.
99. CUL Add. 2427/31. *TG*, 23, 35–6. On the general influence of de Maistre, see Pottmeyer, *Unfehlbarkeit und Souveränität*, 61–72.
100. CUL Add. 4909/302.
101. See Thomas Nipperdey's helpful discussion of the "revolution of historicism," in *Germany from Napoleon to Bismark, 1800–1866*, trans. Daniel Nolan (Princeton: Princeton University Press, 1996), 441–71. In the middle decades of the nineteenth century, as Acton wrote, "the idea of development was in the air." CUL Add. 4907/259.
102. Maurice Mandelbaum, *History, Man, & Reason: A Study in Nineteenth-Century Thought* (Baltimore: Johns Hopkins University Press, 1971), 42. Cf. Georg G. Iggers, "Historicism: The History and Meaning of the Term," *JHI* 56 (January 1995): 129–52.
103. Acton, "Döllinger's Historical Work," 416, 426ff. On historicism and German academic culture in the nineteenth century, see Thomas Albert Howard, *Protestant Theology and the Making of the Modern German University* (Oxford: Oxford University Press, 2006), 324f.
104. CUL Add. 4906/35, 41; CUL Add. 4907/195.
105. Leonard Krieger, "Elements of Early Historicism: Experience, Theory, and History in Ranke," *HT* 14 (December 1975), 1ff.
106. Leopold von Ranke, *Geschichte der romanischen und germanischen Völker von 1494 bis 1514* (Leipzig, 1874), iv–vii. A nice introdution to Ranke's significance is provided in Georg G. Iggers and James M. Powell, eds., *Leopold von Ranke and the Shaping of the Historical Discipline* (Syracuse, NY: Syracuse University Press, 1990).
107. Leopold von Ranke, *Die römischen Päpste in den letzten vier Jahrhunderten*, vol. 1, 8th ed. (Leipzig, 1885), 4.
108. Ranke, *Die römischen Päpste*, vol. 1, xi.
109. Ranke as quoted by M. A. Fitzsimmons in "Ranke: History as Worship," *RP* 42 (October 1980): 546.
110. See Hubert Wolf, *Rankes Päpste auf dem Index: Dogma und Historie in Widerstreit* (Paderborn: Schöningh, 2003), 11–12. On Acton and Döllinger's stance

toward Ranke (one of both praise and criticism), see Roland Hill, *Lord Acton* (New Haven: Yale University Press, 2000), 103–6. Cf. Acton, "Döllinger's Historical Work," 429.

111. Döllinger, *Die Universitäten, sonst und jetzt*, 2nd ed. (Munich, 1871), 39.

112. Döllinger, *Die Universitäten*, 36–40.

113. CUL Add. 4909/338, 365.

114. As Lord Acton succinctly summed up Döllinger's critical view of neo-Thomism: "Historismus in der Kirche, statt Philosophie." CUL Add. 4910/72.

115. James Pereiro, *Cardinal Manning: From Anglican Archdeacon to Council Father at Vatican I* (Oxford: Clarendon Press, 1998), 204–7.

116. E. S. Purcell, "Papal Allocutions and Revolutionary Principles," *DR* 51 (1862): 206.

117. On Mazzini's religious outlook and the role of anti-papalism therein, see Frank Coppa, "The Religious Basis of Giuseppe Mazzini's Political Thought," *JCS* 12 (1970): 237ff., 244.

118. Spencer M. Di Scala, *Italy: From Revolution to Republic, 1700 to the Present*, 4th ed. (Boulder, CO: Westview Press, 2009), 69ff. In the context of the *Risorgimento*, mention should also be made of the movement of "neo-Guelphism," associated with the liberal priest Vincenzo Gioberti (1801–52), who advocated for Italy to unite around the presidency of the Pope. His ideas gained some saliency but were rejected by Pius IX in an allocution of 1848. The key publication in this movement was Gioberti's book, *Del primato civile e morale degli italiani* (Brussels, 1843).

119. *PE*, vol. 1, 278.

120. See Alasdair MacIntyre, *God, Philosophy, Universities: A Selective History of the Catholic Philosophical Tradition* (Lanham, MD: Rowman & Littlefield, 2009), 151ff. and Paolo Dezza, *Alle origini nel neotomismo* (Milan: Fratelli Bocca, 1940). On Pius IX's role in reviving Thomism, see *Pio IX e la rinascita del tomismo* (Vatican City: Libreria editrice vaticana, 1974).

121. On the different trajectories of religious liberty set in motion by the American and French revolutions, see Thomas Albert Howard, *God and the Atlantic: America, Europe, and the Religious Divide* (Oxford: Oxford University Press, 2011), 193–205.

122. See "indifferentismo" in *EC*, vol. 6 (1951), 1830–2. Cf. the essays in Karl Gabriel, Christian Spieß, and Katja Winkler, eds., *Religionsfreiheit und Pluralismus: Entwicklungslinien eines katholischen Lernprozesses* (Paderborn: Ferdinand Schöningh, 2010).

123. On Passaglia, see Gianluca Carlin, *L'ecclesiologia di Carlo Passaglia (1812–1887) mit einer deutschen Zusammenfassung* (Münster: Lit, 2001).

124. "Worse than Attila" was Bishop Ullathorne of Birmingham's assessment of the challenges facing the papacy of Pius IX. See his "Letter Addressed to the Clergy and Laity of the Diocese of Birmingham," printed in the *Weekly Register* (November 19, 1870). BAB Döllinger 5 270/17.

125. Wiseman, *Recollections of the Last Four Popes*, 197ff.

126. On the Jews in the Papal States at this time, see Thomas Brechenmacher, *Das Ende der doppelten Schutzherrschaft: der Heilige Stuhl und die Juden am Übergang zur Moderne, 1775–1870* (Stuttgart: Anton Hiersemann, 2004).

127. Mario Caravale and Alberto Caracciolo, *Lo stato pontificio da Martino V a Pio IX* (Torino: UTET, 1978), 609–10 and Wiseman, *Recollections of the Last Four Popes*, 209ff.

128. While Freemasonry varied in outlook from country to country, it took on a profoundly anticlerical and anti-papal character on the Italian peninsula and in many Catholic countries and therefore was vehemently denounced by Rome. See the entry on "Freemasonry and papacy" in *EVP*, 167–9. A classic work on this topic for Italy is Rosario F. Eposito, *La Massoneria de l'Italia dal 1800 ai nostri giorni*, 5th ed. (Rome: Paoline, 1979).

129. *PE*, vol. 1, 199–203.

130. *PE*, vol. 1, 221–3.

131. The order dates from the early 1000s; its monks, quasi-hermits, observed the barest minimum of communal ties. See Emanuele Bargellini, *Camaldoli iere et oggi: l'identità camaldolese nel nuovo millennio* (Camaldoli: Monastero di Camaldoli, 2000) and *ODCC*, 269–70.

132. On the Papal States under his pontificate, see Caravale and Caracciolo, *Lo stato pontificio*, 615ff.

133. Coppa, *The Modern Papacy since 1789*, 67–83.

134. A decade prior to this, it should be noted, revolts took place in Piedmont and the Kingdom of the Two Sicilies; both were suppressed by troops of the Holy Alliance.

135. Domenico Demarco, *Il tramonto dello Stato pontificio: Il papato di Gregorio XVI* (Turin: G. Einaudi, 1949), 234f. and Caravale and Caracciolo, *Lo stato pontificio*, 620–5.

136. ASV Fondo Particulare Pio IX, Cassetta 5, busta 3.

137. *AGP*, vol. 2, 34–5.

138. *AGP*, vol. 1, 299.

139. On the context of Lamennais's writings, see especially Vincent Viaene, *Belgium and the Holy See from Gregory XVI to Pius IX (1831–1859): Catholic Revival, Society and Politics in 19th-Century Europe* (Leuven: Leuven University Press, 2001).

140. See, for example, *Articles de l'Avenir*, vol. 2 (Louvain, 1831), 163–4.

141. "Atque ex hoc putidissimo indifferentismi fonte absurda illa fluit ac erronea sententia, seu potius deliramentum asserendam esse ac vindicandam cuilibet libertatem conscientiae." *AGP*, vol. 1, 172; cf. English translation in *PE*, vol. 1, 238 (translation modified).

142. *AGP*, vol. 1, 172–3; *PE*, vol. 1, 238–9.

143. *PE*, vol. 1, 250.

144. *RPP*, vol. 6, 97–9.

145. Gerald A. McCool, *Catholic Theology in the Nineteenth Century* (New York: Seabury Press, 1977), 23, 135–9. On the importance of *La Civiltà Cattolica*, see Francesco Dante, *Storia della "Civiltà Cattolica" (1850–1891): Il laboratorio del Papa* (Rome: Edizioni Studium, 1990). Cf. *Saggi sulla rinascita del Tomismo nel secolo XIX* (Vatican City, 1974).

146. Otto Weiß, "Döllinger, Rom und Italien," in *GG*, 254–6.

147. Roger Aubert, *Le pontificat de Pie IX (1846–1878)* (Paris: Bloud & Gay, 1952), 12–16.

148. See Döllinger's fragment on Pius IX in H. F. Reusch, ed., *Kleinere Schriften, gedruckte und ungedruckte, von J. J. I. von Döllinger* (Stuttgart: Cotta, 1890), 560.

149. Aubert, *Le pontificat de Pie IX*, 20–1.

150. Caravale and Caracciolo, *Lo stato pontificio*, 641–9 and "The Jews of Rome," *London Daily News* (September 8, 1849). On Pius IX's fraught relations with Jews, see David Kertzer, *The Popes against the Jews: The Vatican's Role in the Rise of Modern Anti-Semitism* (New York: Alfred A. Knopf, 2001). For a criticism of Kertzer's work, see Justus George Lawler, *Were the Popes against the Jews?* (Grand Rapids, MI: Eerdmans, 2012).

151. Aubert, *Le pontificat de Pie IX*, 16–18. See the first-hand account of Pius's reception shortly after 1846 in Frances Elliot, *Roman Gossip* (London, 1894), 41–9.

152. Leo F. Stock, ed., *Consular Relations between the United States and the Papal States* (Washington, DC: American Catholic Historical Association, 1945), 92, 114.

153. On the dramatic events of 1848 and Pius IX's escape to Gaeta, see Aubert, *Le pontificat de Pie IX*, 27–71 and Owen Chadwick, *A History of the Popes, 1830–1914* (Oxford: Oxford University Press, 1998), 82–91.

154. From his exile in London, Mazzini had written an "Open Letter to the Pope," in which he urged the Pope to help unify Italy, for "such was the will of God." See Giuseppe Mazzini, *Scritti editi ed inediti*, vol. 77 (Imola: P. Galeati, 1940), 341.

155. Quoted in Roland Sarti, "Giuseppe Mazzini and his Opponents," in John A. Davis, ed., *Italy in the Nineteenth Century* (Oxford: Oxford University Press, 2000), 94.

156. Article 8 of the Constitution reads: "*Il Capo della Chiesa Cattolica avrà dalla Republica tutte le guarentigie necessarie per l'esercizio indipendente del potere spirituale.*" The Constitution can be found at <http://web.archive.org/web/20070928075639/http://www.domusmazziniana.it/materiali/costirep.htm>.

157. See Carlo Falconi, *Il Cardinale Antonelli: vita e carriere del Richelieu italiano nella Chiesa di Pio IX* (Milan: A. Mondadori, 1983). Prior to 1849, Rosmini had been a key liberal voice supporting the reforms after 1846. His book *Delle cinque piaghe della Santa Chiesa* (Five Wounds of the Holy Church), published in 1849 but written much earlier, became a staple among reformist Catholics, influencing Döllinger and Lord Acton among others. See *GT*, 75–6.

158. But some violence and desecrations did take place. Perhaps the most notorious was when an anticlerical gang forced its way into the monastery of San Callisto in Trastevere and killed ten monks. See Chadwick, *A History of the Popes, 1830–1914*, 87.

159. *AP*, vol. 1, 174, 183–4.

160. Quoted in Frank Coppa, *Politics and the Papacy in the Modern World* (Westport, CT: Praeger, 2008), 45.

161. On Garibaldi's defense of Rome and the collapse of the Republic, see G. M. Trevelyan, *Garibaldi's Defence of the Roman Republic* (London: Longman, 1907).

162. Friedrich Engel-Janosi, "The Return of Pius IX in 1850," *CHR* 36 (July 1950): 129–62.

163. Thomas Aquinas died at this monastery on March 7, 1274.

164. Raffaele de Cesare, *The Last Days of Papal Rome, 1850–1870*, trans. Helen Zimmern (London: Constable, 1909), 4, 10.

165. A. C. Jemolo, *Chiesa e Stato in Italia negli ultimi cento anni* (Turin: Einaudi, 1949), 123ff. and Giacomo Martina, *Pio IX (1851–1866)*, vol. 2 (Rome: Editrice Pontificia Università Gregoriana, 1986), 49–84.

166. *Punch* (November 18, 1859): 203.

167. E. About, *The Roman Question*, trans. H. C. Coape (New York, 1859), 90.

168. Charles Eliot Norton, *Notes of Study and Travel in Italy* (Boston: Houghton Mifflin, 1957), 164.

169. *Kleinere Schriften*, 581.

170. *PE*, vol. 1, 295.

171. *PE*, vol. 1, 298.

172. *PE*, vol. 1, 302.

173. Caravele and Caracciolo, *Lo stato pontificio*, 672–82 and Martina, *Pio IX*, vol. 2, 1–3.

174. Cf. Gordon Albion, "The Restoration of the Hierarchy," in George Andrew Beck, ed., *The English Catholics, 1850–1950* (London: Burns & Oates, 1950), 86–115 and Aubert, *Le pontificat de Pie IX*, 67–71.

175. Luigi Gambero, *Mary and the Fathers of the Church*, trans. Thomas Buffer (San Francisco: Ignatius Press, 1999).

176. See Basil Cole and Francis Belanger, "The Immaculate Conception, St. Thomas, and Blessed Pius IX," *Nova et Vetera* 4 (2006): 473–94. For more on the history of the dogma, see *ODCC*, 821–2, Jaroslav Pelikan, *Mary through the Centuries: Her Place in the History of Culture* (New Haven: Yale University Press, 1996), and Hilda C. Graef, *Mary: A History of Doctrine and Devotion* (Notre Dame: Christian Classics, 2009).

177. Aubert, *Le pontificat de Pie IX*, 466f.

178. See Ruth Harris, *Lourdes: Body and Spirit in a Secular Age* (New York: Vintage Books, 1999).

179. Martina, *Pio IX*, vol. 2, 261–82. Cf. Veronika Maria Seifert's exhaustive study of Pius's Marian piety: *Pius IX, der Immaculata-Papst: von der Marienverehrung Giovanni Maria Mastai Ferrettis zur Definierung des Immaculata-Dogmas* (Göttingen: Vandenhoeck & Ruprecht, 2013).

180. *PE*, vol. 1, 292.

181. Martina, *Pio IX*, vol. 2, 263–6.

182. The full text of *Ineffabilis Deus* can be found at <http://www.papalencyclicals.net/Pius09/p9ineff.htm> (accessed June 15, 2012).

183. One may view the room at <http://mv.vatican.va/3_EN/pages/z-Info/MV_Info_Restauro04.html> (accessed June 15, 2012). Copies of *Ineffabilis Deus*, in practically every language in the world, are stored in the room. The central fresco shows Pius IX defining dogma with the heavenly host rejoicing. The paintings were done by the artist Francesco Podesti, who witnessed the original proclamation in St. Peter's in 1854. See *La sala dell'immacolata di Francesco Podesti* (Vatican City: Edizioni Musei Vaticani, 2010).

184. This symbolism is a reference to Genesis 3:15 when God says to the serpent: "I will put enmity between you and the woman, and between your seed and her

seed; he [the Christ child, symbolically understood] shall bruise your head" (RSV).

185. Martina, *Pio IX*, vol. 2, 282–6.

186. Gerhard Müller, "Die Immaculata Conceptio im Urteil der mitteleuropäischen Bischöfe," *KD* 14 (1968): 46–70.

187. Johann Friedrich, *Ignaz von Döllinger: Sein Leben auf Grund seines schriftlichen Nachlasses*, vol. 3 (Munich: C. H. Beck, 1901), 144–9.

188. Heinrich Reusch, ed., *Bericht über die am 14., 15. und 16. September zu Bonn gehalten Unions-Conferenzen* (Bonn, 1874), 39. Cf. *Kleinere Schriften*, 601–2.

189. Alfred Plummer, *Conversations with Dr. Döllinger, 1870–1890*, ed. Robrecht Boudens (Louvain: Louvain University Press, 1985), 107. In 1874 Döllinger wrote Henry Nutcombe Oxenham: "The dogmatic decree of 1854 was the calculated precursor to that of 1870, the first completely open break with the tradition of the entire ancient Church." Quoted in CUL Add. 4909/293.

CHAPTER 2

1. Johann Friedrich, *Ignaz von Döllinger: Sein Leben auf Grund seines schriftlichen Nachlasses*, vol. 1 (Munich: C. H. Beck, 1899), 64.

2. For one of the most astute critiques of this motif, see Timothy Larsen, *Crisis of Doubt: Honest Faith in Nineteenth-Century England* (Oxford: Oxford University Press, 2006), 1–3.

3. For a breakdown of the confessional topography and demographics at the beginning of the nineteenth century, see Peter Claus Hartmann, "Bevölkerungszahlen und Konfessionsverhältnisse des Heiligen Römischen Reiches Deutscher Nation und der Reichkreise am Ende des 18. Jahrhunderts," *ZHF* 22 (1995): 345–69.

4. Karl Buchheim, *Ultramontanismus und Demokratie: der Weg der deutschen Katholiken im 19. Jahrhundert* (Munich: Kösel Verlag, 1963), 35ff.

5. Thomas Albert Howard, *Protestant Theology and the Making of the Modern German University* (Oxford: Oxford University Press, 2006), 326.

6. On Döllinger's father, see Eckhard Struck, "Ignaz Döllinger: Ein Physiologe der Goethe-Zeit und der Entwicklungsgedanke in seinem Leben und Werk" (Dissertation, Munich, 1977) and *ADB*, vol. 5, 315–18.

7. Josef Urban, "Döllinger und Bamberg," in *GG*, 171ff.

8. On Döllinger's early years and family relations, see Friedrich, *Döllinger*, vol. 1, 60–9 and Angela Berlis, "Blicke zurück: Vom Totenbett Döllingers in sein Leben," in Elisabeth Bach, Angela Berlis, and Siegfried J. Thuringer, eds., *Ignaz von Döllinger zum 125. Todestag* (Munich: Alt-Katholische Kirchengemeinde St. Wilibrord, 2015), 74–8.

9. This work was heavily indebted to the French scholar Antonine Arnauld's *La perpétuité de la foi de l'Église touchant l'Eucharistie*, 3 vols. (Paris, 1669–74).

10. Friedrich, *Döllinger*, vol. 1, 105.

11. Carl Prantl, *Geschichte der Ludwig-Maximilians-Universität in Ingolstadt, Landshut, München* (Munich, 1872), 725.

12. Franz Herre, *Ludwig I: ein Romantiker auf Bayerns Thron* (Stuttgart: Hohenheim, 2005), 177–90.

13. Roland Hill, *Lord Acton* (New Haven: Yale University Press, 2000), 27ff.

14. See Lawrence G. Duggan, "The Church as an Institution in the Reich," in James A. Vann and Steven Rowan, eds., *The Old Reich: Essays on German Political Institutions, 1495–1806* (Brussels: Éditions de la librairie encyclopédique, 1974), 151–64 and Joachim Whaley, *Germany and the Holy Roman Empire, vol. 2: The Peace of Westphalia to the Dissolution of the Reich, 1648–1806* (Oxford: Oxford University Press, 2013), 150ff., 257ff.

15. Romuald Bauerreiss, *Kirchengeschichte Bayerns, vol. 7: 1600–1803* (Augsburg: Verlag Winfried-Werk, 1970), 416–19 and Michael Printy, *Enlightenment and the Creation of German Catholicism* (Cambridge: Cambridge University Press, 2009), 14.

16. On Josephism, see *EVP*, 246–7.

17. For one of the best treatments of these dissolutions, see Derek Beales, *Prosperity and Plunder: European Catholic Monasteries in the Age of Revolution, 1650–1815* (Cambridge: Cambridge University Press, 2003), 192ff.

18. Derek Beales, *Joseph II*, vol. 2 (Cambridge: Cambridge University Press, 1987), 271ff. and Owen Chadwick, *The Popes and European Revolution* (Oxford: Clarendon Press, 1981), 411–17.

19. The suppression took place during the papacy of Clement XIV (r. 1769–74). On the far-reaching repercussions of this event, see Jeffrey D. Burson and Jonathan Wright, eds., *The Jesuit Suppression in Global Context: Causes, Events, Consequences* (New York: Cambridge University Press, 2015).

20. Elisabeth Kovás, *Der Pabst in Teuschland: die Reise Pius VI. im Jahre 1782* (Vienna: Verlag für Geschichte und Politik, 1983).

21. On Febronianism, see *EVP*, 159–60.

22. Marc R. Forster, *Catholic Germany from the Reformation to the Enlightenment* (New York: Palgrave Macmillan, 2007), 189–90.

23. Hajo Holborn, *A History of Modern Germany, 1648–1840*, vol. 1 (Princeton: Princeton University Press, 1982), 223. On the term "Catholic Enlightenment" and the influence of Hontheim's book, see also Harm Klueting, ed., *Katholische Aufklärung: Aufklärung im katholischen Deutschland* (Hamburg: Meiner, 1993). Cf. Jeffrey D. Burson and Ulrich L. Lehner, eds., *Enlightenment and Catholicism in Europe: A Transnational History* (Notre Dame: University of Notre Dame Press, 2014).

24. In the summary of Hontheim's work that follows, I recognize a debt to Ulrich L. Lehner's introduction to Johann Nikolaus von Hontheim, *Justini Febronii commentarius in suam retractionem (1781)*, ed. Ulrich L. Lehner (Nordhausen: Verlag Traugott Bautz, 2008), i–lv and to Printy, *Enlightenment and the Creation of German Catholicism*, 25–54.

25. Quoted in Printy, *Enlightenment and the Creation of German Catholicism*, 25.

26. The "False Decretals" are a collection of canon law documents said to be the work of a so-called Isidore Mercator, "Pseudo-Isidore." Part of the Decretals are authentic, but other parts—the ones containing the (false) Donation of Constantine and other documents and letters suggesting papal supremacy—are spurious. See *ODCC*, 598.

27. For an excellent discussion of Hontheim's proto-ecumenical ideas in historical context and their later influence, see Christopher Spehr, *Aufklärung und*

Ökumene: Reunionsversuche zwischen Katholiken und Protestanten im deutsch-sprachigen Raum des späteren 18. Jahrhunderts (Tübingen: Mohr Siebeck, 2005), 34–48.

28. Chadwick, *Popes and European Revolution*, 409.

29. Quoted in Chadwick, *Popes and European Revolution*, 411. On Fénelon, whom Döllinger deeply admired, see Sabine Melchior-Bonnet, *Fénelon* (Paris: Perrin, 2008).

30. Bauerreiss, *Kirchengeschichte Bayerns, vol. 7: 1600–1803*, 416ff.

31. Ernst H. J. Münch, *Vollständige Sammlung aller älteren und neueren Concordate*, vol. 1 (Leipzig, 1831), 407 (emphasis added).

32. Ernst Hermann Münch, *Geschichte des Emser Kongresses und seiner Punktate* (Karlsruhe: Müller Verlag, 1840), 1ff.

33. Printy, *Enlightenment and the Creation of German Catholicism*, 26, 51.

34. Chadwick, *Popes and European Revolution*, 411.

35. H. Raab, "Zur Geschichte und Bedeutung des Schlagwortes Ultramontan im 18. und frühen 19. Jahrhundert," *Historisches Jahrbuch der Görres-Gesellschaft* 81 (1962): 159–73.

36. Franz Schnabel, *Deutsche Geschichte im neunzehnten Jahrhundert, vol. 4: Die religiösen Kräfte* (Freiburg im Breisgau: Herder, 1936), 5–20.

37. E. R. Huber and W. Huber, eds., *Staat und Kirche im 19. und 20. Jahrhundert: Dokumente zur Geschichte des deutschen Staatskirchenrechts*, vol. 1 (Berlin: Duncker & Humblot, 1973), 14–15.

38. Chadwick, *Popes and European Revolution*, 496.

39. Klaus Schatz, *Zwischen Säkularisation und zweitem Vatikanum: Der Weg des deutschen Katholizismus im 19. und 20. Jahrhundert* (Frankfurt am Main: Verlag Josef Knecht, 1986), 22–7.

40. Huber and Huber, eds., *Staat und Kirche im 19. und 20. Jahrhundert*, vol. 1, 17–19.

41. Beales, *Prosperity and Plunder*, 286, 289.

42. Huber and Huber, eds., *Staat und Kirche im 19. und 20. Jahrhundert*, vol. 1, 20.

43. Brian E. Vick, *The Congress of Vienna: Power and Politics after Napoleon* (Cambridge, MA: Harvard University Press, 2014), 153ff.

44. Quoted in Karl Hausberger and Benno Hubensteiner, *Bayerische Kirchengeschichte* (Munich: Süddeutscher Verlag, 1985), 281–2.

45. On Montgelas in general, see Franz Herre, *Montgelas: Gründer des bayerischen Staates* (Weilheim: Stöppel, 1988) and Wolfgang Gimbel, "Der Wandel der Rechtsbeziehung von Kirche und Staat unter Montgelas" (Dissertation, Munich, 1966).

46. Some monasteries had already been closed under Elector Karl Theodor; see Jahn, *Klosteraufhebungen und Klosterpolitik in Bayern unter Kürfürst Karl Theodor, 1778–1784*.

47. Among many sources, see Alois Schmid, ed., *Säkularisation in Bayern: Kultur-bruch oder Modernisierung?* (Munich: C. H. Beck, 2003).

48. Quoted in Hausberger and Hubensteiner, *Bayerische Kirchengeschichte*, 277.

49. Thomas Nipperdey, *Germany from Napoleon to Bismarck, 1800–1866*, trans. Daniel Nolan (Princeton: Princeton University Press, 1983), 59.

50. Chester Penn Higby, *The Religious Policy of the Bavarian Government during the Napoleonic Period* (New York: Columbia University, 1919), 18.

51. Huber and Huber, eds., *Staat und Kirche im 19. und 20. Jahrhundert*, vol. 1, 59–60.

52. Higby, *The Religious Policy of the Bavarian Government*, 309f.

53. See Wilhelm Liebhart, *Bayerns Könige: Königtum und Politik in Bayern*, 2nd ed. (Frankfurt am Main: Peter Lang, 1997).

54. On the "concordat system" in general at this time, see Nicholas Atkin and Frank Tallett, *Priests, Prelates, and People: A History of European Catholicism since 1750* (London: I. B. Tauris, 2003), 89–92.

55. See Georg Schwaiger, ed., *Das Erzbistum München und Freising im 19. und 20. Jahrhundert* (Munich: Erich Wewel Verlag, 1989), 11–16.

56. Erwin Gatz, *Die Bistümer der deutschsprachigen Länder von der Säkularisation bis zur Gegenwart* (Freiburg im Breisgau: Herder, 2005), 68ff., 507ff.

57. Bishops are given "unrestricted power" (*ungehinderte Gewalt*) to discipline clergy without interference from the state. See article 12.d especially in *Konkordat zwischen den heiligen Stuhle zu Rom, und dem Königreich Baiern, geschlossen am 5.ten und publicirt im Consistorium zum Rom am 15. Nov. 1817* (Passau, 1817), 22–4.

58. Max Braubach, "Die katholischen Universitäten Deutschlands und die französische Revolution," *HJB* 49 (1929): 263–303. Cf. Karl Theodor von Hegel, *Die Verlegung der Ludwig-Maximilians-Universität nach München* (Munich, 1897).

59. Howard, *Protestant Theology and the Making of the Modern German University*, 130ff.

60. Heinrich Joseph Floss, *Denkschrift über die Parität an der Universität Bonn mit einem Hinblick auf die übrigen Preussischen Hoschschulen* (Freiburg im Breisgau, 1862).

61. On Döllinger's calling, see Ursula Huber, "Döllinger und die Verwaltung der Universität München," in *GG*, 13–20 and Friedrich, *Döllinger*, vol. 1, 183ff.

62. Ludwig I had in fact attended lectures by Sailer at Landshut and developed there a strong admiration for him. He and his ministers looked to Sailer for advice after his ascension to the throne in 1825. On Sailer's role during this time, see Schnabel, *Deutsche Geschichte*, vol. 4, 58ff.

63. Schwaiger, "Ignaz von Döllinger," in *KTD*, 15.

64. See Schnabel, *Deutsche Geschichte*, vol. 4, 196ff.

65. CUL Add. 4093/56. Cf. Friedrich, *Döllinger*, vol. 1, 196ff. On Görres in general, see Jon Vandel Heuvel, *A German Life in the Age of Revolution: Joseph Görres, 1776–1848* (Washington, DC: Catholic University of America Press, 2001).

66. CUL Add. 4093 and Friedrich, *Döllinger*, vol. 1, 191–3. On what we might call Baader's proto-ecumenism, see especially his *Der morgenländische und abendländische Katholicismus: mehr in seinem inner wesentlichen als in mseinem äussern Verhältnisse dargestellt* (Stuttgart, 1840–1).

67. For a list of Döllinger's writings in *Eos*, see Stefan Lösch, *Döllinger und Frankreich: Eine geistige Allianz, 1823–1871* (Munich: C. H. Beck, 1955), 502–13. Cf. Friedrich, *Döllinger*, vol. 1, 206ff.

68. On the journal *Eos* and its contributors more generally, see Karl Pörnbacher, *"Kräftig in die Zeit eingreifen": die katholische Zeitschrift "Eos" und ihr Kreis*

(Munich: Bayer, 1989) and Hans Kapfinger, *Der Eoskreis 1828 bis 1832: Ein Beitrag zur Vorgeschichte des politischen Katholizimus in Deutschland* (Munich: Franz A. Pfeiffer Verlag, 1928).

69. Alexander Dru, *The Contribution of German Catholicism* (New York: Hawthorn Books, 1963), 70. On Döllinger's relations to Lamennais and Montalembert, see Lösch, *Döllinger und Frankreich*, 88ff., 138ff.

70. Buchheim, *Ultramontanismus und Demokratie*, 48.

71. Richard Schaefer, "'Thoughts on the Founding of a Catholic Science': Science, Society and the Syllabus of Errors in German Catholicism, 1820–1869" (PhD Dissertation, Cornell University, 2005), 170–1.

72. For a list of authors and topics treated in the journal, see Bernhard Weber and Dieter Albrecht, *Die Mitarbeiter der Historisch-politischen Blätter für das katholische Deutschland* (Mainz: Matthias-Grünewald Verlag, 1990).

73. Jonathan Israel, *Radical Enlightenment: Philosophy and the Making of Modernity, 1650–1750* (Oxford: Oxford University Press, 2001). Cf. Richard Schaefer, "True and False Enlightenment: German Scholars and the Discourse of Catholicism in the Nineteenth Century," *CHR* 97 (2011): 24–45.

74. G. W. F. Hegel, "Glauben und Wissen," in *Hauptwerke*, vol. 1 (Darmstadt: Wissenschaftliche Buchgesellschaft, 1999), 316.

75. Friedrich, *Döllinger*, vol. 1, 206ff.

76. Günther was actually Bohemian, but lived in Vienna.

77. Wilhelm Mauer, "Der Organismusgedanke bei Schelling und in der Theologie der katholischen Tübinger Schule," *KD* 8 (1962): 202–16.

78. Stephan Lösch, *Die Anfänge der Tübinger Theologischen Quartalschrift (1819–1931): Gedenkgabe zum 100. Todestag Johann Adam Möhlers* (Rottenburg: Bader'sche Verlagsbuchhandlung, 1938).

79. Thomas F. O'Meara, *Romantic Idealism and Roman Catholicism: Schelling and the Theologians* (Notre Dame: University of Notre Dame Press, 1982), 96–7.

80. The quotes from Drey are taken from James Tunstead Burtchaell, "Drey, Möhler, and the Catholic School of Tübingen," in Ninian Smart, John Clayton, Patrick Sherry, and Steven T. Katz, eds., *Nineteenth-Century Religious Thought in the West*, vol. 2 (Cambridge: Cambridge University Press, 1985), 119–20.

81. Johann Sebastian Drey, *Kurze Einleitung in das Studium der Theologie* (Tübingen, 1819), 156–7.

82. On this trip, see Rudolf Padberg, "Johann Adam Möhlers 'Literarische' Reise 1822/23," *Catholica* 42 (1988): 108–18.

83. Möhler is widely heralded as a forerunner of the Second Vatican Council, especially as mediated through the writings of Henri de Lubac and Yves Congar, among others. He has also been regarded as an influence on Catholic Modernism. See *ODCC*, 1098–1100. On the link to Modernism, see Edmond Vermeil, *Jean-Adam Möhler et l'École catholique de Tübingue, 1815–1840* (Paris: Armand Colin, 1913).

84. Dru, *The Contribution of German Catholicism*, 64.

85. See Joseph Fitzer, *Möhler and Baur in Controversy, 1832–38* (Tallahassee, FL: American Academy of Religion, 1974).

86. Burtchaell, "Drey, Möhler, and the Catholic School of Tübingen," 131 (emphasis added). Cf. Michael Himes, *Ongoing Incarnation: Johann Adam Möhler and the Beginnings of Modern Ecclesiology* (New York: Crossroad, 1997).

87. Noted in Paul-Werner Scheele, "Johann Adam Möhler," in *KTD*, 70.

88. Quoted in Friedrich, *Döllinger*, vol. 1, 150. Cf. CUL Add. 4906/1.

89. See the letters from Möhler to Döllinger (September 20, 1834, November 22, 1834, and January 11, 1835) in BSB Döllingerinia II.

90. See Döllinger, ed., *J. A. Möhlers gesammelte Schriften und Aufsätze*, 2 vols. (Regensburg, 1839–40).

91. Döllinger, *Akademische Vorträge*, vol. 2 (Nördlingen: C. H. Beck, 1889), 80.

92. Schatz, *Zwischen Säkularisation und zweitem Vatikanum*, 82. Cf. Erich Garhammer, *Seminaridee und Klerusbildung bei Karl August Graf von Reisach: Eine pastoralgeschichtliche Studie zum Ultramontanismus des 19. Jahrhunderts* (Stuttgart: Verlag Kohlhammer, 1990), 20ff.

93. Johann Adam Möhler, "Ein Wort in der Sache des philosophischen Collegiums zu Löwen," *TQ* 8 (1826): 91–2.

94. Witness the importance Alasdair MacIntyre attributes to *Aeterni Patris* in his *Three Rival Versions of Moral Inquiry* (Notre Dame: University of Notre Dame Press, 1990), 2, 72, passim.

95. John Paul II, *Fides et Ratio*, <http://www.vatican.va/holy_father/john_paul_ii/encyclicals/documents/hf_jp-ii_enc_15101998_fides-et-ratio-en.html> (accessed September 19, 2012).

96. On Liebermann and the origins of the Mainz circle, see Ludwig Lenhart, "Die erste Mainzer Theologen-Schule des 19. Jahrhunderts," *JBM* 6 (1951–4): 93–186; 7 (1955–7): 9–130.

97. *TG*, 17–18.

98. Schnabel, *Deutsche Geschichte*, vol. 4, 80.

99. Schnabel, *Deutsche Geschichte*, vol. 4, 77. On the founding of *Der Katholik*, see Rudolf Pesch, *Die kirchlich-politische Presse der Katholiken in Deutschland vor 1848* (Stuttgart: H. E. Walter, 1964), 140–3.

100. On the early history of this institution, see Francesco C. Cesareo, "The Collegium Germanicum and the Ignatian Vision of Education," *Sixteenth Century Journal* 24 (1993): 829–41.

101. Robert Aubert, *Le pontificat de Pie IX (1846–1878)* (Paris: Bloud & Gay, 1952), 189.

102. Kleutgen has not been the subject of serious biographical treatment in recent decades. See F. Lakner, "Kleutgen und die kirchliche Wissenschaft in Deutschland im XIX. Jahrhundert," *ZKT* 57 (1933): 161–214.

103. Gerald McCool, *The Neo-Thomists* (Milwaukee: Marquette University Press, 1994), 2, 25. Cf. Alasdair MacIntyre, *God, Philosophy, Universities: A Selective History of the Catholic Philosophical Tradition* (Lanham, MD: Rowman & Littlefield, 2011), 152ff.

104. Hans Jürgen Brandt, *Eine katholische Universität in Deutschland? Das Ringen der Katholiken in Deutschland um eine Universitätsbildung im 19. Jahrhundert* (Cologne: Böhlau, 1981), 127ff.

105. *PE*, vol. 1, 278.

106. While Thomas Aquinas was of foremost importance to Kleutgen, he did not follow Thomas on every point. Some regard Kleutgen as a "Suárezian," a follower of the great Spanish Thomist scholar Francisco Suárez (1548–1617). Suárez agreed with Thomas on most points, but when Thomas deviated from opinions generally held by other scholastics, Suárez—and later Kleutgen—tended to side with the consensus viewpoint and/or attempted to reconcile Thomas's positions with those of others. On Suárez, see *ODCC*, 1550–1.

107. On Kleutgen's engagement with Tübingen theologians, see Gerald A. McCool, *Catholic Theology in the Nineteenth Century: The Quest for a Unitary Method* (New York: Seabury Press, 1977), 188ff.

108. Kleutgen, *Die Philosophie der Vorzeit*, 2nd ed., vol. 1 (Innsbruck, 1878), 4.

109. Kleutgen, *Die Philosophie der Vorzeit*, vol. 1, 358ff., 444ff. Cf. Fergus Kerr, *After Aquinas* (Oxford: Blackwell, 2002), 18–21.

110. Kleutgen, *Die Theologie der Vorzeit*, rev. ed., vol. 2 (Münster, 1872), 160–78.

111. See Ralph McInerny, *Praeambula fidei: Thomism and the God of the Philosophers* (Washington, DC: Catholic University of America Press, 2006).

112. McCool, *Catholic Theology in the Nineteenth Century*, 143.

113. Norman P. Tanner, S.J., ed., *Decrees of the Ecumenical Councils: Volume Two, Trent to Vatican II* (London: Sheed & Ward, 1990), 808–9.

114. Aubert, *Le pontificat de Pie IX*, 193–5.

115. See Otto Weiß, "La 'scienza tedesca' e l'Italia nell'Ottocento," *Annali dell'Instituto storico italo-germanico in Trento/Jahrbuch des Italienisch-Deutschen Historischen Instituts in Trient* 9 (1983): 9–85 and Rudolf Reinhardt, "Teologia romana nella Germania de XIX secolo," *CnS* 12 (1991): 553–67.

116. McCool, *Catholic Theology in the Nineteenth Century*, 132, 168ff.

117. Schnabel, *Deutsche Geschichte*, vol. 4, 129.

118. *ESDD*, 562–3 (translation modified). Cf. Herman H. Schwedt, *Das römische Urteil über Georg Hermes (1775–1831): Ein Beitrag zur Geschichte der Inquisition im 19. Jahrhundert* (Rome: Herder, 1980) and Leonhard Gillen, "Joseph Kleutgen und die philosophische Prinzipienlehre bei Hermes," *Scholastik* 37 (1962): 1–31.

119. A notable example is that of Franz Peter Knoodt (1811–89), who wrote a biography of Günther: *Anton Günther: eine Biographie* (Vienna, 1881).

120. *ESDD*, 577–8 (translation modified). Cf. Aubert, *Le pontificat de Pie IX*, 200–2.

121. My discussion of Frohschammer owes a debt to John P. Boyle, "Faith and Reason: The Case of Jacob Froschhammer," in Anthony J. Cernera, ed., *Continuity and Plurality in Catholic Theology* (Fairfield, CT: Sacred Heart University Press, 1998), 1–12.

122. See *Die Philosophie der Vorzeit*, vol. 2, 583–92.

123. Letter from Ernst von Moy de Sons to Döllinger (June 9, 1863), BSB Döllingeriana II. The memorandum, "Meinungsäußerung ueber das Verfahren gegen den Prof. Froschhammer" (Munich, April 15, 1863) is noted in *TG*, 66–7. However, in this memorandum, Döllinger also expressed the concern that "German scholarship, indeed how Germans think and view the world" was in large part alien to theologians in Rome.

124. Frohschammer, *Über die Freiheit der Wissenschaft* (Munich, 1861), 4.

125. *ESDD*, 581–4.

126. Aubert, *Le pontificat de Pie IX*, 193.
127. Giacomo Martina, *Pio IX (1851–1866)*, vol. 2 (Rome: Editrice Pontificia Università Gregoriana, 1986), 314ff.
128. ASV SS, 1864 rubr. 255, fasc. 1.
129. Letter from Döllinger to Jörg (September 25, 1862) in Joseph Edmund Jörg, *Briefwechsel, 1846–1901*, ed. Dieter Albrecht (Mainz: Matthias-Grünewald Verlag, 1988), 211.
130. For a list of Döllinger's publications in this journal, see *TG*, xiii.
131. See Döllinger, *Die Reformation: ihre innere Entwicklung und ihre Wirkungen im Umfange des lutherischen Bekentnisses* (Regensburg: G. Joseph Manz, 1846–8).
132. *GG*, 483–4.
133. This was reported in *Der Katholik*. See Herman H. Schwedt, "Vom ultramontanen zum liberalen Döllinger," *GG*, 109.4. Cf. Friedrich, *Döllinger*, vol. 3, 69–70.
134. Charles Mercy d'Argenteau, nuncio in Munich from 1827 to 1837, to Döllinger (October 9, 1847). BSB Döllingeriana II.
135. On the scandal and abdication, see Heinz Gollwitzer, *Ludwig I. von Bayern: Königtum im Vormärz: Eine politische Biographie* (Munich: Süddeutscher Verlag, 1986), 658–88.
136. On Döllinger's activities in Frankfurt, see Friedrich, *Döllinger*, vol. 2, 363–422 and Schwedt, "Vom ultramontanen zum liberalen Döllinger," *GG*, 118ff.
137. On the role of Catholics in general at the Frankfurt Assembly, see Herman H. Schwedt, "Die katholischen Abgeordneten der Paulskirche und Frankfurt," *Archiv für mittelrheinische Kirchengeschichte* 34 (1982): 143–66. Döllinger "caucused" with the conservative wing which met regularly at Café Milano. See Nipperdey, *Germany from Napoleon to Bismarck*, 542–3.
138. For Döllinger's experiences and writings during and shortly after 1848, I owe a debt to Bradford D. Whitner, "Varieties of Historical Consciousness in Nineteenth-Century Germany: Ranke, Döllinger, Marx" (PhD Dissertation, University of Virginia, 2005) and Schwedt, "Vom ultramontanen zum liberalen Döllinger," *GG*, 107–67.
139. Döllinger delivered his address at the Frankfurt Parliament on August 22, 1848. For the address and the anonymously published essay on "Church and State," see Ignaz von Döllinger, *Kleinere Schriften, gedruckte und ungedruckte*, ed. F. H. Reusch (Stuttgart: Cotta, 1890), 3–41.
140. Buchheim, *Ultramontanismus und Demokratie*, 61–2.
141. On the background to this meeting of Catholic laity—the first so-called "Katholikentag" in Germany—see L. Lenhart, ed., *Idee, Gestalt und Gestalter des ersten deutschen Katholikentags in Mainz* (Mainz: Verlag Kirchheim, 1948).
142. Döllinger, *Kleinere Schriften*, 42ff.
143. Friedrich, *Döllinger*, vol. 2, 436–67 and Schatz, *Zwischen Säkularisation und zweitem Vatikanum*, 100.
144. Döllinger, *Kleinere Schriften*, 63–4.
145. Döllinger, *Kleinere Schriften*, 64–5.
146. *TG*, 40 and Rudolf Lill, "Die ersten deutschen Bischofskonferenzen," *RQ* 59 (1964): 127–85; 60 (1965): 1–70. On Sacconi, see Christoph Weber, *Kardinäle*

und Prälaten in den letzten Jahrzehnten des Kirchenstaates, vol. 2 (Stuttgart: Hiersemann, 1978), 514–15.

147. Writing of Sacconi (November 15, 1848). AAES Germania pos. 638 fasc. 357.

148. James J. Sheehan, *German History, 1770–1866* (Oxford: Clarendon Press, 1989), 691ff.

149. Döllinger, *Die Universitäten sonst und jetzt*, 2nd ed. (Mainz, 1871), 37.

150. For more on Hippolytus, see *ODCC*, 771–3.

151. C. Russell, "Callistus and his Accuser," *DR* 35 (1853): 450.

152. I provide the titles of the English translations of these books. The German titles are *Heidenthum und Judenthum. Vorhalle zur Geschichte des Christenthums* (1857) and *Christenthum und Kirche in der Zeit der Grundlegung* (1860).

153. Döllinger, *Christenthum und Kirche in der Zeit der Grundlegung*, 2nd ed. (Regensburg, 1868), iv.

154. Döllinger, *Christenthum und Kirche in der Zeit der Grundlegung*, 223.

155. *TG*, 46.

156. "... [Döllinger] non ha idee ben ferme sul Primato del Papa, e sostiene opinione non giuste, e censurabili sull'infallibilità del Papa ... " Letter of Sacconi to Fornari (June 5, 1852), ASV NM, 82, fasc. 132; the letter is printed in Schwedt, "Vom ultramontanen zum liberalen Döllinger," in *GG*, 141–2.

157. Döllinger, *Kleinere Schriften*, 108–9; *TG*, 48.

158. Döllinger had written about this movement as early as 1841; see Döllinger, "Die katholische Bewegung in der protestantisch-bischöflichen Kirche von England," *HBKD* 8 (1841): 688–701.

159. Quoted in John Morley, *The Life of William Ewart Gladstone*, vol. 1 (London: Macmillan, 1903), 318–19.

160. Letter of Newman to Döllinger (December 5, 1853). BSB Döllingeriana II.

161. Roland Hill, *Lord Acton* (New Haven: Yale University Press, 2000), 39.

162. Oxenham and Plummer were the principal translators of Döllinger's early works.

163. Alfred Plummer, *Conversations with Dr. Döllinger, 1870–1890*, ed. Robrecht Boudens (Leuven: Leuven University Press, 1985). For more on Döllinger's relations with Anglicans, see Angle Berlis, "Ignaz von Döllinger and the Anglicans," in Stewart J. Brown and Peter B. Nockles, eds., *The Oxford Movement and the Wider World* (Cambridge: Cambridge University Press, 2012).

164. CUL Add. 8120/2. The quote from 1879 is according to the memoir of Blennerhasset, a confidante of Döllinger and Lord Acton. For more on the Döllinger–Blennerhassett relationship, see Chapter 3.

165. Quoted in Hill, *Lord Acton*, 28.

166. Hill, *Lord Acton*, 318–32.

167. Acton to Döllinger (September/October 1878) in *Briefwechsel*, vol. 3, ed. Victor Conzemius (Munich: C. H. Beck, 1971), 207.

168. The original journal is found among the Acton papers in the archives of the Cambridge University Library. In what follows, I also draw from the edited and published version of Herbert Butterfield, "Journal of Lord Acton: Rome 1857," *CHJ* 3 (1946): 186–204.

169. Hill, *Lord Acton*, 72.

170. Döllinger to Charlotte Leydon (January 21, 1870), *Briefwechsel*, vol. 4, 454. CUL Add. 4903/144.
171. CUL Add. 4912/52.
172. Butterfield, "Journal of Lord Acton: Rome 1857," 194. Döllinger requested and was granted the right to read books on the Index. BAB Döllinger 5.11. On Theiner, whose anti-papalist tendencies later cost him his post, see *ADB*, vol. 37, 674–7 and Owen Chadwick, *Acton and History* (Cambridge: Cambridge University Press, 1998), 46–54.
173. CUL Add. 5644/71.
174. CUL Add. 5001/188. Cf. CUL Add. 4904/52: "1857—[Döllinger] not struck, but deeply interested. Pondered over it all—and somewhat taken aback by what he found."
175. Acton, "Döllinger's Historical Work," in Lord Acton, *Selected Writings of Lord Acton*, ed. J. Rufus Fears, vol. 2 (Indianapolis: Liberty Classics, 1986), 441.
176. Butterfield, "Journal of Lord Acton: Rome 1857," 190; Friedrich, *Döllinger*, vol. 3, 181.
177. Luise von Kobell, *Ignaz von Döllinger: Erinnerungen* (Munich, 1891), 71–2. On von Kobell's place in the "high society" of Munich, see Kurt Wilhelm, ed., *Luise von Kobell und die Könige von Bayern* (Munich: Ehrenwirth, 1980).
178. Kobell, *Ignaz von Döllinger: Erinnerungen*, 72–3.
179. In question at this point was Frohschammer's *Ursprung der menschlichen Seelen* (Salzburg, 1854).
180. This exchange is reconstructed and narrated in Friedrich, *Döllinger*, vol. 3, 181. It is important to remember that as an Old Catholic Friedrich often sought to portray Rome in the worst light possible.
181. Acton, "Döllinger's Historical Work," 44.
182. Quoted in Butterfield, "Journal of Lord Acton: Rome 1857," 192.
183. Hill, *Lord Acton*, 80 and Friedrich, *Döllinger*, vol. 3, 185–6.
184. Friedrich, *Döllinger*, vol. 3, 233–51 and *TG*, 53–5.
185. Aubert, *Le pontificat de Pie IX*, 91–2.
186. On Carlo Passaglia, S.J. (1812–87) and his efforts at this time, see Owen Chadwick, *A History of the Popes, 1830–1914* (Oxford: Oxford University Press, 1998), 152–3.
187. Quoted in Chadwick, *A History of the Popes, 1830–1914*, 152.
188. *PE*, vol. 1, 360–1.
189. Döllinger's two "Odeon lectures" of 1861 are included as an appendix in Ignaz von Döllinger, *Kirche und Kirchen: Papstthum und Kirchenstaat. Historisch-politische Betrachtungen*, 2nd ed. (Munich, 1861), 666–84.
190. *Kirche und Kirchen*, 668.
191. *Kirche und Kirchen*, 679.
192. *Kirche und Kirchen*, 684.
193. Schatz, *Zwischen Säkularisation und Zweitem Vatikanum*, 112.
194. Chigi to Antonelli (April 12, 1861), ASV SS 1861. On Chigi, see Giuseppe de Marchi, *Le nunziature apostoliche dal 1800 al 1956* (Vatican City: Liberia Editrice Vaticana, 2006), 55.
195. Acton to Döllinger (May 4, 1861) in *Briefwechsel*, vol. 1, 200. Britain's *Saturday Review* summed up Döllinger's lectures as follows: "[Döllinger] startled his

audience by the crushing indictment of the Pontifical Government. Its worst enemy never would have composed a more overwhelming indictment, or a more hopeless horoscope for its [the Church's temporal power] future than has been done by this...gentleman, a sincere and enthusiastic servant of the Church." "The Ecclesiastical Reaction against the Pope's Temporal Power," *Saturday Review* no. 288 (May 4, 1861): 443-4.

196. Quoted material taken from *TG*, 55-6.

197. Joseph Hergenröther, "Der Zeitgeist und die Souveränität des Papstes," *Katholik* 41.1 (1861): 513-43. See *KTD*, vol. 2, 513ff.

198. Moy to Döllinger (April 17, 1861) as quoted in Friedrich, *Döllinger*, vol. 3, 241.

199. On the combative, arch-ultramontane Veuillot, see Marvin Luther Brown, *Louis Veuillot: French Ultramontane Catholic Journist and Laymen, 1813-1883* (Durham, NC: Moore Publishing, 1977).

200. E. S. Purcell, "Döllinger and the Temporal Power of the Popes," *DR* 50 (1861): 199.

201. Döllinger, *Kirche und Kirchen*, xvii.

202. Döllinger, *Kirche und Kirchen*, xxvii.

203. Döllinger, *Kirche und Kirchen*, xviii–xix.

204. Döllinger, *Kirche und Kirchen*, vi–xi.

205. Acton, "Döllinger on the Temporal Power," *The Rambler* 6 (1861): 3, 13.

206. Gladstone to Döllinger (June 22, 1862). BL Gladstone Papers Add. 44140/266.

207. Döllinger to Theiner (October 14, 1861) in Hubert Jedin, "Kirchenhistoriker-briefe an Augustin Theiner," *RQ* 6 (1971): 210.

208. Döllinger mentions this report in a letter to Charles René de Montalembert (March 21, 1862): "Zu Rom ließ sich der Papst von P. Theiner über mein Buch erstatten und dieser Bericht fiel in der Hauptsache günstig aus." Lösch, *Döllinger und Frankreich*, 450-1.

209. See Döllinger to Gladstone (January 19, 1862). BL Gladstone Papers Add. 44398.

210. *TG*, 59-61.

211. Jörg to Döllinger (October 28, 1861) in Dieter Albrecht, ed., *Joseph Edmund Jörg: Briefwechsel, 1846-1901* (Mainz: Matthias-Grünewald Verlag, 1988), 169.

212. Noted in *TG*, 59.

213. Döllinger to Jörg (October 31, 1861) in Albrecht, ed., *Joseph Edmund Jörg: Briefwechsel*, 172.

214. See Jacob Clemens, *De scholasticorum sententia, philosophia esse theologiae ancillam* (Monasterii Guestphalorum: Academia Achendorffia, 1856). Clemens's harshest critic was Johannes von Kuhn (1806–87) of Tübingen. On Kuhn, see Grant Kaplan, *Answering the Enlightenment: The Catholic Recovery of Historical Revelation* (New York: Crossroad, 2006), 111–49. In the late 1850s and early 1860s, the two, Clemens and Kuhn, clashed frequently in the pages of *Der Katholik* and the Tübingen *Theologische Quartalschrift*. See Whitner, "Varieties of Historical Consciousness," 266-7.

215. Roger Aubert, "L'intervention de Montalembert au congrès de Malines en 1863," *Collectanea Mechlisiensia* 20 (1950): 525-51.

216. Lord Acton, "The Munich Congress," in Acton, *Selected Writings of Lord Acton: Essays in Religion, Politics, and Morality*, ed. J. Rufus Fears (Indianapolis: Liberty

Classics, 1988), 206–7. On Gonella, see Marchi, *Le nunziature apostoliche dal 1800 al 1956*, 55f.

217. The invitation letter is printed in Pius Gams, ed., *Verhandlung der Versammlung katholischer Gelehrten in München von 28. September bis 1. Oktober 1863* (Regensburg, 1863), 5–8.

218. The list of participants is provided in Gams, ed., *Verhandlung*, 10–12.

219. Gams, ed., *Verhandlung*, 9–25.

220. Acton, "The Munich Congress," 207, 220. The participants reflect a wide array of intellectual outlooks; notably absent, however, were representatives from Tübingen, with the exception of Johann Baptist Alzog (1808–78). Still, many others present sympathized with the "Tübingen School," not least Döllinger himself. Cf. Anton Landersdorfer, *Gregor von Scherr (1804–1877): Erzbischof von München und Freising in der Zeit des Ersten Vatikanums und des Kulturkampfes* (Munich: Verlag des Vereins, 1995), 288–9. Scherr himself did not participate in the congress.

221. Acton, "The Munich Congress," 223.

222. The speech is found in Gams, ed., *Verhandlung*, 25–59. It is reprinted in Johann Finsterhölzl, ed., *Ignaz von Döllinger: Wegbereiter heutiger Theologie* (Graz: Verlag Styria, 1969), 227–63. I cite from the Finsterhölzl printing.

223. Döllinger, "Die Vergangenheit und Gegenwart der katholischen Theologie," 227ff.

224. Döllinger, "Die Vergangenheit und Gegenwart der katholischen Theologie," 235–7.

225. Döllinger, "Die Vergangenheit und Gegenwart der katholischen Theologie," 238.

226. Döllinger, "Die Vergangenheit und Gegenwart der katholischen Theologie," 239–42.

227. Döllinger, "Die Vergangenheit und Gegenwart der katholischen Theologie," 242–6.

228. Döllinger, "Die Vergangenheit und Gegenwart der katholischen Theologie," 247–8, 260.

229. Döllinger, "Die Vergangenheit und Gegenwart der katholischen Theologie," 249.

230. Döllinger, "Die Vergangenheit und Gegenwart der katholischen Theologie," 250–3.

231. Döllinger, "Die Vergangenheit und Gegenwart der katholischen Theologie," 251.

232. Döllinger, "Die Vergangenheit und Gegenwart der katholischen Theologie," 251.

233. McCool, *Catholic Theology in the Nineteenth Century*, 131–2.

234. Döllinger, "Die Vergangenheit und Gegenwart der katholischen Theologie," 254–63.

235. On the many topics discussed, see Gams, ed., *Verhandlungen*, 59ff. Still, Döllinger's address was the "big story" of the conference.

236. Landersdorfer, *Gregor von Scherr*, 290. The statement of protest is printed as an appendix in Christoph Moufang, *Die Kirche und die Versammlung katholischer Gelehrten* (Mainz, 1864), 42–6. The eight signatories to this document were Johann Baptist Heinrich, Christoph Moufang, Paul Leopold Haffner, Joseph Hergenröther, Franz Seraph Hettinger, Matthias Joseph Scheeben, George Phillips, and Constantin Freiherr von Schätzler.

237. Gams, ed., *Verhandlungen*, 67.

238. ASV NM 1864, fasc. 20 and ASV SS 1864 rubr. 255, fasc. 2.

239. Gams, ed., *Verhandlungen*, 130–3.

240. Gams, ed., *Verhandlungen*, 137.

241. ASV SS 1863 rubr. 255, fasc. 2.

242. ASV SS 1863 rubr. 255, fasc. 2. Cf. Friedrich, *Döllinger*, vol. 3, 335 and Land-ersdorfer, *Gregor von Scherr*, 292. The communication with the Pope was mediated by the Bavarian Gustav Adolf Fürst von Hohenlohe Schillungsfürst (1823–96), then in Rome serving as Almoner of the Pope [i.e., the Holy See's distributor of charity] and titular bishop of Edessa in Mesopotamia. On him, see *NDB*, vol. 9, 490–1.

243. Gonella to Antonelli (August 21, 1863), ASV SS 1864 rubr. 254, fasc. 1. The Frohschammer affair was very much still alive in Gonella's mind; he mentions Frohschammer several times in the letter. Frohschammer was not invited to take part in the congress.

244. Gonella to Antonelli (August 21, 1863), ASV SS 1864 rubr. 254, fasc. 1.

245. Martina, *Pio IX*, vol. 2, 317ff.

246. ASV SS 1864 rubr. 255, fasc. 1. Cf. John P. Boyle, "The Ordinary Magisterium: Towards a History of the Concept," *HJ* 4 (1979): 386ff.

247. AAES Germania pos. 942 fasc. 518.

248. AAES Germania pos. 942 fasc. 518 (emphasis added).

249. Antonelli to Gonella (September 9, 1863), ASV NM 98 (No. 20).

250. In a letter to Joseph Floß of Bonn, Döllinger mentions the concerns at Rome about the congress. See Friedrich, *Döllinger*, vol. 3, 306f.

251. See Gonella to Scherr (September 11, 1863), Scherr to Gonella (September 14, 1863), and Gonella to Antonelli (September 18, 1863), ASV NM 98 (No. 20). Cf. Boyle, "The Ordinary Magisterium I," 385–6; *GT*, 88–95. It is noteworthy, too, that Gonella sent a report (October 2, 1863) of the congress to Rome, in which he expressed alarm at the want of firm ecclesiastical oversight. Scherr also sent a report (October 7, 1863) indicating that the congress had done no harm. Land-ersdorfer, *Gregor von Scherr*, 293–4. Reisach commented critically on Scherr's report. See "Osservazioni sulla lettera dell' Archepiscopo di Monaco 'Sua San-tita'" (October 10, 1863), AAES pos. 942 fasc. 518. Reisach had independently queried two other scholars—Joseph Ernst of Eichstätt and Christoph Moufang of Mainz—about the congress. See Garhammer, *Seminaridee und Klerusbildung*, 196–8, 301n43.

252. Frank J. Coppa, *Pope Pius IX: Crusader in a Secular Age* (Boston: Twayne Publishers, 1979), 140–53.

253. Reisach played a significant role in its drafting. See Garhammer, *Seminaridee und Klerusbildung*, 198ff. and Schatz, *Zwischen Säkularisation und zweitem Vatika-num*, 114. Joseph Kleutgen played a role as well. See Hubert Wolf, "Joseph Kleutgen, das Breve *Tuas libenter* (1863) und die Folgen für die katholische Theologie," in Franz Xaver Bischof and Georg Essen, eds., *Theologie, kirchliches Lehramt und öffentliche Meinung: Die Münchener Gelehrtenversammlung von 1863 und ihre Folgen* (Stuttgart: Kohlhammer, 2015), 49–70.

254. *ESDD*, 584–5.

255. *ESDD*, 585.

256. See Boyle, "The Ordinary Magisterium I," *HJ* 20 (1979): 380–98 and "The Ordinary Magisterium II," *HJ* 21 (1980): 14–29.

257. *ESDD*, 586–7.

258. Acton to Döllinger (March 9, 1864), *Briefwechsel*, vol. 1, 335.

259. Acton to Simpson (March 8, 1864) in Josef L. Altholz and Damian McElrath, eds., *The Correspondence of Lord Acton and Richard Simpson*, vol. 3 (Cambridge: Cambridge University Press, 1975), 185.

260. For the text of the edict, see Brandt, *Eine katholische Universität in Deutschland?*, 418–20.

261. And not just in Germany. *Tuas libenter* led Lord Acton to suspend operations of the English-language liberal Catholic journal, *Home and Foreign Review*. Döllinger disagreed with Acton over doing this. See Hill, *Lord Acton*, 150–1.

262. Landersdorfer, *Gregor von Scherr*, 296–7.

263. Letter of Lierheimer to unspecified recipient (April 15, 1864); quoted in Landersdorfer, *Gregor von Scherr*, 297.

264. "Il congresso dei dotti cattoloci in Monaco in Baviera e le scienze sacre," *La Civiltà Cattolica* 5.9 (1864): 385–406, 513–33, 657–76; 5.10 (1864): 24–36. Cf. Christoph Moufang, "Die Versammlung katholischer Gelehrten," *Der Katholik* 44.1 (1864): 95–111, 196–221.

265. Döllinger to Dinkel (July 9, 1864); quoted in Landersdorfer, *Gregor von Scherr*, 299.

266. *ESDD*, 592.

267. Döllinger to Charlotte von Leyden (August 2, 1866), *Briefwechsel*, vol. 4, 139.

268. CUL Add. 4903/142.

269. Article 45 of the Syllabus had questioned the role of the "civil authority" in educating priests. See *ESDD*, 595. Cf. Garhammer, *Seminaridee und Klerusbildung*, 201ff.

270. Döllinger, "Die Speyerische Seminarfrage und der Syllabus," *Kleinere Schriften*, ed. F. H. Reusch (Stuttgart: Cotta, 1890), 199, 206. This scathing article was penned in 1865, but not published until 1890.

271. Döllinger, "Die Speyerische Seminarfrage und der Syllabus," *Kleinere Schriften*, 215.

272. On Arbués, see *RPP*, vol. 1, 44.

273. Döllinger, "Rom und die Inquisition," *Kleinere Schriften*, 291; see *TG*, 119. Cf. Louise von Kobell, *Conversations of Dr. Döllinger*, trans. Katherine Gould (London, 1892), 221.

274. *TG*, 109.

275. Jansen to Döllinger (November 22, 1864). BSB Döllingeriana II.

276. This is Mermillod's account as provided to Döllinger in a letter of December 4, 1864; see *Briefwechsel*, vol. 1, 377.

277. This story was conveyed by Cardinal d'Andrea to Lord Acton. See *Briefwechsel*, vol. 1, 393.

278. Janssen to Maria von Sydow (December 29, 1863) in Ludwig von Pastor, ed., *Janssens Briefe*, vol. 1 (Freiburg im Breisgau: Herder, 1920), 215. Cf. Friedrich, *Döllinger*, vol. 3, 375.

279. *TG*, 109.
280. Döllinger to Kathinka von Münich (October 9, 1864). BSB Döllingeriana V.250; *TG*, 107.
281. Sheehan, *German History*, 899ff.
282. Döllinger, *Ignaz von Döllingers Briefe an eine junge Freundin. Mit zwei Bildnissen*, ed. Heinrich Schrörs (Kempten: J. Kösel, 1914), 195.
283. Döllinger to Reusch (July 29, 1867), BAB Reusch 7.11.

CHAPTER 3

1. *ESDD*, 616 (translation modified).
2. Roger Aubert, *Le pontificat de Pie IX (1846-1878)* (Paris: Bloud & Gay, 1953), 358-9 and Robert McClory, *Power and the Papacy: The People and Politics behind the Doctrine of Infallibility* (Liguori, MO: Triumph, 1997), 121-2. The two dissenting bishops—Aloisio Riccio of Sicily and Edward Fitzgerald of Little Rock, Arkansas—subsequently submitted to the decree.
3. Pius IX as quoted in McClory, *Power and the Papacy*, 122.
4. From the *Tribuno* as quoted in Fiorella Bartoccini, *Roma nell'Ottocento: il tramonto della "città santa," nascita di una capitale* (Bologna: Cappelli Editore, 1985), 418.
5. On the details of the last days of papal Rome, see David I. Kertzer, *Prisoner of the Vatican: The Popes, the Kings, and Garibaldi's Rebels in the Struggle to Rule Modern Italy* (Boston: Houghton Mifflin, 2004), 33-58. On the Lateran Treaties of 1929, which created the present-day Vatican City, see Peter King, *The Pope and the Duce: The International Impact of the Lateran Agreements* (New York: St. Martin's Press, 1981).
6. Ignaz von Döllinger, *Lectures on the Reunion of the Churches*, trans. H. N. Oxenham (London, 1872), 135.
7. H. P. Liddon, *Report of the Proceedings at the Reunion Conference Held at Bonn Between the 10th and 16th of August, 1875* (London, 1876), 42-3.
8. Döllinger to Acton (July 23, 1870), *Briefwechsel, 1850-1890*, vol. 2 (Munich: C. H. Beck, 1965), 436-7.
9. John Henry Newman to Alfred Plummer (April 3, 1871), in Charles Stephen Dessain and Thomas Gornall, S.J., eds., *The Letters and Diaries of John Henry Newman*, vol. 25 (Oxford: Clarendon Press, 1973), 308.
10. *CCC*, paragraph #882, 254.
11. On Passaglia, see Gianluca Carlin, *L'ecclesiologia di Carlo Passaglia (1812-1887): mit einer deutschen Zusammenfassung* (Münster: Lit, 2001).
12. Quoted material from Giacomo Martina, *Pio IX (1851-1866)*, vol. 2 (Rome: Editrice Pontificia Università Gregoriana, 1986), 85ff.
13. Christopher Duggan, *A Concise History of Italy* (Cambridge: Cambridge University Press, 1984), 135.
14. Renato Mori, *Il tramonto del potere temporale, 1866-1870* (Rome: Edizioni di storia e letteratura, 1967), 11ff.
15. Alfonso Scirocco, *Garibaldi: Citizen of the World*, trans. Allan Cameron (Princeton: Princeton University Press, 2007), 328-30, 354-7. On the papal zouaves (the

Pope's international volunteer army), see the English Catholic Joseph Powell's fascinating acount, *Two Years in the Pontifical Zouaves: A Narrative of Travel, Residence, and Experience in the Roman States* (London: R. Washbourne, 1871).

16. Mori, *Il tramonto del potere temporale, 1866–1870*, 268–76 and A. C. Jemolo, *Church and State in Italy, 1850–1950*, trans. David Moore (Oxford: Blackwell, 1960), 29–32.

17. *PE*, vol. 1, 389. Cf. *AP* 1, 4: 371–8; *AAS*, 3: 197–202.

18. Aubert, *Le pontificat de Pie IX*, 295–303 and Carol E. Harrison, *Romantic Catholics: France's Postrevolutionary Generation and the Search for a Modern Faith* (Ithaca: Cornell University Press, 2014), 266.

19. Quoted in Klaus Schatz, *Papal Primacy*, 151.

20. See, e.g., II Timothy 3:12: "Indeed, all who desire to live a godly life in Christ Jesus will be persecuted" (RSV).

21. Schatz, *Papal Primacy*, 154.

22. Luigi Tosi, "Un nuovo tributo a San Pietro," *La Civiltà Cattolica* 18 (1867), ser. 7, 3: 528–30.

23. Edmund S. Purcell, *Life of Cardinal Manning*, vol. 2 (London: Macmillan, 1896), 240.

24. Manning as quoted in James Pereiro, *Cardinal Manning: From Anglican Archdeacon to Council Father at Vatican I* (Herefordshire: Gracewing, 2008), 248, 253.

25. See Senestrey's *Wie es zur Definition der päpstlichen Unfehlbarkeit kam: Tagebuch vom I. Vatikanischen Konzil*, ed. Klaus Schatz (Frankfurt am Main: Knecht, 1977). On Senestrey generally, see *NDB*, vol. 24, 252–3.

26. Henry Edward Manning, *The True Story of the Vatican Council* (London, 1877), 67.

27. August Bernhard Hasler, *How the Pope Became Infallible: Pius IX and the Politics of Persuasion*, trans. Peter Heinegg (Garden City, NY: Doubleday, 1982), 83.

28. Aubert, *Le pontificat de Pie IX*, 302. On Ward's life and influence, see W. P. Ward, *William George Ward and the Catholic Revival* (London: Longmans, Green & Co., 1893). Cf. Edmund Sheridan Purcell, "Döllinger and the Temporal Power of the Popes," *DR* 99 (May 1861): 200ff.

29. Quoted in James C. Livingstone, *Modern Christian Thought: The Enlightenment and the Nineteenth Century*, 2nd ed., vol. 1 (Minneapolis: Fortress Press, 2006), 333.

30. Waldemar Gurian, "Louis Veuillot," *CHR* 36 (January 1951): 407. On Veuillot's life and times, see Pierre Peirrard, *Louis Veuillot* (Paris: Beuchesne, 1998). Veuillot helped put into circulation the story that Döllinger's father once said that his son had two heads and no heart, and also that in the cathedral stall, Döllinger did not know his breviary and often read proofs of his books. See William Arthur and W. B. Neatby, *The Popes, the Kings, and the People* (London: Hodder & Stoughton, 1903), 472.

31. Bellarmine as quoted in Richard F. Costigan, *The Consensus of the Church and Papal Infallibility: A Study in the Background of Vatican I* (Washington, DC: Catholic University of America Press, 2005), 24.

32. Alexius M. Driscoll, ed., *The Quaestiones quodlibetales of Thomas Aquinas* (Washington, DC: Catholic University of America Press, 1930), 100–1. Cf.

Gregory Rocca, "Thomas Aquinas on Papal Authority," *Angelicum* 62 (1986): 472–84.

33. On some of the earlier debates on papal authority, see Terrence V. Smith, *Petrine Controversies in Early Christianity* (Tübingen: Mohr, 1985), Brian Tierney, *Origins of Papal Infallibility, 1150–1350: A Study on the Concepts of Infallibility, Sovereignty, and Tradition in the Middle Ages* (Leiden: E. J. Brill, 1972), and James Heft, *John XXII and Papal Teaching Authority* (Lewiston, NY: Edwin Mellen Press, 1986). Cf. *RPP*, vol. 6, 478–81.

34. CUL Add. 4909/60.

35. Acton to Döllinger (June 30, 1863), *Briefwechsel*, vol. 1, 313.

36. Acton, "Döllinger's Historical Work," in Lord Acton, *Essays in the Study and Writing of History*, ed. J. Rufus Fears (Indianapolis: Liberty Classics, 1986), 424–8 and CUL Add. 4094/351.

37. *TG*, 110.

38. This book sought to show, as Acton later put it, "that the story of papal power had been a story of disgrace." CUL Add. 5644/83.

39. Ignaz von Döllinger, *Die Papst-Fabeln des Mittelalters. Ein Beitrag zur Kirchengeschichte*, 2nd ed. (Stuttgart, 1890), iii.

40. Döllinger, *Papst-Fabeln des Mittelalters*, iii–iv.

41. Döllinger, *Papst-Fabeln des Mittelalters*, 57ff.

42. See W. T. Townsend, "The So-Called Symmachian Forgeries," *JR* 13 (April 1933): 165–74.

43. Döllinger, *Papst-Fabeln des Mittelalters*, 59. For fuller treatment of the forgeries, see James M. Moynihan, *Papal Immunity and Liability in the Writings of the Medieval Canonists* (Rome: Gregorian University Press, 1961), 3ff. and Brett Edward Whalen, *The Medieval Papacy* (New York: Palgrave Macmillan, 2014), 42–4.

44. Döllinger, *Papst-Fabeln des Mittelalters*, 60.

45. Lorenzo Valla, *On the Donation of Constantine*, trans. G. W. Bowersock (Cambridge, MA: Harvard University Press, 2007).

46. Döllinger, *Papst-Fabeln des Mittelalters*, 78.

47. Döllinger, *Papst-Fabeln des Mittelalters*, 81.

48. On the False or Pseudo-Isidorian Decretals, see *ODCC*, 598.

49. Bradford Whitner, "Varieties of Historical Consciousness in Nineteenth-Century Germany: Ranke, Döllinger, Marx" (PhD Dissertation, University of Virginia, 2005), 317.

50. Döllinger, *Papst-Fabeln des Mittelalters*, 173.

51. Döllinger, *Papst-Fabeln des Mittelalters*, 170.

52. On the "Honorius Question," see Remigius Bäumer, "Die Wiederentdeckung der Honoriusfrage im Abendland," *RQ* 56 (1961): 200–14 and *ODCC*, 787, 1106. At the time of the Council, Peter le Page Renouf published *The Case of Pope Honorius, Reconsidered with Reference to Recent Apologies* (London: Longman, 1869). It caused quite a stir.

53. On Böhmer, see Johannes Janssen, *J. F. Böhmers Leben, Briefe und kleinere Schriften* (Freiburg im Breisgau, 1868).

54. Acton, "Döllinger's Historical Work," 430 and CUL Add. 4903/269.

55. CUL Add. 4909/85.

56. Acton, "Döllinger's Historical Work," 450 (emphasis added).

57. Acton mentions this, but does not give the name of the journal. See "Döllinger's Historical Work," 447.

58. "Plummer's Translation of Döllinger on the Popes," *DR* 18 (1872): 363.

59. Acton, "Döllinger's Historical Work," 449.

60. Döllinger to Henry Nutcombe Oxenham (February 21, 1869), CUL Add. 4911/112.

61. On Stefan Lösch, *Döllinger und Frankreich: Eine geistige Allianz, 1823–1871* (Munich: C. H. Beck, 1955), 215–16 and *TG*, 135.

62. Friedrich, *Döllinger*, vol. 3, 466. On Maret, see Andrea Riccardi, *Neo-gallicanesimo e cattolicesimo borghese: Henri Maret e il Concilio vaticano* (Bologna: Il Mulino, 1976).

63. Döllinger to Acton (December 21, 1868), in *Briefwechsel*, vol. 1, 532–3.

64. Döllinger to Acton (December 21, 1868), in *Briefwechsel*, vol. 1, 530.

65. Acton to Döllinger (July 15, 1868), in *Briefwechsel*, vol. 1, 511.

66. The doctrine of the Assumption of Mary was not dogmatically (and infallibly) proclaimed until 1950 in Pius XII's bull, *Munificentissimus Deus*. See Jaroslav Pelikan, *Mary through the Centuries* (New Haven: Yale University Press, 1996), 201–14.

67. See "Corrispondenza dalla Francia," *La Civiltà Cattolica* 7.5 (1869): 345–52. Cf. Martina, *Pio IX*, vol. 3, 154–7 and Owen Chadwick, *A History of the Popes, 1830–1914* (Oxford: Oxford University Press, 1998), 189–90.

68. Martina, *Pio IX*, vol. 3, 116ff.

69. *RPP*, vol. 13, 277 and *KGV*, vol. 1, 3.

70. Cf. Frank Coppa, *Pope Pius IX: Crusader in a Secular Age* (Boston: Twayne Publishers, 1979), 157 and *RPP*, vol. 13, 277.

71. Cited in Dom Cuthbert Butler, *The Vatican Council, 1869–1870, Based on Bishop Ullathorne's Letters* (London: Collins and Harvill Press, 1962), 56.

72. Acton, "The Next General Council," in Lord Acton, *Essays in Religion, Politics, and Morality*, ed. J. Rufus Fears (Indianapolis: Liberty Classics, 1988), 263, 265.

73. These commissions focused on dogma, church discipline, matters of church policy, religious orders, Oriental churches, and missions. They drew up preliminary drafts of 65 decrees by late 1969. *RPP*, vol. 13, 277.

74. *TG*, 123–4. On the eve of that council, Hefele published *Causa Honorii Papae* (Naples, 1869), which focused on the case of Pope Honorius I and aimed to demonstrate the moral and historical inadmissibility of Papal Infallibility.

75. Cited in McClory, *Power and the Papacy*, 76.

76. Döllinger to Maret (December 10, 1868), cited in *TG*, 124, n. 16.

77. Hefele to Schwarzenberg (May 10, 1869), ASV CVI Lettere Schwarzenberg.

78. Antonelli to Schwarzenberg (July 15, 1868), ADSC, vol. 7, 1048.

79. Martina, *Pio IX*, vol. 3, 143 and Aubert, *Le pontificat de Pie IX*, 313.

80. Cited in Lösch, *Döllinger und Frankreich*, 282.

81. See Montalembert to Döllinger (November 7, 1869) and Döllinger to Montalembert (November 23, 1869), in Lösch, *Döllinger und Frankreich*, 475–80.

82. Gladstone to Döllinger (March 25, 1870), BL Add. 44140.

83. Döllinger to Leyden (March 1, 1869), *Briefwechsel*, vol. 4, 374. On June 9, 1870, she married Sir Rowland Blennerhasset, the fourth of the (Catholic) Blennerhassett baronets and a close friend of Acton and Döllinger. Döllinger performed the wedding ceremony. On Lady Blennerhassett, who met Döllinger in 1865 and stood in close correspondence with him in his later years, see Victor Conzemius's introduction to *Briefwechsel*, vol. 4, ix–xxxii. Cf. Heinz-Jürgen Vogels, "Döllinger mit Herz: Zum Briefwechsel Döllinger-Blennerhassett," *IKZ* 74 (1984): 170–86 and Victor Conzemius, "Charlotte Lady Blennerhasset. Eine bayerische Kosmopolitin," *SdS* (1981): 612–26.

84. Döllinger's colleague at Munich, Johann Nepomuk Huber, assisted Döllinger with the articles. *TG*, 147–8. The articles are reprinted in Walter Brandmüller, *Ignaz von Döllinger am Vorabend des I.Vatikanums* (St. Ottilien: Eos Verlag, 1977), 147–80. On the *Allgemeine Zeitung*, which reached about 5,400 people at the time of Döllinger's writing, see Brandmüller, *Ignaz von Döllinger am Vorabend des I.Vatikanums*, 14ff.

85. *Allgemeine Zeitung* (March 15, 1869) in Brandmüller, *Ignaz von Döllinger am Vorabend des I.Vatikanums*, 180.

86. Cited in McClory, *Power and Papacy*, 74.

87. Döllinger to Acton (July 23, 1869), *Briefwechsel*, vol. 1, 567.

88. Döllinger to Oxenham (July 6, 1869) excerpted in CUL Add. 4919/79. Cf. Döllinger to Gladstone (March 15, 1870), BSB Döllingeriana II.

89. Brandmüller, *Ignaz von Döllinger am Vorabend des I.Vatikanums*, 56ff. His colleague Johann Nepomuk Huber assisted with the book.

90. *Der Papst und das Concil* (Leipzig: E. F. Steinacker, 1869), iv.

91. Döllinger had great admiration for Dante as a critic of the Church hierarchy. See Döllinger, "Dante as Prophet," in *Studies in European History*, trans. Margaret Warre (London, 1890), 80–118. Döllinger has also been likened to Dante by contemporaries and subsequent critics alike. See William H. Cooper, "A Nineteenth-Century Dante," *Crozer Quarterly* 23 (October 1946): 355–62.

92. *Der Papst und das Concil*, x–xi.

93. *Der Papst und das Concil*, xvii.

94. Roland Hill, *Lord Acton* (New Haven: Yale University Press, 2000), 189.

95. On Gregory VII and the *Dictatus Papae*, see Colin Morris, *The Papal Monarchy: The Western Church from 1050 to 1250* (Oxford: Clarendon Press, 1989). Cf. *EVP*, 186–7.

96. *Der Papst und das Concil*, 154.

97. Döllinger gave some thought to writing a "Janus II," to focus on papal developments in the post-Reformation era, but this was never completed. See Döllinger to Acton (August 8, 1869), *Briefwechsel*, vol. 1, 571.

98. *Der Papst und das Concil*, viii. For an evaluation of Döllinger's historical analysis, see Tierney, *The Origins of Papal Infallibility, 1150–1350*, 10ff.

99. *Der Papst und das Concil*, xv.

100. A Hungarian translation followed in 1870. *TG*, 155.

101. Acton to Döllinger (August 10, 1869), *Briefwechsel*, vol. 1, 572f.

102. Gladstone to Döllinger (October 10, 1869), BL Gladstone Papers Add. 44426 (Add. 44140).

103. Brandmüller, *Ignaz von Döllinger am Vorabend des I.Vatikanums*, 89ff.

104. Quoted in Butler, *The Vatican Council*, 89.

105. Josef Hergenröther, *Anti-Janus, eine historisch-theologische Kritik der Schrift "Der Papst und das Concil"* (Freiburg im Breisgau, 1870).

106. Brandmüller, *Ignaz von Döllinger am Vorabend des I.Vatikanums*, 99ff.

107. Manning, *The True Story of the Vatican Council*, 67.

108. Meglia to Antonelli (August 30, 1869), ASV SS 1869 rubr. 1, fasc. 5.

109. *KGV*, vol. 1, 278–9.

110. Already in 1868, Döllinger had expressed his worries to Acton and Maret about the political implications of the Council if "the ultramontane-Jesuit interpretation [of the 'Syllabus'] became Council Decrees." See Döllinger to Acton (September 1, 1868), *Briefwechsel*, vol. 1, 516 and Döllinger to Maret (December 10, 1868), Lösch, *Döllinger und Frankreich*, 469.

111. Volker Stalmann, *Fürst Chlodwig zu Hohenlohe-Schillingsfürst, 1819–1901* (Paderborn: Ferdinand Schöningh, 2009), 109–16. On Döllinger's role, see *TG*, 170–4. The possibility of action by Europe's heads of state caused great concern in Rome. See Meglia to Antonelli (July 8, 1869), ASV SS rubr. 1, fasc. 5. Cf. J. Grisar, "Die Circulardepesche des Fürsten von Hohenlohe vom 9. April 1869 über das bevorstehende Vatikanische Konzil," *Archiv und Wissenschaft* 3 (1961): 216–40 and *KGV*, vol. 1, 277–84.

112. On the Fulda conference and its broader context, see *KGV*, vol. 1, 232–46.

113. *ADSC*, vol. 7, 1196–7.

114. Dupanloup's *Lettre au clergé de son diocèse. Observations sur la controverse soulevée relativement à la définition de l'infaillibilité au prochain concile* (Paris, 1869) represents one of the most forceful arguments for the "inopportunist" position.

115. *KGV*, vol. 1, 241–6 and Butler, *The Vatican Council*, 91.

116. Döllinger to Leyden (August 21, 1869), *Briefwechsel*, vol. 4, 414–15.

117. Döllinger to Leyden (August 21, 1869), *Briefwechsel*, vol. 4, 414–15. On the meeting at Herrnsheim, see Hill, *Lord Acton*, 189.

118. On the so-called "Vincentian Canon," see Thomas G. Guarino, "St. Vincent of Lérins and the Development of Christian Doctrine," *Logos: A Journal of Catholic Thought and Culture* 17 (2014): 103–17.

119. See "Erwägungen für die Bischöfe des Conciliums über die Frage der päpstlichen Unfehlbarkeit," in Döllinger, *Briefe und Erklärungen über die Vaticanischen Decrete, 1869–1887* (Munich, 1890), 1–28.

120. *TG*, 193ff.

121. Döllinger to Leyden (November 22, 1869), *Briefwechsel*, vol. 4, 440.

122. See the letters from Meglia to Antonelli (November 8, 13, 21, and 23, 1869), ASV SS 1869 rubr. 1, fasc. 5.

123. This exchange was reported without providing a source in Anon., "Dr. Döllinger and the Papacy," *Quarterly Review* 172 (1891): 42. I emphasize "reportedly" for this is the only place that I've documented this utterance.

124. Meglia to Antonelli (August 30, 1869), ASV SS 1869 rubr. 1, fasc. 5.

125. Walter Brandmüller, "'Janus' auf dem Index," in Albert Portmann-Tinguely, ed., *Kirche, Staat und katholische Wissenschaft in der Neuzeit, Festschrift für Heribert Raab zum 65.Geburtstag am 16. März 1988* (Paderborn: Ferdinand Schöningh, 1988), 426.

126. Brandmüller, "'Janus' auf dem Index," 427.

127. ASV NM 133, Busta 2. Decree of the Congregation of the Index (November 30, 1869), ASV SS 5 (1869/70), 390. Brandmüller, "'Janus' auf dem Index," 432. Cf. Hubert Wolf, ed., *Römische Inquisition und Indexkongregation* (Paderborn: Ferdinand Schöningh, 2005), 353.

128. *KGV*, vol. 1, 124–5 and Coppa, *Pope Pius IX*, 161f.

129. *The Vatican: A Weekly Record of the Council* (supplement to the *Tablet*, December 18, 1869).

130. Butler, *The Vatican Council, 1869–1870*, 135.

131. On the atmosphere in Rome at this time, see Ferdinand Gregorovius, *The Roman Journals of Ferdinand Gregorovius, 1852–1874*, trans. Mrs. Gusatvus V. Hamilton (London, 1907), 342ff.

132. Chadwick, *A History of the Popes, 1830–1914*, 197–8 and *RPP*, vol. 13, 278. In addition to bishops, superior generals and abbot generals of monastic congregations were also eligible participants. A complete listing of participants in the Council is found as an appendix in *KGV*, vol. 2, 360–92.

133. Some members of the Curia, notably Antonelli, were actually worried about the consequences of defining Infallibility, though they maintained a diplomatic reticence about it.

134. Aubert, *Le pontificat de Pie IX*, 326–9. On Strossmayer, see Ivo Sivric, *Bishop J. G. Strossmayer: New Light on Vatican I* (Chicago: Franciscan Herald Press, 1975).

135. Hill, *Lord Acton*, 198.

136. Acton to Gladstone (January 1, 1870) in Damian McElrath, James C. Holland, Sue Katzman, and Ward White, eds., *Lord Acton: The Decisive Decade, 1864–1874: Essays and Documents* (Louvain: Bureaux de la R. H. E., Bibliothèque de l'Université & Publications Universitaires de Louvain, 1970), 170.

137. Victor Conzemius, "Die Minorität auf dem Ersten Vatikanischen Konzil: Vorhut des Zweiten Vatikanums," *Theologie und Philosophie* 45 (1970): 416–18 and Anton Landersdorfer, "Im Umkreis des I.Vatikanischen Konzils und des Kulturkampfes," in Georg Schwaiger, ed., *Das Erzbistum München und Freising im 19. und 20. Jahrhundert* (Munich: Erich Wewel Verlag, 1989), 135–41.

138. *Generalien-Sammlung der Erzdiöcese München und Freising, III, Die oberhirtlichen Verordnungen und allgemeinen Erlasse von 23. Juli 1856 bis 6. Mai 1878* (Munich, 1878), 1133–7.

139. Landersdorfer, "Im Umkreis des I.Vatikanischen Konzils und des Kulturkampfes," 138.

140. On Friedrich's role at the Council and his collaboration with Döllinger, see Ewald Kessler, *Johann Friedrich (1836–1917): ein Beitrag zur Geschichte des Altkatholizismus* (Munich: Kommissionsbuchhandlung R. Wölfe, 1975), 172ff.

141. Hill, *Lord Acton*, 203.

142. Hill, *Lord Acton*, 192–9.

143. Odo Russell to Lord Clarendon (December 22, 1869) in Odo Russell, *The Roman Question: Extracts from the Despatches of Odo Russell from Rome, 1858–1870* (London: Chapman & Hall, 1962), 375.

144. Quoted in Hill, *Lord Acton*, 210.

145. Hill, *Lord Acton*, 197–8.

146. *Römische Briefe vom Concil von Quirinus* (Munich: Rudolph Oldenbourg, 1870). In addition to Friedrich, Count Louis Arco-Valley (1845–91), the Bavarian diplomat in Rome and Acton's brother-in-law, also contributed to "Quirinus." But the lion's share of the letters was composed by Döllinger and Acton. Determining exactly who wrote what, however, has not proven easy to figure out, but undertaken admirably by Victor Conzemius; see his "Die Verfasser der 'Römischen Briefe vom Konzil' des 'Quirinus,'" in *Festschrift für Hans Förster: Freiburger Geschichtsblätter* 52 (1963–4): 229–56 and Victor Conzemius, "Die Römischen Briefe vom Konzil. Eine entstehungsgeschichtliche und quellenkritische Untersuchung zum Konzilsjournalismus Ignaz v. Döllingers und Lord Actons," *RQ* 59 (1964): 186–229; 60 (1965): 76–119.

147. CUL Add. 7727/58.

148. CUL Add. 7727/16, 63. Cf. Gregorovius, *Roman Journals*, 353.

149. From Acton's Vatican Diary. CUL Add. 7727/56.

150. Quoted in J. V. Conzemius, "Lord Acton at the First Vatican Council," *JEH* 20 (October 1969): 278.

151. *Römische Briefe vom Concil von Quirinus*, 64–5; *Letters from Rome on the Council by Quirinus*, vol. 1 (London: Rivingtons, 1870), 74.

152. *Römische Briefe vom Concil von Quirinus*, 62–4, 85–6.

153. *Römische Briefe vom Concil von Quirinus*, 71.

154. *Römische Briefe vom Concil von Quirinus*, 65.

155. *Römische Briefe vom Concil von Quirinus*, 61.

156. *Römische Briefe vom Concil von Quirinus*, 80.

157. Aubert, *Le pontificat de Pie IX*, 346.

158. Hill, *Lord Acton*, 201.

159. Acton to Döllinger (February 13, 1870), *Briefwechsel*, vol. 2, 163.

160. *Römische Briefe vom Concil von Quirinus*, v.

161. Strossmayer to Döllinger (March 4, 1871) in *AK*, 254.

162. *KGV*, vol. 2, 145.

163. See Ignaz von Döllinger, "Einige Worte über die Unfehlbarkeitsadresse 19. Jan. 1870," in *Briefe und Erklärungen*, 34.

164. On the Council of Florence, see *ODCC*, 619–20. Cf. André de Halleux, "Le Concile de Florence: Union ou Uniatisme?" *Patristic and Byzantine Review* 13 (1994): 29–48, Donald W. Norwood, "A Reunion Council?" *ER* 45 (1993): 482–9, and Carl Krauthauser, "The Council of Florence Revisited," *Eastern Churches Journal: A Journal of Eastern Christendom* 4 (1997): 141–54.

165. Döllinger, *Briefe und Erklärungen*, 32–9.

166. J. B. Bury, *History of the Papacy in the 19th Century: Liberty and Authority in the Roman Catholic Church* (New York: Schocken Books, 1964), 99.

167. *KGV*, vol. 2, 233.

168. Meglia to Antonelli (February 25, 1870), ASV NM 128.

169. See Wilhelm Emmanuel Ketteler, "Erklärung des Hochwürdigsten Herrn Bischofs von Mainz auf die Veröffentlichung des Herrn Stiftspropst v. Döllinger in der *All[gemeine] Z[eitung]* vom 27. Januar 1870," *Der Katholik* 50 (1870): 252–6.

170. On the historiography of the Council of Florence, see Henry Chadwick, *East and West: The Making of a Rift in the Church from Apostolic Times to the Council of Florence* (Oxford: Oxford University Press, 2003), 263–73 and Aristeides

Papadakis and John Meyendorff, *The Christian East and the Rise of the Papacy* (Crestwood, NY: St. Vladimir's Seminary Press, 1994), 379–408. Döllinger's claims were especially contested by Eugenio Cecconi, author of *Studi storici sul Concilio di Firenze; con documenti inediti o nuovamente dati alla luce sui manoscritti di Firenze e di Roma* (Florence, 1869).

171. Quoted in Otto Weiß, "Döllinger, Rom, und Italien," in *GG*, 246.

172. Meglia to Antonelli (January 29, 1870), ASV CVI 1870/71 fasc. monaco and Meglia to Antonelli (February 18, 1870), ASV CVI 1870/71 fasc. monaco.

173. Acton quoted here, conveying to Döllinger what Hohenlohe had heard from the Pope. See Acton to Döllinger (February 13, 1870), *Briefwechsel*, vol. 2, 164.

174. Matteo Liberatore, "Il Dottor Döllinger e la petizione dei vescovi al Concilio," *La Civiltà Cattolica* 7–9 (1870): 384–400.

175. *Pastoral-Blatt für die Erzdiöcese München-Freising vom 17. Februar 1870* (No. 72), 42.

176. Döllinger, *Briefe und Erklärungen*, 40–57. The article appeared in the *Allgemeine Zeitung* on March 11, 1870.

177. Karim Schelkens, John A. Dick, and Jürgen Mettepenningen, *Aggiornamento? Catholicism from Gregory XVI to Benedict XVI* (Leiden: Brill, 2013), 49–52.

178. *Römische Briefe vom Concil von Quirinus*, 396.

179. Döllinger to Acton (April 8, 1870). Döllinger here quotes a letter from Hefele. *Briefwechsel*, vol. 2, 290.

180. The French foreign minister, Napoleon Daru, a devout Catholic, eventually sent an envoy to the Council threatening the withdrawal of French troops if the decisions of the Councils violated the rights of governments. But this threat never materialized as French majority bishops prevailed against the government. Hill, *Lord Acton*, 214.

181. Christopher McIntosh, *The Swan King: Ludwig II of Bavaria*, rev. ed. (London: I. B. Tauris, 2012), 161–3.

182. Bismarck's words are referred to in a letter from Döllinger to Acton (April 8, 1870), *Briefwechsel*, vol. 2, 289. Cf. Massimiliano Valente, *Diplomazia pontificia e Kulturkampf: la Santa Sede e la Prussia tra Pio IX e Bismarck, 1862–1878* (Rome: Studium, 2004), 71ff.

183. Acton to Gladstone (March 10, 1870), McElrath et al., eds., *Lord Acton: The Decisive Decade*, 177–8.

184. Döllinger to Gladstone (March 15, 1870), BL Gladstone Papers, Add. 44140/273. Michael Candler, "The Significance of the Friendship between W. E. Gladstone and Ignaz von Döllinger," *IKZ* 90 (2000): 158.

185. Gladstone to Döllinger (March 25, 1870), BL Gladstone Papers, Add. 44140/274.

186. Clarendon to Gladstone (March 23, 1870), *Briefwechsel*, vol. 2, 243–4, n.2 and Hill, *Lord Acton*, 213.

187. Acton to Gladstone (March 20, 1870), McElrath et al., eds., *Lord Acton: The Decisive Decade*, 181.

188. Döllinger to Acton (March 31, 1870), *Briefwechsel*, vol. 2, 277.

189. Mark E. Powell, *Papal Infallibility: A Protestant Evaluation of an Ecumenical Issue* (Grand Rapids, MI: Eerdmans, 209), 104 and Avery Dulles, S.J., "Newman on Infallibility," *TS* 51 (1990): 434–49.

190. Döllinger to Newman (March 19, 1870), *Letters and Diaries of John Henry Newman*, vol. 25, 84. Döllinger refers here to the Belgian Archbishop Victore-August-Isidor Dechamps (1810–83), a strong defender of Infallibility.

191. Newman to Döllinger (April 9, 1870), *Letters and Diaries of John Henry Newman*, vol. 25, 85.

192. Newman to Alfred Plummer (January 15, 1871), *Letters and Diaries of John Henry Newman*, vol. 25, 269.

193. Newman to Plummer (April 3, 1871), *Letters and Diaries of John Henry Newman*, vol. 25, 309.

194. For Newman and Döllinger more generally at this time, see Franz Xaver Bischof, "John Henry Newman und Ignaz von Döllinger: Papstdogmen und Gewissen," in Mariano Delgado, Volker Leppin, and David Neuhold, eds., *Ringen um die Wahrheit: Gewissenskonflikte in der Christentumsgeschichte* (Stuttgart: Kohlhammer, 2011), 271–86.

195. *Römische Briefe vom Concil von Quirinus*, 402–3.

196. *Römische Briefe vom Concil von Quirinus*, 415.

197. *Römische Briefe vom Concil von Quirinus*, 341.

198. On Schrader, see *NDB*, vol. 23, 510–11.

199. *RPP*, vol. 13, 279 and *KGV*, vol. 3, 28–75.

200. Schatz, *Papal Primacy*, 160.

201. Cited in Schatz, *Papal Primacy*, 160.

202. The most detailed investigation of Guidi's intervention is found in Ulrich Horst, "Kardinalerzbischof Filippo Maria Guidi OP und das 1. Vatikanischen Konzil," *Archivum Fratrum Praedicatorum* 49 (1979): 429–511; cf. *KGV*, vol. 3, 99–109 and *RPP*, vol. 13, 279.

203. *Römische Briefe vom Concil von Quirinus*, 556.

204. Acton to Döllinger (June 10, 1870), *Briefwechsel*, vol. 3, 422.

205. Tauffkirchen as quoted in Hill, *Lord Acton*, 222.

206. *KGV*, vol. 3, 140–52. On Gasser's intervention and its subsequent theological significance at the time of Vatican II, see Lawrence J. King, "Newman and Gasser on Infallibility: Vatican I and Vatican II," *NSJ* 9 (2011): 27–32.

207. *ESDD*, 616. The phrasing was directed against Gallicanism in general and particularly against article four of the Gallican Articles (1682), which Rome had accepted in negotiations with France in the seventeenth century. This article reads as follows: "Although the pope has the chief part in questions of faith, and his decrees apply to all the Churches, and to each Church in particular, yet his judgment is not irreformable, at least pending the consent of the Church."

208. George G. Windell, *The Catholics and German Unity, 1866–1871* (Minneapolis: University of Minnesota Press, 1954), 227.

209. Chadwick, *History of the Popes, 1830–1914*, 213–14.

210. *The Times* as quoted in E. E. Y. Hales, *Pio Nono* (Garden City, NY: Image Books, 1962), 324.

211. Christopher Hibbert, *Rome: Biography of a City* (New York: W. W. Norton, 1985), 273.

212. *Römische Briefe vom Concil von Quirinus*, 636–7.

213. Döllinger to Acton (July 23, 1870), *Briefwechsel*, vol. 2, 436–7.

214. "Wir sind Ketzer wenn er Recht hat. Er ist wenn er Unrecht hat." Acton to Döllinger (July 25, 1870), *Briefwechsel*, vol. 2, 438.

215. Chadwick, *History of the Popes, 1830–1914*, 215–16.

216. Döllinger to Acton (September 18, 1870), *Briefwechsel*, vol. 2, 455.

217. Quoted in Antonio Monti, *Pio IX nel Risorgimento: con documenti inediti ed illustrazioni* (Bari: G. Laterza, 1928), 194.

218. Coppa, *Pope Pius IX*, 171.

219. Quoted in Chadwick, *History of the Popes, 1830–1914*, 217.

220. Quoted in Ernest Vercesi, *Pio IX* (Milan: Edzioni Carbaccio, 1930), 257.

221. *AP*, vol. 5, 263–77; *AAS*, vol. 6, 136–46.

222. BSB Döllingeriana IX.3.

223. Meglia to Antonelli (July 22, 1870), ASV SS rubr. 255, fasc. 1.

224. This is according to Johann Friedrich, *Tagebuch während des Vaticanischen Concils* (Nördlingen, 1871), 389.

225. Friedrich, *Döllinger*, vol. 3, 347–58.

226. Meglia to Antonelli (July 28, 1870), ASV CVI 1870/71 fasc. monaco.

227. See the letter of Liddon to Oxenham (July 29, 1870) in J. O. Johnston, *The Life and Letters of Henry Parry Liddon, Canon of St. Paul's Cathedral and Sometime Ireland Professor in the University of Oxford*, 2nd ed. (London: Longmans, Green & Co., 1904), 138–9. On Liddon and Oxenham, see *ODNB*, vol. 11, 1102–7 and vol. 15, 13–15.

228. Döllinger to Schulte (July 24, 1870), BAB Schulte 6/14.

229. Scherr to Rauscher (August 4, 1870), CVI 1870 fasc. 4.

230. Meglia to Antonelli (July 22, 1870), ASV SS rubr. 255, fasc. 1.

231. *KGV*, vol. 3, 222–3. On the Edict of 1818, see Karl Hausberger, *Staat und Kirche nach der Säkularisation. Zur bayerischen Konkordatspolitik im frühen 19. Jahrhundert* (St. Ottilien: Eos Verlag, 1983), 331–44. On Lutz, see *NDB*, vol. 15, 568–70.

232. *KGV*, vol. 2, 233. Dieter Albrecht, "Döllinger, die Bayerische Regierung und das Erste Vatikanische Konzil," in Konrad Repgen and Stephan Skalweit, eds., *Spiegel der Geschichte: Festgabe für Max Braubach zum 10. April 1964* (Münster: Verlag Aschendorff, 1964), 810ff. and Fritz von Rummel, *Das Ministerium Lutz und seine Gegner, 1871–1882* (Munich: C. H. Beck, 1935), 27ff. and BAB Döllinger 5.162.

233. Hefele to Döllinger (August 10, 1870 and September 14, 1870) in *AK*, 222–3. On Döllinger's relations with Hefele more generally, see Rudolf Reinhardt, "Johannes Joseph Ignaz von Döllinger und Carl Joseph Hefele," *ZBL* 33 (1970): 439–46.

234. *AK*, 223.

235. For the text of the "Nuremberg Declaration," see *CL*, vol. 7, 1731–2. Cf. *AK*, 14–16. An Italian translation was sent to Rome by Meglia on August 27, 1870. ASV CVI 1870/71 fasc. monaco.

236. Johann Michael Raich, "Die Nürnberger Erklärung," *Der Katholik* 50 (1870): 370–2.

237. Of particular significance was the so-called "Königswinter Deklaration" (August 14, 1871), a rejection of the Vatican decrees, signed by numerous high-ranking laity. See *AK*, 105–7.

238. *KGV*, vol. 3, 222.

239. Scherr to Melchers (August 13, 1870) as quoted in Anton Landersdorfer, *Gregor von Scherr (1804–1877): Erzbischöf von München und Freising in der Zeit des Ersten Vatikanums und des Kulturkampfes* (Munich: Verein für Diözesangeschichte von München und Freising, 1995), 426, n.321.

240. Landersdorfer, *Gregor von Scherr*, 427.

241. *KGV*, vol. 3, 230f. See Wilhelm Emmanuel Ketteler, *Die unfehlbare Lehre nach der Entscheidung des vaticanischen Concils* (Mainz, 1871) and Josef Fessler, *Die wahre und die falsche Unfehlbarkeit der Päpste* (Vienna, 1871). On Fessler, see Anton Erdinger, *Dr. Joseph Fessler, Bischof von St. Pölten und Sekretär des Vatikanischen Concils: ein Lebensbild* (Brixen: A. Weger, 1874).

242. Karl Josef Rivinius, "Kettelers Kirchenverständnis auf dem Ersten Vatikanischen Konzil im Kontext der Unfehlbarkeitsdiskussion," *ZKG* 76 (1979): 281–97.

243. *CL*, vol. 7, 1733–5 and Butler, *The Vatican Council, 1869–1870*, 430–1. Cf. *KGV*, vol. 3, 226, n.113. This letter, and the publications of Ketteler and Fessler, which received approbation from Rome, proved influential in obtaining affirmation of the Council by the French minority bishops as well. See Margaret O'Gara, *Triumph in Defeat: Infallibility, Vatican I, and the French Minority Bishops* (Washington, DC: Catholic University of America Press, 1988), 204–5.

244. Butler, *The Vatican Council, 1869–1870*, 432.

245. *AP*, vol. 5, 257–62 and *KGV*, vol. 3, 228.

246. BAB Reusch 7.320. Hefele indicated that he submitted because of the "high good" of church unity and in the hope that a future council would make clearer the compatibility of the recent Vatican Council with previous tradition.

247. Hefele to Döllinger (September 14, 1870) in *AK*, 223. Bishop Strossmayer of Croatia was the last to submit and then only faintly. On his submission, see Sivric, *Bishop J. G. Strossmayer*, 243ff.

248. See Lord Acton, *Sendschreiben an einen deutschen Bischof des Vaticanischen Concils* (Nördlingen, 1870). For Ketteler's response, see his *Die Minorität auf dem Concil. Antwort auf Lord Actons Sendschreiben an einen deutschen Bischof des Vaticanischen Concils* (Mainz, 1871) in Ketteler, *Sämtliche Werke und Briefe*, vol. 3 (Mainz: Hase und Koehler, 1982), 821–33. Cf. *KGV*, vol. 3, 228.

249. Johann Friedrich, *Die Wortbrüchigkeit und Unwahrhaftigkeit deutscher Bischöfe. Offenes Sendschreiben an W. E. Freiherr von Ketteler in Mainz* (Constance, 1873).

250. Joseph Hubert Reinkens, *Die Unterwerfung der deutschen Bischöfe zu Fulda* (Münster, 1871), 17, 20.

251. Butler, *The Vatican Council, 1869–1870*, 431.

252. On this, see August Franzen, *Die katholisch-Theologische Fakultät Bonn im Streit um das Erste Vatikanische Konzil.Zugleich ein Beitrag zur Entstehungsgeschichte des Altkatholizismus am Niederrheim* (Cologne: Böhlau, 1974), 182–213.

253. Interestingly, according to Friedrich, Döllinger and Scherr crossed paths in the English Garden in Munich on October 17, 1870 and then Scherr had indicated that he would *not* take measures against Döllinger. If this story is true, then Scherr presumably had a rather sudden change of mind. See Friedrich, *Döllinger*, vol. 3, 559 and *TG*, 251.

254. *Briefe und Erklärungen*, 59–61.

255. Meglia to Antonelli (December 1, 1870). ASV CVI 1870/71 fasc. monaco. Cf. Georg Denzler, "Das I. Vatikanische Konzil und die Theologische Fakultät der Universität München," *Annuarium Historiae Conciliorum* 1 (1969): 427 and Landersdorfer, *Gregor von Scherr*, 433.

256. Kessler, *Johann Friedrich*, 299–305.

257. *TG*, 259 and Landersdorfer, *Gregor von Scherr*, 433.

258. See the letter of compliance in *Aktenstücke des Ordinariates des Erzbisthums München und Freising betreffend das allgemeine Vatikanische Concil* (Regensburg, 1871), 50–2. The letter was soon translated into Italian and sent to Rome. ASV SS 1870 rubr. fasc. 1. Munich's canon lawyer Isidor Silbernagl represents a special case. He did not gainsay the validity of the Vatican decrees per se, but he disputed on a purely legal basis that the Archbishop possessed the juridical authority to intervene in matters of the theological faculty. See Landersdorfer, *Gregor von Scherr*, 434, n.351.

259. Friedrich's letter is found in *Aktenstücke des Ordinariates des Erzbisthums München und Freising*, 52–9. *TG*, 262. Cf. Kessler, *Johann Friedrich*, 299–305.

260. Hefele to Döllinger (December 17, 1870) in Schulte, *AK*, 226–7.

261. BAB Reusch 7.320; *TG*, 249.

262. The letter was released January 5, 1871. *Aktenstücke des Ordinariates des Erzbisthums München und Freising*, 84–5. Cf. Landersdorfer, *Gregor von Scherr*, 430–1.

263. Meglia to Antonelli (January 8, 1871), ASV SS 1870 rubr. 1 fasc 2.

264. *TG*, 264, n.24.

265. Scherr to Döllinger (January 4, 1871), *Briefe und Erklärungen*, 62–5.

266. Döllinger to Acton (January 10, 1871), *Briefwechsel*, vol. 3, 8.

267. Döllinger to Scherr (January 29, 1871), *Briefe und Erklärungen*, 67–8.

268. Scherr to Döllinger (February 14, 1871), *Briefe und Erklärungen*, 69.

269. Döllinger to Scherr (March 14, 1871), *Briefe und Erklärungen*, 70–1.

270. Scherr to Döllinger (March 17, 1871), *Briefe und Erklärungen*, 72.

271. Meglia to Antonelli (March 18, 1871), ASV SS 1870 rubr. 1, fasc. 2.

272. Louise von Kobell, *Conversations with Dr. Döllinger*, trans. Katherine Gould (London, 1892), 15–16.

273. Lady Blennerhassett to Sir Rowland Blennerhassett (March 26, 1871), Blennerhassett Papers, CUL Add. 7486/50.

274. Hefele to Döllinger (March 11, 1871), in Friedrich, *Döllinger*, vol. 3, 567.

275. Döllinger to Scherr (March 14, 1871), *Briefe und Erklärungen*, 73–92.

276. Döllinger to Scherr (March 28, 1871), *Briefe und Erklärungen*, 73–92.

277. Dönniges to Ludwig II (April 8, 1871) in Nobert Miko, ed., *Das Ende des Kirchenstaates*, vol. 4 (Vienna: Verlag Harold, 1970), 120.

278. *Rheinischer Merkur* (April 9, 1871): 137.

279. Many can be found at BAB Döllinger 5.30–152. Cf. BSB Döllingeriana I.1.2–5.

280. BSB Döllingeriana I.1.2.

281. *Thüringer Presse* (April 6, 1871), BAB Döllinger 5.268/4.

282. Meglia to Antonelli (March 31, 1871), ASV SS 1870 rubr. 1, fasc. 2.

283. See the Open Letter of Catholic Clergy in Munich, ASV SS rubr. 1, fasc. 2 and Miko, ed., *Das Ende des Kirchenstaates*, vol. 4, 156.

284. BAB Döllinger 5.268/8 and 5.268/13; BSB Döllingeriana VI.16.

285. *Pastoral-Blatt für die Erzdiöcese München-Freising* (April 2, 1871), ASV SS 1870 rubr. 1, fasc. 2; *Briefe und Erklärungen*, 72–97.

286. Antonelli to Meglia (April 12, 1871), ASV NM 129.

287. March 31, 1871. ASV SS 1870 rubr. 1, fasc. 2: "L'Atto Dolinger [!] mettendo fuori della chiesa è naturale che non può esercitare il ministero qualunque sia la posizione che occupa." In attributing this remark to the Pope, I follow the scholarship of Mario Belardinelli, "Döllinger e L'Italia; per una storia del dibattito sull' liberta nella Chiesa nell'Ottocento," *Rivista di storia della chiesa in Italia* 37 (1983): 106. In a second communiqué, of April 5, 1871, Meglia worried about the king supporting "the German teaching of Döllinger" (*la doctrina tedesca del Döllinger*). See Meglia to Antonelli (April 5, 1871), ASV SS 1870 rubr. 1, fasc. 2.

288. Antonelli to Meglia (April 5, 1871), ASV NM 129.

289. Antonelli to Meglia (April 8, 1871), ASV NM 129.

290. Antonelli to Meglia (April 8, 1871), ASV NM 129.

291. *TG*, 276. Cf. Franzen, *Die Katholisch-Theologische Fakultät Bonn im Streit um das Erste Vatikanische Konzil*, 183ff.

292. Döllinger to Ruffo Scilla (October 12, 1887), *Briefe und Erklärungen*, 147–54.

293. Quoted material comes from two birthday greetings from Ludwig II to Döllinger (February 28, 1870 and February 28, 1871) as quoted in Margot Weber, *Das I. Vatikanische Konzil im Spiegel der bayerischen Politik* (Munich: Kommissionsbuchhandlung R. Wölfe, 1970), 208ff. Cf. McIntosh, *Swan King*, 161.

294. Various relevant diplomatic communiqués are found at BHSA Ministerium des Äußeren 642. Cf. Landersdorfer, *Gregor von Scherr*, 440–1 and *TG*, 273–5.

295. Scherr to Ludwig II (April 15, 1871), in *Aktenstücke des Ordinariates des Erzbisthums München und Freising*, 132–4.

296. Meglia to Antonelli (April 17, 1871), ASV SS 1870 rubr. 1, fasc. 2.

297. Meglia to Antonelli (April 22, 1871), ASV NM 129.

298. *Aktenstücke des Ordinariates des Erzbisthums München und Freising*, 136.

299. BAB Döllinger 5.155; *Briefe und Erklärungen*, 98–9.

300. "Heute habe ich das letzte Hochamt gehalten … ; ich werde die Herren in keine Verlegenheit bringen, ich betrachte mich als den, zu welchem mich der Erzbischof machen wird." These words are according to Friedrich, *Döllinger*, vol. 3, 581.

301. Newman to Döllinger (April 9, 1871), BSB Döllingeriana II.

302. BAB Döllinger 5.156; *Briefe und Erklärungen*, 100–2.

303. *TG*, 286.

304. Meglia to Antonelli (April 17, 1871), ASV SS 1870 rubr. 1, fasc. 2: "Egli è triste e agitatissimo; ad una persona diceva l'altro ieri: 'Io sono l'uomo il più disgraziato del mondo: se torno indietro sono perduto, se continuo ad andare innanzi, sono perduto egualmente.'" The source of this self-description by Döllinger is unfortunately not given.

305. Giuseppe di Lampedusa, *The Leopard*, trans. Archibald Colquhoun (New York: Pantheon Books, 2007), 96.

CHAPTER 4

1. Emphases added.
2. Robert Wilken, *Christianity: The First One Thousand Years—A Global History of Christianity* (New Haven: Yale University Press, 2012), 195–205.
3. Henry Chadwick, *East and West: The Making of a Rift in the Church from Apostolic Times to the Council of Florence* (Oxford: Oxford University Press, 2003) and Vladimir Kharlamov, "Vatican II and the Eastern Orthodox Church," *JEC* 38 (2001): 168–88.
4. Karl Heinx Voigt, *Ökumene in Deutschland: Internationale Einflüsse und Netzwerkbildung, 1848–1945* (Göttingen: Vandenhoeck & Ruprecht, 2014) and Stan M. Landry, *Ecumenism, Memory, and German Nationalism, 1817–1917* (Syracuse: Syracuse University Press, 2014), 79ff.
5. Michael B. Gross, *The War Against Catholicism: Liberalism and the Anti-Catholic Imagination in Nineteenth-Century Germany* (Ann Arbor: University of Michigan Press, 2005), 240ff.
6. Ronald J. Ross, *The Failure of Bismarck's Kulturkampf: Catholicism and State Power in Imperial Germany, 1871–1887* (Washington, DC: Catholic University of America Press, 1998), 35ff. and Massimilano Valente, *Diplomazia pontificia e kulturkampf: La Santa Sede e la Prussia tra Pio IX e Bismarck, 1862–1878* (Rome: Edizioni Studium, 2004), 196ff.
7. John A. Radano, ed., *Celebrating a Century of Ecumenism: Exploring the Achievements of International Dialogue in Commemoration of the Centenary of the 1910 Edinburgh World Missionary Conference* (Grand Rapids, MI: Eerdmans, 2012); Mauro Velati, "Il secolo dell'ecumenismo cristiano," *CnS* 22 (2001): 605–31; and Cecil M. Robeck, "Evangelism and Ecumenism: One Hundred Years after Edinburgh," *Lutheran Forum* 4 (2010): 33–8.
8. Olaf Blaschke, "Das 19. Jahrhundert: Ein zweites konfessionelles Zeitalter?" *Geschichte und Gesellschaft* 26 (2000): 38–75. Cf. Helmut Walser Smith, ed., *Protestants, Catholics, and Jews in Germany, 1800–1914* (Oxford: Berg, 2001).
9. Mark D. Chapman's *The Fantasy of Reunion: Anglicans, Catholics, and Ecumenism, 1833–1882* (Oxford: Oxford University Press, 2014) is one of the few substantive treatments of ecumenism in the nineteenth century.
10. *ODCC*, 225, 619.
11. Peter Neuner, *Döllinger als Theologe der Ökumene* (Paderborn: Ferdinand Schöningh, 1979), 115–31.
12. August Boudinhon, "Excommunication," *CE*, vol. 5 (New York: Robert Appleton, 1909), 671–98 and Joseph Hollweck, *Die kirchlichen Strafgesetze* (Mainz: Franz Kirchheim, 1899), 114ff.
13. Louise von Kobell, *Conversations with Dr. Döllinger*, trans. Katherine Gould (London, 1892), 261.
14. Döllinger to Steichele (March 1, 1887) in *Briefe und Erklärungenüber die Vaticanischen Decrete* (Munich, 1890), 130. Excommunication or "the ban" in canon law derived, inter alia, from a passage in I Corinthians 5:5 where Paul provides instructions for dealing with the unrepentant sinner: "[Y]ou are to deliver this man to Satan for the destruction of the flesh, that his spirit may be saved in the day of the Lord Jesus" (RSV). Cf. I Timothy 1:20. On the theology and history of

excommunication, see *ODCC*, 584–5, Francis Edward Hyland, *Excommunication: Its Nature, Historical Development and Effects* (Washington, DC: Catholic University of America Press, 1928), Jean-Marie Kilumby Mayimby-Kil, *Excommunication et communion avec l'église catholique* (Rome: Pontificia Universitas Urbaniana, 2001), and Elisabeth Vodola, *Excommunication in the Middle Ages* (Berkeley: University of California Press, 1986).

15. Döllinger to Blennerhassett (June 6, 1871), *Briefwechsel*, vol. 4, 502.

16. In the Döllinger papers in the archives of the Bayerische Staatsbibliothek in Munich, there is a small (undated) card with the images of Luther, Hus, and Döllinger. The inscription on it reads: "three fighters for spiritual freedom" (*drei Kämpfer für Geistesfreiheit*). BSB Döllingeriana XX.1.

17. *Kladderadatsch: Humoristisch-satyrisches Wochenblatt* (April 16, 1871): 72.

18. "Dr. Döllinger von München," *National- Zeitung* (April 12, 1871), BSB Döllingeriana XXI.7.

19. "Die Döllinger'sche Angelegenheit," *Braunschweiger Volksfreund* (May 26, 1871), BSB Döllingeriana XXI.7.

20. "J. von Döllinger und seine Gegner," *Süddeutsche Telegraph* (April 9, 1871), BSB Döllingeriana XXI.7.

21. "Döllinger und die deutschen Katholiken," *Norddeutsches Protestantenblatt* (April, 15 1871), BAB Döllinger 5.259.20.

22. *Rheinischer Merkur: Kirchlich-politisches Wochenblatt* (April 9, 1871), 137. Cf. Róisín Healy, *The Jesuit Specter in Imperial Germany* (Boston: Brill Academic, 2003), 60.

23. *Rheinischer Merkur: Kirchlich-politisches Wochenblatt* (April 30, 1871), 165. Founded in Cologne in 1870, this paper was renamed the *Deutsche Merkur* in 1872. See Joseph Troxler, *Die neuere Entwicklung des Altkatholizimus* (Cologne: J. P. Bachem, 1908), 24.

24. *Münchener Punsch* 24, no. 20 (May 14, 1871). There is a third, unidentifiable figure being burned with them.

25. The letter from Koblenz is dated April 18, 1871, BAB Döllinger 5.80.

26. BSB Döllingeriana I.13.1, 1.3.1.s, 1.5, and BAB Döllinger 5.30–65.

27. BAB Döllinger 5.54.

28. Michael Winichner, "*Die Unterzeichneten verwerfen die Unfehlbarkeit des Pabstes*": *Die alt-katholische Gemeinde von Simbach am Inn* (Bonn: Alt-Katholischer Bistumsverlag, 2009), 28ff.

29. "Die Erklärung Döllingers," *Die Vaterland-Zeitung für dieösterreichische Monarchie* (April 7, 1871), BSB Döllingeriana XXI.7. Cf. Dieter Albrecht, "Döllinger, die Bayerische Regierung und das Erste Vatikanische Konzil," in Konrad Repgen and Stephan Skalweit, eds., *Spiegel der Geschichte: Festgabe für Max Braubach zum 10. April 1964* (Münster: Verlag Aschendorff, 1964), 815.

30. BAB Döllinger 5.154.

31. Joseph Hergenröther, *Kritik der von Döllinger'schen Erklärung vom 28 März* (Freiburg im Breisgau, 1871), 2.

32. *TG*, 297–8.

33. Noted in Alfred Plummer, *Conversations with Dr. Döllinger, 1870–1890* (Leuven: Leuven University Press, 1985), 18–19.

34. *Pastoral-Blatt für die Erzdiöcese München-Freising vom 30. Mai 1871* in *Aktenstücke des Ordinariates des Erzbistums München und Freising betreffend das allgemeine Vatikanische Concil* (Regensberg, 1871), 113ff.

35. *TG*, 297.

36. *GG*, 485.

37. *TG*, 287.

38. He had previously served as rector in 1844–5 and 1866–7. *GG*, 484–5. Cf. "Dr. Dollinger [sic]: Significance of the Election at Munich," *New York Times* (August 29, 1871).

39. *Kladderadatsch* (August 6, 1871), printed in Elisabeth Bach, "Stadtspaziergang," in Elisabeth Bach, Angela Berlis, and Siegfried J. Thuringer, eds., *Ignaz von Döllinger zum 125. Todestag: Spurensuche, Schlaglichter auf ein außergwöhnliches Leben* (Bonn: Alt-Katholischer Bistumsverlag, 2015), 24.

40. "Die Bedeutung der großen Zeitereignisse für die deutschen Hochschulen. Rektoratesrede, gehalten am 23. Dezember 1871 in der Aula der Universität München," in Döllinger, *Akademische Vorträge*, 3 vols. (Nördlingen: C. H. Beck, 1889–91), vol. 3, 20.

41. *GG*, 485.

42. "Erklärung der Mitglieder der theologischen Facultät." *Pastoral-Blatt für die Erzdiöcese München-Freising* (July 13, 1871), BAB Döllinger 5.160.

43. *TG*, 305.

44. The letter is printed in Stefan Lösch, *Döllinger und Frankreich: Eine geistige Allianz, 1823–1871* (Munich: C. H. Beck, 1955), 490–3.

45. Quoted in Theodorus [James Bass Mullinger], *The New Reformation: A Narrative of the Old Catholic Movement* (London: Longmans, Green and Co., 1875), 111.

46. On the general influence of Döllinger in Italy, see Cesare Milaneschi, *Il vecchio cattolicesimo in Italia* (Cosenza: Luigi Pellegrini, 2014), 35–66.

47. *GG*, 268.

48. BSB Döllingeriana I.1.2 and "Dr. Döllinger and the Professors of the University of Rome," *New York Times* (May 8, 1871).

49. BAB Döllinger 5.101 and 5.102.

50. *GG*, 260–1.

51. *Il Fischietto* (May 18, 1871).

52. See Alois Pichler to Döllinger (July 11, 1871), BSB Döllingeriana II. and "L'opposizione all'infallibilità in Germania e in Italia," *Voce della Verità* (May 18, 1871), quoted in *GG*, 269.

53. See, inter alia, "Un eretico di più o la dichiarazione del dottor Döllinger," *L'Unitá Cattolica* (April 1, 1871) and "L'Anatema contro Döllinger," *L'Unitá Cattolica* (April 21, 1871); quoted in *GG*, 259.

54. "L'opposizione all'infallibilità in Germania e in Italia," *Voce della Verità* (May 18, 1871), quoted in *GG*, 259.

55. [Giuseppe Fantoni], *La Civiltà Cattolica*, 8.3 (1871): 746ff.

56. *Il Fischietto* (April 29, 1871). Cf. Wolfgang Suchanek, *Das Deutschlandbild in der italienischen Presse 1870/71* (Bonn: Suchanek, 1975), 162f.

57. "Mr. Plummer's Translation of Dr. Döllinger on the Popes," *DR* 18 (1872): 363.

58. "The Vatican Council: Its Authority, Its Work," *DR* 20 (1873): 159.
59. W. B. Ullathorne, *The Döllingerites, Mr. Gladstone, and Apostates from the Faith* (London: T. Richardson, 1874).
60. Josef L. Altholz, *The Liberal Catholic Movement in England* (London: Burns & Oates, 1962), 241f. Cf. Roland Hill, *Lord Acton* (New Haven: Yale University Press, 2000), 226ff.
61. Newman to Alfred Plummer (April 3, 1871), in Charles Stephen Dessain and Thomas Gornall, S.J., eds., *The Letters and Diaries of John Henry Newman*, vol. 25 (Oxford: Clarendon Press, 1973), 308.
62. Newman to Döllinger (April 9, 1871), BSB Döllingeriana II.
63. BSB Döllingeriana I.5 (Marburg). For a negative reaction to Oxford's conferral of an honorary degree on Döllinger, see "Oxford and Dr. Döllinger," *Tablet* (June 10, 1871). BSB Döllingeriana XIX.10.
64. Plummer to Döllinger (June 4, 1872), BSB Döllingeriana II.
65. "Dr. Döllinger's Fables Respecting the Medieval Popes," *Christian Observer* (London, 1872), 141. Cf. Angela Berlis, "Ignaz von Döllinger and the Anglicans," in Stewart J. Brown and Peter B. Nockles, eds., *The Oxford Movement: Europe and the Wider World, 1830–1930* (Cambridge: Cambridge University Press, 2012), 236–48.
66. "The Excommunication of Dr. Döllinger," *The Guardian* (April 26, 1871), BSB Döllingeriana XI.3.
67. For an American (German-language) ultramontane view, see "Döllinger der Gründer und das sichtbare Oberhaupt der Zukunftskirche," *Der Herold des Glaubens: Ein katholisches Sonntagsblatt* (May 14, 1871), BAB Döllinger 5.262/1. The paper was published in St. Louis. With irony, the author skewers "German science" and Döllinger's "infallible" utterances. Another, outspoken American critic of Döllinger's actions was Orestes Brownson. See Patrick W. Carey, *Orestes A. Brownson: American Religious Weathervane* (Grand Rapids, MI: Eerdmans, 2004), 314–15. Brownson called the Old Catholic movement the religion of "proud German professors."
68. Charles Neville et al. to Döllinger (May 22, 1871), BSB Döllingeriana II.
69. *Harper's Weekly* (July 15, 1871): 648.
70. John W. Nevin, "The Old Catholic Movement," *MR* 21 (April 1873): 252–5.
71. Much previous attention by this newspaper and others had focused on the Council. See J. Ryan Beiser, *The Vatican Council and the American Secular Newspapers, 1869–70* (Washington, DC: Catholic University of America Press, 1941).
72. "The Catholic Party in Germany—Dr. Döllinger's Reply to his Archbishop," *New York Herald* (April 20, 1871).
73. "Doctor Dollinger's Excommunication," *New York Herald* (April 20, 1871).
74. "Dr. Dollinger and the King of Bavaria," *New York Herald* (April 26, 1871).
75. "Dr. Döllinger and the Pope," *New York Times* (April 22, 1871).
76. "A New Reformation," *Trenton State Gazette* (March 29, 1871).
77. *Hartford Daily Courant* (April 28, 1871).
78. "Roman Infallibility," *New Hampshire Sentinel* (May 11, 1871).
79. "The Infallibility Dogma in Bavaria," *San Francisco Bulletin* (May 15, 1871).

80. Klaus Schatz, *Zwischen Säkularisation und Zweitem Vatikanum: Der Weg des deutschen Katholizismus im 19. und 20. Jahrhundert* (Frankfurt am Main: Verlag Josef Knecht, 1986), 128 and David Blackbourn, *The Long Nineteenth Century: A History of Germany, 1780–1918* (New York: Oxford University Press, 1998), 261. On the religious demographics and geography of Catholicism of Germany after 1871, see Helmut Walser Smith, *German Nationalism and Religious Conflict: Culture, Ideology, Politics, 1870–1914* (Princeton: Princeton University Press, 1995), 42ff.

81. See, e.g., Rudolf Keussen, "Döllinger und die altkatholische Kirche," *IKZ* 26 (1936): 168–92; Wolfgang Krahl, "Döllinger als Altkatholik," *IKZ* 62 (1972): 219–30; and, more recently, Christian Oeyen, "Döllinger als Altkatholik: Eine Bestandaufnahme," *IKZ* 80 (1990): 67–105.

82. See Victor Conzemius, "Döllinger, Ignaz," *TRE*, vol. 9, 20–6.

83. Olaf Blaschke, "Der Altkatholizismus 1870 bis 1945: Nationalismus, Antisemitismus und Nationalsozialismus," *HZ* 261 (1995): 60–1.

84. Urs Küry, *Die altkatholische Kirche: Ihre Geschichte, ihre Lehre, ihr Anliegen* (Stuttgart: Evangelisches Verlagswerk Stuttgart, 1966), 62.

85. C. B. Moss, *The Old Catholic Movement: Its Origins and History*, 2nd ed. (Berkeley: Apocriphile Press, 1964), 231.

86. Report from Bruch to Friedrich Ferdinand von Beust, Minister of Foreign Affairs in Vienna (March 31, 1871), in Nobert Miko, *Das Ende des Kirchenstaates*, vol. 4 (Vienna: Verlag Herold, 1970), 112.

87. Report from Dönniges to Ludwig II (April 8, 1871), in Miko, *Das Ende des Kirchenstaates*, vol. 4, 119. On Dönniges, see *ADB*, vol. 5, 339–41.

88. Report of Tauffkirchen to Bismarck (May 10, 1871), in Miko, *Das Ende des Kirchenstaates*, vol. 4, 156.

89. Report of Tauffkirchen to Bismarck (August 11, 1871), in Miko, *Das Ende des Kirchenstaates*, vol. 4, 222–3.

90. Quoted material taken from John Newenham Hoare, *The Old Catholic Movement in Bavaria* (Dublin, 1872), 16–17. Cf. *TG*, 307f.

91. *KGV*, vol. 3.

92. *Pastoralblatt für die Erzdiöcese München-Freising* (May 20, 1871), 113.

93. Theodorus, *The New Reformation*, 116 and Moss, *The Old Catholic Movement*, 232–3.

94. Moss, *The Old Catholic Movement*, 234.

95. "Quis nobis dabit videre ecclesiam sicut erat in diebus antiquis?" See "Die Münchner Erklärung von Pfingsten 1871," in *AK*, 20.

96. "Die Münchner Erklärung von Pfingsten 1871," in *AK*, 16ff.

97. *Allgemeine Zeitung* (June 13, 1871), noted in *TG*, 310.

98. Döllinger to Oxenham (August 22, 1870) as quoted in Victor Conzemius, "Aspects ecclésiologiques de l'évolution de Döllinger et du vieux catholicisme," *Revue des Sciences Religieuses* 34 (1960): 247–79. Cf. Hill, *Lord Acton*, 229.

99. Moss, *Old Catholic Movement*, 233.

100. Ewald Kessler, *Johann Friedrich (1836–1917): Ein Beitrag zur Geschichte des Altkatholizismus* (Munich: Kommissionsbuchhandlung R. Wölfe, 1975), 339f.; Johann Friedrich von Schulte, *Lebenserinnerungen: Mein Wirken als*

Rechtslehrer, mein Anteil in der Politik und Staat, vol. 1 (Giessen: Verlag von Emil Roth, 1909), 271f.; and *TG*, 312.

101. Johann Friedrich, *Ignaz von Döllinger: Sein Leben auf Grund seines schriftlichen Nachlasses*, vol. 3 (Munich: C. H. Beck, 1901), 611.

102. Theodorus, *New Reformation*, 117–19.

103. J. Lowry Whittle, *Catholicism after the Vatican. With a Narrative of the Old Catholic Congress at Munich* (London: Henry S. King & Co., 1872), 42.

104. Peter Neuner, *Stationen einer Kirchenspaltung: Der Fall Döllinger—ein Lehrstück für die heutige Kirchenkrise* (Frankfurt am Main: Verlag Josef Knecht, 1990), 133.

105. This committee included Döllinger, Friedrich, and J. N. Huber of Munich; Schulte of Prague; Friedrich Maasen of Vienna; Reinkens of Breslau; and Josef Langen of Bonn. Whittle, *Catholicism after the Vatican*, 49.

106. Küry, *Die Altkatholische Kirche*, 79ff.

107. On the Church of Utrecht, see n.117.

108. The full list of delegates is found in *Stenographischer Bericht über die Verhandlungen des Katholiken-Congresses, abgehalten vom 22. bis 24. September 1871* (Munich, 1871), xvi–xx.

109. *Stenographischer Bericht*, 104–5.

110. *Stenographischer Bericht*, 110, 129. Cf. Ferdinand Ribbeck, *Donatus und Augustinus, oder der erste entscheidende Kampf zwischen Separatismus und Kirche* (Elberfeld, 1858), 218.

111. *Stenographischer Bericht*, 131. On November 17, 1871 Döllinger wrote Schulte: "Wir müssen als der reformatorische Sauerteig innerhalb der Kirche bleiben." This was in response to a letter that Schulte sent Döllinger on November 2, 1871, seeking solidarity with him after the Munich Congress. See Schulte, *Lebenserinnerungen*, vol. 1, 297–9.

112. *Stenographischer Bericht*, 110, 131. Cf. Hubert Huppertz, "*Döllinger und der Protestantismus*," *IKZ* 89 (1999): 2ff.

113. *Stenographischer Bericht*, 131–2.

114. This creed, also identified as the *professio fidei Tridentina*, known for its strongly anti-Protestant bent, was issued on November 13, 1565 by Pope Pius IV in his bull "Iniunctum nobis" under the auspices of the Council of Trent (1545–63). See Philip Schaff, *A History of the Creeds of Christendom*, vol. 2 (New York: Harper, 1877), 96ff.

115. For a contemporary Old Catholic view of Rome, see Angela Berlis, "Überlegungen zur ökumenischen Zukunft des Petrusdienstes aus altkatholischer Sicht," *TQ* 178 (1998): 149–54.

116. *Stenographischer Bericht*, 221ff.

117. On the (rather complex) origins of the Church of Utrecht amid the Jansenist controversies of the late seventeenth and early eighteenth century, see Küry, *Die Altkatholische Kirche*, 32ff. and Moss, *The Old Catholic Movement*, 90–140. The first "Old Catholic" Archbishop of Utrecht was Cornelius van Steenoven (r. 1723–5), ordained without the consent of Rome by the Jansenist-friendly French bishop Dominique Marie Varlet. On Varlet and his thought, see Serge A. Thériault, "La Sainte Trinité dans la théologie de Dominique Varlet, aux origines du vieux-catholicisme," *IKZ* 73 (1983): 234–45.

118. Moss, *The Old Catholic Movement*, 234.
119. For statements from the present, see, e.g., "Address of Welcome from the Bishops of the Union of Utrecht on the Occassion of the 125th Anniversary of its Founding" at <http://www.utrechter-union.org/page/420/building_bridges> (accessed January 19, 2015). In this document, the Old Catholic bishops state: "The break with the church was not something that was sought at that time [after Vatican I] .... It was a matter of survival for the Old Catholic movement that they organize themselves..."
120. Reinkens, "Conscience and the Vatican," trans. J. S. Stahl, *MR* 20 (1873): 117, 138.
121. Döllinger only addressed those gathered at Cologne once and this was to oppose a proposal by Friedrich Maasen of Cologne, who wanted to declare that the Pope and Roman bishops were heretics. See Neuner, *Stationen einer Kirchenspaltung*, 135.
122. *AK*, 353ff.; Moss, *Old Catholic Movement*, 238–9.
123. *Die Verhandlungen des zweiten Alt-Katholiken-Congresses zu Köln* (Cologne and Leipzig, 1872), vii–xxii and *AK*, 25–41.
124. Neuner, *Döllinger als Theologe der Ökumene*, 111.
125. Friedrich, *Döllinger*, vol. 3, 614f.
126. John James Lias, "Döllinger, Ignaz," *Encyclopaedia Britannica*, 11th ed. (New York, 1910), 341.
127. On the other candidates and procedures of the vote, see Moss, *Old Catholic Movement*, 241.
128. *AK*, 361.
129. Neuner, *Stationen einer Kirchenspaltung*, 136.
130. *AK*, 360ff. and Victor Conzemius, *Katholizismus ohne Rom* (Zurich: Benziger Verlag, 1969), 64–5.
131. Acton to Döllinger (September 15, 1871), *Briefwechsel*, vol. 3, 35.
132. Döllinger to Acton (September 19, 1871), *Briefwechsel*, vol. 3, 36–7 (emphasis added).
133. Cf. Hill, *Lord Acton*, 230–3.
134. Wilhelm Kahle, *Westliche Orthodoxie: Leben und Ziele Julian Joseph Overbecks* (Leiden: E. J. Brill, 1968), 124ff.
135. Willibald Beyschlag, *Der Altkatholicismus. Eine Denk- und Schutzschrift an das evangelische Deutschland* (Halle, 1882), 49.
136. Nevin, "The Old Catholic Movement," 240, 277–8.
137. Frederick Meyrick to Döllinger (April 5, 1872), BSB Döllingeriana II. On the Anglo-Continental Society and its aims, see Chapman, *Fantasy of Reunion*, 220–2.
138. Hoare, *The Old Catholic Movement in Bavaria*, 38–9.
139. Christopher Wordsworth, *The Old Catholics and the Cologne Congress of 1872* (Lincoln: James Williamson, 1872), 3.
140. E. R. Huber and W. Huber, eds., *Staat und Kirche im 19. und 20. Jahrhundert: Dokumente zur Geschichte des deutschen Staatskirchenrechts, vol. 2: Staat und Kirche im Zeitalter des Hochkonstitutionalismus und des Kulturkampfs, 1848–1890* (Berlin: Duncker & Humblot, 1976), 624–67.

141. Quoted in Ross, *The Failure of Bismarck's Kulturkampf*, 38.

142. Only in 1890 were Old Catholics in Bavaria granted separate status as a "Privatkirchengesellschaf"; they received full official legal recognition in 1920. See Huber and Huber, eds., *Staat und Kirche*, vol. 2, 911–12.

143. Friedrich, *Döllinger*, vol. 3, 615 and Neuner, *Döllinger als Theologe der Ökumene*, 115.

144. Huber and Huber, eds., *Staat und Kirche*, 627–8, 668–70, 738–40, 746; *TG*, 331.

145. Huber and Huber, eds., *Staat und Kirche*, 668–70.

146. A quote found in Frederick Meyrick, "To the Editor of 'The Hour'" (November 22, 1875), BSB Döllingeriana II.

147. Blaschke, "Der Altkatholizismus 1870 bis 1945," *HZ* 261 (1995): 60–1, n.18. Today, there are less than 20,000 members of the German Old Catholic Church. See the German Old Catholic website at <http://www.alt-katholisch.de/> (accessed July 22, 2015).

148. Blaschke, "Der Altkatholizismus 1870 bis 1945," 62.

149. Ross, *The Failure of Bismarck's Kulturkampf*, 47.

150. Willibald Beyschlag, "The Origin and Development of the Old Catholic Movement," *AJT* 2 (July 1898): 513.

151. Quoted in Jonathan Sperber, *Popular Catholicism in Nineteenth-Century Germany* (Princeton: Princeton University Press, 1984), 236.

152. *AAS* 7: 496–513; *AP* 6: 264–5. See Reinkens's blistering response to this encyclical: J. H. Reinkens, *Second Pastoral Letter in Reply to the Encyclical of Pope Pius IX*, trans. J. E. B. Mayor (London, 1874).

153. On the celibacy question, see Angela Berlis, "Seelsorge verträgt keine Teilung. Ignaz von Döllinger und die Frage des Zölibats," *Annali di studi religiosi* 6 (2005): 249–81.

154. Neuner, *Döllinger als Theologe der Ökumene*, 151ff.

155. Günther Eßer, "Ignaz von Döllinger, der Altkatholizismus und die Ökumene," *IKZ* 91 (2001): 137–57.

156. Conzemius, *Katholizimus ohne Rom*, 119ff.

157. *Der Papst und das Concil* (Leipzig: E. F. Steinacker, 1869), xvii.

158. *AK*, 15, 22.

159. Döllinger to Plummer (November 29, 1871), noted in CUL Add. 4911/107.

160. "Die Bedeutung der großen Zeitereignisse für die deutschen Hochschulen. Rektoratsrede, gehalten am 23. Dezember 1871 in der Aula der Universität München," in Döllinger, *Akademische Vorträge*, 3 vols. (Nördlingen: C. H. Beck, 1889–91), vol. 3, 11–38.

161. Olaf Blaschke, "Das 19. Jahrhundert: Ein zweites konfessionelles Zeitalter," *Geschichte und Gesellschaft* 26 (2000): 38–75. Cf. Helmut Walser Smith, ed., *Protestants, Catholics, and Jews in Germany* (Oxford: Berg, 2001).

162. Noted in Robbert Stupperich, *Melanchthon*, trans. Robert H. Fischer (Philadelphia: Westminster Press, 1965), 105.

163. From Calvin's *Institutes*; quoted in George H. Tavard, *Two Centuries of Ecumenism: The Search for Unity*, trans. Royce W. Hughes (Notre Dame: Mentor-Omega, 1960), 13.

164. Heinz Duchhardt and Gerhard May, eds., *Union-Konversion-Toleranz. Dimensionen der Annäherung zwischen den christlichen Konfessionen im 17. und 18.*

Jahrhundert (Mainz: Philipp von Zabern, 2000) and Harm Klueting, ed., *Irenik und Antikonfessionalismus im 17. und 18. Jahrhundert* (Hildesheim: Georg Olms Verlag, 2003).

165. Döllinger, *Ueber der Wiedervereinigung der christlichen Kirchen* (Nördlingen, 1888), 74–5. Cf. Christoph Böttigheimer, "Das Unionskonzept des Helmstedter Irenikers Georg Calixt (1586–1656)," in Harm Klueting, ed., *Irenik und Antikonfessionalismus im 17. und 18. Jahrhundert* (Hildesheim: Olms, 2003), 55–70.

166. Martin Schmidt, "Ecumenical Activity on the Continent of Europe in the Seventeenth and Eighteenth Centuries," in Ruth Rouse and Stephen Charles Neill, eds., *A History of the Ecumenical Movement, 1517–1948* (Philadelphia: Westminster Press, 1954), 93ff., 112ff.

167. Arthur Freeman, "Count Nicholas Ludwig von Zinzendorf: An Ecumenical Pioneer," *JES* 36 (1999): 287–302.

168. On Döllinger's high regard for Bossuet, see *Wiedervereinigung*, 77–8.

169. On the German scene in the late eighteenth century, see Christopher Spehr's fine study, *Aufklärung und Ökumene: Reunionsversuche zwischen Katholiken und Protestanten im deutschsprachigen Raum des späteren 18. Jahrhunderts* (Tübingen: Mohr Siebeck, 2005).

170. While the Holy Alliance is widely seen as the brainchild of Tsar Alexander I, it should be noted that he drew heavily on German pietistic and mystical currents in the early nineteenth century. See especially Franz von Baader, *Ueber das durch die französische Revolution herbeigeführte Bedürfnis einer neuen und innigeren Verbindung der Religion mit der Politik* (Munich, 1815), a work that proposed the unity of Christian monarchies throughout Europe against the "ideas of 1789." Baader, it will be remembered, strongly influenced the young Döllinger.

171. Döllinger to King Maximilian II (November 6, 1848); *TG*, 385.

172. Friedrich, *Döllinger*, vol. 1, 150 and Reinhold Rieger, "Johann Adam Möhler, 'Wegbereiter der Ökumene?'" *ZKG* 101 (1990): 267–86.

173. Eugène Michaud, *Programme de réforme de l'Eglise d'Occident aux anciens catholiques et autres communions chrétiennes* (Paris: Sandoz et Fischbacker, 1872). On Michaud, see Raoul Dederen, *Un réformateur catholique au XIX siècle: Eugène Michaud, 1839–1917* (Geneva: Librairie Droz, 1963).

174. Georges Florovsky, "Orthodox Ecumenism in the Nineteenth Century," *St. Vladimir's Seminary Quarterly* 4 (1956): 2–53.

175. E. B. Pusey, *An Eirenicon in a Letter to the Author of "The Christian Year"* (Oxford, 1865). Pusey would go on to publish two more "Eirenicons."

176. Chapman, *Fantasy of Reunion*, 79.

177. Döllinger to Pusey (May 30, 1866) in Henry Parry Liddon and John Octavius Johnston, *Life of Edward Bouverie Pusey, Doctor of Divinity, Canon of Christ Church, Regius Professor of Hebrew in the University of Oxford*, 4 vols. (London, 1893–7), vol. 2, 118. In the 1840s, Döllinger had written several articles on "Puseyism" for the *Historisch-politische Blätter für das katholische Deutschland*.

178. It merits mentioning that Döllinger himself attended a conference of Protestants and Catholics on the subject of reunion in Erfurt in 1860. See *Die Zusammenkunft gläubiger Protestanten und Katholiken zu Erfurt im Herbste 1860 und deren Verlauf: Eine auf eigene Theilname und sämmtliche bekannt gewordene Quellen*

gegründete Darstellung und Mahnung zur Fortsetzung des Werkes (Paderborn: Junsermann, 1867). For the broader context of this conference, see also Manfred Fleischer, "Lutheran and Catholic Reunionists in the Age of Bismarck," *CH* 38 (1969): 43–66.

179. The lectures were given respectively on January 31; February 7, 14, 21, 28; and March 13, 20 (1872). These were published (in unauthorized, stenogaphic form) in the *Allgemeine Zeitung* and translated into English and published as *Lectures on the Reunion of the Churches*, trans. Henry Nutcombe Oxenham (New York, 1872). Only in 1888 were they published in book form in German as *Ueber die Wiedervereinigung der christlichen Kirchen: Sieben Vorträge gehalten zu München im Jahr 1872* (Nördlingen, 1888). (I cite from the German version, but have consulted Oxenham's translations in making my own.)

180. *Wiedervereinigung*, 7.

181. *Wiedervereinigung*, 27.

182. *Wiedervereinigung*, 43.

183. *Wiedervereinigung*, 52ff. "Apostolic Succession" refers to the method whereby the ministry of ecclesiastical offices has been passed down from the original apostles by continuous succession. See *ODCC*, 91.

184. See St. Cyprian, *De ecclesia catholicae unitate* [English and Latin], trans. Maurice Bévenot (Oxford: Clarendon Press, 1971).

185. *Wiedervereinigung*, 64. For a more recent treatment of the "catholicity" of the early Reformation, see Carl Braaten and Robert W. Jenson, eds., *The Catholicity of the Reformation* (Grand Rapids, MI: Eerdmans, 1996).

186. On Gerhard Wolter Molanus (1633–1722), see *NDB*, vol. 17, 719–20. To put Döllinger's often severe anti-Jesuitism into broader context, see Michael Gross, "*Kulturkampf* and Unification: German Liberalism and the War against the Jesuits," *Central European History* 30 (1997): 545–66 and Geoffrey Cubitt, *The Jesuit Myth: Conspiracy and Politics in Nineteenth-Century France* (Oxford: Clarendon Press, 1993).

187. *Wiedervereinigung*, 69, 78.

188. *Wiedervereinigung*, 115.

189. *Wiedervereinigung*, 30.

190. *Wiedervereinigung*, 136f.

191. *Wiedervereinigung*, 114–15.

192. *Wiedervereinigung*, 137.

193. *Wiedervereinigung*, 123ff.

194. *Wiedervereinigung*, 31.

195. *Wiedervereinigung*, 124.

196. *Wiedervereinigung*, 139.

197. See, e.g., Valentino Steccanella, "La reunione delle chiese. Proposta dal Döllinger," *La Civiltà Cattolica* 6 (1872): 565–96, 673–88; 7 (1872): 55–68; *GG*, 272.

198. Alfred Plummer to Döllinger (June 4, 1872), BSB Döllingeriana II.

199. *Report of the Proceedings of the Reunion Conference held at Bonn on September 14, 15, and 16, 1874*, trans. E. M. B. (London, 1875), preface.

200. Döllinger to Eugène Michaud (February 16, 1872), BSB Döllingeriana II.

201. William Chauncy Langdon, *The Restoration of Christian Unity and the Approaching Alt-Catholic Congress at Cologne: A Letter to J. J. Ignatius Döllinger* (London: Rivingtons, 1872), 3, 25. On Langdon, see *DAB*, vol. 10, 239f.

202. Wordsworth, *The Old Catholics and the Cologne Congress of 1872*, 3–5.

203. *Die Verhandlungen des zweiten Altkatholiken-Congresses zu Köln* (Cologne: Verlag von Eduard Heinrich Meyer, 1872), 73ff. (hereafter *Verhandlungen*). Cf. Theodorus, *New Reformation*, 162.

204. *Verhandlungen*, xi–xii and *AK*, 355–6.

205. Küry, *Die Altkatholische Kirche*, 432.

206. Christian Oeyen, "Die Entstehung der Bonner Unions-Konferenzen im Jahr 1874," Habilitationsschrift at the "Christ Catholic" Theological Faculty at Bern (Constance, 1971), 43–67.

207. At this Council, the Commission in fact was further organized into two sub-commissions: one, seated at Munich and led by Döllinger, to focus on Anglicanism; the other, seated at Bonn and led by Josef Langen, to focus on Eastern Orthodoxy. See *Der dritte Altkatholiken-Kongress in Konstanz im Jahre 1873. Offizieller stenographischer Bericht der Verhandlungen vom 12. bis 14. September 1873* (Constance, 1873), 18ff.

208. Oeyen, "Die Entstehung der Bonner Unions-Konferenzen im Jahr 1874," 54–6.

209. Heinrich Reusch, *Bericht über die am 14. 15. und 16. September zu Bonn gehaltenen Unions-Conferenzen im Auftrage des Vorsitzenden Dr. von Döllinger* (Bonn, 1874), 1.

210. See Richard Shannon, *Gladstone: God and Politics* (London: Hambledon & Continuum, 2007), 263–5.

211. Gladstone, "The Right Rev. Dr. von Döllinger," *The Speaker* (January 18, 1890): 57–60.

212. Meyrick to Döllinger (September 5, 1874), cited in Oeyen, "Die Enstehung der Bonner Unions-Konferenzen," 133.

213. John James Lias to Döllinger (2 July 1875), BSB Döllingeriana II.

214. *Bonner Zeitung* (13 September 1874), cited in Oeyen, "Die Enstehung der Bonner Unions-Konferenzen," 166.

215. BAB Reusch 7.1 and Theodorus, *New Reformation*, 232–4. Officially, there were 56 participants, but the conversations were dominated by roughly a dozen. Many came simply to hear the learned discourse of a few. The following countries were represented: Germany, Russia, Greece, England, Switzerland, Denmark, France, and the United States.

216. Heinrich Reusch kept notes in German and G. F. Broade, an English chaplain in Düsseldorf and correspondent for *The Guardian*, kept notes in English. The original notes may be found at BAB Nachlaß Reusch. After the conference, Reusch took the English and German notes, had Döllinger approve them, and then published them. See full citation at n.209. The English translation appeared in 1875. Hereafter I draw from the English, citing it as *Proceedings* 1875, consulting the German too when necessary. It should be kept in mind though that while utterances are attributed to specific individuals at the conference, these are reconstructions based on notes and may likely not represent *exactly* what was said.

217. Plummer, *Conversations with Döllinger*, 100–1, 116.

218. The "filioque" (literally, "and the Son") refers to the dogmatic formulation expressing the "double procession" of the Holy Spirit that was added by the Western Christian Church to the Nicene-Constantinopolitan Creed immediately after the words "the Holy Spirit... who proceeds from the Father." It was not part of the original Creed, but came into usage in the West after the Third Council of Toledo (589). It was regularly sung at mass by monks in the Frankish Empire, and eventually adopted at Rome around 1000. Eastern Christian have never accepted this formulation, viewing it as an unwarranted addition. This issue has been and remains one of the leading theological points of contention between Western and Orthodox Christians. For the history and theology behind the "filioque controversy," see Bernd Oberdorfer, *Filioque: Geschichte und Theologie einesökumenischen Problems* (Göttingen: Vandenhoeck & Ruprecht, 2001) and Edward A. Siecienski, *The Filioque: History of a Doctrinal Controversy* (Oxford: Oxford University Press, 2010).

219. *Proceedings* 1875, 23. Cf. Owen Chadwick, "Döllinger and Reunion," in G. R. Evans, ed., *Christian Authority: Essays in Honour of Henry Chadwick* (Oxford: Clarendon Press, 1988), 321.

220. *Proceedings* 1875, 17.

221. Moss, *Old Catholic Movement*, 262.

222. Chapman, *Fantasy of Reunion*, 232.

223. BAB Reusch 4a. The formula on the "filioque" and all fourteen articles are printed in English and German in Philip Schaff, *The Creeds of Christendom with History and Critical Notes*, vol. 2 (New York, 1877), 545–51.

224. *Proceedings* 1875, 20.

225. See Leo Donald Davis, *The First Seven Ecumenical Councils (325–787): Their History and Theology* (Collegeville, MN: The Liturgical Press, 1990), 290ff.

226. Moss, *Old Catholic Movement*, 264. Döllinger proposed the following article: "We acknowledge that the invocation of saints is not commanded as a duty necessary to salvation for every Christian." But due to Orthodox opposition, he decided to withdraw it.

227. Plummer, *Conversations with Döllinger*, 107.

228. Schaff, *Creeds of Christendom*, vol. 2, 549.

229. *Proceedings* 1875, 55–7.

230. Schaff, *Creeds of Christendom*, vol. 2, 550–1.

231. Plummer, *Conversations with Döllinger*, 104; Schaff, *Creeds of Christendom*, vol. 2, 550; Moss, *The Old Catholic Movement*, 266. "Transubstantiation" refers to the Roman Catholic Church's theology of the Eucharist, as developed in the Middle Ages, which posits that the "substance" of the Body and Blood of Christ appear in the Eucharist at the moment of consecration, while the "accidents" (i.e., the external appearances of bread and wine) remain the same. See *ODCC*, 1647 and J. F. McCue, "The Doctrine of Transubstantiation from Berengar through Trent: The Point at Issue," *Harvard Theological Review* 61 (1968): 385–430.

232. *Proceedings* 1875, 54.

233. BAB Reusch 7.15.

234. BAB Reusch 7.22.

235. Plummer, *Conversations with Döllinger*, 116.

236. See, e.g., "The Old Catholic Conference," *The Times* (September 18, 1874); "The Old Catholics: Harmony at the Bonn Conference—Dr. Döllinger Complimented," *New York Times* (September 17 1874); and *The Guardian* (September 23, 1874).

237. As Robert Jenkins Nevin wrote to Döllinger (November 17, 1874): "I do not know anything that has assured me more of the usefulness of the impulse you have given toward Catholic unity by the Bonn conferences than the irritability of the Ultramontane party in regard to it. It seems by last weeks [sic] papers that it even betrayed Monsig. Manning into expressing the bitterness of his heart about you [Döllinger]." BSB Döllingeriana II. Cf. B. Negri, "I cattolici e i dissenti," *Rivista universale* 24 (1874): 240.

238. Döllinger to Lady Blennerhassett (November 10, 1874), in *Briefwechsel*, vol. 4, 576.

239. Plummer (citing a letter from Newman) to Döllinger (November 2, 1874). BSB Döllingeriana II.

240. *Proceedings* 1875, xxvi.

241. On the May Laws (1873–6), see Robert Lougee, "The *Kulturkampf* and Historical Positivism," *CH* 23 (1954): 219–35.

242. Sperber, *Popular Catholicism*, 234–6.

243. *Gravibus Ecclesiae* (December 24, 1874), *PE*, vol. 1, 443–6; *AP* 6: 347–60; *AAS* 8: 181–92.

244. *Quod nunquam* (February 5, 1875), *PE*, vol. 1, 447–9; *AP* 7: 6–12; *AAS* 8: 251–5. In *Graves ac diuturnae*, Pius more explicitly lambasted the "new heretics," i.e., Old Catholics; see *PE*, vol. 1, 451–3; *AP* 7: 44–9.

245. Gladstone, *The Vatican Decrees in their Bearing on Civil Authority* (1874), in J. F. Maclear, ed., *Church and State in the Modern Age: A Documentary History* (New York: Oxford University Press, 1995), 177–80.

246. For an overview, see Josef L. Altholz, "The Vatican Decrees Controversy, 1874–1875," *CHR* 57 (1972): 593–605.

247. Bismarck to Gladstone (March 1, 1875), BL Add. 44446/293, cited in Hill, *Lord Acton*, 258.

248. Manning's reply to Gladstone, *The Times* (November 7, 1874) in Maclear, ed., *Church and State in the Modern Age*, 181–2.

249. The Duke was Henry Fitzalan Howard (1847–1917), the fifteenth Duke of Norfolk.

250. On the contrast between Manning and Newman on Infallibility explored from a theological perspective, see Mark E. Powell, *Papal Infallibility: A Protestant Evaluation of an Ecumenical Issue* (Grand Rapids, MI: Eerdmans, 2009), 49–122.

251. John Henry Newman, *Newman's Reply to the Pamphlet by Gladstone: To His Grace the Duke of Norfolk* (Toronto, 1874), 43. Cf. John T. Ford, "Newman's *Letter to the Duke of Norfolk*: Citizenship, Church, and Conscience," *Josephinum Journal of Theology* 8 (2001): 38–50.

252. Some of their letters are preseved in *Correspondence between the Secretaries of the Friends of Spiritual Enlightenment and the Anglo-Continental Society Containing*

Statements on the Validity of Anglican Orders, the Eternal Procession of the Holy Ghost and Invocation of Saints (London: Rivingstons, 1875).

253. Gladstone to Döllinger (July 24, 1875), BL Gladstone Papers Add. 44140/392.
254. Gladstone to Döllinger (July 24, 1875), BL Gladstone Papers Add. 44140/396 and Döllinger to Gladstone (August 2, 1875), BSB Döllingeriana II.
255. Originally, the conference was to last until 14 August, but it was extended for two days.
256. *Report of the Proceedings at the Reunion Conference held at Bonn between the 10th and 16th of August, 1875 with a Preface by H. P. Liddon* (London, 1876), liv (hereafter *Proceedings* 1876).
257. Heinrich Reusch, ed., *Bericht über die vom 10. bis 16. August zu Bonn gehaltenen Unions-Conferenzen im Auftrage des Vorsitzenden Dr. von Döllinger* (Bonn, 1875), 1–2 (hereafter *Bericht*). An English translation quickly appeared. Cf. *Proceedings* 1876, liii–liv.
258. Letter of March 8, 1875, *Proceedings* 1875, 136.
259. A partial list of participants can be found at *Proceedings* 1876, lv–lxix.
260. On Herzog and his consecration as bishop in 1876, see Küry, *Die altkatholische Kirche*, 79ff.
261. The bishopric of Gibraltar was only founded in 1842 to provide spiritual oversight to Anglicans on the Continent and in North Africa. See H. J. C. Knight, *The Diocese of Gibraltar: A Sketch of its History, Work, and Tasks* (London: SPCK, 1917).
262. Perry also referred to Döllinger as "the greatest man of the age." William Stevens Perry, "The Second Reunion Conference at Bonn, August, 1874," *American Church Review* 28 (1876): 371–3.
263. Plummer, *Conversations with Döllinger*, 121.
264. Gladstone's letter is included in *Proceedings* 1875, 143–6.
265. Undated letter written prior to the second conference. *Proceedings* 1875, 137.
266. On John of Damascus, see *ODCC*, 891.
267. According to Plummer: "Overbeck rose and…asked whether it would not be better to insert in the first article the number of Councils intended to be included under the term ecumenical. Here was a bombshell! Döllinger looked aghast." Plummer, *Conversations with Döllinger*, 140. The Seventh Ecumenical Council (the second Council of Nicea, 787) is embraced by Catholic and Orthodox Christians, but disputes about it arose during the Reformation, including in the English Reformation.
268. On these, see Chapman, *Fantasy of Reunion*, 244–50.
269. Schaff, *Creeds of Christendom* (translation modified).
270. Schaff, *Creeds of Christendom*, 552–4 and Moss, *Old Catholic Movement*, 268–9.
271. Frederick Meyrick, *Memories of Life at Oxford, and Experiences in Italy, Greece, Turkey, Germany, Spain, and Elsewhere* (London: John Murray, 1905), 266.
272. *Bericht*, 90.
273. *Bericht*, 113–15.
274. Meyrick, *Memories*, 262.
275. Perry, "The Second Reunion Conference at Bonn, August, 1875," 371–3.
276. *Brixener Kirchenblatt* (November 3, 1875), BAB Döllinger 5.276.

277. BSB Döllingeriana I.7.

278. BSB Döllingeriana I.8.

279. Döllinger to Gladstone (August 20, 1875), BSB Döllingeriana II.

280. Döllinger to Acton (August 18, 1875), *Briefwechsel*, vol. 3, 150.

281. Neuner, *Döllinger als Theologe der Ökumene*, 211.

282. Wilhelm Kahle, *Westliche Orthodoxie: Leben und Ziele Julian Joseph Overbecks* (Leiden: E. J. Brill, 1968), 145ff.

283. Kahle, *Westliche Orthodoxie*, 124–56.

284. See J. J. Overbeck, *Die Bonner Unions Conferenz, oder Altkatholizismus und Anglikanismus in ihrem Verhältnis zur Orthodoxie. Eine Appelation an die Patriarchen und Heiligen Synoden der orthodoxen-katholischen Kirche* (Halle: H. W. Schmidt, 1876). Cf. J. J. Overbeck, *The Bonn Conferences. Impressions Produced by their Transactions* (London, 1875); "The Bonn Conference and the Filioque Question," *Orthodox Catholic Review* 4 (1875): 217–63; and *TG*, 430–2. Interestingly, in 1892 the Russian Orthodox Church decided to revisit the results at Bonn and set up a special commission to do so. It concluded, however, that the Bonn formulation had made the Son a "cause" or a "co-cause" of the procession of the Spirit—a view that the Orthodox considered untenable. See Siecienski, *Filioque: History of a Doctrinal Controversy*, 188.

285. Pusey to Liddon (August 19, 1875) quoted in Chapman, *Fantasy of Reunion*, 251.

286. As Liddon recorded in his diary: "Dr. Pusey told me that if the English Church gave up the *Filioque*, he must either shut his eyes and go to Rome or trust that God would save him out of any Church at all. He could have no part in it." Quoted in John Octavius Johnston, *The Life and Letters of Henry Parry Liddon, Canon of St. Paul's Cathedral and Sometime Ireland Professor in the University of Oxford* (London: Longmans, Green and Co., 1904), 189.

287. Quoted in *TG*, 433.

288. E. B. Pusey, *On the Clause "and the Son" in Regard to the Eastern Church and the Bonn Conference: A Letter to the Rev. H. P. Liddon* (London, 1876), 4.

289. Liddon's diary from September 9, 1876 as quoted in Chapman, *Fantasy of Reunion*, 260.

290. Döllinger to Acton (June 29, 1876), *Briefwechsel*, vol. 3, 166–7. Despite his esteem for Döllinger, Liddon recognized the validity of Pusey's concerns.

291. See Georgi Georgiev, *The Russo-Turkish War of Liberation (1877–1878) and the World Public*, trans. Ventisislav Konstantinov Venkov (Bulgaria: Sofia Press, 1987). For both political and religious reasons, Gladstone vehemently contested Disraeli's policy. See W. E. Gladstone, *Bulgarian Horrors and the Question of the East* (London: John Murray, 1876).

292. Quoted in Liddon and Johnston, *Life of Edward Bouverie Pusey*, vol. 4, 300.

293. *TG*, 437.

294. Meyrick to Döllinger (June 24, 1879), BSB Döllingeriana II.

295. It should be noted, however, that the legacy of the Bonn conferences of 1874 and 1875 played a role in the Bonn Union of 1931, which established full communion between the Anglican and Old Catholic Churches. See Moss, *The Old Catholic Movement*, 340–51. Cf. Gordon Huelin, *Old Catholics and Anglicans, 1931–1981* (Oxford: Oxford University Press, 1983).

CHAPTER 5

1. Guglielmo Matthiae, *San Lorenzo fuori le mura* (Rome: Marietti, 1966).
2. Owen Chadwick, *A History of the Popes, 1830–1914* (Oxford: Oxford University Press, 1998), 268–72.
3. On the "back story" of this beatification, see Kenneth Woodward, *Making Saints: How the Catholic Church Determines Who Becomes a Saint, Who Doesn't, and Why* (New York: Simon & Schuster, 1996), 309ff. For a critical reaction to the beatification, see John W. O'Malley, "The Beatification of Pope Pius IX," *America* 26 (2000): 6–11.
4. Homily of September 3, 2000 at <http://w2.vatican.va/content/john-paul-ii/en/homilies/2000/documents/hf_jp-ii_hom_20000903_beatification.html> (accessed July 27, 2015) (emphases in the original).
5. Franz Xaver Bischof treats these very well; see *TG*, 352–83.
6. Édouard Naville, *The Life Work of Sir Peter Le Page Renouf*, vol. 4 (Paris: E. Leroux, 1907), lxxxviii—c and *TG*, 368–74.
7. The letters from the Renoufs to Döllinger, especially from May and June 1885, may be found at BSB Döllingeriana II. and in Kevin J. Catchcart, ed., *The Letters of Peter le Page Renouf (1822–1897)*, vol. 4 (Dublin: University College Dublin Press, 2004), 210–14. Cf. J. Savignac and M. Stracmans, "Lettre de Sir Peter le Page Renouf au Chanoine Döllinger," *Revue d'histoire et de philosophie religieuses* 36 (1956): 61–72.
8. Peter le Page Renouf to Döllinger (May 14, 1885), in Catchcart, ed., *Letters of Peter le Page Renouf*, 211.
9. BSB Döllingeriana VII.86 and Johann Friedrich, *Ignaz von Döllinger: Sein Leben auf Grund seines schriftlichen Nachlasses*, vol. 3 (Munich: C. H. Beck, 1901), 595.
10. Moufang to Leo XII (July 7, 1885); the letter is found in the Nachlaß Moufang at the Diözesan- und Domarchiv in Mainz and is quoted in *TG*, 372–3, n.120 and n.121.
11. Steichele to Döllinger (July 30, 1886), in Döllinger, ed., *Briefe und Erklärungen über die Vaticanischen Decrete, 1869–1886* (Munich, 1890), 127–8.
12. A "Lady of High Rank" to Döllinger (February 15 and 28, 1880), in *Briefe und Erklärungen*, 114.
13. Döllinger to a "Lady of High Rank" (1880), *Briefe und Erklärungen*, 120.
14. Döllinger to Steichele (March 1, 1887), *Briefe und Erklärungen*, 135–6.
15. Döllinger to Steichele (March 1, 1887), *Briefe und Erklärungen*, 142 (emphasis added).
16. Döllinger to Steichele (March 1, 1887), *Briefe und Erklärungen*, 141.
17. Döllinger to Steichele (March 1, 1887), *Briefe und Erklärungen*, 129–30.
18. Döllinger to Steichele (March 1, 1887), *Briefe und Erklärungen*, 132.
19. Döllinger to Scilla (October 12, 1887), *Briefe und Erklärungen*, 148.
20. Döllinger to Scilla (October 12, 1887), *Briefe und Erklärungen*, 150–1.
21. See August Boudinhon, "Excommunication," *CE*, vol. 5, 671–98.
22. Döllinger to Scilla (October 12, 1887), *Briefe und Erklärungen*, 147, 154.
23. BSB Döllingeriana II.1.
24. Letter of February 24, 1889, BSB Döllingeriana II.1.
25. *Church Times* (March 8, 1889), BAB Döllinger 5.253.

26. *Deutsche Merkur* (March 2, 1889), BAB Döllinger 5.169.
27. *Der Katholik* (March 2, 1889), BAB Döllinger 5.171.
28. *Allgemeine Zeitung* (March 7, 1889).
29. Roland Hill, *Lord Acton* (New Haven: Yale University Press, 2000), 324–6.
30. Quoted in Friedrich, *Döllinger*, vol. 3, 709, n.5.
31. Alfred Plummer, *Conversations with Dr. Döllinger* (Leuven: Leuven University Press, 1985), 237.
32. Hill, *Lord Acton*, 329.
33. The then nuncio of Munich and future Vatican Secretary of State Antoni Agliardi reported to Rome that Munich's capitular vicar Michael Rampf (Archbishop Steichele had recently passed away) had dutifully forbidden any liturgical function and any participation by the clergy. ASV SS 1890 rubr. 255, fasc. 3.
34. Döllinger had written quite presciently about the problem of anti-Semitism in European history. See Jacques Kornberg, "Ignaz von Döllinger's *Die Juden in Europa*: A Catholic Polemic against Antisemitism," *JHMT* 6 (1999): 223–45.
35. Hill, *Lord Acton*, 328 and *TG*, 487. Döllinger was buried in Munich's Old South Cemetery (*Alter Südfriedhof*) only several gravesites away from his former colleague and kindred spirit, Johann Adam Möhler.
36. Victor Conzemius, "Der Tod Ignaz von Döllingers in den Briefen der Freunde," *KJB* 9 (1968): 300–16. Newspapers as far away as Australia carried news of Döllinger's death. See "Death of Dr. Döllinger," *Sydney Morning Herald* (January 13, 1890): 7.
37. Acton to Mamy Acton (January 11, 1890), CUL Add. 7956/40.
38. Acton to Mamy Acton (January 27, 1890), CUL Add. 7956/45.
39. Acton, "Döllinger's Historical Work," *EHR* 5 (October 1890): 700–44.
40. Gladstone, "The Right Rev. Dr. von Döllinger," *The Speaker* (January 18, 1890): 57–60. Gladstone also acquired a painting of Döllinger as an act of remembrance. It hangs today in the St. Deiniol's Library, Hawarden (UK). Gladstone wrote another reflection: "Dr. Döllinger's Posthumous Remains," *The Speaker* (August 30, 1890): 231–3.
41. *Deutscher Merkur* (January 18, 1990), BAB Döllinger 5.173. An English translation of Friedrich's funeral speech appeared in *The Guardian* (January 22, 1890).
42. *The Guardian* (January 22, 1890), BAB Reusch 7.316.
43. John Owen, "The Life and Writings of Ignatius von Döllinger: The German Theologian," *Edinburgh Review* 175 (1892): 48–50.
44. E. P. Evans, "Ignatius von Döllinger," *Atlantic Monthly* 68 (October 1891): 553–65. On Evans, see George Harvey Genzmer, "Evans, Edward Payson," *DAB*, vol. 6, 197–8.
45. Charles Dickens, *A Tale of Two Cities* (New York: Bantam Books, 1981), 9.
46. On these distinctions, see Avery Dulles, S.J., *Magisterium: Teacher and Guardian of the Faith* (Naples, FL: Sapienta Press, 2007), 28–39 and Yves Congar, O.P., "A Brief History of the Forms of the Magisterium and its Relations with Scholars," in Charles E. Curran and Richard A. McCormick, S.J., eds., *Readings in Moral Theology, vol. 3: The Magisterium and Morality* (New York: Paulist Press, 1982), 314–31.
47. Dulles, *Magisterium*, 37.

48. Claude Welch, *Protestant Thought in the Nineteenth Century, 1799–1870*, vol. 1 (New Haven: Yale University Press, 1972), 152.

49. On Troeltsch and historicism, see Ernst Troeltsch, *Historismus und seine Probleme* (Tübingen: C. B. Mohr, 1922).

50. John Henry Newman, *On Consulting the Faithful in Matters of Doctrine* (New York: Sheed & Ward, 1961), 17.

51. Acton, "Döllinger's Historical Work," 729, 734 (emphasis added).

52. Acton, "Döllinger's Historical Work," 714.

53. *TG*, 436.

54. Owen Chadwick, *The Secularisation of the European Mind in the Nineteenth Century* (Cambridge: Cambridge University Press, 1975).

55. Olaf Blaschke, "Das 19. Jahrhundert: eine zweites konfessionelles Zeitalter," *Geschichte und Gesellschaft* 26 (2000): 38–75.

56. Thomas Albert Howard, "Neither a Secular nor a Confessional Age: Ignaz von Döllinger, Vatican I, and the Bonn Reunion Conferences of 1874 and 1875," *JHS* 11 (March 2011): 59–84.

57. Giuseppe Alberigo, *A Brief History of Vatican II*, trans. Matthew Sherry (Maryknoll, NY: Orbis, 2005), 9–10, 123–4. For a contrary position, see Kristin M. Colberg, *Vatican I and Vatican II: Councils in the Living Tradition* (Collegeville, MN: Liturgical Press, 2016).

58. Hans Küng, *Disputed Truth: Memoirs*, trans. John Bowden (New York: Continuum, 2008), 168–9.

59. On Döllinger and modern ecumenism, see Peter Neuner, *Döllinger als Theologe der Ökumene* (Paderborn: Schöningh, 1979) and Hubert Huppertz, "Döllingers Bedeutung für die ökumenische Bewegung," *IKZ* 89 (1999): 182–200.

60. Jerome-Michael Vereb, C.P., *"Because he was a German": Cardinal Bea and the Origins of Roman Catholic Engagement with the Ecumenical Movement* (Grand Rapids, MI: Eerdmans, 2006), 137. For Döllinger's role in the thinking of Yves Congar, see Yves Congar, *My Journal of the Council*, trans. Mary John Ronayne and Mary Cecily Boulding (Collegeville, MN: Liturgical Press, 2012), 82, 109–10, 140, 490. On Möhler and the origins of Catholic ecumenism, see Reinhold Rieger, "Johann Adam Möhler: Wegbereiter der Ökumene," *ZKG* 101 (1990): 267–86.

61. *Mortalium animos* (January 6, 1928), in *PE*, vol. 3, 313–19.

62. "Decree on Ecumenism," in Austin Flannery, O.P., ed., *The Vatican Council II, vol. 1: The Conciliar and Post-Conciliar Documents*, new rev. ed. (Northport, NY: Costello Publishing, 1996), 452. Additionally, Döllinger and many of the minority bishops at Vatican I were prescient in recognizing that Papal Infallibility would become a vexing, indeed neuralgic, issue in the ecumenical enterprise. See Margaret O'Gara, *Triumph in Defeat: Infallibility, Vatican I, and the French Minority Bishops* (Washington, DC: Catholic University of America Press, 1988), 202ff.

63. <https://www.catholicculture.org/culture/library/view.cfm?RecNum=3233> (accessed July 31, 2015).

64. John Rawls, *A Theory of Justice* (Cambridge, MA: The Belknap Press of Harvard University Press, 1971), 205–11. Cf. Reinhard Hütter, "Conscience 'Truly so Called' and its Counterfeits: John Henry Newman and Thomas Aquinas on What Conscience is and Why it Matters," *Nova et Vetera* 12 (2014): 701–67.

65. John Henry Newman, *Newman's Reply to the Pamphlet by Gladstone: To His Grace the Duke of Norfolk* (Toronto, 1874), 43. On Newman's gamut of positions on Infallibility, see Avery Dulles, S.J., "Newman on Infallibility," *TS* 51 (1990): 434–48.

66. *Gaudium et Spes*, §16 in Flannery, ed., *Vatican Council II*, 916–17. Cf. *CCC*, 490–5.

67. *Disputed Questions on Truth*, 17 (1256–17) in Ralph McInerny, ed. and trans., *Thomas Aquinas: Selected Writings* (New York: Penguin Books, 1998), 218–31. Cf. *Summa Theologiae* I-I, Q. 79, A. 13.

68. *Disputed Questions on Truth*, 17 in McInerny, ed., *Thomas Aquinas: Selected Writings*, 233 (emphasis added).

69. Massimo Faggioli, *Vatican II: The Battle for Meaning* (New York: Paulist Press, 2012) and Hans Urs von Balthasar, *The Office of Peter and the Structure of the Church*, 2nd ed., trans. Andrée Emery (San Francisco: Ignatius Press, 2007), 279.

70. Flannery, ed., *Vatican Council II*, 350–426. Cf. Giuseppe Alberigo, "The Authority of the Church in the Documents of Vatican I and Vatican II," trans. Anthony Matteo, *JES* 19 (1982): 119–45 and John Ford, "Infallibility: From Vatican I to the Present," *JES* 8 (1971): 768–91.

71. Newman to Alfred Plummer (April 3, 1871), noted in Dulles, "Newman on Infallibility," 445.

72. Balthasar, *The Office of Peter*, 177. Of Vatican I and Döllinger, Balthasar has this to say: "A long list of unnecessary human tragedies attested to the uneasy and unclarifed relationship between theology and the Magisterium [after Vatican I]....In a special 'grave' lies Döllinger" (Balthasar, *The Office of Peter*, 280–1).

73. Charles Taylor, *A Catholic Modernity?*, ed. James L. Heft (New York: Oxford University Press, 1999), 37.

Select Bibliography

Primary Sources

Ignaz von Döllinger: in German

Akademische Vorträge. 3 vols. Nördlingen: C. H. Beck, 1889–91.

Bibliotheca Döllingeriana: Katalog der Bibliothek des verstorbenen Kgl. Universitäts-Professors J. J. J. von Döllinger, Stiftspropstes bei St. Cajetan, Reichsrathes der Krone Bayern, Vorstandes der Kgl. Akademie der Wissenschaften. Munich: J. Lindauer, 1893.

Briefe und Erklärungen über die Vatikanischen Decrete, 1869–1887. Munich: C. H. Beck, 1890.

Briefwechsel von Ignaz von Döllinger. Edited by Victor Conzemius. 4 vols. Munich: C. H. Beck, 1963–81.

Christentum und Kirche in der Zeit der Grundlegung. 2nd ed. Regensburg: G. J. Manz, 1868.

[Janus] *Der Papst und das Concil.* Leipzig: E. F. Steinacker, 1869.

Die Papst-Fabeln des Mittelalters. Ein Beitrag zur Kirchengeschichte. Munich: J. G. Cotta, 1863.

Die Reformation: Ihre innere Entwicklung und ihre Wirkungen im Umfange des lutherischen Bekenntnisses. 3 vols. Regensburg: G. Joseph Manz, 1846–8.

Die Universitäten, Sonst und Jetzt. 2nd ed. Munich: G. J. Manz, 1871.

Fries, Heinrich and Johann Finsterhölzl, eds. *Ignaz von Döllinger* (Wegbereiter Heutiger Theologie). Graz: Verlag Styria, 1969.

Heidenthum und Judenthum. Vorhalle zur Geschichte des Christenthums. Regensburg, 1857.

Ignaz von Döllingers Briefe an eine junge Freundin. Mit zwei Bildnissen. Edited by Heinrich Schrörs. Kempten: J. Kösel, 1914.

Kirche und Kirchen: Papstthum und Kirchenstaat. Historisch-politische Betrachtungen. 2nd ed. Munich: J. G. Cotta, 1861.

Kleinere Schriften: Gedruckte und Ungedruckte. Edited by Franz Heinrich Reusch. Stuttgart: Cotta, 1890.

[Quirinus] *Römische Briefe vom Concil.* Munich: F. Kirchheim, 1870.

Ignaz von Döllinger: English Translations

Addresses on Historical and Literary Subjects. Translated by Margaret Warre. London: J. Murray, 1894.

The Church and the Churches, or the Papacy and the Temporal Power: An Historical and Political Review. Translated by William Bernard MacCabe. London: Hurst and Blackett, 1862.

Conversations of Dr. Döllinger Recorded by Louise von Kobell. Translated by Katharine Gould. London: R. Bentley, 1892.

Fables Respecting the Popes in the Middle Ages: A Contribution to Ecclesiastical History. Translated by Alfred Plummer. London: Rivingtons, 1871.

The First Age of Christianity and the Church. Translated by Henry Nutcombe Oxenham. 4th ed. London: Gibbings, 1906.

Hippolytus and Callistus, or, The Church of Rome in the First Half of the Third Century: with Special Reference to the Writings of Bunsen, Wordsworth, Baur, and Gieseler. Translated by Alfred Plummer. Edinburgh: T. & T. Clark, 1876.

A History of the Church. Translated by Edward Cox. London: C. Dolman, 1840–2.

Lectures on the Reunion of the Churches. Translated by Henry Nutcombe Oxenham. New York: Dodd and Mead, 1872.

Studies in European History: Being Academic Addresses Delivered by John Ignatius von Döllinger. Translated by Margaret Warre. London: J. Murray, 1890.

Universities Past and Present: a Lecture Delivered December 22nd, 1866 in the University Hall at Munich. Translated by C. E. C. B. Appleton. Oxford: Rivingtons, 1867.

Papal Documents of the Nineteenth Century

Acta et decreta sacrorum conciliorum recentiorum: collectio lacensis. 7 vols. Freiburg im Breisgau: Herder, 1870–90.

Acta sanctae sedis; ephemerides romanae a SSMO D.N. Pio PP. X authenticae et officales Apostolicae Sedis actis publice evulgandis declaratae. 36 vols. Rome: Ex Typographia Polyglotta S. C. de Propaganda Fide, 1870–1908.

Benedictine Monks of Solesmes, eds. *Papal Teachings: The Church.* Translated by Mother E. O'Gorman, R. S. C. J. Boston: St. Paul's, 1962.

Carlen, Claudia, ed. *The Papal Encyclicals.* 5 vols. Wilmington, NC: McGrath Publishing Co., 1981.

Denzinger, Heinrich, ed. *Enchiridion symbolorum definitionum et declarationum de rebus fidei et morum. Kompendium der Glaubensbekenntnisse und kirchlichen Lehrentscheidungen.* Freiburg im Breisgau: Herder, 1991.

Gregory XVI, Pope. *Il trionfo della Santa Sede e della Chiesa contro gli assalti de' novatori respinti e combattuti stesse loro armi.* Rome, 1799.

Gregory XVI, Pope. *Acta Gregorii Papae XVI, scilicet constitutiones, bullae, litterae apostolicae, epistolae.* 4 vols. Rome: S. C. de Propaganda Fide, 1901–4.

Pius IX, Pope. *Pii IX Pontificis Maximi Acta.* 9 vols. Rome: Ex Typographia Bonarum Artium, 1854–78.

Wiseman, Cardinal Nicholas. *Recollections of the Last Four Popes and Rome in their Times.* London, 1858.

Other Primary Sources

Acton, John Emerich Edward Dalberg, Baron. "The Munich Congress." *Home and Foreign Review* 4 (1864): 209–44.

Acton, John Emerich Edward Dalberg, Baron. "Döllinger's Historical Work." *English Historical Review* 5 (1890): 700–44.

Acton, John Emerich Edward Dalberg, Baron. *Letters of Lord Acton to Mary Gladstone.* Edited by Herbert Paul. New York: Macmillan, 1904.

Acton, John Emerich Edward Dalberg, Baron. *Selections from the Correspondence of the First Lord Action.* Edited by John Neville Figgis and Reginald Vere Laurence. London: Longmans, Green, 1917.

Acton, John Emerich Edward Dalberg, Baron. *Lord Acton and the First Vatican Council: A Journal.* Edited by Edmund Campion. Sydney: Catholic Theological Faculty, 1975.

Acton, John Emerich Edward Dalberg, Baron. *Selected Writings of Lord Acton.* Edited by J. Rufus Fears. 3 vols. Indianapolis: Liberty Classics, 1985–8.

Aktenstücke des Ordinariates des Erzbisthmus München und Freising betreffend das allgemeine Vatikanische Concil. Regensburg, 1871.

Albrecht, Dieter, ed. *Joseph Edmund Jörg: Briefwechsel, 1846–1901.* Mainz: Matthias-Grünewald Verlag, 1988.

Altholz, Josef L. and Damian McElrath, eds. *The Correspondence of Lord Acton and Richard Simpson.* Vol. 3. Cambridge: Cambridge University Press, 1975.

Beyschlag, Willibald. *Der Altkatholicismus. Eine Denk- und Schutzschrift an das evangelische Deutschland.* Halle, 1882.

Blennerhassett, Charlotte Lady. "In Memoriam. I. von Döllinger." *Deutsche Rundschau* 25 (1899): 459–63.

Blennerhassett, Charlotte Lady. "Lord Acton (1834–1902)." *Deutsche Rundschau* 122 (1905): 64–92.

Blennerhassett, Rowland Sir. "Dr. von Döllinger." *The Guardian,* January 22, 1890.

Catchcart, Kevin J., ed. *The Letters of Peter le Page Renouf (1822–1897).* Vol. 4. Dublin: University College Dublin Press, 2004.

Cecconi, Eugenio. *Storia del Concilio Ecumenico Vaticano scritta sui documenti orginali.* 4 vols. Rome: Tipografia Vaticana, 1872–8.

Congar, Yves, *My Journal of the Council,* trans. Mary John Ronayne and Mary Cecily Boulding. Collegeville, MN: Liturgical Press, 2012.

Consalvi, Ercole. "Memoire sul Conclave in Venezia." *Archivum Historiae Pontificiae* 3 (1965): 239–308.

Cornelius, Carl Adolf von. *Gedächtnisrede auf J. von Döllinger, gehalten in der öffentlichen Sitzung der k.b. Akademie der Wissenschaften zu München am 28. März 1890.* Munich: Verlag der k.b. Akademie, 1890.

De Maistre, Joseph. *Du Pape.* Lyons, 1836.

De Maistre, Joseph. *The Works of Joseph de Maistre.* Translated by Jack Lively. New York: Macmillan, 1965.

De Maistre, Joseph. *Considérations sur la France.* Paris: Garnier, 1980.

Denzinger, Heinrich. *The Sources of Catholic Dogma.* Translated by Roy J. Deferrari. St. Louis: Herder, 1957.

Der dritte Altkatholiken-Congreß in Constanz im Jahre 1873. Stenographischer Bericht. Officielle Ausgabe. Constanz, 1873.

Der Kirchenstaat: Eine Historisch-Politisch-Statistische Skizze, mit dem Portrait des Papstes Pius IX. Leipzig: C. B. Lorck, 1859.

Dessain, C. S. and Vincent Ferrer Blehl, S.J., eds. *The Letters and Diaries of John Henry Newman.* 32 vols. London: Thomas Nelson and Sons, 1961–2006.

Donovan, J., ed. *Catechism of the Council of Trent.* Dublin: James Duffy, 1914.

Drey, Johann Sebastian von. *Kurze Einleitung in das Studium der Theologie: Mit Rücksicht auf den wissenschaftlichen Standpunct und das Katholische System.* Tübingen: Heinrich Laupp, 1819.

Dupanloup, Félix. *Lettre sur le futur concile oecuménique adressée par l'Évêque d'Orléans au clergé de son diocèse.* Paris: C. Douniol, 1870.

Erdinger, Anton. *Dr. Joseph Fessler, Bischof von St. Pölten und Sekretär des Vatika-nischen Concils: ein Lebensbild.* Brixen: A. Weger, 1874.

Evans, E. P. "Ignatius von Döllinger." *Atlantic Monthly* 68 (October 1891): 553–65.

Friedberg, Emil. *Sammlung der Aktenstücke zum Ersten Vatikanischen Concil: Mit Einem Grundrisse der Geschichte Desselben.* Tübingen: H. Laupp, 1872.

Friedrich, Johann. *Tagebuch während des Vaticanischen Concils geführt.* Nördlingen, 1871.

Friedrich, Johann. *Geschichte des Vatikanischen Konzils.* 3 vols. Bonn: P. Neusser, 1877–87.

Friedrich, Johann. "Johann Joseph Ignaz von Döllinger." *Nord und Süd* 11 (1879): 296–316.

Friedrich, Johann. *Ignaz von Döllinger: Sein Leben auf Grund seines schriftlichen Nachlasses.* 3 vols. Munich: C. H. Beck, 1899–1901.

Friedrich, Johann. "Meine Briefe an Döllinger aus dem Konzilsjahre 1869/1870." *Internationale kirchliche Zeitschrift* 6 (1916) 27–55, 174–214, 300–34, 401–53.

Gams, Pius, ed. *Verhandlungen der Versammlung katholischer Gelehrten in München von 28. September bis 1. Oktober 1863.* Regensburg, 1863.

Gladstone, William Ewart. *The Vatican Decrees in their Bearing on Civil Authority.* New York: D. Appleton, 1874.

Gladstone, William Ewart. "The Right Rev. Dr. von Döllinger." *The Speaker* 18 (1890): 57–60.

Gladstone, William Ewart. *Correspondence on Church and Religion of William Ewart Gladstone.* Edited by D. C. Lathbury. London: J. Murray, 1910.

Gladstone, William Ewart. *The Gladstone Diaries.* 14 vols. Edited by M. R. D. Foot. Oxford: Clarendon Press, 1968–94.

Granderath, Theodore. *Geschichte des Vaticanischen Konzils von seiner ersten Ankün-digung bis zu seiner Vertagung.* 3 vols. Edited by Conrad Kirch. Freiburg im Breisgau: Herder, 1903–6.

Gregorovius, Ferdinand. *Römische Tagebücher, 1852–1889.* Edited by Hanno-Walter Kruft and Markus Völkel. Munich: C. H. Beck, 1991.

Hefele, Karl Joseph von. *A History of the Christian Councils: From the Original Docu-ments.* Edited and translated by William R. Clark. Edinburgh: T. & T. Clark, 1872–96.

Hergenröther, Joseph. "Der Zeitgeist und die Souveränität des Papstes." *Der Katholik* 41 (1861): 513–43.

Hergenröther, Joseph. "Döllinger über den Kirchenstaat." *Der Katholik* 41 (1861): 536–75, 641–79.

Hergenröther, Joseph. *Anti-Janus: An Historico-Theological Criticism of the Work, Entitled "The Pope and the Council."* Translated by J. B. Robertson. New York: Catholic Publishing Society, 1870.

Hergenröther, Joseph. "Die Conciliums-Briefe der Allgemeinen Zeitung." *Historisch-Politische Blätter für das Katholische Deutschland* 65 (1870): 707–23, 737–61, 865–86; 66 (1870): 21–40, 132–57, 198–223, 421–47.

Hergenröther, Joseph. *Kritik der v. Döllinger'schen Erklärung vom 28. März d. J., Freiburg 1871.* Freiburg im Breisgau: Herder, 1871.

Hinschius, Paul. *Das Kirchenrecht der Katholiken und Protestanten in Deutschland.* Berlin: Guttentag, 1869.

Huber, E. R. and W. Huber, eds. *Staat und Kirche im 19. und 20. Jahrhundert: Dokumente zur Geschichte des deutschen Staatskirchenrechts.* Vol. 1. Berlin: Duncker & Humblot, 1973.

Janssen, Johannes. *Briefe.* Edited by Ludwig Freiherrn von Pastor. 2 vols. Freiburg: Herber, 1920.

Jedin, Hubert. "Kirchenhistorikerbriefe an Augustin Theiner." *Roman Quartalschrift* 6 (1971): 210.

Johnston, John Octavius. *The Life and Letters of Henry Parry Liddon, Canon of St. Paul's Cathedral and Sometime Ireland Professor of Exegesis in the University of Oxford.* London: Longmans, Green and Co., 1904.

Jörg, Joseph Edmund. "Herr Stiftspropst von Döllinger und seine kirchlich-politische Publikation." *Historisch-Politische Blätter für das Katholische Deutschland* 48 (1861): 807–54.

Jörg, Joseph Edmund. "Döllinger. Erinnerungen seines alten Amanuensis." *Historisch-Politische Blätter für das Katholische Deutschland* 105 (1890): 237–62.

Jörg, Joseph Edmund. *Briefwechsel, 1846–1901.* Edited by Dieter Albrecht. Mainz: Matthias-Grünewald Verlag, 1988.

Ketteler, Wilhelm Emmanuel, Freiherr von. *Freiheit, Autorität und Kirche: Erörterungen über die grossen Probleme der Gegenwart.* Mainz: F. Kirchheim, 1862.

Ketteler, Wilhelm Emmanuel, Freiherr von. *Die Unwahrheiten der Römischen Briefe vom Concil in der "Allgemeinen Zeitung."* Mainz: F. Kirchheim, 1870.

Ketteler, Wilhelm Emmanuel, Freiherr von. *Briefwechsel und öffentliche Erklärungen.* 6 vols. Edited by Erwin Iserloh. Mainz: Hase und Koehler, 1977–2001.

Ketteler, Wilhelm Emmanuel, Freiherr von. *Sämtliche Werke und Briefe.* 11 vols. Edited by Erwin Iserloh. Mainz: Hase und Koehler, 1977–2001.

Kleutgen, Joseph. *Die Theologie der Vorzeit verteidigt,* 2nd ed. 5 vols. Münster, 1867–74.

Kleutgen, Joseph. *Die Philosophie der Vorzeit verteidigt,* 2nd ed. 2 vols. Innsbruck, 1878.

Kobell, Luise von. *Ignaz von Döllinger: Erinnerungen.* Munich, 1891.

Langdon, William Chauncy. *Letter in Regard to the Reform Movement in the Church of Italy.* London, 1868.

Liddon, Henry Parry. "Dr. von Döllinger." *The Guardian,* January 22, 1890.

Liddon, Henry Parry and John Octavius Johnston. *Life of Edward Bouverie Pusey, Doctor of Divinity, Canon of Christ Church, Regius Professor of Hebrew in the University of Oxford.* 4 vols. London: Longmans, Green & Co., 1893–7.

Lill, Rudolf, ed. *Vatikanische Akten zur Geschichte des deutschen Kulturkampfes; Leo XIII.* Tübingen: M. Niemeyer, 1970.

Lösch, Stephan, ed. *Johann Adam Möhler: Gesammelte Aktenstücke und Briefe.* Vol. 1. Munich: Josef Kösel & Friedrich Pustet, 1928.

MacClear, J. F., ed. *Church and State in the Modern Age: A Documentary History.* New York: Oxford University Press, 1995.

McElrath, Damian, James C. Holland, Sue Katzman, and Ward White, eds. *Lord Acton: The Decisive Decade, 1864–1874: Essays and Documents.* Louvain: Bureaux de la R. H. E., Bibliothèque de l'Université & Publications Universitaires de Louvain, 1970.

Maret, Henri-Louis-Charles. *Du Concile général et de la paix religieuse. Première partie, la constitution de l'église et la périodicité des conciles généraux; mémoire soumis au prochain concile ecuménique du Vatican.* Paris: Henri Plon, 1869.

Marshall, T. W. M. *The Old Catholics at Cologne.* New York: J. A. McGee, 1873.

Meyrick, Frederick. *Memories of Life at Oxford and Experiences in Italy, Greece, Turkey, Germany, Spain, and Elsewhere.* London: J. Murray, 1905.

Michael, Emil. *Ignaz von Döllinger: Eine Charakteristik.* Innsbruck: Fel. Rauch, 1894.

Möhler, Johann Adam. *Unity in the Church or the Principle of Catholicism: Presented in the Sprit of the Church Fathers of the First Three Centuries.* Edited and translated by Peter C. Erb. Washington, DC: Catholic University of America Press, 1996.

Münch, Ernst H. J. *Vollständige Sammlung aller älteren und neueren Concordate.* Vol. 1. Leipzig, 1831.

Newman, John Henry. *A Letter Addressed to His Grace the Duke of Norfolk on Occasion of Mr. Gladstone's Recent Expostulation.* London: B. M. Pickering, 1875.

Newman, John Henry. *Conscience, Consensus, and the Development of Doctrine: Revolutionary Texts.* Edited by James Gaffney. New York: Image Books, 1992.

Overbeck, Julian Joseph. *Catholic Orthodoxy and Anglo-Catholicism: A Word about Intercommunion between the English and the Orthodox Churches.* London: N. Trübner, 1866.

Perry, William Stevens. *The Reunion Conference at Bonn, 1875. A Personal Narrative.* Hartford, CT, 1876.

Plummer, Alfred. *Conversations with Dr. Döllinger, 1870–1890.* Edited by Robrecht Boudens. Lovain: Louvain University Press, 1985.

Powell, Joseph. *Two Years in the Pontifical Zouaves: A Narrative of Travel, Residence, and Experience in the Roman States.* London: R. Washbourne, 1871.

Prantl, Carl. *Geschichte der Ludwig-Maximilians-Universität in Ingolstadt, Landshut, München.* Munich, 1872.

Pusey, E. B. *On the Clause "and the Son" in Regard to the Eastern Church and the Bonn Conference: A Letter to the Rev. H. P. Liddon.* London: J. Parker, 1876.

Pusey, E. B. *Spiritual Letters of Edward Bouverie Pusey: Doctor of Divinity, Canon of Christ Church, Regius Professor of Hebrew in the University of Oxford.* Edited by J. O Johnston and W. C. E. Newbolt. London: Longmans, Green & Co, 1898.

Ranke, Leopold von. *Die römische Päpste in den letzten vier Jahrhunderten.* 8th ed. 3 vols. Leipzig, 1885.

Ranke, Leopold von. *The History of the Popes During the Last Four Centuries.* Translated by G. R. Dennis. London: G. Bell & Sons, 1912.

Rauschenbusch, Walter. "The Life of Döllinger." *American Journal of Theology* 7 (October 1903): 734.

Reinkens, Joseph Hubert. *Second Pastoral Letter, in Reply to the Encyclical of Pope Pius IX.* Translated by J. E. B. Mayor. London, 1874.

Reinkens, Joseph Hubert. *Joseph Hubert Reinkens, ein Lebensbild.* Gotha: F. A. Perthes, 1906.

Reinkens, Joseph Hubert. *Briefe an seinen Bruder Wilhelm: 1840–1873; eine Quellen-publikation zum rheinischen und schlesischen Katholizismus des 19. Jahrhunderts und zu den Anfängen der Altkatholischen Bewegung.* Cologne: Böhlau, 1979.

Renouf, P. Le Page. *The Case of Pope Honorius: Reconsidered with Reference to Recent Apologies*. London: Longmans, Green, Reader, and Dyer, 1869.

Reusch, Heinrich F., ed. *Bericht über die am 14., 15. und 16. September zu Bonn gehaltenen Unions-Conferenzen*. Bonn, 1874.

Reusch, Heinrich F., ed. *Bericht über die vom 10. bis 16 August 1875 zu Bonn gehaltenen Unions-Conferenzen, im Auftrage des Vorsitzenden Dr. von Döllinger*. Bonn, 1875.

Reusch, Heinrich F., ed. *Report of the Proceedings at the Reunion Conference held at Bonn on September 14, 15, and 16, 1874*. Translated by E. M. B. London: Rivingtons, 1875.

Reusch, Heinrich F., ed. *Report of the Union Conferences held from August 10 to 16, 1875, at Bonn under the Presidency of Dr. von Döllinger*. Translated by Samuel Buel. New York: T. Whittaker, 1876.

Rosmini, Antonio. *Delle cinque piaghe della Santa Chiesa*. Genova: Presso G. Grondona, 1849.

Russell, Odo William Leopold. *The Roman Question: Extracts from the Despatches of Odo Russell from Rome, 1858–1870*. Edited by Noel Blakiston. London: Chapman & Hall, 1962.

Sammlung Kirchlicher und Staatlicher Vorschriften und Abriss des Kirchenrechts für die Altkatholischen Kirchengemeinschaften. Bonn: Synodalrepräsentanz, 1898.

Scheeben, Matthias Joseph. *Schulte und Döllinger gegen das Concil: Kritische Beleuchtung der Schulte'schen Broschüre über die Macht der Päpste und der jüngste Erklärung Döllingers*. Regensburg: Friedrich Pustet, 1871.

Scheeben, Matthias Joseph. "Aus den Akten der Bonner Unionsconferenz." *Periodische Blätter zur wissenschaftlichen Besprechung der großen religiösen Fragen der Gegenwart 3*, 513–28. Regensburg, 1874.

Schulte, Johann Friedrich von. *Der Altkatholicismus: Geschichte seiner Entwicklung, innere Gestaltung und rechtlichen Stellung in Deutschland: Aus den Akten und anderen authentischen Quellen*. Giessen: Emil Roth, 1887.

Schulte, Johann Friedrich von. *Lebenserinnerungen: Mein Wirken als Rechtslehrer, mein Anteil an der Politik in Kirche und Staat*. Giessen, 1908.

Senestrey, Ignatius von. *Wie es zur Definition der päpstlichen Unfehlbarkeit kam: Tagebuch vom I.* Vatikanischen Konzil. Edited by Klaus Schatz. Frankfurt am Main: Knecht, 1977.

Stenographischer Bericht über die Verhandlungen des Katholiken-Congresses, abgehalten vom 22. bis 24. September 1871. Munich, 1871.

Strossmayer, Josip Juraj. *Bishop Strossmayer's Speech in the Vatican Council of 1870*. New York: Agora Publishing, 1941.

Tanner, S.J., Norman P., ed. *Decrees of the Ecumenical Councils: Volume Two, Trent to Vatican II*. London: Sheed & Ward, 1990.

Theiner, Augustin, ed. *Documents inédits relatifs aux affaires religieuses de la France 1790 à 1800 extraits des archives secrètes du Vatican*. Vol. 1. Paris, 1857.

Tizanni, Vincenzo. *Il Concilio Vaticano I: Diario di Vincenzo Tizzani*. Edited by Lajos Pásztor. Stuttgart: A. Hiersemann, 1991.

Ullathorne, William Bernard. *The Döllingerites, Mr. Gladstone, and the Apostates from the Faith: A Letter to the Catholics of his Diocese*. London: T. Richardson, 1874.

Ullathorne, William Bernard. *Letters of Archbishop Ullathorne.* Edited by Mother Francis Raphael. London: Burns & Oates. 1892.

Secondary Sources

Adams, Nicholas, George Pattison, and Graham Ward, eds. *The Oxford Handbook of Theology and Modern European Thought.* Oxford: Oxford University Press, 2013.

Alberigo, Giuseppe. "The Authority of the Church in the Documents of Vatican I and Vatican II." *Journal of Ecumenical Studies* 19 (1982): 119–45.

Albrecht, Dieter. "Döllinger, die bayerische Regierung und das Erste Vatikanische Konzil," in Konrad Repgen and Stephan Skalweit, eds., *Spiegel der Geschichte: Festgabe für Max Braubach zum 10. April 1964,* 795–815. Münster: Aschendorff, 1964.

Alexander, Jeffrey, Ron Eyerman, Bernhard Giesen, Neil J. Smelser, and Piotr Sztompka. *Cultural Trauma: Theory and Applications.* Berkeley: University of California Press, 2004.

Altholz, Joseph L. *The Liberal Catholic Movement in England: The "Rambler" and its Contributors, 1848–1864.* London: Burns & Oates, 1962.

Anderson, Margaret Lavinia. "The Limits of Secularization: On the Problem of the Catholic Revival in Nineteenth-Century Germany." *Historical Journal* 38 (September 1995): 647–70.

Anderson, Robin. *Pope Pius VII (1800–1823): His Life, His Times and His Struggle with Napoleon.* Rockford, IL: TAN Books, 2000.

Arnold, Claus. *Kleine Geschichte des Modernismus.* Freiburg: Herder, 2007.

Astarita, Tommaso. *Between Salt Water and Holy Water: A History of Southern Italy.* New York: W. W. Norton, 2005.

Atkin, Nicholas and Frank Tallett. *Priests, Prelates, and People: A History of European Catholicism since 1750.* London: I. B. Tauris, 2003.

Aubert, Roger. *Le pontificat de Pie IX (1846–1878).* Paris: Bloud & Gay, 1952.

Aubert, Roger. *The Church in a Secularised Society.* Translated by Janet Sondheimer. New York: Paulist Press, 1978.

Aubert, Roger. *The Church Between Revolution and Restoration.* Translated by Peter Becker. New York: Crossroad, 1981.

Bach, Elisabeth, Angela Berlis, and Siegfried J. Thuringer, eds. *Ignaz von Döllinger zum 125. Todestag: Spurensuche, Schlaglichter auf ein außergewöhnliches Leben.* Bonn: Alt-Katholischer Bistumsverlag, 2015.

Balthasar, Hans Urs von. *The Office of Peter and the Structure of the Church.* 2nd ed. Translated by Andrée Emery. San Francisco: Ignatius Press, 2007.

Bastable, James D., ed. *Newman and Gladstone: Centennial Essays.* Dublin: Veritas Publications, 1978.

Bauerreiss, Romuald. *Kirchengeschichte Bayerns.* St. Ottilien: EOS Verlag, 1949.

Bauerreiss, Romuald. *Kirchengeschichte Bayerns, vol. 7: 1600–1803.* Augsburg: Verlag Winfried-Werk, 1970.

Beales, Derek. *Prosperity and Plunder: European Catholic Monasteries in the Age of Revolution, 1650–1815.* Cambridge: Cambridge University Press, 2003.

Belardinelli, Mario. "Döllinger e l'Italia: per una storia del dibattito sulla 'libertà nella chiesa' nell'Ottocento." *Rivista di storia della Chiesa in Italia* 36 (1982): 381–407; 37 (1983) 72–116.

Bennette, Rebecca Ayako. *Fighting for the Soul of Germany: The Catholic Struggle for Inclusion after Unification.* Cambridge, MA: Harvard University Press, 2012.

Berger, Stefan, ed. *A Companion to Nineteenth-Century Europe, 1789–1914.* Malden, MA: Blackwell, 2006.

Berlis, Angela. Frauen im Prozess der Kirchwerdung. Eine historisch-theologische Studie zur Anfangsphase des deutschen Altkatholizismus (1850–1890). Frankfurt am Main: Peter Lang, 1998.

Berlis, Angela."Seelensorge verträgt keine Teilung. Ignaz von Döllinger (1799–1890) und die Frage des Zölibats." *Annali di studi religiosi* 6 (2005): 249–81.

Bischof, F. X. *Theologie und Geschichte: Ignaz von Döllinger (1799–1890) in der zweiten Hälfte seines Leben. Ein Beitrag zu seiner Biographie.* Stuttgart: Kohlhammer, 1997.

Bischof, F. X. "John Henry Newman und Ignaz von Döllinger: Papstdogmen und Gewissen." In Mariano Delgado, Volker Leppin, and David Neuhold, eds., *Ringen um die Wahrheit: Gewissenskonflikte in der Christentumsgeschichte,* 271–86. Stuttgart: Kohlhammer, 2011.

Bischof, F. X. and Georg Essen, eds. *Theologie, kirchliches Lehramt und öffentliche Meinung: Die Münchener Gelertenversammlung von 1863 und ihre Folgen.* Stuttgart: Kohlhammer, 2015.

Blackbourn, David. "The Catholic Church in Europe since the French Revolution: A Review Article." *Comparative Studies in Society and History* 33 (1991): 778–90.

Blackbourn, David. *The Long Nineteenth Century: A History of Germany, 1780–1918.* New York: Oxford University Press, 1998.

Blaschke, Olaf. "Der Altkatholizismus 1870 bis 1945: Nationalismus, Antisemitismus und Nationalsozialismus." *Historische Zeitschrift* 261 (1995): 51–99.

Blaschke, Olaf. "Das 19. Jahrhundert: Ein zweites konfessionelles Zeitalter?" *Geschichte und Gesellschaft* 26 (2000): 38–75.

Blouin, Francis X., ed. *Vatican Archives: An Inventory and Guide to Historical Documents of the Holy See.* New York: Oxford University Press, 1998.

Boyle, John P. "The Ordinary Magisterium: Towards a History of the Concept." *The Heythrop Journal* 20 (1979): 380–98; 21 (1980): 14–19.

Boyle, John P. *Church Teaching Authority: Historical and Theological Studies.* Notre Dame: University of Notre Dame Press, 1995.

Boyle, John P. "Faith and Reason: The Case of Jacob Frohschammer." In Anthony J. Cernera, ed., *Continuity and Plurality in Catholic Theology,* 1–12. Fairfield, CT: Sacred Heart University Press, 1998.

Brandmüller, Walter. "Die Publikation des 1. Vatikanischen Konzils in Bayern: Aus den Anfängen des bayerischen Kulturkampfes." *Zeitschrift für bayerische Landesgeschichte* 31 (1968): 197–258, 575–634.

Brandmüller, Walter. *Ignaz v. Döllinger am Vorabend des I. Vatikanums: Herausforderung und Antwort.* St. Ottilien: EOS Verlag, 1977.

Brandmüller, Walter. *Handbuch der bayerischen Kirchengeschichte.* St. Ottilien: EOS Verlag, 1991–8.

Brandt, Hans Jürgen. *Eine katholische Universität in Deutschland? Das Ringen der Katholiken in Deutschland um eine Universitätsbildung im 19. Jahrhundert.* Cologne: Böhlau, 1981.

Braubach, Max. "Die katholischen Universitäten Deutschlands und die Französische Revolution." *Historisches Jahrbuch* 49 (1929): 263–303.

Brezik, Victor B., ed. *One Hundred Years of Thomism: Aeterni Patris and Afterwards.* Houston, TX: Center for Thomistic Studies, University of St. Thomas, 1981.

Broers, Michael. *The Politics of Religion in Napoleonic Italy: The War against God, 1801–1814.* London: Routledge, 2002.

Brown, Marvin Luther. *Louis Veuillot, French Ultramontane Catholic Journalist and Layman, 1813–1883.* Durham, NC: Moore Publishing, 1977.

Brown, Stewart J. and Peter B. Nockles, eds. *The Oxford Movement: Europe and the Wider World, 1830–1930.* Cambridge: Cambridge University Press, 2012.

Buchheim, Karl. *Ultramontanismus und Demokratie: der Weg der deutschen Katholiken im 19. Jahrhundert.* Munich: Kösel Verlag, 1963.

Bunnell, Adam. *Before Infallibility: Liberal Catholicism in Biedermeier Vienna.* Rutherford, NJ: Fairleigh Dickinson University Press, 1990.

Burleigh, Michael. *Earthly Powers: The Clash of Religion and Politics from the French Revolution to the Great War.* New York: HarperCollins, 2005.

Burson, Jeffery D. and Ulrich L. Lehner, eds. *Enlightenment and Catholicism in Europe: A Transnational History.* Notre Dame: University of Notre Dame Press, 2014.

Bury, J. B. *History of the Papacy in the 19th Century: Liberty and Authority in the Roman Catholic Church.* New York: Schocken Books, 1964.

Butler, Cuthbert. *The Vatican Council, 1869–1870, Based on Bishop Ullathorne's Letters.* London: Collins and Harvill Press, 1962.

Butterfield, Herbert. "Journal of Lord Acton: Rome 1857." *Cambridge Historical Journal* 3 (1946): 186–204.

Calkins, Arthur Burton. "John Henry Newman on Conscience and the Magisterium." *Downside Review* 87 (1969): 358–69.

Caravale, Mario and Alberto Caracciolo. *Lo Stato Pontificio da Martino V a Pio IX.* Torino: UTET, 1978.

Carlen, Claudia. *Papal Pronouncements, a Guide, 1740–1978.* Ann Arbor: Pierian Press, 1990.

Carlin, Gianluca. *L'Ecclesiologia di Carlo Passaglia (1812–1887): Mit Einer Deutschen Zusammenfassung.* Münster: Lit, 2001.

Cessario, Romanus O.P. *A Short History of Thomism.* Washington, DC: Catholic University of America Press, 2003.

Chadwick, Owen. *Catholicism and History: The Opening of the Vatican Archives.* Cambridge: Cambridge University Press, 1978.

Chadwick, Owen. *The Popes and European Revolution.* Oxford: Clarendon Press, 1982.

Chadwick, Owen. "Döllinger and Reunion." In *Christian Authority: Essays of Henry Chadwick.* Edited by G. R. Evans, 296–334. Oxford: Clarendon Press, 1988.

Chadwick, Owen. *Acton and History.* Cambridge: Cambridge University Press, 1998.

Chadwick, Owen. *A History of the Popes, 1830–1914.* Oxford: Oxford University Press, 1998.

Chandler, Michael. *The Life and Work of Henry Parry Liddon (1829–1890).* Leominster: Gracewing, 2000.

Chandler, Michael. "The Significance of the Friendship between William E. Gladstone and Ignaz von Döllinger." *Internationale kirchliche Zeitschrift* 90 (2000): 153–67.

Chapman, Alister, John Coffey, and Brad S. Gregory, eds. *Seeing Things their Way: Intellectual History and the Return of Religion.* Notre Dame: University of Notre Dame Press, 2009.

Chapman, Mark D. *The Fantasy of Reunion: Anglicans, Catholics, and Ecumenism, 1833–1882.* Oxford: Oxford University Press, 2014.

Clark, Christopher and Wolfram Kaiser, eds. *Culture Wars: Secular–Catholic Conflict in Nineteenth-Century Europe.* Cambridge: Cambridge University Press, 2003.

Conzemius, Victor. "Aspects Ecclésiologiques de l'Évolution de Döllinger et du Vieux Catholicisme." *Revue des Sciences Religieuses* 34 (1960): 247–79.

Conzemius, Victor. "Römische Briefe vom Konzil." *Theological Quartalschrift* 14 (1960): 427–62.

Conzemius, Victor. "Acton, Döllinger und Ketteler. Zum Verständnis des Ketteler-Bildes in den Quirinusbriefen und zur Kritik an Vigneners Darstellung Kettelers auf dem Vatikanum I." *Archiv für Mittelrheinische Kirchengeschichte* 14 (1962): 194–238.

Conzemius, Victor. "Die 'Römischen Briefe vom Konzil.' Eine Entstehungsgeschichtliche und Quellenkritische Untersuchung zum Konzilsjournalismus Ignaz v. Döllingers und Lord Actons." *Roman Quartalschrift* 59 (1964): 186–229; 60 (1965) 76–119.

Conzemius, Victor. "Die Verfasser der 'Römischen Briefe vom Konzil.'" *Festschrift Hans Foerster* 52 (1964): 229–56.

Conzemius, Victor. "Zwischen Rom, Canterbury und Konstantinopel: Der Altkatholizismus in römischkatholischer Sicht." *Theological Quartalschrift* 145 (1965): 188–234.

Conzemius, Victor. "Der Tod Ignaz von Döllingers in Briefen der Freunde." *Kurtrierisches Jahrbuch* 8 (1968): 303–4.

Conzemius, Victor. *Katholizismus ohne Rom: die Altkatholische Kirchengemeinschaft.* Zürich: Benziger, 1969.

Conzemius, Victor. "Ignaz v. Döllinger: The Development of a XIX. Century Ecumenist." *Hundert Jahre Christkatholische-Theologische Fakultät der Universität Bern. Beiheft zur Internationale Kirchliche Zeitschrift* 64 (1974): 110–27.

Conzemius, Victor. "Liberaler Katholizismus in England." In Martin Schmidt and Georg Schwaiger, eds., *Kirchen und Liberalismus im 19. Jahrhundert,* 173–96. Göttingen: Vandenhoeck & Ruprecht, 1976.

Conzemius, Victor. "Die Kirchenkrise Ignaz von Döllingers: deutsche gegen römische Theologie?" *Historisches Jahrbuch* 108 (1988): 406–29.

Coppa, Frank. *Cardinal Giacomo Antonelli and Papal Politics in European Affairs.* Albany, NY: State University of New York Press, 1990.

Coppa, Frank. *The Modern Papacy Since 1789.* New York: Longman, 1998.

Coppa, Frank. *Politics and the Papacy in the Modern World.* Westport, CT: Praeger, 2008.

Costigan, Richard F. *The Consensus of the Church and Papal Infallibility: A Study in the Background of Vatican I.* Washington, DC: Catholic University of America Press, 2005.

Croce, Giuseppe M. "Una fonte importante per la storia del pontificato di Pio IX e del Concilio Vaticano. I: I manoscritti inediti di Vincenzo Tizzani." *Archivum Historiae Pontificiae* 23 (1985): 217–345; 24 (1986); 273–363; 25 (1987): 263–363.

Cwiekowski, Frederick J. *The English Bishops and the First Vatican Council.* Louvain: Bibliothèque de l'Université. Publications Universitaires de Louvain, 1971.

Dante, Francesco. *Storia della "Civiltá Cattolica" (1850–1891): Il laboratorio del Papa.* Rome: Edizioni Studium, 1990.

Danz, Christian, ed. *Schelling und die historische Theologie des 19. Jahrhunderts.* Tübingen: Mohr Siebeck, 2013.

De Cesare, Raffaele. *The Last Days of Papal Rome, 1850–1870.* Translated by Helen Zimmern. London: Constable, 1909.

De Marchi, Giuseppe. *Le nunziature apostoliche dal 1800 al 1956.* Vatican City: Liberia Editrice Vaticana, 2006.

Dederen, Raoul. *Eugène Michaud, 1839–1917, un réformateur catholique au XIXe siècle.* Geneva: Droz, 1963.

Demarco, Domenico. *Il Tramonto dello Stato Pontificio: Il Papato di Gregorio XVI.* Turin: G. Einaudi, 1949.

Denzler, Georg. "Das I. Vatikanische Konzil und die theologische Fakultät der Universität München." *Annuarium Historiae Conciliorum* 1 (1969): 412–55.

Denzler, Georg and Ernst Ludwig Grasmück, eds. *Geschichtlichkeit und Glaube: zum 100. Todestag Johann Joseph Ignaz von Döllingers (1799–1890).* Munich: E. Wewel, 1990.

Dezza, Paolo. *Alle origini nel neotomismo.* Milan: Fratelli Bocca, 1940.

Dirrigl, Michael. *Ludwig I: König von Bayern, 1825–1848.* Munich: Hugendubel, 1980.

Dirrigl, Michael. *Maximilian II: König von Bayern, 1848–1864.* Munich: Hugendubel, 1984.

Dotzler, Ludwig. "Über das Verhältnis Martin Deutingers zu Ignaz Döllinger." *Beiträge zur Altbayerischen Kirchengeschichte* 23 (1963): 130–47.

Dru, Alexander. *The Contribution of German Catholicism.* New York: Hawthorn Books, 1963.

Dru, Alexander. "Lord Acton, Döllinger, und der Münchner Kongreß." *Hochland* 56 (1963): 49–58.

Duffy, Eamon. *Saints and Sinners: A History of the Popes.* New Haven: Yale University Press, 2006.

Dulles, Avery, S.J. "Newman on Infallibility." *Theological Studies* 51 (1990): 434–49.

Dulles, Avery, S.J. *Magisterium: Teacher and Guardian of the Faith.* Naples, FL: Sapienta Press, 2007.

Egelhaaf, Gottlob. "Zum Gedächtniß Döllinger's." *Deutsche Rundschau* 72 (1890): 287–91.

Engel-Janosi, Friedrich. "The Return of Pius IX in 1850." *Catholic Historical Review* 36 (July 1950): 129–62.

Falconi, Carlo. *Il Cardinale Antonelli: vita e carriere del Richelieu italiano nella Chiesa di Pio IX.* Milan: A. Mondadori, 1983.

Finsterhölzl, Johann, ed. *Ignaz von Döllinger.* Graz: Verlag Styria, 1969.

Finsterhölzl, Johann. *Die Kirche in der Theologie Ignaz von Döllingers bis zum ersten Vatikanum.* Göttingen: Vandenhoeck & Ruprecht, 1975.

Fleischer, Manfred P. *Katholische und lutherische Ireniker, Unter Besonderer Berücksichtigung des 19. Jahrhunderts.* Göttingen: Musterschmidt-Verlag, 1968.

Ford, John. "Infallibility: From Vatican I to the Present." *Journal of Ecumenical Studies* 8 (1971): 768–91.

Forster, Marc R. *Catholic Germany from the Reformation to the Enlightenment.* New York: Palgrave Macmillan, 2007.

Franzen, August. *Die katholisch-Theologische Fakultät Bonn im Streit um das Erste Vatikanische Konzil: Zugleich eines Beitrag zum Entstehungsgeschichte des Altkatholizismus am Niederrhein.* Cologne: Böhlau, 1974.

Fries, Heinrich. "Newman und Döllinger." *Newman Studien* 1 (1948): 26–76.

Fries, Heinrich and Georg Schwaiger, eds. *Katholische Theologen Deutschlands im 19. Jahrhundert.* 3 vols. Munich: Kösel, 1975.

Fuhrmann, Horst. "Päpstlicher Primat und Pseudoisidorische Dekretalen." *Quellen und Forschungen aus Italienischen Archiven und Bibliotheken* 49 (1969): 313–29.

Fuhrmann, Horst. *Ignaz von Döllinger: Ein exkommunizierter Theologe als Akademiepräsident und Historiker.* Leipzig: Verlag der Sächsischen Akademie der Wissenschaften zu Leipzig, 1999.

Garhammer, Erich. *Seminaridee und Klerusbildung bei Karl August Graf von Reisach: Eine pastoralgeschichtliche Studie zum Ultramontanismus des 19. Jahrhunderts.* Stuttgart: Kohlhammer, 1990.

Gatz, Erwin, ed. *Die Bischöfe der deutschsprachigen Länder 1785/1803 bis 1945: Ein Biographisches Lexikon.* Berlin: Duncker & Humblot, 2002.

Gatz, Erwin. *Die Bistümer der deutschsprachigen Länder von der Säkularisation bis zur Gegenwart.* Freiburg im Breisgau: Herder, 2005.

Godet, P. "Doellinger." *Revue du Clergé Français* 36 (1903): 17–41, 125–50, 367–95.

Goetz, Leopold Karl. *Franz Heinrich Reusch, 1825–1900: Eine Darstellung seiner Lebensarbeit.* Gotha: F. A. Perthes, 1901.

Gollwitzer, Heinz. *Ludwig I. von Bayern, Königtum im Vormärz: Eine Politische Biographie.* Munich: Süddeutscher Verlag, 1986.

Greschat, Martin, ed. *Gestalten der Kirchengeschichte.* Stuttgart: Kohlhammer, 1981–6.

Grisar, Josef. "Die Circulardepesche des Fürsten Hohenlohe vom 9. April 1869 über das bevorstehende Vatikanische Konzil." *Archiv und Wissenschaft* 3 (1961): 216–40.

Gross, Michael B. *The War against Catholicism: Liberalism and the Anti-Catholic Imagination in Nineteenth-Century Germany.* Ann Arbor: University of Michigan Press, 2005.

Guarino, Thomas G. *Vincent of Lérins and the Development of Christian Doctrine.* Grand Rapids, MI: Baker Academic, 2013.

Hales, E. E. Y. *Revolution and Papacy, 1769–1846.* Notre Dame: University of Notre Dame Press, 1966.

Hanus, Franciscus. *Die preussische Vatikangesandtschaft, 1747–1920.* Munich: Pohl, 1954.

Hartmann, Peter Claus. "Bevölkerungszahlen und Konfessionsverhältnisse des Heiligen Römischen Reiches Deutscher Nation und der Reichkreise am Ende des 18. Jahrhunderts." *Zeitschrift für historische Forschung* 22 (1995): 345–69.

Hasler, August Bernhard. *How the Pope Became Infallible: Pius IX and the Politics of Persuasion.* Translated by Peter Heinegg. Garden City, NY: Doubleday & Co., 1981.

Hausberger, Karl and Benno Hubensteiner. *Bayerische Kirchengeschichte.* Munich: Süddeutscher Verlag, 1985.

Hennesey, James J. *The First Council of the Vatican: The American Experience.* New York: Herder and Herder, 1963.

Henrici, Peter. "Matteo Liberatore und Joseph Kleutgen: Zwei Pioniere der Neuscholastik." *Gregorianum* 91 (2010): 768–89.

Herre, Franz. *Ludwig I: ein Romantiker auf Bayerns Thron*. Stuttgart: Hohenheim, 2005.

Hill, Roland. *Lord Acton*. New Haven: Yale University Press, 2000.

Himes, Michael. *Ongoing Incarnation: Johann Adam Möhler and the Beginnings of Modern Ecclesiology*. New York: Crossroad, 1997.

Hinske, Norbert and Karl Hengst, eds. *Katholische Aufklärung: Aufklärung im Katholischen Deutschland*. Hamburg: Meiner, 1993.

Hollweck, Joseph. *Die Kirchlichen Strafgesetze*. Mainz: Franz Kirchheim, 1899.

Howard, Thomas Albert. *Religion and the Rise of Historicism*. Cambridge: Cambridge University Press, 1999.

Howard, Thomas Albert. "A 'Religious Turn' in Modern European Historiography?" *Historically Speaking* 4 (June 2003): 24–6.

Howard, Thomas Albert. *Protestant Theology and the Making of the Modern German University*. Oxford: Oxford University Press, 2006.

Howard, Thomas Albert. *God and the Atlantic: America, Europe, and the Religious Divide*. Oxford: Oxford University Press, 2011.

Howard, Thomas Albert. "Neither a Secular nor Confessional Age: The Bonn Reunion Conferences of 1874 and 1875." *Journal of the Historical Society* 11 (March 2011): 59–84.

Huber, Ernst Rudolf. *Deutsche Verfassungsgeschichte seit 1789. Der Kampf um Einheit und Freiheit: 1830 bis 1850*. 2 vols. Stuttgart: Kohlhammer, 1988.

Huppertz, Hubert. "Döllingers Bedeutung für die ökumenische Bewegung." *Internationale kirchliche Zeitschrift* 89 (1999): 182–200.

Hütter, Reinhard. "Conscience 'Truly so Called' and its Counterfeits: John Henry Newman and Thomas Aquinas on What Conscience is and Why it Matters." *Nova et Vetera* 12 (2014): 701–67.

Hyland, Francis Edward. *Excommunication: Its Nature, Historical Development and Effects*. Washington, DC: Catholic University of America Press, 1928.

Iggers, Georg G. "Historicism: The History and Meaning of the Term." *Journal of the History of Ideas* 56 (January 1995): 129–52.

Israel, Jonathan I. *Radical Enlightenment: Philosophy and the Making of Modernity, 1650–1750*. New York: Oxford University Press, 2001.

Jahn, Cornelia. *Klosteraufhebungen und Klosterpolitik in Bayern unter Kurfürst Karl Theodore, 1778–1784*. Munich: C. H. Beck, 1994.

Jemolo, A. C. *Chiesa e stato in Italia negli ultimi cento anni*. Turin: G. Einaudi, 1949.

Jodock, Darrell, ed. *Catholicism Contending with Modernity: Roman Catholic Modernism and Anti-Modernism in Historical Context*. Cambridge: Cambridge University Press, 2000.

Kahle, Wilhelm. *Westliche Orthodoxie. Leben und Ziele Julian Joseph Overbecks*. Leiden: E. J. Brill, 1968.

Kapfinger, Hans. *Der Eoskreis 1828–1832: Ein Beitrag zur Vorgeschichte des politischen Katholizismus in Deutschland*. Munich: Dr. Franz A. Pfeiffer, 1928.

Kaplan, Grant. *Answering the Enlightenment: The Catholic Recovery of Historical Revelation*. New York: Crossroad, 2006.

Kerr, Fergus. *After Aquinas: Versions of Thomism.* Oxford: Blackwell Publishing, 2002.

Kertzer, David I. *Prisoner of the Vatican: The Popes, the Kings, and Garibaldi's Rebels in the Struggle to Rule Modern Italy.* Boston: Houghton Mifflin, 2004.

Kessler, Ewald. *Johann Friedrich (1836–1917): ein Beitrag zur Geschichte des Alkatholizismus.* Munich: Kommissionsbuchhandlung R. Wölfe, 1975.

Kessler, Ewald. "Ergänzungen und Berichtigungen zur Döllinger-Biographie von Stephan Lösch." *Internationale kirchliche Zeitschrift* 98 (1990): 137–53.

Kessler, Ewald. "Herzog Max in Bayern. Eine Gedenkrede von Ignaz v. Döllinger." *Zeitschrift für Bayerische Landesgeschichte* 53 (1990): 149–54.

Kessler, Ewald. "Döllinger und der Protestantismus." *Internationale kirchliche Zeitschrift* 89 (1999): 2–22, 96–113.

Kilumby Mayimby-Kil, Jean-Marie. *Exommunication et communion avec l'église catholique.* Rome: Pontificia Universitas Urbaniana, Facultas Iuris Canonici, 2001.

King, Lawrence J. "Newman and Gasser on Infallibility: Vatican I and Vatican II." *Newman Studies Journal* 8 (2011): 27–39.

Kirmeier, Josef and Manfred Treml, eds. *Glanz und Ende der alten Klöster: Säkularisation im bayerischen Oberland 1803.* Munich: Süddeutscher Verlag, 1991.

Klausnitzer, Wolfgang. *Päpstliche Unfehlbarkeit bei Newman und Döllinger: ein Historisch-Systematischer Vergleich.* Innsbruck: Tyrolia Verlag, 1980.

Kleineidam, Erich. *Die katholisch-theologische Fakultät der Universität Breslau 1811–1945.* Cologne: Wienand, 1961.

Kley, Dale Van. *The Religious Origins of the French Revolution: From Calvin to the Civil Constitution, 1560–1791.* New Haven: Yale University Press, 1996.

Klueting, Harm, ed. *Irenik und Antikonfessionalismus im 17. und 18. Jahrhundert.* New York: Olms, 2003.

Komonchak, Joseph A. "Modernity and the Construction of Roman Catholicism." *Cristianesmo nella Storia* 18 (1997): 353–85.

Kornberg, Jacques. "Ignaz von Döllinger's *Die Juden in Europa*: A Catholic Polemic against Antisemitism." *Journal for the History of Modern Theology/Zeitschrift für neuere Theologieschichte* 6 (1999): 223–45.

Kreuzer, Georg. *Die Honoriusfrage im Mittelalter und in der Neuzeit.* Stuttgart: A. Hiersemann, 1975.

Küng, Hans. *Infallible? An Inquiry.* Translated by Edward Quinn. Garden City, NY: Doubleday, 1983.

Küppers, Werner. "Döllinger, Johann Joseph Ignaz v." *Neue Deutsche Biographie* 4 (1959): 21–5.

Küry, Urs. *Die Altkatholische Kirche: Ihre Geschichte, ihre Lehre, ihr Anliegen.* Stuttgart: Evangelisches Verlagswerk, 1966.

Lakner, F. "Kleutgen und die kirchliche Wissenschaft in Deutschland im XIX. Jahrhundert." *Zeitschrift für katholische Theologie* 57 (1933): 161–214.

Landersdorfer, Anton. "Gregor von Scherr, Erzbishof von München und Freising (1856–1877)." In Georg Schwaiger, ed., *Christenleben im Wandel der Zeit,* 138–60. Munich: E. Wewel, 1987.

Landersdorfer, Anton. *Gregor von Scherr (1804–1877): Erzbischof von München und Freising in der Zeit der Ersten Vatikanums und des Kulturkampfes.* Munich: Verlag des Vereins, 1995.

Leb, Ioan-Vasile. "The Reunification of Churches According to Ignaz von Döllinger." *Revista Teologica* 22 (2012): 173–88.

Lehner, Ulrich L. *The Catholic Enlightenment: The Forgotten History of a Global Movement*. New York: Oxford University Press, 2016.

Leoni, Francesco. *Storia della Controrivoluzione in Italia*. Naples: Guida, 1975.

Liebhart, Wilhelm. *Bayerns Könige: Königtum und Politik in Bayern*. Frankfurt am Main: Peter Lang, 1997.

Lill, Rudolf. "Die ersten deutschen Bischofskonferenzen." *Roman Quartalschrift* 59 (1964): 127–85; 60 (1965): 1–70.

Lill, Rudolf. "Die deutschen Theologieprofessoren vor dem Vatikanum I in Urteil des Münchener Nuntius." In Erwin Iserloh and Konrad Repgen, eds., *Reformata Reformanda: Festgabe für Hubert Jedin zum 17. Juni 1965*, vol. 2, 483–508. Münster: Aschendorff, 1965.

Lill, Rudolf. "Die Anfänge der katholischen Bewegung in Deutschland und der Schweiz." In Hubert Jedin, ed., *Handbuch der Kirchengeschichte*, vol. 6, 259–86. Freiburg: Herder, 1999.

Lindbeck, George A. *Infallibility*. Milwaukee: Marquette University Press, 1972.

Lonergan, Bernard. *A Second Collection: Papers*. Toronto: Toronto University Press, 1996.

Loome, Thomas Michael. *Liberal Catholicism, Reform Catholicism, Modernism: A Contribution to a New Orientation in Modernist Research*. Mainz: Matthias-Grünewald Verlag, 1979.

Lösch, Stephan. *Döllinger und Frankreich, eine geistige Allianz, 1823–1871*. Munich: C. H. Beck, 1955.

McClory, Robert. *Power and the Papacy: The People and Politics behind the Doctrine of Papal Infallibility*. Liguori, MO: Triumph Press, 1997.

McCool, Gerald A. *Catholic Theology in the Nineteenth Century*. New York: Seabury Press, 1977.

McCool, Gerald A. *The Neo-Thomists*. Milwaukee: Marquette University Press, 1994.

McIntosh, Christopher. *The Swan King: Ludwig II of Bavaria*. London: I. B. Tauris, 2012.

MacIntyre, Alasdair. *Three Rival Forms of Moral Enquiry*. Notre Dame: University of Notre Dame Press, 1990.

MacIntyre, Alasdair. *God, Philosophy, Universities: A Selective History of the Catholic Philosophical Tradition*. Lanham, MD: Rowman & Littlefield, 2009.

McMahon, Darrin M. *Enemies of the Enlightenment: The French Counter-Enlightenment and the Making of Modernity*. Oxford: Oxford University Press, 2001.

McManners, John. *The French Revolution and the Church*. London: Harper & Row, 1969.

Mandelbaum, Maurice. *History, Man, & Reason: A Study in Nineteenth-Century Thought*. Baltimore: Johns Hopkins University Press, 1971.

Marguery-Melin, Bruno. *La destruction de l'Abbaye de Cluny: 1789–1823*. Cluny: Centre d'Études Clunisiennes, 1985.

Martina, Giacomo. *Pio IX*. 3 vols. Rome: Editrice Pontificia Università Gregoriana, 1974–90.

Menozzi, D. "L'orginazzazione della chiesa italiana in età Napoleonica." *Cristianesmo nella Storia* 14 (1993): 405–45.

Mettenpenningen, Jürgen. *Nouvelle théologie—New Theology: Inheritor of Modernism, Precursor of Vatican II.* London: T. & T. Clark, 2010.

Miko, Norbert. *Das Ende des Kirchenstaates.* 4 vols. Vienna: Verlag Herold, 1962.

Miko, Norbert. "Zur Frage der Publikation des Dogmas von der Unfehlbarkeit des Papstes durch den deutschen Episkopat im Sommer 1870. Aktenstücke aus dem Historischen Archiv der Erzdiözese Köln." *Roman Quartalschrift* 58 (1963): 28–50.

Milaneschi, Cesare. *Il vecchio cattolicesimo in Italia.* Consenza: Luigi Pellegrini, 2014.

Monti, Antonio. *Pio IX nel Risorgimento Italiano: con documenti inediti e illustrazioni.* Bari: G. Laterza, 1928.

Mori, Renato. *Il tramonto del potere temporale, 1866–1870.* Rome: Edizioni di Storia e Letteratura, 1967.

Morley, John. *The Life of William Ewart Gladstone.* Vol. 1. London, 1903.

Morris, Colin. *The Papal Monarchy: The Western Church from 1050 to 1250.* Oxford: Clarendon Press, 1989.

Moss, C. B. *The Old Catholic Movement: Its Origins and History*, 2nd ed. London: SPCK, 1964.

Müller, Gerhard. "Die Immaculata Conceptio im Urteil der mitteleuropäischen Bischöfe. Zur Entstehung des mariologischen Dogmas von 1854." *Kerygma und Dogma* 14 (1968): 46–68.

Neuner, Peter. *Döllinger als Theologe der Ökumene.* Paderborn: Schöningh, 1979.

Neuner, Peter. "Die 'Papstfabeln' im Rahmen der Biographie Döllingers." In Georg Schawiger, ed., *Historische Kritik in der Theologie: Beiträge zu ihrer Geschichte*, 285–306. Göttingen: Vandenhoeck & Ruprecht, 1980.

Neuner, Peter. *Stationen einer Kirchenspaltung: Der Fall Döllinger, ein Lehrstück für die heutige Kirchenkrise.* Frankfurt: Verlag Josef Knecht, 1990.

Nipperdey, Thomas. *Germany from Napoleon to Bismark, 1800–1866.* Translated by Daniel Nolan. Princeton: Princeton University Press, 1996.

O'Dwyer, Margaret. *The Papacy in the Age of Napoleon and the Restoration: Pius VII, 1800–1823.* Lanham, MD: University Press of America, 1985.

O'Gara, Margaret. *Triumph in Defeat: Infallibility, Vatican I, and the French Minority Bishops.* Washington, DC: Catholic University of America Press, 1988.

O'Meara, Thomas F. *Romantic Idealism and Roman Catholicism: Schelling and the Theologians.* Notre Dame: University of Notre Dame Press, 1982.

O'Meara, Thomas F. *Church and Culture: German Catholic Theology, 1860–1914.* Notre Dame: University of Notre Dame Press, 1991.

Oeyen, Christian. "Die Entstehung der Bonner Unions-Konferenzen im Jahr 1874." Unpublished Habilitationsschrift, University of Bern, 1971.

Oeyen, Christian. "Döllinger als Altkatholik: Eine Bestandsaufnahme." *Internationale kirchliche Zeitschrift* 80 (1990): 67–105.

Osterhammel, Jürgen. *The Transformation of the World: A Global History of the Nineteenth Century.* Translated by Patrick Camiller. Princeton: Princeton University Press, 2014.

Parker, Kenneth L. and Erick H. Moser. *The Rise of Historical Consciousness among the Christian Churches.* Lanham, MD: University Press of America, 2013.

Pelikan, Jaroslav. *Mary through the Centuries: Her Place in the History of Culture.* New Haven: Yale University Press, 1996.

Pereiro, James. *Cardinal Manning: From Anglican Archdeacon to Council Father at Vatican I.* Herefordshire: Gracewing, 2008.

Pörnbacher, Karl. *"Kräftig in die Zeit eingreifen": Die katholische Zeitschrift "Eos" und ihr Kreis.* Munich: Bayer, 1989.

Pottmeyer, Hermann Josef. *Unfehlbarkeit und Souveränität: Die päpstliche Unfehlbarkeit im System der ultramontanen Ekklesiologie des. 19. Jahrhunderts.* Mainz: Matthias-Grünewald Verlag, 1975.

Pottmeyer, Hermann Josef. "Ultramontanismo ed ecclesiologia." *Christianesimo nella Storia* 12 (1991): 527–52.

Powell, Mark E. *Papal Infallibility: A Protestant Evaluation of an Ecumenical Issue.* Grand Rapids, MI: Eerdmans, 2009.

Printy, Michael. *Enlightenment and the Creation of German Catholicism.* Cambridge: Cambridge University Press, 2009.

Raab, H. "Zur Geschichte und Bedeutung des Schlagwortes 'Ultramontan' im 18. und frühen 19. Jahrhundert." *Historisches Jahrbuch der Görres-Gesellschaft* 81 (1962): 159–73.

Raab, H. and Albert Portmann-Tinguely, eds. *Kirche, Staat und katholische Wissenschaft in der Neuzeit: Festschrift für Heribert Raab zum 65. Geburtstag am 16. März 1988.* Paderborn: F. Schöningh, 1988.

Reinhardt, Rudolf. "Teologia romana nella germania de XIX secolo." *Christianesimo nella Storia* 12 (1991): 553–67.

Rémond, René. *Religion et société en Europe: La sécularisation aux XIXe et XXe siècles.* Paris: Éditions du Seuil, 1998.

Rocca, Gregory. "Thomas Aquinas on Papal Authority." *Angelicum* 62 (1985): 472–84.

Rouse, Ruth and Stephen Charles Neill, eds. *A History of the Ecumenical Movement, 1517–1948.* Philadelphia: Westminster Press, 1954.

Roveri, Alessandro. *La Santa Sede tra Rivoluzione e Restaurazione: il Cardinal Consalvi 1813–1815.* Florence: La Nuova Italia, 1974.

Rummel, Fritz, Freiherr von. *Das Ministerium Lutz und Seine Gegner, 1871–1882: ein Kampf um Staatskirchentum, Reichstreue und Parlamentscherrschaft in Bayern.* Munich: C. H. Beck, 1935.

Sailer, Johann Michael. *Bischof Sailer und Ludwig I. von Bayern: mit ihrem Briefwechsel.* Regensburg: Manz, 1932.

Schaefer, Richard. "'Thoughts on the Founding of a Catholic Science': Science, Society and the Syllabus of Errors in German Catholicism, 1820–1869." PhD Dissertation, Cornell University, 2005.

Schaefer, Richard. "Infallibility and Intentionality: Franz Brentano's Diagnosis of German Catholicism." *Journal of the History of Ideas* 68 (July 2007): 477–99.

Schaefer, Richard. "Program for a New Catholic Wissenschaft: Devotional Activism and Catholic Modernity in the Nineteenth Century." *Modern Intellectual History* 62 (November 2007): 433–62.

Schaefer, Richard. "Intellectual History and the Return of Religion." *Historically Speaking* 12 (2011): 30–1.

Schaefer, Richard. "True and False Enlightenment: German Scholars and the Discourse of Catholicism in the Nineteenth Century." *Catholic Historical Review* 97 (January 2011): 24–45.

Schatz, Klaus. *Zwischen Säkularisation und zweitem Vatikanum: Der Weg des deutschen Katholizismus im 19. und 20. Jahrhundert.* Frankfurt am Main: Verlag Josef Knecht, 1986.

Schatz, Klaus. *Vaticanum I, 1869–1870.* 3 vols. Paderborn: F. Schöningh, 1992–4.

Schatz, Klaus. *Der Päpstliche Primat: Seine Geschichte von den Ursprüngen bis zur Gegenwart.* Würzburg: Echter Verlag, 1996.

Schelkens, K., John A. Dick, and Jürgen Mettepenningen. *Aggiornamento? Catholicism from Gregory XVI to Benedict XVI.* Leiden: Brill, 2013.

Schnabel, Franz. *Deutsche Geschichte im neunzehnten Jahrhundert, vol. 4: Die religiösen Kräfte.* Freiburg im Breisgau: Herder, 1936.

Schoenl, William J. *The Intellectual Crisis in English Catholicism: Liberal Catholics, Modernists, and the Vatican in the Late Nineteenth and Early Twentieth Centuries.* New York: Garland, 1982.

Schoof, Mark O.P. *A Survey of Catholic Theology, 1800–1970.* Translated by N. D. Smith. Glen Rock, NJ: Paulist Newman Press, 1970.

Schwaiger, Georg. "Ignaz von Döllinger im Lichte der neueren Forschung." *Münchener Theologische Zeitschrift* 18 (1967): 143–51.

Schwaiger, Georg. "Die Münchener Gelehrtenversammlung von 1863 in den Strömungen der Katholischen Theologie des 19. Jahrhunderts." In Max Seckler et al., eds., *Kirche und Theologie im 19. Jahrhundert: Referate und Berichte des Arbeitskreises Katholische Theologie,* 735–48. Göttingen: Vandenhoeck & Ruprecht, 1975.

Schwedt, Herman H. *Das römische Urteil über Georg Hermes (1775–1831): Ein Beitrag zur Geschichte der Inquisition im 19. Jahrhundert.* Rome: Herder, 1980.

Schwedt, Herman H. "Die katholischen Abgeordneten der Paulskirche und Frankfurt." *Archiv für mittelrheinische Kirchengeschichte* 34 (1982): 143–66.

Seifert, Veronika Maria. *Pius IX, der Immaculata-Papst: von der Marienverehrung Giovanni Maria Mastai Ferrettis zur Definierung des Immaculata-Dogmas.* Göttingen: Vandenhoeck & Ruprecht, 2013.

Sheehan, James J. *German History, 1770–1866.* Oxford: Clarendon Press, 1989.

Siecienski, Edward A. *The Filioque: History of a Doctrinal Controversy.* Oxford: Oxford University Press, 2010.

Silbernagl, Ludwig. *Die kirchenpolitischen und religiösen Zustände im neunzehnten Jahrhundert. Ein Kulturbild.* Landshut: Krüll'schen Universitätsbuchhandlung, 1901.

Sivric, Ivo. *Bishop J. G. Strossmayer: New Light on Vatican I.* Chicago: Franciscan Herald Press, 1975.

Smart, Ninian, John Clayton, Patrick Sherry, and Steven T. Katz, eds. *Nineteenth-Century Religious Thought in the West.* Vol. 2. Cambridge: Cambridge University Press, 1985.

Smith, Helmut Walser, ed. *German Nationalism and Religious Conflict: Culture, Ideology, Politics, 1870–1914.* Princeton: Princeton University Press, 1995.

Smith, Helmut Walser, ed. *Protestants, Catholics, and Jews in Germany, 1800–1914.* Oxford: Berg, 2001.

Southern, Gilbert Edwin. "The Bavarian *Kulturkampf:* A Chapter in Government, Church, and Society in the Early Bismarckreich." PhD Dissertation, University of Massachusetts, 1977.

Spehr, Christopher. *Aufklärung und Ökumene: Reunionsversuche zwischen Katholiken und Protestanten im deutschsprachigen Raum des späteren 18. Jahrhunderts.* Tübingen: Mohr Siebeck, 2005.

Speigl, Jakob. *Die Traditionslehre und Traditionsbeweis in der historischen Theologie Ignaz von Döllinger.* Essen: Ludgerus-Verlag Hubert Wingen, 1964.

Sperber, Jonathan. *Popular Catholicism in Nineteenth-Century Germany.* Princeton: Princeton University Press, 1984.

Tackett, Timothy. *La Révolution, l'Église, la France.* Paris: Du Cerf, 1986.

Taylor, Charles. *A Catholic Modernity?* Edited by James L. Heft. New York: Oxford University Press, 1999.

Taylor, Charles. *A Secular Age.* Cambridge, MA: The Belknap Press of Harvard University Press, 2007.

Tierney, Brian. "The Origins of Papal Infallibility." *Journal of Ecumenical Studies* 8 (1971): 841–64.

Tierney, Brian. *Origins of Papal Infallibility, 1150–1350: A Study on the Concepts of Infallibility, Sovereignty, and Tradition in the Middle Ages.* Leiden: E. J. Brill, 1972.

Troxler, Joseph. *Die neuere Entwicklung des Altkatholizismus: ein Beitrag zur Sektengeschichte der Gegenwart.* Cologne: J. P. Bachem, 1908.

Turner, Frank M. *John Henry Newman: The Challenge to Evangelical Religion.* New Haven: Yale University Press, 2002.

Turner, James. *Philology: The Forgotten Origin of the Modern Humanities.* Princeton: Princeton University Press, 2014.

Valente, Massimiliano. *Diplomazia Pontificia e Kulturkampf: la Santa Sede e la Prussia tra Pio IX e Bismarck, 1862–1878.* Rome: Studium, 2004.

Viaene, Vincent. *Belgium and the Holy See from Gregory XVI to Pius IX (1831–1859): Catholic Revival, Society, and Politics in 19th-Century Europe.* Leuven: Leuven University Press, 2001.

Vick, Brian E. *The Congress of Vienna: Power and Politics after Napoleon.* Cambridge, MA: Harvard University Press, 2014.

Vidler, Alec. *The Modernist Movement in the Roman Church.* Cambridge: Cambridge University Press, 1934.

Vigener, Fritz. *Drei Gestalten aus dem modernen Katholizismus: Möhler, Diepenbrock, Döllinger.* Munich and Berlin: R. Oldenbourg, 1926.

Vogels, Heinz-Jürgen. "Döllinger mit Herz: Zum Briefwechsel Döllinger-Blennerhassett." *Internationale kirchliche Zeitschrift* 74 (1984): 170–86.

Wallace, Lillian Parker. *The Papacy and European Diplomacy, 1869–1878.* Chapel Hill: University of North Carolina Press, 1948.

Ward, W. P. *William George Ward and the Catholic Revival.* London: Longmans, Green and Co., 1893.

Weber, Bernhard and Dieter Albrecht. *Die Mitarbeiter der Historisch-politische Blätter für das katholische Deutschland.* Mainz: Matthias-Grünewald Verlag, 1990.

Weber, Christoph. *Kardinäle und Prälaten in den letzten Jahrzehnten des Kirchenstaates: Elite-Rekrutierung.* Vol. 2: *Karriere-Muster u. Soziale Zusammensetzung d. Kurialen Führungsschicht zur Zeit Pius' IX. (1846–1878).* Stuttgart: Hiersemann, 1978.

Weber, Margot. *Das I. Vatikanische Konzil im Spiegel der bayerischen Politik.* Munich: Kommissionsbuchhandlung R. Wölfe, 1970.

Weigand, Katharina, ed. *Münchner Historiker zwischen Politik und Wissenschaft.* Munich: Hervert Utz Verlag, 2010.

Weis, Eberhard. *Montgelas, 1759–1799.* Munich: C. H. Beck, 2005.

Weiß, Otto. "Der Ultramontanismus. Grundlagen—Vorgeschichte—Struktur." *Zeitschrift für Bayerische Landesgeschichte* 41 (1978): 821–77.

Weiß, Otto. *Die Redemptoristen in Bayern (1790–1909): Ein Beitrag zur Geschichte des Ultramontanism.* St. Ottilien: Verlag Erzabtei St. Ottilien, 1983.

Weiß, Otto. "La 'scienza tedesca' e l'Italia nell'Ottocento." *Annali dell'Instituto storico italo-germanico in Trento/Jahrbuch des Italienisch-Deutschen Historischen Instituts in Trient* 9 (1983): 9–85.

Weiß, Otto. "Das Gedächtnis des 100. Todestages Johann Joseph Ignaz von Döllingers. Ein Forschungsbericht." *Historisches Jahrbuch* 112 (1992): 482–95.

Weitlauff, Manfred. "Ignaz von Döllinger—Im Schatten des ersten Vatikanums." *Münchener theologische Zeitschrift* 41 (1990): 215–43.

Whaley, Joachim. *Germany and the Holy Roman Empire, vol. 2: The Peace of Westphalia to the Dissolution of the Reich, 1648–1806.* Oxford: Oxford University Press, 2013.

Windell, George G. *The Catholics and German Unity, 1866–1871.* Minneapolis: University of Minnesota Press, 1954.

Witetschek, Helmut. "Die Bedeutung der theologischen Fakultät der Universität München für die kirchliche Erneuerung in der ersten Hälfte des 19. Jahrhunderts." *Historisches Jahrbuch* 86 (1966): 107–37.

Wolf, Hubert. "Kardinal Gustav Adolf von Hohenlohe (1823–1896) als Mitinitiator der 'Zirkulardepesche' vom 9. April 1869?" *Zeitschrift für Kirchengeschichte* 101 (1990): 380–4.

Wolf, Hubert. "Rekonziliation Döllingers durch Johann Heinrich Floß?" *Theological Quartalschrift* 172 (1992): 121–5.

Wolf, Hubert. *Rankes Päpste auf dem Index: Dogma und Historie in Widerstreit.* Paderborn: Schöningh, 2003.

Wolf, Hubert, ed. *Römische Inquisition und Indexkongregation: Grundlagenforschung, 1814–1917: Einleitung.* Paderborn: Schöningh, 2005.

Zachhuber, Johannes. *Theology as Science in Nineteenth-Century Germany.* Oxford: Oxford University Press, 2013.

Index

Printed and bound by CPI Group (UK) Ltd, Croydon, CR0 4YY